D1108264

Religion
Under The
State Constitutions

by

Chester James Antieau, S.J.D.
Professor of Law, Georgetown University

Phillip Mark Carroll, L.L.M.
of the Virginia Bar; Assistant Director
of the Institute for Church-State Law,
Georgetown University

Thomas Carroll Burke, L.L.B.
of the New York Bar; Fellow of the
Institute for Church-State Law,
Georgetown University

A Publication Of The
Institute for Church-State Law
Georgetown University

1 9 6 5
CENTRAL BOOK COMPANY, INC.
BROOKLYN, N. Y.

PRINTED IN U.S.A.   THE ALPERT PRESS INC., BROOKLYN, N. Y.

TABLE OF CONTENTS

Chapter One

Chapter Two

Chapter Three

Chapter Four

Chapter Five

Chapter Six

Appendix

Footnotes

NOTE TO THE READER

Some of the most pressing problems facing Americans today are those arising in the area of church-state relations. The issues of religious freedom and the problems of aid to the churches are both national and local. While much of the current controversy has been with us for a long time, a number of novel questions have arisen only recently. Illustrative are the experiments in shared education now being conducted throughout the country.

There exists a wealth of material on the stands taken by the Supreme Court of the United States on the various questions of church-state relations. While the Supreme Court remains the final arbiter of issues involving the United States Constitution, there are many areas of church and state where, either by choice or lack of opportunity, it has not ruled. Consequently, until the Court does rule, it is to the constitutions of the several states and the judicial decisions of the state courts interpreting these constitutions that we must look for the resolution of these problems. Additionally, although the Supreme Court has made a decision under the United States Constitution, the state courts remain the final judges of the permissability of state, church, or individual action under their own constitutions. While the state courts cannot condone what the Supreme Court has condemned, they may be more restrictive than the federal tribunal and deny the validity of certain practices under their constitutions which have been permitted under the Federal Constitution. Thus, the constitutional clauses of the several states, and the interpretations and construction of these clauses by the highest tribunals in the states are vital to a knowledge of the law of church and state.

A note concerning the methodology utilized in preparing this study will be helpful. First, where the Supreme Court has ruled in a given area, the decision of that tribunal is reported and analyzed. Complete treatment of the United States Supreme Court rulings is not attempted, however; that is left, instead, to the numerous commentaries on that body of the law. Second, the constitutional clauses of the several states that deal with religion are discussed. For the most part, these clauses are discussed in their contemporary application rather than historical origin, except where it was thought helpful to note changes in constitutional text from constitution to constitution. The clauses are then examined in light of the interpretations given them by the high courts of the various states, as well as by the rulings of Attorneys General, and, to a limited extent, the practices in different localities. The rulings of government bodies and officials of specific application, such as the regulations made by superintendents of schools, are also noted. This study does not, however, contain all of the materials necessary to a complete treatment of any one problem of church and state. Unreported cases, cases not decided directly under constitutional clauses relating to religion, and many collateral rulings not directly based on the constitutions are not considered. Counsel is invited to pursue questions in whatever depth is necessary in his own jurisdiction.

The format of this book is topical, and to some extent limited by that approach. The topics and subdivisions were selected for the convenience of the reader and consequently are somewhat arbitrary. It must be kept in mind that there are many areas which overlap, and the reader should remain aware that a particular principle of law may have valid application in a number of different situations. Within each topical heading, the constitutional clause, or one which typifies the majority of clauses in the state constitutions, is set forth. The clause itself is then analyzed. Secondly, the extent to which it controlled the outcome of litigation is discussed, and the construction given the clause by the tribunal is set forth. Emphasis is given to those problems of current importance. No attempt has been made to give textual treatment to every case decided under every state constitutional clause dealing with religion, with the exception of the chapter on tax exemptions. Only the most significant cases have been discussed in the text, while those of lesser importance will be found in the footnotes.

In many instances the wording of the constitutional clause will control the outcome of litigation. However, where the clause is general or vague, the practitioner must seek out the interpretations expressed by the highest tribunal in his jurisdiction. In addition, many of the states have identically worded clauses. In such a case, an interpretation given a constitutional clause in one state may very well provide a clue as to how the court in a neighboring state would react. However, as would be expected, there is often a division of opinion among the courts of different states on the construction to be given an identically worded clause. Here, lawyers and litigants must make a decision as to which of two or more conflicting lines of authority is most favorable, and urge its choice upon the court. Extremely useful analogically are the decisions of the United States Supreme Court rendered under the First Amendment. A number of states have constitutional clauses identical to, or comparable with, the First Amendment to the Federal Constitution. In those states, a great deal of weight may well be attached to the rulings and interpretations of the nation's highest tribunal.

Wherever possible, the authors have indicated what the status of the law presently is in each area of discussion. Furthermore, whenever a trend in the law is discernible, they have endeavored to state what the law may very well become. In the presence of conflicting lines of authority, the authors, when comment appeared warranted, have set forth an opinion as to the better reasoned solution. The authors have, for the most part, refrained from making judgments regarding the desirability of the current status of the law in any given area, except where they believed that some comment would be helpful.

Finally, this work is not a definitive treatise on the law or practice in each or any state. A complete catalogue of existing legal and non-legal materials in the area of religion would fill considerably more than this modest volume. It is intended only as a general survey of religious questions as they have arisen under the state constitutions. It will provide the general reader with a more detailed insight into the issues and answers to the problems of church and state, and the practitioner with a starting point in doing research in this area. The practitioner is cautioned to investigate fully the local unreported cases, rulings of attorneys general and other state and local officials, the local custom and practice, and the proceedings of constitutional conventions.

Washington, D.C.

Chapter One

Constitutional Clauses Banning Aid to Churches and Religious Institutions

Generally

State or local government aid to churches and church-related institutions assumes a number of possible forms. Most obviously a governmental unit may attempt to make a direct cash grant or its equivalent to a religious entity. A governmental unit may also allow a church or church-related organization to occupy unused public property. Finally, a number of states and their local municipalities have undertaken to make grants to such church-related organizations and institutions as hospitals, orphanages, and other child-care homes. Since a great many of the states have constitutional clauses which prohibit aid to churches and religious institutions, the validity of such practices has become the subject of considerable litigation.

The type of state constitutional clause under which the propriety of such aid has been litigated varies. Many of the states have adopted very specific constitutional language which appears to preclude any public aid to institutions or organizations which are characterized as "sectarian." In some instances, this term is defined in the constitution itself, usually by listing the types of institutions which are considered "sectarian." Most often, however, this is left for the courts to construe and interpret. Other states have adopted only general clauses which simply prohibit an "establishment" or any preferential treatment of one faith.

Often of importance to the state tribunals faced with such questions has been their own individual assessment of the social utility of the particular institution or organization involved. This is borne out by the frequency with which courts distinguish between the giving of aid to a church and the making of a grant to a hospital, orphanage, or other welfare institution run by that church. Aid in the latter case is frequently allowed, whereas it is prohibited in the former.

1

In ruling on issues involving these types of aid, courts are usually faced with two common contentions. First, proponents often will argue that the aid is purely *incidental*. The direct beneficiaries of such aid are the members of the public, not the institution or its sponsor. To hold, they assert, that such aid is invalid because it helps, indirectly, the organization performing a necessary public service indicates an unwarranted hostility towards religion never intended by the framers of the different state constitutions. This leads to the second proposition, that such organizations are merely "conduits", acting only as vehicles for the dispensation of such aid to the individuals who are in need of it. Many cases in this area present close questions of fact, and consequently must be examined carefully. As in many areas of constitutional interpretation, the difference between permitting and disallowing a particular type of aid to an institution is one of degree. Slight changes in factual patterns may often spell the difference between aid and no aid.

Cash Grant or Its Equivalent

Virtually every state constitution forbids direct cash aid, or its equivalent, to institutions devoted solely to worship, and attempts by states to grant direct aid to sectarian institutions are unusual. The California Consitution provision is typical:

> Neither the Legislature, nor any country, city and county, . . . or other municipal corporation, shall ever make any appropriation, or pay from any public fund whatever, or grant anything to or in aid of any religious sect, church, creed, or sectarian purpose . . . . [1]

Under this provision, the State Attorney General has ruled that use of tax funds in support of a Pilgrimage Play, a dramatization of the life of Jesus Christ, is unconstitutional.[2] Similarly, the California Supreme Court has held that a legislative appropriation of $10,000 to restore the San Diego Mission, then under the ownership and control of the Catholic Church, was unconstitutional under the same provision.[3] The court rejected the contention that the historical and educational value of the mission gave it a public purpose, thereby making the appropriation permissible. Since the Mission belonged to the Catholic Church, under the Archbishop of San Francisco, rather than the State, the appropriation was violative of the California Constitution. The same Court examined Verdi's "Nabucco" and a Festival of Faith and Freedom Foundation, and found the former not to be a religious work and the latter not a religious organization, and thus constitutionally able to receive County aid.[4]

The Georgia Constitution is equally explicit, stating that ". . . No money shall ever be taken from the public treasury, directly or indirectly, in aid of any church, sect, or denomination . . . ."[5] Not surprisingly, payment of a paving assessment on church property from the city treasury has been held to violate this provision.[6]

Under the comparable Illinois provision,[7] it has been held that the prohibition against the use of public funds in aid of churches extends only to funds which form a part of the public revenues of the state, and does not preclude the use by a church of funds derived from leasing a commons held by a Roman Catholic parish under an original French land grant.[8]

The Constitutional provisions and cases decided thereunder are clear, then; cash aid by the state, or subdivisions thereof, to purely religious organizations, for the benefit of those organizations, is forbidden.

Use of Government Property by Churches

Where public property—usually a school building—is rented or leased to church related groups for fair value, apparenly no constitutional problem is raised. Rental of unused government property has usually been held permissible,[9] and there is no apparent constitutionally cognizable distinction in renting for fair value to religious organizations rather than to a non-sectarian group.[10]

There is a substantial body of state case law on the subject of *gratuitous* use of government owned property by religious groups, whether for actual religious services or merely as a meeting place.[11] Much of the litigation, however, involves the authority of local school boards to permit or deny use of school facilities by religious groups, and is thus beyond the scope of this work.[12] Claims by religious groups that denial of such use is, in effect, a denial of their religious freedom have thus far been unsuccessful.[13] Similarly, cases involving the denial of the use of park facilities and the like are usually litigated under Freedom of Religion clauses, and are treated elsewhere in this work. Only those cases where the constitutionality of church use of government property has been litigated in a strictly aid context are considered herein. Where the constitutionality of such use has been litigated under "no aid" provisions, the courts are divided, with a majority upholding its permissibility.

The Florida Constitution provides that "No preference shall ever be given by law to any church, sect, or mode of worship, and no money shall ever be taken from the public treasury directly or indirectly in aid of any church, sect or religious denomination . . . ."[14] A Florida statute permitting the trustees of a school district to authorize the use of schools for "any legal assembly" has been held not to violate this provision in a taxpayers suit to enjoin the temporary use of public school buildings for religious meetings.[15] The Florida Court noted that:

> While admittedly, there are some differences of view regarding the matter of religious meetings in school houses during non-school

> periods, . . . logic, as well as our traditional attitudes toward the
> importance of religious worship, justifies our alignment with those
> courts which permit such use. The cases where this type of use
> of school property is permitted, usually involve the application of
> statutes similar to [ours]. The cases which deny such use cus-
> tomarily involve situations where there has been no such statutory
> authorization.[16]

The Court further observed that "an incidental benefit to a religious
group resulting from an appropriate use of public property is not violative . . . of the Florida Constitution,"[17] and that any wear and tear
suffered in the process of use of the school by the religious group did
not constitute an indirect appropriation to that group, applying the
maxim *de minimis non curat lex.* The Court does note, however, by way
of dictum, that such use for prolonged periods, or with no intent to
build a church, would probably violate the state Constitution.
    Finally, the Court points out that a stricter rule would invalidate
the

> traditional Easter Sunrise Service observed in many communities
> throughout Florida. We know that such services are customarily
> held in public parks or playgrounds and, in some instances, in
> public school and state university stadia. The Easter Sunrise
> Service is dedicated to memorializing the Resurrection of Christ,
> a distinguishing aspect of the dogma of Christianity as contrasted
> to Judaism. An application of the rule . . . (banning use of gov-
> ernment property by religious groups) . . . would result in prohibit-
> ing such services, not only on school grounds or stadia but in any
> public park. We think that when the rule is reduced to such ab-
> surd application its fallacies and weaknesses become obvious.[18]

Similarly, Florida has also allowed the use of public lakes and streams
for baptisms.[19] The Court there held that a county could accept land
devised it under a will which further provided that a church in the
vicinity should have the privilege of baptizing in a lake therein. In
holding that this arrangement did not violate either the establishment
clause of the First Amendment or the instant Flordia Constitutional provision, the Court observed that these baptisms were a colorful part of
the history of our country, and that to prohibit "such use of public
waters would, in effect, prohibit many groups from carrying out the tenets
of their faith . . ."[20]
    In a case holding that a school building may not be leased for other
than school purposes, the Kansas Court noted that:

> The public school house cannot be used for any private purposes.
> The argument is a short one. Taxation is invoked to raise funds
> to erect the building; but taxation is illegitimate to provide for
> any private purpose. Taxation will not lie to raise funds to build
> a place for a religious society, a political society, or a social club.

What cannot be done directly cannot be done indirectly. As you
may not lay taxes to build a church, no more may you levy taxes
to build a school-house and then lease it for a church. Nor is it
an answer to say that its use for school purposes is not interfered
with, and that the use for other purposes works little . . . injury
to the building, and results in immediate pecuniary benefit. The
extent of the injury or the benefit is something into which the
courts will not inquire.[21]

The court disposed of the defendant's *de minimis* argument thus:
"The character of the use is the only legitimate question . . . . The use
of a public school-house for a single religious . . . gathering is legally
as unauthorized as its constant use therefor."[22]

The Illinois Constitution provides that "No person shall be required
to attend or support any place of worship against his consent."[23] Additionally, it decrees that school funds and property "shall be faithfully
applied to the objects for which such gifts or grants were made,"[24] and
further bans the "grant or donation of land, money, or other personal
property . . .to any church, or for any sectarian purpose."[25] An Illinois
statute giving the Board of School Directors power to grant the use of
public school houses," . . . when not occupied by schools, for religious
meetings and Sunday schools . . ."[26] has been upheld as not being repugnant to these provisions.[27] The Court observed that temporary
use of schools for religious meetings might confer an incidental benefit on
the religious group, but noted that the Constitution did not ban ". . . any
incidental benefit whatsoever from the public bodies or authorities of the
State,"[28] and argued that this incidental benefit was not unlike that given
by the tax exemption granted by the legislature pursuant to the state
constitution.

The Indiana Court originally held similarly,[29] but in a later case held
that the phrase "when unoccupied for common school purpose" had
reference only to the time intervening between terms of school, and did
not authorize a religious organization to use a school house on Sundays
and evenings during the school term, when the school was not actually
in session.[30]

On two occasions[31] the Iowa Court has sustained school authorities
in permitting religious uses, remarking in the later case that

. . . such occasional use does not convert the school-house into a
building for worship, within the meaning of the constitution. The
same reasoning would make our halls of legislation places of worship, because in them, each morning, prayers are offered by
chaplains.[32]

The Iowa Constitution, which provides:

The General Assembly shall make no law respecting an establishment of religion, or prohibiting the free exercise thereof; nor shall

> any person be compelled to attend any place of worship, pay tithes, taxes, or other rates for building or repairing places of worship, ...[33]

was held not to have been violated by such religious use of school property.

The Iowa Court also apparently applied the rule of *de minimis non curat lex* to this constitutional prohibition against aid to religion when it remarked:

> . . . we incline to think that the use of a public school building for Sabbath schools, religious meetings, . . . which of necessity must be occasional and temporary, is not so palpably a violation of the fundamental law as to justify the courts in interfering. Especially is this so where . . . abundant provision is made for securing any damages which the taxpayer may suffer by reason of the use. . . . With such precaution, the amount of taxes anyone could be compelled to pay by reason of such use would never amount to any appreciable sum.[34]

The Nebraska Court, under a typical no preference or support provision, [35] refused mandamus to stop the Board of Education from allowing the use of a schoolhouse three or four times a year as a place of worship.[36]

In a New York case,[37] the use of public school buildings as meeting places for sectarian societies (Newman Clubs, YMCA, and Junior Hadassah Clubs) was held permissible. The court expressly grounded the constitutionality of such use on the fact that the groups were not permitted to ". . . hold any religious denominational services in any of the public schools . . . and that . . . [they] are only and solely permitted to have meetings . . . for the purpose of conducting ethical, educational and cultural discourses and lectures. . . ."[38]

Under the New York Constitution's no preference provision,[39] it has been held constitutional for a local school board to permit the erection on Junior High School property of a Nativity scene, erected and maintained by private funds, and present only during the Christmas recess.[40] A recent New York case held likewise.[41] In an earlier decision, a New York court ruled that the use of the second floor of a public firehouse for religious services pending erection or repair of the Congregation's permanent home, was not unconstitutional.[42] In the absence of a ruling by New York's highest Court, the inconsistency between allowing the use of some government property—a public firehouse—for religious services, and apparently denying the permissibility of use of other government property—a schoolhouse, would seem irreconcilable.

Pennsylvania would appear to have determined that use of schools for a sectarian purpose is unconstitutional[43] (although the specific constitutional clause violated by such use was left in doubt); but a Pennsylvania statute, the constitutionality of which has apparently not been litigated with reference to use of government property by churches, provides that a school board may permit the use of school buildings ". . . for social, recreation, and other purposes. . . ."[44]

There are no discoverable California cases dealing with the use of schools by religious groups, but the State Attorney General has ruled that a county may not grant the use of its rooms, courthouse, and public grounds surrounding the courthouse to private, public, religious, or charitable groups[45] under the California Constitutional "no aid for sectarian purposes" provision.[46]

Louisiana manifestly has not decided the question of the use of schools by religious groups, but, in an action to compel the removal of a memorial statute to St. Frances [Mother] Cabrini, a member of the Missionary Sisters of the Sacred Heart, the Louisiana Supreme Court refused to compel the removal of the monument, holding not only that the presence of the statute on public ground did not violate the Louisiana Constitutional provision forbidding establishment or the giving of a preference to any sect,[47] but that "to deny the right of the city to erect a statute to a public figure solely because of the honoree's religion . . . would be to violate the constitutional mandate that there be no discrimination against anyone because of his race or religion."[48] The Court further observed that the incidental religious significance of the statute would not violate the constitutional inhibition unless the memorial was intended as a public shrine or place of worship, or for the propagation of a particular religious faith. According to the Court, the only test of the permissibility of such a statute is whether the person contributed to the public welfare: charitable, scientific, social, health or otherwise.

The decisions, then, do not appear to be based upon the type of government property involved. It is seemingly not significant in determining the constitutionality of the use government property by religious groups, gratis, whether it is a school or civic building that is involved. Observations in this area, then, may be made irrespective of the type of government property involved.

If the use of government property by a church or church-related organization is accompanied by the payment of a fair rental, there is no valid constitutional objection fairly raised under the specific "no aid to sectarian institutions" clauses or the broader "no preference" type provisions. In addition, it would appear that if the use of this property, by the organization, is without charge, but is for a non-religious purpose, e.g., a lecture or movie, no constitutional problem is raised thereby.

If, however, the use of this property is for a religious purpose and no rental is paid, the courts disagree as to its constitutionality. A number of states have categorized the practice as direct aid to the church and have ruled the use unconstitutional. A considerable number of others, however, justify the aid as but an *incidental* benefit to the church, dismiss taxpayer objections as *de minimis,* and hold the free use of the property constitutional. It must be noted that the holdings in the latter states are almost unanimously limited to factual situations where the use of the property is only *temporary* or *periodic.* Dictum in the decisions of these state courts indicates that should such use be permanent or regular in nature, or without evidence of any intention to locate and construct other permanent quarters, it would be unconstitutional.

It is submitted that the holdings (and probable holdings in factual situations involving more regular use) of the latter courts are better reasoned and more socially desirable. The constitutional clauses—whether specifically banning aid to sectarian institutions or more generally banning preference or establishment—are but a starting point for discussion in this area. Their wording is not clearly determinative of the permissibility of the free use of government property by churches in any but extreme factual situations. Clearly, as we have seen in discussing cash grants, *direct* aid to churches is unconstitutional. It seems equally clear that if there is but a minor, or what courts are inclined to term "incidental", benefit to the religious body, with little attendant taxpayer expense or inconvenience, state action which, as a matter of fact, benefits the religious organization should not be held unconstitutional.

When the use of government property by a church is temporary, or merely periodic, it would seem that the benefit to the church is less than substantial, that taxpayer objections are *de minimis,* and that the use of the property is not unconstitutional.[49] Regular use, however, approaches direct aid to the religious organization. Looked at from the standpoint of the church itself, regular use of government property would surely eliminate the need (if not the desire) for construction and maintenance of its own house of worship. This, it is suggested, is more than an "incidental" or insubstantial benefit; the effect of the government action in permitting the regular use of its property is not dissimilar from that of a direct cash grant to the religious organization.[50] Additionally, as use of the government property without the payment of a fair rental becomes more regular, taxpayer objections become more substantial; wear and tear on property used by a church weekly or even daily cannot easily be dismissed as *de minimis.*[51] From a constitutional standpoint, then, the "permissible when periodic" rule is consistent: permission is denied when the use of government property approximates unconstitutional direct aid to the religious body, and granted when the religious body derives but a minor benefit therefrom.

Complete prohibition of the use of government property by churches is undesirable. Emergency situations, delays in construction, and comparable problems do arise. Even a strict view of the separation of church and state should not dictate that the government withhold use of its property under such circumstances.[52] The traditionally recognized value of churches in our society does not permit a hostility between government and religion: in a spirit of "neighborliness" and charity the government ought to be allowed to lend its property to anyone deserving thereof,[53] whether the circumstances involve victims of a flood or members of the congregation of a church destroyed by a fire, or otherwise temporarily without a permanent home.

The undesirability of regular free use of government property by churches is no less clear.[54] With regular use of government property by such groups, taxpayer expenses—for heat, light, air-conditioning and the like—are bound to rise. With regular use of government property by these groups the possibility of government interference becomes more likely—whether it be in regulating the rituals involved in religious ceremonies, or the articles useable in the government lent houses of worship. The possibility of competing for prime time for holding services and meetings, with the necessarily resulting friction and divisiveness in the community, would also make such regular use socially impractical and undesirable.

Certain obvious problems are created by the "permissible but periodic" rule. Determinations of when the use is truly occasional may be difficult, government intervention or control is not inconceivable, competition for times is still possible, and inter-faith friction might still arise. The rule, however, avoids the dangers implicit in either extreme: it allows churches to use government property when they need it most, yet denies them such use when the social and community ramifications thereof are most dangerous.

Aid To Charitable Institutions Operated By Religious Societies

Historically, churches and church related organizations have been intimately involved in caring for the sick, infirm, aged, and destitute. While the field has been somewhat pre-empted by government supported institutions, there is still a clear need of, and place for, private, sectarian charitable institutions. If the institution is merely private, there is no church-state problem, but where, as is frequently the case, a particular religious denomination controls the institution, constitutional problems in the area of church-state law arise.

Many states have seen fit to include very specific provisions in their constitutions in the area of governmental aid to charitable organizations. Some approach the problem by banning appropriations to charitable organizations not under the control of the state, while others phrase the prohibition purely in terms of sectarian institutions. New Mexico is typical of the former approach, with its provision that "No appropriation shall be made for charitable, educational or other benevolent purpose to any person, corporation, association, institution, or community, not under the absolute control of the state . . .",[55] while South Carolina typifies the latter:

The property or credit of the State . . . or any . . . subdivision of
the state, or any public money . . . shall not, by gift, donation,
loan, . . . or otherwise be used, directly or indirectly, in aid or
maintenance of any college, school, hospital, orphan house, or other
institution, . . . of whatever kind, which is wholly or in part under
the direction or control of any church or of any religion or sectarian denomination, society or organization.[56]

A third approach would seem to be that of Wyoming, which bans
aid to charitable institutions not under the control of the state, but specifically mentions sectarian institutions: "No appropriation shall be made
for charitable, industrial, educational, or benevolent purposes to any
person, corporation, or community not under the absolute control of the
state, nor to any denominational or sectarian institution or association."[57]
This provision goes beyond that of New Mexico in that it not only excludes non-state controlled charitable institutions from state aid, but also
specifically lists sectarian institutions as excluded.

Two states seemingly permit appropriations to sectarian institutions
run by religious societies by the wording of their state constitutions,[58]
and many states have broad exceptions to their constitutional prohibitions
against governmental aid to sectarian charitable organizations.[59]

The cases in this area, whether arising under the instant constitutional provisions or under the broader "no preference" provisions, fall into
three areas: 1) Hospitals, 2) Custodial Institutions, and 3) Welfare
Organizations, run by church-related organizations. Where the specific
constitutional ban is at issue, the general rule seems to be that contracts
between a state or city and a sectarian charitable institution, whereby
the governmental unit agrees to re-imburse the institution for services
rendered or expenses incurred, are unconstitutional.[60] Where a more
general constitutional inhibition is at issue, these appropriations are
generally upheld.

1. Hospitals

There has been a good deal of litigation in the area of state grants
to sectarian hospitals, and, of the states having specific constitutional
provisions banning aid to sectarian charitable institutions, most of the
litigation has occurred in Pennsylvania. The constitution of that state,
which is typical, provides: "No appropriation shall be made for charitable, educational or benevolent purposes to any person or community nor
to any denominational and sectarian institution, corporation or association. . . ."[61] The leading case decided under this provision held that state
appropriations to hospitals operated by the Lutheran, Catholic, Episcopal, and Jewish denominations were unconstitutional.[62] The Court, in
discussing this constitutional clause, noted that:

The intent of these provisions was, and therefore still is, to forbid the state from giving, either directly or indirectly, any recognition to a religious sect or denomination, even in the fields of public charity and education: They in effect provide that, to serve charitable educational or benevolent purposes, the money of the people shall not be put under denominational control or into sectarian hands, for administration or distribution, no matter how worthy the end in view. It will be noted the Constitution does not say merely that no appropriations shall be made for sectarian or denominational purposes, nor does it confirm the limitation against state aid to those institutions which actually teach sectarian doctrines or promote denominational interests. What it provides is that "no appropriation shall be made to any denominational or sectarian institution." These words, when taken at their face value, are most comprehensive in scope. They plainly forbid state aid to institutions affiliated with a particular religious sect or denomination, or which are under the control, domination, or governing influence of any religious sect or denomination, the ordinary understanding of the phrase "sect or denomination" being a church, or body of persons in some way united for purposes of worship, who profess a common religious faith, and are distinguished from those composing other such bodies by a name of their own.[63]

The Pennsylvania Court concluded

that, when a charitable, benevolent, or educational establishment is "denominational or sectarian" according to the meaning of these terms as understood by the average man, even though the institution in question may bestow its benefits on others, and permits those outside the ranks of the sect or denomination involved to take part in its management, it is none the less a sectarian or denominational institution, within the inhibition of the Constitution against state aid.[64]

The doctrine of this case has been followed in later Pennsylvania rulings and, indeed, the Court has refused to permit the payment of per diem charges by the state to such hospitals caring for indigents under contract with the public welfare authorities.[65] However, in a case where the hospital was named after a saint, staffed by Roman Catholic nursing sisters wearing their distinctive garb, and it occupied a building leased from a religious corporation, the Pennsylvania Court ruled it was not sectarian, apparently largely influenced by an independent board of trustees that, according to the hospital's answer, "at all times exercised exclusive and complete supervision and control over all the affairs thereof, and at no time has any preference been given for any denominational or sectarian purpose."[66]

New Mexico is another state specifically banning aid to charitable or benevolent institutions not under control of the state.[67] Although there appear to be no court decisions hereunder, the Attorney General of New Mexico has given rulings (1) that county funds may not be given to a county hospital owned by a private corporation;[68] and (2) that hospitals leased by a county to private organizations may not be maintained with public funds.[69]

The South Carolina constitution bans aid to sectarian organizations.[70] Although there has been no case decided directly under this clause, the South Carolina Supreme Court has said by way of dictum:

> . . . we think the plain meaning of our Constitution is that no public funds be allocated in any manner to any hospital or health center which is 'under the direction or control of any church or of any religious or sectarian denomination, society or organization.'[71]

Much of the litigation concerning the constitutionality of grants to charitable and benevolent institutions associated with particular denominations has arisen in states not having the kind of clause here described. There is, for instance, a Georgia decision holding that a city could not appropriate funds to pay a hospital operated by the Sisters of Mercy a monthly rental and pro rata sum for each charity patient, as well as patients with contagious diseases.[72] The result was thought to follow from Georgia's general constitutional clause banning aid to sectarian institutions.[73] The North Carolina Court has held that state aid may not be given to privately operated hospitals, the decision flowing from a constitutional clause prohibiting the use of private laws.[74]

On the other hand, states have been permitted to make appropriations for hospitals in other states with varying worded constitutional clauses. The Mississippi Constitution, for example, provides:

> No law granting a donation or gratuity in favor of any person or object shall be enacted except by the concurrence of two-thirds of the members elect of each branch of the legislature, nor by any vote for a sectarian purpose or use.[75]

Under this clause, the Mississippi Supreme Court has sustained the grant of state funds to a hospital operated by the Sisters of Mercy for the care of indigent sick.[76] Chief Justice McGhee explained:

> Our Constitution does not say "no appropriation," or "no public funds," or "no money of the state" may be used "for a sectarian purpose or use," but the provision is that no "donation or gratuity" shall be made for such purpose. Nor does our Constitution prohibit a grant being made to any "sectarian institution" as do the constitutions of many other states. Even so, the grant here involved is not to the Sisters of Mercy of Vicksburg, as aforesaid, but to the appellee hospital corporation, engaged in operating a general hospital on a nonsectarian basis. However, money may be handled by a "sectarian institution" and still not be devoted to a "sectarian

purpose or use." Administering to the sick is not sectarian; it is done by governmental and secular agencies.[77]

The court added:

> The operating of a hospital may be for a charitable, benevolent, and philanthropic purpose without being operated for a sectarian purpose . . . the charter powers of a corporation control, and not the religious beliefs of its stockholders, as to whether it is operated in a secular activity.[78]

Comparably, New Hampshire, whose constitution provides: "that no money raised by taxation shall ever be granted or applied for the use of the schools or institutions of any religious sect or denomination,"[79] has sustained the use of public funds for scholarships and grants in aid to all hospitals offering approved nursing training without regard to the auspices under which they are operated, so long as the hospital training programs are devoid of sectarian doctrine and purposes.[80] Said the New Hampshire Court:

> A hospital operated under the auspices of a religious denomination which receives funds under the provisions of this bill acts merely as a conduit for the expenditure of public funds for training which serves exclusively the public purpose of public health and is completely devoid of sectarian doctrine and purposes. This does not violate the Constitution.[81]

The Court continued:

> What was intended to be forbidden . . . was support of a particular sect or denomination by the state, at the expense of taxpayers of other denominations or of no denomination. It was not intended that members of a denomination should be deprived of public benefits because of their beliefs. . . . If some denomination incidentally derives a benefit through the release of other funds for other uses, this result is immaterial.[82]

Kentucky's Constitution provides: " . . . nor shall any person be compelled . . . to contribute to the erection or maintenance of any such place of worship, or to the support of any minister of religion."[83] Under this clause the Kentucky Court has ruled that state tax funds can be given to hospitals operated by religious groups so long as they are open to the public and there is no teaching of religion therein.[84] Chief Justice Sims, speaking for the Court, stated:

> The fact that members of the governing bodies of these hospitals, which perform a recognized public service to all people regardless of faith or creed, are all of one religious faith does not signify that the money allotted the hospitals is to aid their particular denomina-

tion. On the contrary, governing boards of such hospitals are but the channels through which the funds flow. Courts will look at the use to which these funds are put rather than the *conduits* through which they run. If that use is a public one and is calculated to aid all people in the State, it will not be held in contravention of section five merely because the hospitals carry the name or are governed by the members of a particular faith.[85]

The Court added:

Manifestly, the drafters of our Constitution did not intend to go so far as to prevent a public benefit, like a hospital in which the followers of all faiths and creeds are admitted, from receiving State aid merely because it was originally founded by a certain denomination whose members now serve on its board of trustees . . . Certainly, it was never the intention of the framers of section five of our Constitution to prevent the State from aiding with money raised by taxes an institution rendering public service merely because the governing body of the institution is composed of one denomination.[86]

On authority of the *Effron* decision, the Kentucky Court later sustained the lease of a public hospital to an order of nursing nuns at a nominal rental.[87] Noting that all were to be admitted regardless of creed, and that the hospital was to be operated as a non-profit venture, the Court found no violation of the Kentucky constitution in the arrangement.

A recent Alaska case,[88] decided under Alaska's establishment and free exercise provision,[89] held that the state constitution was not violated by leasing a community owned hospital to a non-profit corporation, organized for charitable purposes. The Court observed that the leasing of the hospital to a group incorporated as the Sisters of St. Joseph of Newark

. . . was not designed, nor does it have the effect by its nature, of promoting or giving a preferred position to whatever religious beliefs the individual members of the corporation may have. The fact that specific sectarian beliefs may be entertained by those persons does not bar the city from achieving its valid secular goal of caring for the sick.[90]

Thus, generalizing, it would appear that where a grant to a sectarian hospital is contested under the specific type of constitutional clause barring aid to sectarian charitable institutions, such aid might be invalidated. On the other hand, where the grant is questioned with reference to a more general "no aid" provision, it may well be upheld.

The United States Supreme Court decision in the well-known case of *Bradfield v. Roberts*[91] is illustrative in this connection. There, a taxpayer sued to enjoin the Federal Government from carrying out a contract whereby it agreed to, erect a building on the grounds of, and pay for poor patients at, Providence Hospital in the District of Columbia. The court upheld the contract, noting that the corporation which owned the hosptal, while consisting exclusively of Catholic Sisters of Charity, was an entity distinct from its shareholders. The Court said:

> . . . [A]ssuming that the hospital is a private eleemosynary corporation, the fact that its members . . . are members of a monastic order or sisterhood of the Roman Catholic Church, and the further fact that the hospital is conducted under the auspices of said church is wholly immaterial. . . . Whether the individuals who compose the corporation under its charter happen to be all Roman Catholics, or all Methodists, or Presbyterions, or Unitarians, or members of any other religious organization, or of no organization at all, is not of the slightest consequence with reference to the law of its incorporation, nor can the religious beliefs upon religious matters of the various incorporators be inquired into.[92]

The Court further observed:

> Nor is it material that the hospital may be conducted under the auspices of the Roman Catholic Church. To be conducted under the auspices is to be conducted under the influence or patronage of that church. The meaning of the allegation is that the church exercises great and perhaps controlling influence over the management of the hospital. It must, however, be managed pursuant to the law of its being. That the influence of any particular church may be powerful over the members of a non-sectarian and secular corporation, incorporated for a certain defined purpose and with clearly stated power, is surely not sufficient to convert such a corporation into a sectarian body. That fact does not alter the legal character of the corporation. . . .[93]

Finally, the Court noted that:

> There is no allegation that its hospital work is confined to members of that church or that in its management the hospital has been conducted so as to violate its character in the smallest degree. It is simply the case of a secular corporation being managed by people who hold to the doctrines of the Roman Catholic Church, but who nevertheless are managing the corporation according to the law under which it exists. . . .[94]

So, where there is a specific constitutional clause banning aid to sectarian charitable institutions, there would seem to be little basis for sustaining such aid. Where there is no such provision, however, this aid may be justified under a number of possible rationales. Courts attempting to justify such appropriations have relied on the "conduit" theory and refused to look beyond the purpose and composition of the corporation controlling the hospital as it was incorporated.

It would seem reasonable to deny aid to sectarian hospitals where there is a specific constitutional provision forbidding such aid, but the reasoning of the courts allowing this aid where there is no specific constitutional inhibition would seem more valid, in light of the nature of these hospitals and social function which they perform.

2. Custodial Institutions

There is some authority from states having constitutional clauses of this type that would indicate the permissibility of assistance by the state to custodial institutions operated by religious organizations. The cases, however, are decided under unique exceptions to the instant constitutional provisions, and are therefore poor authority elsewhere for sustaining such aid.

New York has a typical clause: "The money of the state shall not be given or loaned to or in aid of any private corporation or association . . ."[95]; but a very broad, and not at all typical, exception thereto: "Payments by counties, cities or towns to charitable, eleemosynary, correctional and reformatory institutions and agencies, wholly or partly under public or private control, for care, support and maintenance, may be authorized, but shall not be required, by the legislature."[96] Under this provision it has been held that a local Board of Supervisors may collect a tax and pay that sum to a corporation organized to care for and educate orphans, even though the purposes of the corporation include the education of children of poor clergymen.[97] Similarly, the New York Court of Appeals has held that a county was not precluded by the state constitution from appropriating funds for the secular education of the inmates of an orphan asylum by reason of the fact that the orphanage was under the control of a religious organization, and that the teachers in the asylum were members of the sisterhood.[98]

A Pennsylvania case,[99] decided under that state's provision banning appropriations for charitable or benevolent purposes to any sectarian or denominational institution,[100] held that payment of funds by a county Institutional District for care and maintenance of children placed by a Juvenile Court in sectarian homes was constitutional. The court noted that this was not a bequest to the institution, but payment to the home for the children. This view is difficult to reconcile with that taken by the Pennsylvania court in rejecting the permissibility of payment by the state of a per diem charge for indigents to sectarian hospitals.[101] In both cases the fact that the appropriation is for the individual and not for the institution would seem clear. The rejection of the conduit theory in the case of hospitals, and its acceptance in the case of orphanages, is inexplicable in terms of the constitutional language or public policy.

Most of the litigation in the area of governmental grants to sectarian custodial institutions has arisen in states not having the instant clauses.

A large number of these cases arose in Illinois. The religious freedom clause of the Illinois Constitution provides that "No person shall be required to . . . support any ministry or place of worship against his consent, . . ."[102] and another clause forbids the government to appropriate anything "to any church or for any sectarian purpose."[103]

As early as 1882 the Illinois Court had ruled that the industrial schools for girls, authorized by statute, were not sectarian institutions.[104] Six years later, the Court ruled the Chicago Industrial School for Girls, which had no facilities of its own, could not make payments to the House of the Good Shepherd and St. Joseph's Orphange, institutions related to the Catholic Church, for caring for the children.[105] This would be aid of a sectarian purpose, concluded the Court, after noting that the doctrines of the Catholic Church were taught in these homes. The Court said:

> It is an untenable position that public funds may be paid out to help support sectarian schools provided only such schools shall render a quid pro quo for the payments made to them. The constitution declares against the use of public funds to aid sectarian schools independently of the question whether there is or is not a consideration furnished in return for the funds so used.[106]

In 1917, however, the Illinois Court repudiated the reasoning of the 1888 decision and sustained a payment of fifteen dollars per month to the Chicago Industrial School for Girls, a Catholic institution to which Catholic girls were committed by the juvenile courts.[107] The children participated in religious services, but the Court remarked "The people not only did not declare hostility to religion but regard its teachings and practices as a public benefit which might be equal to the payment of taxes."[108] Continuing, the Court ruled that the Illinois Constitution would not be violated *if payments to the religious institution were less than the costs of the public services provided by the government.* The Court noted:

> It would be contrary to the letter and spirit of the constitution to exclude from religious exercises the members of any denomination when the State assumes their control or to prevent the children of members from receiving the religious instruction which they would have received at home. The constitutional prohibition against furnishing aid or preference to any church or sect is to be rigidly enforced but it is contrary to fact and reason to say that paying less than the actual cost of clothing, medical care and attention, education and training in useful arts and sciences, is aiding the institution where such things are furnished.[109]

At the same term of Court, and on the same reasoning, the Illinois Court sustained such payments to the Addison Manual Training School for

Boys, an institution operated by the Lutheran Church, to which children of all faiths were sent. There was no religious instruction and no religious songs were sung, but the school was opened with prayer.[110]

The rationale and decision were repeated the following year when the Court sustained payments to the Kettler Manual Training School for Boys, operated by the German Catholic Orphanage Society,[111] and again in 1919 when the court upheld payments to St. Hedwig's Industrial School for Girls.[112] The court reiterated its oft-repeated rationale: "One who pays less for benefits or services than the actual cost of the same is not making a donation by such payment."[113]

The policy of the Illinois Court is clear then; if the payments by the government to the sectarian custodial institution are less than it would cost the government to furnish the services itself, the appropriations are constitutional. The reasoning is financially utilitarian on the surface, but the "cut-off point" posited by the Illinois Court would seem to be valid in determining when the institution in question stops being a conduit and starts receiving aid for its own purposes.

Maryland, which has only a general clause providing that no ". . . person . . . be compelled to . . . maintain, or contribute . . . to maintain, any place of worship, or any ministry . . . ,"[114] has upheld a contract whereby wards of a city would be cared for in asylums conducted under religious auspices.[115] In sustaining the validity of a contract with the St. Mary's Industrial School for Boys, the Maryland Industrial School for Girls, and the St. Vincent's Infant Asylum of Baltimore, the court observed that "The fact that the institutions may be under denominational or religious control can in no manner affect their qualifications for assuming such relation to the city. . . ."[116] The court went on to note that ". . . . charity, to say the least of the matter, is quite as likely to be fully and faithfully administered under such auspices as it could be under any other. It could therefore be no objection that the institutions are or may be under the control and influence of those belonging to any particular church or denomination."[117]

Florida's Constitution provides that "no money shall ever be taken from the public treasury directly or indirectly in aid of any church, sect or religious denomination or in aid of any sectarian institution."[118] The Florida Court has ruled that, so long as no state monies were to be spent, there could be perpetuated a chapel in buildings of a Negro industrial school taken over by a county board of public instruction.[119]

Oklahoma's Constitution is quite comparable. It provides:

> No public money or property shall ever be appropriated, applied, donated, or used; directly or indirectly, for the use, benefit, or support of any sect, church, denomination, or system of religion, or for the use, benefit, or support of any priest, preacher, minister, or other religious teacher or dignitary, or sectarian institution as such.[120]

Noting that there were state-paid chaplains at the state hospitals and reformatories, as well as at "Girls' Town," a state institution, the Oklahoma Supreme Court held constitutional, under this clause, the construction of a chapel for nonsectarian, nondenominational religious worship on grounds owned by the state and used for an orphans' home.[121] The Court noted that separation of church and state "does not mean to compel or require separation from God." [122]

In another Oklahoma case,[123] a home operated by the Baptists sued the state auditor on a contract whereby the state had promised to support children. The Oklahoma Court sustained the contract and ordered such payments, remarking: ". . . so long as they involve the element of substantial return to the state and do not amount to a gift, donation, or appropriation to the institution having no relevancy to the affairs of the state, there is constitutional provision offended." [124]

An 1882 Nevada case[125] came to an opposite result when Catholic children in attendance at the Nevada Orphan Asylum, operated by a Catholic group, were given instruction in the Catholic faith and every morning said the Lord's Prayer, the Apostles Creed, etc., even though Protestant children were excused from such exercises and instruction. The Nevada Court refused mandamus for the payment of seventy-five dollars per orphan, as promised, under the Constitution which read: "No public funds of any kind or character whatever, state, county, or municipal, shall be used for sectarian purposes." [126]

Illinois, with its general constitutional clause that no person shall be required to support any ministry or place of worship against his consent,[127] has ruled that a county may permit a religious denomination to hold religious services at the county poor farm and to erect a chapel there, without charge to the county.[128] Speaking of the constitutional clause, the Illinois Supreme Court stated:

> This does not mean that religion is abolished. The State undertakes to provide for all the wants of the unfortunate wards whom it has collected at the poor farm . . . . If charitably disposed persons wish to hold religious services in the lecture room or reading room occasionally or regularly, without expense to the county, no constitutional right is interfered with. Religious privileges are brought to the inmates, which may be availed of by each according to his own wishes. No one can be obliged to attend or to contribute, but no one has a right to insist that the services shall not be held. The man of no religion has a right to act in accordance with his lack of religion, but no right to insist that other shall have no religion.[129]

It is difficult to generalize in this area. The only two cases decided under a specific constitutional provision banning aid to sectarian charitable institutions upheld such aid, but as has been noted, both cases are *sui generis*—one invoked New York's unique constitutional exception to the instant prohibition, and the other is quite inconsistent with the substantial body of case law on aid to sectarian hospitals in Pennsylvania.

Where there has been no specific constitutional ban at issue, the cases are divided, with a majority upholding such aid. Here too, however, it is difficult to generalize, as the cases are frequently decided on the basis of the particular facts therein. It seems safe to say, however, that many jurisdictions will allow this aid if they are convinced that the appropriation is for the benefit of individuals, and not for the sectarian institution. Various criteria are used in determining this, but the cost of the care (as compared to what it would cost the state to provide the care itself), and whether or not the individual was committed to the institution by a court, would appear most important.

3. Welfare Organizations

While there is a good deal of case law on the subject of governmental aid to non-Governmental charities, very little of it deals with sectarian charities, and most of the cases dealing with sectarian welfare organizations do not arise under the instant constitutional provisions. Generally, appropriation of public money to a sectarian charitable institution is held unconstitutional under clauses prohibiting the use of state funds for sectarian purposes.[130]

Louisiana is apparently the only state with rulings under a specific clause banning aid to sectarian charitable organizations. Under the Louisiana constitution "No appropriation from the state treasury shall be made for private, charitable or benevolent purposes to any person or community; provided, this shall not apply to . . . public charitable institutions conducted under state authority."[131] In 1898 the Louisiana court ruled that this clause prevents appropriations from the state treasury, but does not prevent municipal corporations in the state from, aiding charitable and benevolent institutions.[132] Rulings of the State Attorney General seem to find constitutional local contributions to orphanages, the Red Cross, the Salvation Army and other welfare agencies,[133] but leave in doubt the permissibility of donations to the Boy Scouts and Knights of Columbus.[134]

Some states not having specific bans on contribtutions to charitable and benevolent organizations have had to resolve controversies in this area under their more general constitutional clauses. Nebraska, for example, with a general clause that no one shall be compelled to "support any place of worship against his consent,"[135] and a clause banning aid to "sectarian or denominational" educational institutions,[136] has ruled that a public power district could not make pledges to the local Community Chest since this charity passed on funds to religious organizations doing charitable work.[137] The Court observed that:

> If by giving to agencies of this character, even though the money given is designated to be used for activities non-sectarian in char-

acter, it makes available to such agency for religious or educational purposes money it has on hand to an extent not otherwise possible, thus indirectly doing what the Constitution prohibits, we think it would be bad.[138]

Comparably, the Georgia Court has declared unconstitutional a contract between a city and the Salvation Army, whereby the latter would assume responsibility for the charitable work of the city.[139] The Georgia Constitution states "No money shall ever be taken from the pubilc treasury, directly or indirectly, in aid of any church, sect, or denomination of religionists, or of any sectarian institution."[140] The Court noted that the Salvation Army was a sectarian institution within the meaning of the state constitution, and that paying that organization for caring for the poor, although at actual cost, was giving a great advantage and substantial aid to that institution in the prosecution of its religious and benevolent purposes.

On the other hand, Utah, with a general clause quite like Georgia's [141] has ruled that an appropriation to the Daughters of the Utah Pioneers was not violative of the state constitution, even though the historical display planned by that organization would be largely representative of the Mormon Church.[142] The court characterized this as "a coincidence of history rather than a deliberate attempt to further that faith."[143]

Because of the scarcity of material in the area of governmental aid to church-related welfare organizations, either under the instant specific constitutional prohibiiton or under broader clauses, it is truly impossible to generalize here. The scant authority under specific constitutional bans would seem to permit appropriations by local governments to sectarian welfare organizations, while, curiously, the cases decided under broader provisions would seem, generally, to deny the constitutionality of such aid. Because of this scarcity of material, and the anomalous nature of what there is of it, it is submitted that the much more varied and authoritative body of case law discussed under hospitals and custodial institutions, *supra*, is the most valid source of precedent in this area.

In summary, it is true on the one hand that the state constitutional clauses herein discussed effectively restrict state aid to churches and related institutions. However, they do not necessarily prohibit all such aid. As the courts have frequently pointed out, interpretations attempting to preclude any practice which might in some fashion benefit a religious group or church are as undesirable as the practice of giving direct aid.

As was seen, the validity of any aid practice seems to turn primarily on the type of aid granted and the nature of the recipient institution. It is apparent that direct grants of cash or its equivalent are prohibited under the constitutions of all states. Aid of this kind was denied even where the money would have been used for the purpose of restoring historical monuments on the ground that such monuments still had religious significance.

The issue is less sharp with regard to the use of public property by religious groups. Predictably, the states are divided on this question. In a number of states, especially those with restrictive constitutional clauses, any use of this property by a religious organization is improper. This is true whether or not any rental is paid. Many states, however, have upheld the use of such property when the use was adjudged to be only temporary or periodic. Normally, the payment of a fair rental is also required. Moreover, the likelihood that the use will be permitted is greater in states which have only a general "no aid" clause. Some courts are influenced further if taxpayer objections are only *de minimis*, or if the benefit received is only *incidental*. Neither test is very certain, and, oftentimes, a slight change of degree in either direction will effect the validity of any aid practice.

The states are divided also on the extent to which aid should be granted to charitable agencies operated by religious groups. Apparently instrumental in the determination of the propriety of such aid to these entities has been the language of the constitutional clause itself. This is especially evident in the case of the hospitals. Special attention is paid to the way in which the hospitals are operated, as well as the nature of the control exercised by the sectarian body. It is safe to say that in the majority of jurisdictions, the mere fact that a hospital or similar institution is under the adminsitrative control of persons who espouse a certain religious belief—even as an organized community—is not sufficient to brand the institution as "sectarian" and preclude it from aid. In the case of hospitals, the courts seem especially receptive to the "conduit" theory, since the patient is clearly the direct beneficiary.

The same is true with regard to other welfare agencies sponsored by religious groups. Such agencies commonly have a lengthy history of public service. Once again the likelihood that the courts will uphold aid to these agencies may ultimately depend upon the type of clause involved. A broad clause gives the courts leeway in interpreting; and when this is the case, they tend to favor an interpretation which allows the aid. In states with narrowly written clauses, the courts rarely have an alternative except to disallow the aid.

In this chapter, we have discussed the various types of aid to religious institutions and organizations in general. Although schools were also included within the scope of this discussion, they raise problems which require more extensive treatment. The next chapter, therefore, is devoted solely to the constitutional clauses which operate to prohibit aid to church-related educational institutions.

Chapter Two

Constitutional Bans Upon Aid To Church-Related Educational Institutions

Generally

Numerous states have constitutional clauses specifically banning aid by the state to church related ("sectarian," "religious," "denominational") educational institutions.[1] In addition, a number of other states have more broadly stated constitutional clauses banning aid to religious or charitable organizations.[2] Cases in the area of aid to church related educational institutions have frequently been litigated under both of these types of clauses. Finally, there is a seemingly endless variety of state constitutional clauses that can limit state aid to church related schools. Amongst these are: the typical freedom of religion clause, general bans upon the establishment of religion, clauses to the effect that no one shall be compelled to support any church, prohibitions on the use of public school funds for any other purpose,[3] bans upon the grant of public funds or property to educational institutions not under state control,[4] bans on the use of public funds for any sectarian purpose,[5] bans upon the use of public funds to aid educational institutions under sectarian control,[6] prohibitions upon state aid to sectarian schools,[7] prohibitions on state aid to private schools,[8] bans upon spending public funds in aid of any school where sectarian doctrine is taught,[9] prohibition upon the control of school funds by religious sects,[10] prohibitions on spending public funds for private purposes, and bans upon lending the public credit.

The cases that have been litigated under these various constitutional clauses are here divided into the following areas:

The grant of funds or property to church related educational institutions.

State provision of textbooks for children attending church-related schools.

23

State provision of transportation for children attending church-related schools.

Payment of rent to church authorities for use of physical facilities by public schools.

Payment of salaries to teachers in church-related schools.

Payment of tuition for students attending church-related schools.

Sale of public property to church-related educational institutions.

Programs whereby the public schools release children for attendance at religious services elsewhere.

Use of public facilities, services, and teachers by church-related schools.

Religious instruction of public school students in public schools outside of school hours.

Shared time.

The Grants of Funds or Property to Church-Related Educational Institutions

Although the early history of the United States was characterized by frequent gifts of both land and money to church-related educational institutions, the overwhelming majority of litigated cases decided in the last century decide, or indicate, that such grants are violative of various state constitutional clauses. Stated somewhat differently, the courts customarily have not permitted the levy of taxes to aid church-related educational institutions.

In a number of instances local authorities have apparently attempted to finance educational institutions closely related to various church groups as "public schools." Courts have denied the use of public funds for such schools when they are convinced that the institutions are under the control of sectarian authorities or are but vehicles for the inculcation of religion.

There is but occasional reception of the thesis that payment can be made to church-related educational institutions because they provide services to those children who are special wards of the state.

From 1821 until until 1917 the Massachusetts Constitution provided:

> All moneys raised by taxation in the towns and cities for the support of public schools, and all moneys which may be appropriated by the state for the support of common schools, shall be applied to, and expended in, no other schools than those which are conducted according to law, under the order and superintendence of the authorities of the town or city in which the money is to be expended; and such moneys shall never be appropriated to any religious sect for the maintenance, exclusively, of its own school.[11]

This clause did not prevent the Massachusetts Supreme Court from upholding the Legislature in spending money raised by taxation for a nonsectarian agricultural school at Amherst. The Court, in passing, explained the purpose of the foregoing constitutional clause:

> The object of the provision is to regulate the expenditure of money raised by town or cities for general educational purposes, and to confine it strictly to the support of the common or public schools, which every town is required to maintain under the general law . . . and also to restrain the raising of money by taxation for the support of schools of a religious and sectarian character.[12]

Three years later the Court ruled that a town could not appropriate money which had been raised by taxation to support, as a public school, an educational institution founded by a charitable bequest which vested power in trustees who, though a majority were to be chosen by the inhabitants of the town, yet were required to be members of certain religious societies.[13] In 1913, the Massachusetts Court ruled that aid to sectarian colleges and universities would be constitutional under the then existing constitutional language. The Court explained:

> Article XVIII of the Amendments to the Constitution was adopted because of a deep-seated conviction of the imperative necessity of preserving the public system in its integrity and of guarding it from attack or change by explicit mandate. Public schools never have been understood to include higher institutions of learning like colleges and universities. All money raised by taxation for the purpose of expenditure within the sphere of the public or common schools, as these words generally have been understood, must not be diverted to any other kind of school maintained in whole or in part by any religious sect. But there is no constitutional prohibition of appropriations for higher educational institutions, societies, or undertakings under sectarian or ecclesiastical control.[14]

Perhaps because of popular dissatisfaction with this ruling, the Massachusetts Constitution was amended in 1917 to read, as presently:

> All moneys raised by taxation in the towns and cities for the support of public schools, and all moneys which may be appropriated by the commonwealth for the support of common schools shall be applied to and expended in, no other schools than those which are conducted according to law, under the order and superintendence of the authorities of the town or city in which the money is expended; and no grant, appropriation or use of public money or property or loan of public credit shall be made or authorized by the commonwealth or any political division thereof for the purpose of founding, maintaining or aiding any school or institution of learning, whether under public control or otherwise, wherein any denominational doctrine is inculcated, or any other school, or any college, infirmary, hospital, institution, or educational, charitable or religious undertaking which is not publicly owned and under the exclusive control, order and superintendence of public officers or public agents authorized by the commowealth or federal authority or both . . . and no such grant, appropriation or use of public money or property or loan of public credit shall be made or authorized for the purpose of

founding, maintaining or aiding any church, religious denomination or society.[15]

Under the amended clause it would appear that state aid to sectarian colleges or universities is now forbidden.

Nebraska's Constitution contains the usual religious freedom clause, with the added guarantee that "No person shall be compelled to . . . support any place of worship against his consent . . . ."[16] Additionally, the Constitution provides:

> No sectarian instruction shall be allowed in any school or institution supported in whole or in part by the public funds set apart for educational purposes, nor shall the state accept any grant, conveyance, or bequest of money, lands or other property to be used for sectarian purposes. Neither the State Legislature nor any county, city or other public corporation, shall ever make any appropriation from any public funds, or grant any public land in aid of any sectarian or denominational school or college, or any educational institution which is not exclusively owned and controlled by the state or a governmental subdivision thereof.[17]

In 1932, the State Superintendant of Public Instruction refused to allocate public funds to a "public school" because he deemed it to be a sectarian institution. His action was upheld by the State Supreme Court which noted that the three rooms in which classes were held were located in a building rented by the school district and belonging to the Catholic Church. The name "St. Boniface School" was inscribed over the entrance, there was a cross on the top of the building, the land belonged to the Catholic Church, the building was across the street from a Catholic Church, the building contained a chapel in its basement, and instruction in the supposedly public school was given by three nuns who wore their distinctive garb.[18]

Missouri's Constitution contains the usual freedom of religion clause,[19] a clause prohibiting the state to compel any person to support any place of worship, priest, minister, preacher or teacher of any sect or church,[20] and a clause providing:

> That no money shall ever be taken from the public treasury, directly or indirectly, in aid of any church, sect or denomination of religion, or in aid of any priest, preacher, minister or teacher thereof, as such; and that no preference shall be given to nor any discrimination made against any church, sect or creed of religion, or any form of religious faith or worship.[21]

Furthermore, the Constitution ordains that:

> Neither the general assembly, nor any county, city, town, township, school district or other municipal corporation, shall ever make an appropriation or pay from any public fund whatever, anything in aid of any religious creed, church or sectarian purpose, or to help

to support or sustain any private or public school, academy, seminary, college, university, or other institution of learning controlled by any religious creed, church or sectarian denomination whatever; nor shall any grant or donation of personal property or real estate ever be made by the state, or any county, city, town or other municipal corporation, for any religious creed, church, or sectarian purpose whatever.[22]

Under these clauses, the Missouri Court has enjoined the use of school funds for a "public school" which was found to be sectarian and religious. A Catholic school building had been taken over by the public authorities, but the institution was still called "St. Cecilia School." The teachers paid by the public school authorities were nuns. The school day commenced with prayer, then the children were marched to the Catholic Church next door for Mass; after this, they were marched back to the school rooms for religious instruction. On half of the school days the parish priest gave religious instruction in the building and on Friday afternoon the children were marched to the church for confession. In the school rooms were pictures and symbols of the Catholic faith, as well as holy water fonts. Usually all of the hundred or more children in attendance at the school were of the Catholic faith, but in some years there were one or two non-Catholics.[23]

Again, in 1953, the Missouri Supreme Court refused to permit the transfer of public funds to a "public school" when the Court concluded that in reality it was a sectarian school administered to promote the interests of the Catholic Church. The following facts were deemed controlling, by the Court, as to the characterization of the institution:

1. The school was owned by the Church and held in the name of the bishop.
2. The buildings were located upon church property.
3. Teaching was by nuns, dressed in distinctive garb and wearing emblems of their religious order.
4. Religious services were conducted daily by priests and nuns at the adjacent church building.
5. There was religious teaching daily in the school building.
6. The same school buses were used to transport children to this "public school" as for Saturday religious instruction.
7. Non-Catholic children were sent to another school district, with the defendant school district paying their tuition.[24]

Similarly, the Kansas Court ruled that a plaintiff had stated a cause of action when he alleged the public school district had in fact operated a sectarian institution. According to the allegations, the school was conducted in a dormitory/home of priests and sisters of the Catholic church, instruction was provided by sisters, and the program was sectarian. In overruling a demurrer of the defendants, the Court suggested that if the allegations could be proved the school would not be "public" and use of public funds to support it would violate the Kansas Constitution.[25] The religious liberty clause provides that no person shall be compelled to support any form of worship.[26] Another clause provides: "No religious sect or sects shall ever control any part of the common school or university funds of the state." [27]

On another occasion the Kansas Court ruled that the City of Atchison could not tax to aid two sectarian colleges in the city. No constitutional clause was cited by the Court, which preferred to rule that this was taxation for a *private* purpose and hence invalid.[28]

The Pennsylvania Court has held that the City of Pittsburgh could not use tax funds to aid Duquesne University.[29] This, ruled the Court, violated Art. III, sec. 18 of the State Constitution, which provides: "No appropriations shall be made for charitable, educational or benevolent purposes to any person or community nor to any denominational and sectarian institution, corporation or association . . . ."

In an early Texas case the plaintiff alleged that the public school was taught by a member of the Baptist Church in a house belonging to the Baptist Association and that daily prayers were said. The Texas Court ruled judicial relief would be improper since the plaintiff had failed to appeal first to the state superintendent of schools for relief.[30]

Relief was denied also to a protestant who thought his public school had been converted into a sectarian institution because four of the six teachers were sisters who wore religious garb while working. The North Dakota Court was unanimous in holding that these facts did not make of the public school a sectarian institution.[31]

The Oklahoma Court has held that the state could pay a sectarian orphanage for housing and educating orphans. Speaking of the terms of the contract, the Court said: ". . . so long as they involve the element of substantial return to the State and do not amount to a gift, donation or appropriation to the institution having no relevance to the affairs of the State, there is no constitutional provision offended."[32] The constitutional clause litigated provides that the State shall not "make donation by gift, subscription to stock, by tax, or otherwise, to any company, association, or corporation." [33]

The New York Constitution provides:

> Neither the State nor any subdivision thereof, shall use its property or credit or any public money, or authorize or permit either to be used, directly or indirectly, in aid or maintenance, other than for examination or inspection, of any school or institution of learning wholly or in part under the control or direction of any religious denomination, or in which any denominational tenet or doctrine is taught.[34]

In 1910 a contract between a municipality and the lessee of its waterworks was held valid as to a provision wherein the lessee became bound to furnish water free of cost to the parochial schools in the town. The above constitutional clause was not violated, said the court, inasmuch as the water became the private property of the lessee who could do with it as he pleased.[35]

Generally then, most courts would deny the constitutionality of appropriations of public money to aid church-related educational institutions. Where the institution is admittedly sectarian, the courts have no problem in prohibiting these grants.[36] Where the institution is called public, but is, in reality, a sectarian school, the courts are split, with the majority, however, looking to the substance of the school rather than its form, and holding such appropriations unconstitutional.

State Provision of Textbooks for Children Attending Church-Related Schools

There are few cases passing upon the permissibility of the state or its political subdivisions providing textbooks to children attending church-related schools. The Mississippi and Louisiana Courts have sustained such provision and the United States Supreme Court has ruled that the Louisiana practice did not violate the Fourteenth Amendment. At that time, however, the First Amendment establishment ban had not yet been made binding upon the states and consequently the current constitutionality of the practice is in some doubt. The New York, New Mexico, and Oregon courts have ruled that their state constitutions preclude the provision of textbooks to children attending church-related schools. Where the practice has been sustained the books were not of a sectarian or religious nature. These courts sustaining the practice looked upon the provision of textbooks, especially by loan, as being for the benefit of the children and the state, not for any religious institution.

Louisiana has a constitutional freedom of religion clause which contains the ban upon establishment in these words:

> No law shall be passed respecting an establishment of religion . . . nor shall any preference ever be given, nor any discrimination made against, any church, sect or creed of religion, or any form of religious faith or worship.[37]

Another clause of the constitution ordains that "No public funds shall be used for the support of any private or sectarian school."[38] The Louisiana Supreme Court ruled in 1927 that neither of these constitutional provisions was violated by the provision of textbooks which were neither sectarian nor religious in nature to children attending church related schools. The court held that the church related schools "are not the beneficiaries of these appropriations," adding that "It was for their (the children's) benefit and the resulting benefit to the state that the appropriations were made."[39] The same ruling was repeated in another case during the same term, and, on appeal to the United States Court, the practice of providing free textbooks to children attending church related schools was held constitutional. The establishment ban of the First Amendment not yet having been made binding on the states through the Fourteenth Amendment, the Court ruled that the purchase of school books for such children was not the spending of public money for a private purpose.[40]

Mississippi's Constitution contains a general freedom of religion clause, with the provision that "no preference shall be given by law to any religious sect or mode of worship." [41] In addition, another clause provides:

> No religious or other sect or sects shall ever control any part of the school or other educational funds of this state; nor shall any funds be appropriated toward the support of any sectarian school, or to any school that at the time of receiving such appropriation is not conducted as a free school.[42]

The Supreme Court of Mississippi has ruled that children attending church-related schools can be provided with free textbooks, in common with children attending the public schools. Justice Alexander observed:

> If the pupil may fulfill its duty to the state by attending a parochial school it is difficult to see why the state may not fulfill its duty to the pupil by encouraging it 'by all suitable means.' The state is under a duty to ignore the child's creed, but not its need . . . . The state which allows the pupil to subscribe to any religious creed should not, because of his exercise of this right, proscribe him from benefits common to all . . . . "Even as there is no religious qualification in its public servants for office there should be no religious disqualification in its private citizens for privileges available to a class to which they belong." [43]

It should be noted that under the Mississippi practice the books were on loan to the children, there was no contention that the books were "sectarian in their content," and they dealt with "health, democracy, good citizenship, history, as well as elemental studies in literature, science, geography, mathematics and language." [44]

New York has a typical constitutional clause prohibiting the use of public property or money in aid to denominational schools.[45] In 1922 the Appellate Division of the Supreme Court ruled that Ogdensburg could not use funds to provide textbooks and school supplies to children attending parochial schools. The court said:

> Even though we accept the statute as meaning that the books and supplies are to be furnished to the pupils and not to the school, we think the act plainly comes within the prohibition of the Constitution; if not directly in aid of the parochial schools, it certainly is indirect aid.[46]

The New Mexico Constitution provides:

> The schools, colleges, universities and other educational institutions
> provided for by this Constitution shall forever remain under the
> exclusive control of the State, and no . . . . funds appropriated,
> levied or collected for educational purposes, shall be used for the
> support of any sectarian, denominational or private school, college
> or university.[47]

Under this clause, the New Mexico Supreme Court affirmed a decree
of a lower court forbidding the furnishing of free textbooks, by the state,
to students attending church-related educational institutions.[48]

Oregon's constitutional clause more generally bans aid to religion.
It provides:

> No money shall be drawn from the Treasury for the benefit of
> any religeous (sic), or theological institution, nor shall any money
> be appropriated for the payment of any religeous (sic) services
> in either house of the Legislative Assembly.[49]

Nevertheless, the Oregon Court reached the identical result as in New
York and New Mexico, namely, that provision of textbooks even on loan
to children attending parochial schools would be unconstitutional.   The
Court refused to accept either the child welfare or public benefit arguments.   It further held that failure to provide textbooks to such children
was not violative of Equal Protection.   The Court explained: "The
classification which excludes such pupils from the State's bounty is not
only reasonable, it is commanded by the Constitution itself."[50]   Legislation has recently been enacted in Rhode Island approving the loan of
textbooks to pupils attending private schools.   Its constitutionally has
not yet been tested.[51]

It would appear that the only possible manner in which provision
of textbooks for students in church-related schools may be constitutionally
permissible is when the books in question are of a non-sectarian nature.
Even here, however, there is a split of authority, with some states,
notably Louisiana and Mississippi, upholding the practice; and others,
specifically New York, New Mexico, and Oregon denying its constitutionality.   Whether the "child benefit" reasoning of courts allowing the provision of testbooks to scholars attending church affiliated schools will withstand the First Amendment ban remains to be litigated before the United
States Supreme Court.

Provision of Transportation for Children Attending Church-Related Schools

Although the United States Supreme Court has ruled that the United
States Constitution permits states and their political subdivisions to
provide transportation for children attending church-related schools,[52]

the state courts are divided as to the constitutionality of such practice under their state constitutions. To some extent the decisions hinge upon the wording of the particular state constitutions, although a number of restrictive clauses have been ruled not violated on the "child-benefit" theory. By constitutional amendment or judicial decision, bus transportation of children attending church-related schools is permissible in New York, New Jersey, California, Connecticut, Kentucky and Maryland. There is some evidence that it is lawful in Massachusetts. On the other hand the practice has been ruled unconstitutional by courts in Alaska, Delaware, Missouri, New Mexico, Oklahoma, Washington and Wisconsin.[53]

After the New York Court of Appeals had disallowed bus transportation for children attending parochial schools[54] the people of that State amended their constitution so as to authorize such transportation. The clause banning public funds for educational institutions under "the control or direction of any religious denomination," now provides, further: "but the legislature may provide for the transportation of children to and from any school or institution of learning."[55] As so amended, the New York constitution permits transportation of children to church-related schools.[56]

The New Jersey Constitution similarly provides: "The Legislature may, within reasonable limitations as to distance to be prescribed, provide for the transportation of children within the ages of five to eighteen years inclusive to and from any school."[57] The Supreme Court of that State has upheld bus transportation for children attending church-related schools[58] and the United States Supreme Court in affirming, has ruled that the practice is constitutional under the United States Constitution.[59]

The remaining states have adjudicated the matter of bus transportation for children attending church-related schools under their general clauses banning aid to religious institutions or educational institutions under religious control. Quite typically, the Alaska Constitution provides: "No money shall be paid from public funds for the direct benefit of any religious or other private educational institution."[60] The Alaska Supreme Court has ruled that this clause was violated by a legislative enactment authorizing bus transportation for children attending church-related schools.[61] The Court observed that if the people of Alaska had desired the result of New York and New Jersey they would have specifically included in the 1959 Alaska Constitution a clause similar to that employed in the two foregoing states. In dissent, Justice Dimond observed that the Court was expanding the constitutional ban upon "direct benefits" to a religious institution to preclude aid only *indirectly* benefitting an educational institution.[62]

California's Constitution very broadly prohibits aid to "any religious sect" or to "any school . . . controlled by any religious creed, church, or sectarian denomination whatever . . . ."[63] But transportation of children to church-related schools has been held not violative of this clause.

Concluding that the principal benefit from the transportation is to the children, the Court noted: ". . . if the benefit from that transportation is to the pupils, then an incidental benefit flowing to a denominational school from free transportation of its pupils should not be sufficient to deprive the legislature of the power to authorize a school district to transport such pupils." [64]

The Connecticut Constitution provides that no person shall be compelled "to support any congregation, church or religious association," [65] and further, that the school fund shall not be diverted "to any other use than the encouragement and support of public or common schools." [66] The Constitution permits, according to the Supreme Court of that State, provision for the transportation of pupils to church-related schools. "The transportation of school children serves a public purpose," said the Court, and added that ". . . a statute which serves a public purpose is not unconstitutional merely because it incidentally benefits a limited number of persons." [67] "In the light of our history and policy," concluded the Court, "it cannot be said to compel support of any church." [68]

However, Delaware, with a constitutional clause providing that the public school fund "shall not be appropriated to, or used by, or in aid of any sectarian church or denominational school" [69] has ruled void a statute appropriating money from the *general* fund for transportation of pupils attending *free* schools supported by any church or religious society. [70]

Kentucky's Constitution prohibits compelling any person "to contribute to the support or maintenance" of any place of worship. [71] The high court of that State has ruled this clause was not violated by a statute providing transportation for children attending church-related schools. The Court stated:

> . . . it cannot be said with any reason or consistency that tax legislation to provide our school children with safe transportation is not tax legislation for a public purpose. Neither can it be said that such legislation or such taxation is an aid of a church, or of a private, sectarian, or parochial school, nor that it is other than what it is designed and purports to be, . . . legislation for the health and safety of our children, the future citizens of our state. The fact that in a strained and technical sense the school might derive an indirect benefit from the enactment, is not sufficient to defeat the declared purpose and the practical and wholesome effect of the law. [72]

Without passing upon the constitutional question the Maine Supreme Court held unauthorized for want of a legislative enabling act a municipal ordinance providing bus transportation for children attending church-related schools, dictum indicates such an act would be constitutional. [73]

Maryland's Constitution contains the typical clause providing that no person shall be compelled to contribute to any ministery or place of worship.[74] Additionally, it has a clause providing that the school fund shall be kept inviolate.[75]   Bus transportation of children to church-related schools violates neither of these clauses, according to the Court of Appeals of that State.   Any aid to such school was but incidental and a by-product of the legitimate legislative activity, namely protecting children on their way to and from school, which they are compelled to attend by law.[76]   The decision was affirmed four years later.[77]

Without openly passing upon the constitutionality of the enactment, the Massachusetts Court gave mandamus ordering authorities to provide transportation for children attending private schools, as required by act of the Legislature.[78]

Missouri's Constitution includes the typical clause that no one shall be compelled to support any place of worship or to maintain or support any priest, minister, preacher or teacher of any sect, church, creed or denomination of religion.[79]   Another clause states that "That no money shall ever be taken from the public treasury, directly or indirectly, in aid of any church, sect or denomination of religion, or in aid of any priest, preacher, minister or teacher thereof, as such." [80]   Other clauses ban diversion of the state university fund to other uses or purposes,[81] and decree that the county school fund shall be "sacredly preserved." [82] Under these clauses the Missouri Court has found "unlawful" the use of public funds to transport children to church-related schools.[83]   In a case decided under the clause in the New Mexico Constitution banning the use of public school funds "for the support of any sectarian, denominational or private school, college or university" [84] a lower court decree enjoining state provision of bus transportation for children attending church related schools was affirmed by the Supreme Court of that State.[85]

Oklahoma has a frequently found constitutional clause banning the use of public money or property for sectarian purposes. It states:

> No public money or property shall ever be appropriated, applied, donated, or used, directly or indirectly, for the use, benefit, or support of any sect, church, denomination, or system of religion, or for the use, benefit, or support of any priest, preacher, minister, or other religious teacher or dignitary, or sectarian institution as such.[86]

According to the Oklahoma Court, such clause forbids the use of public funds to provide transportation to church-related schools.[87]

Pennsylvania's Constitution includes the clause providing the "No money raised for the support of the public schools of the Commonwealth shall be appropriated to or used for the support of any sectarian school." [88] The Pennsylvania Court has never directly ruled on the constitutional issue, but strong dictum in a 1947 case indicates that bus transportation to church-related schools would be unconstitutional.[89]   Again, in 1957, without deciding the constitutionality of legislative permission, the Court ruled that the board of directors of a local school district was without discretionary power to transport non-public school pupils.[90] However, the Attorney General of Pennsylvania has recently noted that a proposed "equal bus" law would be valid under the instant constitutional provision.[91]

The Constitution of the State of Washington provides that "No public money or property shall be appropriated for or applied to any religious worship, exercise or instruction, or the support of any religious establishment."[92] It adds: "All schools maintained or supported wholly or in part by the public funds shall be forever free from sectarian control or influence."[93] Under these clauses the Washington Court has ruled invalid a statute authorizing transportation of pupils to private schools.[94]

The Wisconsin Constitution ordains: ". . . nor shall any money be drawn from the treasury for the benefit of religious societies, or religious or theological seminaries," and adds that no one shall be compelled to support any place of worship or ministry.[95] In 1962 the Wisconsin Court held unconstitutional a statute authorizing the school boards to transport children to parochial schools. The Court said:

> Those parochial schools, which now pay part or all of the cost of transportation of their pupils out of their school funds, stand to benefit financially by the operation of the new act. Others stand to gain through increased enrollment. Such an increase of enrollment is a benefit to these parochial schools."[96]

In a number of states there are rulings of attorneys general on the constitutionality of transporting children to church-related schools. Thus, the Attorney General of Louisiana has ruled that parishes can provide transportation to parochial school children.[97] Similarly, the Michigan Attorney General has ruled constitutional Michigan's new equal bus law.[98] On the other hand, the Minnesota Attorney General has ruled that bus transportation can be provided only for children attending public schools,[99] under that State's Constitution which provides that no portion of the public school fund "or any public moneys or property, be appropriated or used for the support of schools wherein the distinctive doctrines, creeds or tenets of any particular Christian or other religious sect are promulgated or taught."[100] School districts are not authorized in South Dakota to provide bus transportation for children attending church-related schools.[101]

In a somewhat different transportation case, the Oklahoma Court ruled that the language "public schools of said city" in a franchise ordinance embraced the Catholic schools, so that their students could travel at a reduced fare. The Court said it would not assume that the parties intended to discriminate against children "going to schools that were maintained by private agencies by private benevolence for the benefit of the public."[102]

The cases, then, are split on the constitutionality of free bus transportation for children attending church-related schools. While specific constitutional clauses have sometimes been determinative of the result, it seems that, on identical facts, one court may deny the constitutionality of such a practice, while another, usually on the basis of the "child-benefit theory," may permit it.   This division of authority cannot be reconciled, and is apparently not likely to be eliminated by any recognizable trend towards one of the two positions.

Payment of Rent to Church Authorities for Use of Physical Facilities By Public Schools

Standing by itself, there is no constitutional objection, according to the majority of cases, in having the state or its political subdivisions pay rent to ecclesiastical authorities for the use of physical facilities by public schools.   However, rental of facilities seems to have been accompanied at times by a continued permeation of the facilities with religious symbolism and influence, and on occasion, even school district abdication of control to sectarian officials.   It is here that serious constitutional problems arise under all state constitutions, regardless of their wording.

The Illinois Court indicated in 1887 that boards of education can, when necessary, procure buildings for use as public schools, and it matters not that such buildings had been used previously by some religious body and are still owned by a church.   The Court denied equitable relief to a person who did not show that he had any children in such school, even though the public school was in the basement of a Catholic church, children attended mass in the church at eight o'clock, then repaired to their class room and engaged in catechism study for a half hour before the official opening of the school day, and at noon said the Angelus prayer.[103]   Illinois' religious freedom clause contains the provision: "No person shall be required to attend or support any ministry or place of worship against his consent, nor shall any preference be given by law to any religious denomination or mode of worship.[104]

Wisconsin's Constitution provides: ". . . nor shall any money be drawn from the treasury for the benefit of religious societies, or religious or theological seminaries." [105]   This constitutional provision was held not to have been violated by a practice wherein public school authorities rented and used part of a parochial school for a public school.   However, the Court enjoined the continuation of practices that resulted in the public school being pervaded by religious influences.[106]

The Kentucky Constitution provides: "No portion of any fund or tax now existing, or that may hereafter be raised or levied for educational purposes, shall be appropriated to, or used by, or in aid of any church, sectarian or denominational school." [107]   By way of dictum, the Kentucky Court has suggested that public school authorities can pay a fair rental to churches for the use of physical facilities.   Said the Court:

It was never intended by the section of the Constitution, supra, to withhold the right to teach public schools in buildings rented, or their use otherwise acquired, from others, if the circumstances justified it, although the building may be owned by a particular religious denomination. The vice sought to be prevented by the constitutional provision was the teaching of religious sectarianism in schools maintained by public funds, and which it is indisputably shown was not true in this case . . . . [108]

Eleven years earlier the Kentucky Court had voided as unconstitutional a contract between the trustees of a graded school and Stanton College, a sectarian institution, by which the College had leased to the graded school two rooms in its educational building, primarily because the public school authorities had turned over to the head of the sectarian institution effective control of the graded or public school. The Court stated:

It is not essential to the invalidity of agreements between a sectarian school and a common school that it should be shown that any part of the common school fund was paid to the sectarian institution. To so hold would be too narrow a view to take of the broad import of the constitution and does not fairly interpret the spirit of the prohibition against the union of church and school. The constitution not only forbids the appropriation for any purpose or in any manner of the common school funds to sectarian or denominational institutions but it contemplates that the separation between the common school and the sectarian or denominational school or institution shall be so open, notorious and complete that there can be no room for reasonable doubt that the common school is absolutely free from the influence, control or denomination of the sectarian institution or school. And if the arrangement between Stanton College and the graded school should be subjected to the scrutiny of this not too comprehensive or rigid test, the evidence makes it plain that it was of such a nature as to reasonably create the belief that the graded school trustees had abdicated all control and authority over the graded school and delivered its conduct entirely to Mr. Hanley, the head of the sectarian institution. [109]

Iowa's Constitution provides: "The General Assembly shall make no law respecting an establishment of religion, or prohibiting the free exercise thereof; nor shall any person be compelled to attend any place of worship, pay tithes, taxes, or other rates for building or repairing places of worship, or the maintenance of any minister, or ministry." [110] Where a public school district rented a room in a Catholic school building, the arrangement was voided by the Iowa Supreme Court because the walls were decorated with Catholic pictures, nuns taught the classes in the room rented and were paid by the school district. The Court reasoned that the school was, in effect, a parochial rather than a public school and enjoined the school district officials "from directly or indirectly making any appropriation or use of the public school funds for the support or in aid of such parochial school, or of any so-called public school maintained or conducted in connection with such parochial school." [111] Earlier the Iowa Court had acknowledged that public school authorities could rent physical facilities in a building owned by the Catholic Church for public school purposes.[112] The New Mexico Supreme Court has upheld a lower court's injunction against the rental of buildings owned by the Catholic Church which have religious emblems such as crosses, grottos, religious statuary and religious pictures remaining in them,[113] although it is not clear whether the decision is based upon the United States Constitution or that of New Mexico.[114]

It would appear clear, then, that constitutional objections to the payment of rental by public school authorities to churches for the use of the physical facilities are valid only when there is something beyond the mere use, by a public school, of the physical plant of some religious organization. It is only when the building retains some of its original character as a religious entity or house of worship that the practice may become unconstitutional.

Payment of Salaries to Teachers in Church-Related Schools

Some state constitutions specifically prohibit payments of public funds to teachers of religion.[115] Indeed, even broader constitutional clauses may be interpreted as prohibiting state payment of salaries to teachers in church-related schools. The problem has, however, seldom been litigated.

Public schools have at times been determined to be so "sectarian" or "church-related" that they could not receive public funds (discussed supra). Thus, the Nebraska Court invalidated payment to teachers in such schools as violative of the state constitution.[116] The New Mexico Court has held the same in a comparable case[117] as has the Missouri Court.[118] This latter Court's unwillingness to allow the payment of salaries to nuns was influenced by the State's specific constitutional ban upon the payment of public money to any teacher of religion.[119]

Interestingly enough, in the single adjudicated case involving payments to teachers in church-related schools, the appellate court sustained the expenditures. The Indiana Constitution provides: "No money shall be drawn from the treasury, for the benefit of any religious or theological institution."[120] During the depression of the thirties when Catholic schools educating eight hundred students were faced with the threat of closing because of lack of funds, the public school authorities of Vincennes paid the salaries of the teachers, and the Supreme Court of Indiana approved the arrangement since the curriculum was state approved and comparable to that of the government operated schools, and the teachers had been certified by proper state officials. This enabled the Court to characterize the schools as "public" although only attended by Catholic children, and taught by members of religious orders wearing distinctive garb. Additionally there were holy water fonts, crucifixes and religious pictures in the rooms and religious instruction was given to the children who voluntarily attended for a half-hour on mornings before the beginning of the official school day.[121]

In a case analogically relevant to those under discussion, the Utah Supreme Court has decreed that it was permissible for the state legislature to authorize inclusion of time spent teaching in parochial schools towards benefits under that State's teacher retirement act.[122] The Utah Constitution provides: "No public money or property shall be appropriated for or applied to any religious worship, exercise or instruction, or for the support of any ecclesiastical establishment."[123] Additionally, it states: "Neither the Legislature nor any county, city, town, school district or other public corporation, shall make any appropriation to aid in the support of any school, seminary, academy, college, university or other institution, controlled in whole, or in part, by any church, sect or denomination whatsoever."[124] Despite the Indiana case, and the Utah experience permitting time spent teaching in a church-related school to be included in computing retirement benefits, the law would appear to be that payment of salaries to teachers in church related schools is unconstitutional, whether reliance be placed on a specific ban or on a broader constitutional clause.

Payment of Tuition for Students Attending Church-Related Schools

There is no great body of case authority on the subject of the government paying tuition for children attending church-related educational institutions, but the reported cases indicate that the practice would be unconstitutional under many state constitutions. However, there is some authority for holding that state payments to war veterans are constitutional even if they prefer to attend church-related schools and colleges.

In the 1870s the Mississippi Legislature authorized persons to present "pay certificates" to be paid out of the common school fund for children attending private schools. In 1879 the Supreme Court of that State held the legislative act unconstitutional in that "there is no requirement in the law that these private institutions shall be free from sectarian control in religious matters."[125] The Mississippi Constitutional clause deemed violated is as follows:

> No religious or other sect or sects shall ever control any part of the school or other educational funds of this state; nor shall any funds be appropriated toward the support of any sectarian school, or to any school that at the time of receiving such appropriation is not conducted as a free school.[126]

In 1891 the South Dakota Court ruled invalid an act authorizing the legislature to pay tuition fees for students attending Pierre University, a

Presbyterian institution.[127]   Such statute was violative of the South Dakota Constitution which provides: "No money or property of the state shall be given or appropriated for the benefit of any sectarian or religious society or institution.[128]   It adds: "No appropriation of lands, money or other property or credits to aid any sectarian school shall ever be made by the state, or any county or municipality within the state. . . . "[129]   In 1931 the South Dakota Court ruled that a school district that had terminated its public school could not pay to parents a sum of money for sending their children to a parochial school.[130]

After World War II, the Virginia Legislature authorized the payment of tuition for children of dead or disabled veterans. However, the Virginia Court ruled that payment of such tuition for children attending sectarian schools was unconstitutional [131] under the State constitution which provides:

> The general assembly shall not make any appropriation of public funds, or personal property, or of any real estate, to any church, or sectarian society, association, or institution of any kind whatever, which is entirely or partly, directly or indirectly, controlled by any church or sectarian society. . . . [132]

At the end of World War I, Wisconsin by legislative act authorized the payment to veterans of thirty dollars per month for attendance at any school or college in the state, with the payment by the state to particular institutions chosen "on the basis of the actual increased cost of operation in excess of the cost to the institution if such legislation had not been passed." When it was argued that the legislation gave financial aid to religious schools patronized by the veterans, the Wisconsin Court dismissed the challenge, stating:

> The contention that financial benefit accrues to religious schools from the act is equally untenable. Only actual increased cost to such schools occasioned by the attendance of beneficiaries is to be reimbursed. They are not enriched by the services they render. Mere reimbursement is not aid.[133]

Payment by the government of tuition for students attending sectarian institutions would seem to be unconstitutional, then, with a broad exception in the case of payments to veterans who attend church-related institutions. Perhaps there should not be any constitutionally cognizable distinction between veterans and non-veterans, but the cases do indicate that payment of tuition for the former is permissible, while it is not in the case of the latter.

Sale of Public Property to Church-Related Educational Institutions

In what are apparently the only two decided cases in this area, the courts have twice held that state constitutions permit the sale of public lands, as part of redevelopment projects, to church-related educational institutions, so long as the sale was at a fair price. Both cases specifically held there was nothing unconstitutional in the sale of such land at a price below that of the cost to the governmental entity.

The Missouri Constitution provides:

> That no money shall ever be taken from the public treasury, directly or indirectly, in aid of any church, sect or denomination of religion, or in aid of any priest, preacher, minister or teacher thereof, as such; and that no preference shall be given to nor any discrimination made against any church, sect or creed of religion, or any form of religious faith or worship.[134]

This clause, according to the Missouri Supreme Court, was not violated when the City of St. Louis condemned land as part of a redevelopment project and then sold it at a fair price to St. Louis University, a Catholic institution. Allegedly the sale price was less than the cost of condemnation, clearance, etc. to the city but this was not deemed controlling, according to the court, so long as "fair value" was received by the city upon the sale.[135]

The New York Court of Appeals has similarly held that municipal land, condemned as part of a redevelopment project, could be turned over to Fordham University, a Catholic institution, so long as the sale price was fair.[136] The estimated cost to the city was approximately sixteen dollars per square foot and the price paid by Fordham was seven dollars. However, the Court pointed out that Fordham was paying for the "re-use value", and that all appraisers had testified that the "re-use value" was less than the seven dollars Fordham paid. Fordham additionally promised to raze the old buildings, to relocate the tenants and to use the land in prescribed ways. Said the New York Court:

> Since this sale is an exchange of considerations and not a gift or subsidy, no "aid to religion" is involved and a religious corporation cannot be excluded from bidding.[137]

The court added: ". . . Fordham would be deprived of constitutional rights if it alone were excluded from the bidding."[138] It had been argued that the sale violated the New York constitutional prohibition against appropriations for educational institutions under the control of religious denominations.[139]

Thus, in the only two reported cases in this area, it was clearly held constitutionally permissible for a city to sell redevelopment property to sectarian educational institutions at less than its actual value as long as the sale involved "fair value".

Programs Whereby the Public Schools Release Children For Attendance At Religious Services Elsewhere

Religious instruction of public school pupils conducted away from the school itself is customarily spoken of as (1) "released time" and (2) "dismissed time". Released time programs are usually characterized by allowing students who desire to attend religious instruction to depart, while others remain at, the public school. Dismissed time programs customarily are characterized by a dismissal of all the students in the public school at the time desired by some for religious training.

Released time and dismissed time programs can be, and generally have been held to be, constitutional. Constitutional problems only become significant when (1) there is participation by public school authorities, such as urging by teachers to attend; (2) there is cost to the public school system, such as in preparation of cards, forms, records, bus transportation; or (3) there is such an extensive use of the released or dismissed time as to jeopardize the effectiveness of the public school program. Cases have decided the first two practices are sufficient to invalidate a program of this type, but there is no reported decision as yet deciding the constitutionality of a program under the third circumstance. The United States Supreme Court has ruled that a released time program, such as that of New York City's, does not violate anything in the federal constitution.

California's Constitution contains a liberty of conscience section,[140] but no section banning establishment. Released time has been held constitutional by the California Appellate Court. Under the litigated plan the cost of setting up the program was paid for by the school system, teachers kept attendance records, and oversaw the workings of the plan. Said the Court:

> Reference to the debates of the constitutional convention which presented the Constitution of 1879 to the people of California demonstrates that there was no thought whatsoever in the minds of the framers of that document in opposition to or of hostility to religion as such. They proposed to insure separation of church and state, and to provide that the power and the authority of the state should never be devoted to the advancement of any particular religion. Our pioneer forefathers did not have the remotest idea that they were laying the foundations of the great Commonwealth of California that was to be a jejune, godless state; they believed one of the great pillars of our national strength to be the general acceptance of religion by our people.[141]

The Illinois Supreme Court in a case decided under the Illinois establishment clause [142] has sustained a released time program authorizing the local school superintendent to excuse pupils one hour each week to attend religious instruction classes away from the public schools. Said Justice Fulton for the Court:

> We concede that the board of education should not help sustain or support any school controlled by a church or sectarian denomination or aid any church or sectarian purpose. On the other hand, we do not deem it the duty of a school board to be hostile or antagonistic to religion or churches, nor should it interfere with the free exercise and enjoyment of religious freedom.
> The preamble to the constitution . . . recognizes the reliance of the people upon a deity, and while the decisions of the Federal and State courts approve the doctrine of the separation of church and state, it is nowhere stated that there is any conflict between religion and the State, nor any disfavor of any kind upon religion as such.[143]

Article I, section 3 of the New York constitution is a general freedom of religion clause, without any aspect of an establishment ban. However, Article XI, section 4 is a typical clause banning the use of public money or property in aid of denominational schools. In 1925 the trial division of the supreme court ruled that a released time program was unconstitutional because the school authorities used public printing facilities to print the necessary excuse cards.[144] Two years later, when a released time program provided that the cards were not to be printed with public facilities, the appellate division of the supreme court sustained such a program. Teachers issued and collected the cards, but the court found this not objectionable. Said the Court:

> When the wish of parents for weekday religious instruction for their children involves no serious interruption to school attendance, the state can have no purpose to defeat it. If local school authorities render their assistance by methods so innocuous as those detailed here, it does not amount to illegality.[145]

In 1951, in the landmark case of *Zorach v. Clauson,* [146] the Court of Appeals sustained the New York City program of released time. The program authorized the release of students attending religious instruction the last hour of the day on one day each week. The parents requested the release in writing and such cards were filed at the public school. Registration at the religious schools were filed with the public school authorities, and attendance records were filed there weekly. No comment by the teacher or principal on attendance or non-attendance of children was permitted. The Court of Appeals noted that there was "neither supervision nor approval of religious teachers and no solicitation of pupils or distribution of cards"[147] and "no announcement of any kind in the public schools relative to the program."[148] The United States Supreme Court, in affirming, ruled that the practice was consistent with the United States Constitution.[149]

The Oregon Legislature has enacted that:

> Any child attending the public school, on application of his guardian or either of his parents, may be excused from such school for a period or periods not exceeding 120 minutes in any week to attend week day schools giving instruction in religion.[150]

This statute has been sustained by the Oregon Supreme Court in an opinion which does not, however, discuss the constitutionality of the act as possibly violating Oregon's constitutional ban upon establishment.[151]

The Utah State Board of Education has resolved that:

> Credit for Bible history and literature to the extent of one unit may be accepted by any state high school toward graduation, provided such subject has been pursued for the same length of time and with the same thoroughness required for the same credit in any other subject, and provided further that the teacher of such subject shall have full high school certification or its equivalent.[152]

In Utah the Church of the Latter Day Saints maintains seminary classes near the high schools, and classes are conducted five hours per week on a released time basis. A Utah scholar has concluded that "it cannot be said that the constitutionality of the Utah program is free from doubt,"[153] but there is no court decision on the practice.

The State of Washington Constitution bans the expenditure of public money for the support of any religious establishment.[154] In 1959 the State Supreme Court upheld the constitutionality in general of released time programs, but found objectionable a particular practice where a religious representative made announcements concerning the religious classes and distributed cards in the public school classroom, the Court concluding that the pupils were converted thereby into a "captive audience."[155] The Court observed:

> Our State constitution like that of the United States and every state in the Union, by the language used, indicates the framers were men of deep religious beliefs and conviction, recognizing a profound reverence for religion and its influence in all human affairs essential to the well-being of the community.[156]

The Wisconsin Constitution provides: ". . . nor shall . . . any preference be given by law to any religious establishment or modes of worship; nor shall any money be drawn from the treasury for the benefit of religious societies, or religious or theological seminaries.[157] On two occasions Wisconsin Attorneys General have ruled that released time programs are constitutional. In 1926 the Attorney General stated:

> So long as neither the school board nor the teachers, as a part of their school work, have any connection whatever with the dissemmination of religious instruction, there will be no violation of the

constitution . . . the constitution is violated only when the teachers or the school machinery are connected either directly or indirectly with the dissemination of religious instruction.[158]

In 1949 the Wisconsin Attorney General so ruled again, adding that a program of dismissed time would be even more clearly constitutional.[159]

It would seem, then, that released or dismissed time programs in the abstract are constitutionally permissible. When the public schools, teachers in the public schools, or the expenditure of public funds are involved, the constitutionality of these practices is in some doubt. If the role of the teacher, or the community, is essential to the program and/or involves the expenditure of public funds, the plan has usually been held unconstitutional. The distinction would seem to be between merely *permitting* programs whereby public schools release children for attendance at religious instructions elsewhere, and, on the other hand, fostering or financing such plans.

Use of Public Facilities, Services, and Teachers by Church-Related Schools

Church-related schools have used various public buildings and facilities as part of their educational program. The physical facilities used by church related schools include: public school gymnasia for basketball practice and games, public school cafeterias, public libraries, public playgrounds, parks, and recreational centers, public auditoria, public museums, and public swimming pools.[160]

Cases determining the constitutionality of the use of government property by churches and church related organizations generally, are discussed *supra*. No adjudicated case determining the constitutionality of use of such facilities by church-related schools in particular has been found.[161] However, the rules discussed with reference to the use of government property by church-related organizations, *supra*, would seem applicable here. Thus, for example, it would seem that so long as a fair rental is paid to the public authorities no serious constitutional problem is raised.[162]

In an instance of the use of a particular public facility, or, more properly, a public service, namely the extension of publicly supported health services to children attending parochial schools, the Attorney General of Pennsylvania has upheld the use of public funds for this purpose, under a Pennsylvania Constitutional provision banning aid to sectarian schools.[163] Apparently, public health services are "presently available to denominational school pupils" in the state of New York,[164] but the constitutionality of this practice has not been litigated.

The use of teachers employed by the public school district in church related schools is comparable to the use of the physical facilities or services of the school district. The weight of authority would seem to uphold the constitutionality of this practice. In a 1963 New York case,[165] a statute providing home teaching for the physically handicapped "irrespective of the school they legally attend" was held not violative of New York's constitutional ban upon aid to sectarian educational institutions.[166] Justice Levine, in holding that the home teaching of a rheumatic sixth-grader registered in a Catholic elementary school did not violate this constitutional ban, ruled that there was neither direct nor indirect aid to the school: "The benefits of home teaching will inure solely to the pupil. . . . It is difficult to conceive how the parochial school will obtain any real advantage from it."[167]

Comparably, the Missouri Constitution prohibits appropriations to ". . . . help to support or sustain any private or public school, academy, seminary, college, university, or other institution of learning controlled by any religious creed, church or sectarian denomination whatever. . . ."[168] In February 1963, the Attorney General of that state ruled that the St. Louis County Special School District could serve students in independent (including church-related) schools.[169] The teachers involved will primarily be specialists who will work with handicapped children, especially those with hearing or speech defects.

The Oklahoma Attorney General has ruled that a public school district which provides special services, such as remedial reading and speech therapy, for certain of the pupils regularly enrolled in and attending its schools, has authority to furnish similar services to children residing in that school district who are not enrolled in the public schools of the district, but who are enrolled in and attending parochial or other private schools.[170] While the Oklahoma Constitution contains no specific ban on the use of public funds in support of sectarian education, it does prohibit the use of public money or property for sectarian purposes generally.[171]

The Maryland Attorney General has found no constitutional barrier, at least on a state level, to use of the public school closed-circuit class room television network by parochial schools in that state.[172]

While there is no authority directly contra the decisions and rulings of Attorneys General upholding the constitutionality of the use of public facilities, services, and teachers in or by church-related schools, the language of the Supreme Court of Iowa in a 1918 case is thought by some to render suspect the constitutionality of such practices in that state. In holding that the carrying on, with public school funds, of a public school in conjunction with and as a physical part of a Catholic elementary school, was illegal, the court enjoined the public school authorities from ". . . . directly or indirectly making any appropriation or use of the public school funds for the support or in aid of any such parochial school, or of any so called public school maintained or conducted in connection with such public school."[173]

In general, then, courts and Attorneys General have upheld the sharing of facilities, services, and teachers when the use of these facilities has been litigated under state constitutional clauses banning aid to sectarian institutions in general, or sectarian religious institutions in particular. The number of cases and rulings are slight, however, and the sharing has not been too extensive. Whether more complete sharing of public facilities, services, and teachers will withstand objections based on constitutional bans upon aid remains to be litigated.

Religious Instruction of Public School Students in Public Schools Outside Of School Hours

At one time there was apparently considerable instruction in religion of public school students in public schools outside of school hours. The National Education Association reported in 1946 that in sixteen states the public schools were being used by religious groups after school hours.[174] The *McCollum* decision probably influenced some authorities in thinking that public school properties could not be used for such programs even after school hours. This, however, must be deemed at this writing to be an open question so far as the United States Supreme Court is concerned.

Furthermore, there is rather current proof that public school buildings are still being used, outside of school hours, for instruction of the public school students in religion. Thus, the Edison High School in San Antonio, Texas, was reported in 1960 as having a group of fifty students meeting for devotional exercises without adult supervision in a school room three mornings a week from eight to eight twenty-five, classes beginning at eight thirty.[175]

No appellate decision concerned with the constitutionality of religious instruction of public school students in public schools outside of school hours has been discovered.

Shared Time

"Shared time"—a system whereby part of the regular school day finds children from the private (including church-related) schools in attendance at the public schools and/or vice versa[176]—has seldom been litigated under state constitutional clauses dealing with religion.

The Pennyslvania Constitution ordains that "No appropriation shall be made to any charitable or educational institution not under the absolute control of the commonwealth . . . ."[177] and further provides that "No appropriation shall be made for charitable, educational or benevolent purposes to any person or community nor to any denominational or sectarian institution, corporation or association. . . ."[178] In 1913 the Pennsylvania Court held that a child, described only as "a pupil in a private school," could attend public school classes under a statute with a provision that ". . . no pupil shall be refused admission to the courses . . . [in a public school] . . . by reason of the fact that his elementary or academic education is being or has been received in a school other than a public school."[179]   The Attorney General of Pennsylvania has not since ruled on the permissibility of shared time in that state.[180]

The Utah Constitution bans aid to "any ecclesiastical establishment"[181] and forbids appropriations to any educational institution" . . . controlled in whole, or in part, by any church, sect or denomination whatever."[182]   Additionally, "The legislature shall provide for the establishment and maintenance of a uniform system of public schools . . . free from sectarian control."[183]   The Utah Attorney General has ruled on a statute providing that:

> Local school districts maintaining automobile driver education classes shall allow pupils enrolled in grades nine to twelve, inclusive, or regularly established private schools located in said school district to enroll in the most accessible public school in said school district for the purpose of receiving driver instruction.

In ruling that the public school district could not charge a fee of the students, their parents, or the private institutions themselves, the Attorney General noted that:

> It is similar to assuming the costs for private dancing, elocution or musical lessons. . . . Public funds may not be used for such purposes. However, if students of private schools choose to have their education supplemented by the public schools, they certainly are entitled to such privilege. The public school must stand open to all pupils in the community.

Finally, in response to the inquiry as to whether the time of day in which the instruction is offered (during or beyond regular school hours) was relevant, the Attorney General ruled that it was not, observing that "a private school youngster, after enrolling with the public schools, is a public school student." The local Board of Education is then under a duty "to fix the school hours and the training and the education offered so as to be in the best interest of the students," without distinguishing between public and private school pupils.[184]

In 1918, the Supreme Court of the state of Iowa held that the carrying on with public school funds of a public school in conjunction with and as a physical part of a parochial school was illegal. The Catholic school classes were conducted in one room, while the public school classes were held in another, the same building being used in both cases. While the public school paid rent for the room that was used by its school, the room remained adorned with Catholic religious pictures and objects, classes were taught by a Catholic nun, and she was paid by the public school district. The Court enjoined the school district from ". . . directly or indirectly making any appropriation or use of the public school funds for the support or in aid of any such parochial school, or of any so called public school maintained or conducted in connection with such parochial school." [185] It would seem that the decision, language, and philosophy of this case would leave doubtful the constitutionality of a program of shared time in Iowa. Additionally, the Iowa Attorney General has ruled that a "partial high school for the accommodation of three classes [manual training, mathematics, and agriculture] of the parochial school" would be unconstitutional, noting that "It is the policy of this state that neither the public property nor credit nor money may be used directly or indirectly in the aid of any school, wholly or in part under the control of any religious denomination." [186]

There are, then, two conflicting views on the permissibility of shared time under state constitutional clauses dealing with religion. It remains to be seen, as shared time programs become more popular or necessary, whether courts will or will not attempt to reconcile such programs with constitutional clauses dealing with religion.

To summarize: Direct grants of funds or property to church-related schools are probably unconstitutional under most state constitutions today. Textbooks and bus transportation, on the other hand, give rise to issues upon which the states are divided. At least as far as the question has been litigated, there is no indication that giving textbooks to children in sectarian schools is necessarily unconstitutional under state clauses. In the matter of bus transportation, the state courts which have faced the issue have split almost evenly on whether or not the practice is invalid.

Along other lines there appears to be no substantial constitutional objection in the states to the practice of local authorities using the property of a religious organization and paying that organization a fair rental. Conversely, paying the salaries of teachers in church-related schools from the public treasury is most likely unconstitutional in all states. Furthermore, paying the tuition of students attending these schools is likewise invalid in most states. A relevant argument might be raised, however, in a state which abandoned its public school system for a system of private schools and made tuition grants to the students attending these schools. Denial of funds to a student who wished to attend a denominational school under these circumstances might well be a denial of religious freedom and equal protection under both the state and federal constitutions. Somewhat inconsistently, veterans are excepted from the general ban upon the distribution of tuition funds to students attending church-related institutions.

The sale of public property to church-related organizations apparently raises no valid constitutional objection as long as a fair price is paid. Similarly, the sharing of facilities, services, and in some cases, teachers, has been upheld where litigated. Not passed upon by any of the states is the question of use of the public schools for religious instruction after school hours. There appears to be no objection to this practice under

the federal constitution.   Conceivably, a state with a narrowly worded
constitutional prohibition might find the practice invalid.   Shared time
programs are still in a state of experiment.   There is considerable, but
speculative, evidence that such programs may avoid constitutional road-
blocks, and provide an answer to the dilemma facing the church-related
schools.   Studies are presently underway in a number of areas to determine whether such programs are workable.

In the foregoing chapter, we have been concerned with the various
forms of public aid to church-related schools.   The following chapter
will also be devoted to the schools.   Attention will be focused upon the
constitutionality of various religious activities and practices which are
carried on in the public schools.

Chapter Three

Religion in the Public Schools

Generally

The history of the American people is the history of a religious people. Our forebears held the firm belief that good government was dependent on the development of good moral character, and said so frequently in their early constitutional documents. They believed also that moral behavior stemmed from the inculcation of strong religious values. Those views are still shared by a majority of Americans today. Consequently, it is not surprising that parents, educators, and other leaders have attempted to maintain the influence of religion by making it a part of the general educational process.

At the same time, however, this country also boasts a long tradition of religious freedom. This freedom is guaranteed by the national constitution and by each and every state constitution. Essential to this freedom is the right of the individual to completely refrain from taking part in any religious ceremony or practice in which he does not believe or which may violate his creed. This right has been brought sharply into focus by the various religious ceremonies and exercises performed in the public schools. The purpose of this chapter is to assess, principally under the state constitutional guarantees, the validity of the various practices.

Among the practices which have been strenuously opposed on constitutional grounds have been the saying of prayers, reading of verses from the bible, singing of religious hymns and the like. Also objected to upon religious grounds have been the compulsory flag salute requirements and the compulsory education laws. The instruction of children in the public schools by members of a religious sect, or by those wearing religious garb, has come under considerable fire. Finally, commencement and baccalaureate ceremonies, the observance of religious holidays, and other similar practices have been attacked on the same ground. In

51

general, these practices have been litigated either under clauses which forbid the preference of any one faith, or under clauses which simply guarantee the free exercise of religion.

Bible Reading and Prayers in the Public Schools

Religious activity in the public schools is now subject under the Fourteenth Amendment of the United States Constitution to the ban upon the establishment of religion. The Supreme Court of the United States has ruled that no school district can permit reading of any version of the Bible in the schools during school hours, even though unwilling participants are excused.[1] It has further held that neither the Lord's prayer nor state composed official prayers can be read by teachers during school hours, even though children whose parents do not wish them to listen are excused.[2] State constitutional clauses are significant here, not because they can authorize what the United States Supreme Court has forbidden, but because the state clauses may well be *more* restrictive than the United States Constitution as interpreted by the federal court.

Distribution of Gideon Bibles in the public schools has been held violative of state constitutional clauses. The Florida Constitution provides, inter alia, "No preference shall be given by law to any church, sect or mode of worship and no money shall ever be taken from the public treasury directly or indirectly in aid of any church, sect or religious denomination or in aid of any sectarian institution." [3] This clause prevented the distribution in the schools of the Gideon Bible, in a suit brought by a Catholic and a Jew. Said the Florida Court:

> The distribution through the school system each year certainly approximates an annual promotion and endorsement of the religious sects or groups which follow its teachings and precepts. This distribution likewise would tend to impair the rights of plaintiffs and their children to be free from governmental action which discriminates in the free exercise of religious beliefs.[4]

The New Jersey Court agreed that the Gideon Bible cannot be distributed in the public schools. The Court added that the distribution of the King James version of the Bible would be equally invalid.[5] The New Jersey Constitution provides: "There shall be no establishment of one religious sect in preference to another . . . ." [6] Somewhat comparably, the Supreme Court of New Mexico has enjoined the distribution of Presbyterian religious literature in the public schools of that state.[7]

On the other hand, the Supreme Court of California has held that both the King James and Douai versions of the Bible can be purchased and placed on the shelves of public school libraries for reference purposes.[8] The California Constitution provides: "The free exercise and enjoyment of religious profession and worship, without discrimination or preference, shall forever be guaranteed in this State . . . ." [9]

Even before the United States Supreme Court rulings, some state courts had held impermissible the reading of Bibles and the saying of prayers in the public schools, and these rulings continue to be controlling under the state constitutions. Such rulings exist in Illinois,[10] Louisiana,[11] Nebraska,[12] and Wisconsin.[13] In some instances, the result was based upon the "sectarian" nature of the particular version of the Bible employed.[14] The Florida Court, in a case decided under that state's Freedom of Religion clause, had banned *sectarian* comment on the Bible by public school teachers, enjoined the use of public school premises after school hours for Bible instruction, and restrained the exhibition of religious films in the public schools.[15]

A number of earlier state decisions allowing teachers to say prayers or read the Bible in public schools during school hours are apparently no longer valid since the United States Supreme Court decisions. This would seem true of rulings in Colorado,[16] Florida,[17] Georgia,[18] Iowa,[19] Kansas,[20] Kentucky,[21] Maine,[22] Massachusetts,[23] Michigan,[24] Minnesota,[25] New York,[26] Ohio,[27] Pennsylvania,[28] Tennessee,[29] and Texas.[30] Also questionable since the *Schempp* decision is an earlier ruling of the Illinois Court that morning chapel exercises could be held at the State University, with reading from the New Testament, recitation of the Lord's Prayer, singing of religious hymns, and occasional talks, even though those objecting could be excused upon signing a request.[31]

Also worthy of note in this regard is a recent decision of the State Supreme Court of Florida which affirmed an original judgment by upholding the constitutionality of bible reading in the public schools of the state. This occured after the decision had been appealed to the Supreme Court of the United States and remanded by that tribunal for reconsideration in light of the *Murray* and *Schemp* decisions. The Florida Court found that the bible reading statute ". . . was founded upon secular rather than sectarian considerations . . ." and concluded that it was ". . . designed to require moral training and the inculcation of good citizenship, (and) does not offend the establishment clause of the Constitution as written and intended by the authors."[32] This decision was again appealed, and the United States Supreme Court has since reversed the Florida Court.[33]

The Massachusetts Attorney General has ruled, inter alia, that prayers may not be said on a voluntary basis, and that grace may not be said before meals in public school cafeterias. Voluntary gatherings of students to pray are, however, permissible.[34]

Singing Religious Hymns in Public Schools

The singing of religious hymns in public schools is probably unconstitutional since the Schempp decision. In 1902 the Nebraska Court ruled that public school teachers could not sing religious songs in classrooms.[35] The Nebraska Constitution provides: "No sectarian instruction shall be allowed in any school or institution supported in whole or in part by the public funds set apart for educational purposes. . . .[36] In 1910, the Illinois Court held that Catholic children attending the public schools could not be forced to sing Protestant hymns as a condition of attendance.[37] This was deemed violative of the State Constitution which bans appropriations of ". . . anything in aid of any church or sectarian purpose. . . ."[38]

There is an 1884 Iowa decision to the effect that the singing of religious songs at public schools was not unconstitutional.[39] The Iowa Constitution provides:

> The General Assembly shall make no law respecting an establishment of religion, or prohibiting the free exercise thereof; nor shall any person be compelled to attend any place of worship, pay tithes, taxes, or other rates for building or repairing places of worship, or the maintenance of any minister, or ministry.[40]

Public School Credit for Courses in the Bible

◁In a few states public school credit has been given for courses in the Bible, which instruction was given away from the public school.▷ In West Virginia, for instance, such credit can be given by the public high schools under a program where the syllabus is prepared, teachers' qualifications are prescribed, and examinations are given, by the public school authorities.[41]

In the sole reported case, the Washington Supreme Court in 1918 struck down a program under which public high school students were given credit for Bible study away from the school. The students studied "the historical, biographical, narrative, and literary features" of the Bible. They could receive a half credit for study of the Old Testament and another half credit for study of the New, out of 30 to 32 credits required by the public schools for graduation. The outline had been adopted by the board of education which also examined the students in this subject. Said the Washington Court:

> . . . to give a credit in the public school for such instruction, is to give a credit for sectarian teaching and influence which is the very thing outlawed by the Constitution.

The Court found a spending of public money, too, since teachers' time "will be consumed while under the pay of the state in furnishing the syllabus or outline, the conducting of examinations, the rating of papers, and the determining of proper credits."[42]

Religious As Teachers in Public Schools

A study in Texas in 1958-59 showed that some two hundred and thirty-three schools in that state employed Protestant ministers as teachers.[43]   Nuns have been so employed in a number of states.   The weight of authority holds that ministers, nuns, and other religious cannot be denied the opportunity to teach in public schools.

Thus, the Indiana Court has held that:

> No statute or rule prohibiting the employment of teachers belonging to a certain religious denomination or sect could be held valid. The employment of the teachers in this case certainly could not be held invalid because teachers belonged to certain orders of the Catholic Church. . . . Membership in any particular church can neither legally qualify nor disqualify a teacher.[44]

The New York Court of Appeals, while affirming a ban upon the wearing of religious garb by teachers in the public schools, refused to forever ban sisters from teaching there.   The Court indicated that it did—

> not wish to be understood as acquiescing in that part of the opinion below in which it is asserted that "these sisters should never be permitted to teach in our public schools."   There is no reason, either in morals or in law why they or any other qualified persons should not be allowed thus to teach, whatever may be their religious convictions, provided they do not by their acts as teachers promote any denominational doctrine or tenet.[45]

The New Mexico court has held similarly.[46]   Comparably, the Iowa Supreme Court notes that "The law . . . demands no religious test for admission into the teacher's profession." [47]   In some of these cases, then, attempts to ban religious from teaching in public schools would not only offend the state constitutional liberty of religion clauses, but would be violative of the state constitutional clauses prohibiting religious tests for public officers.[48]

In the decisions acknowledging the right of nuns to teach in the public schools, courts have generally added that it is immaterial that the religious turn over their salaries to their religious order.   To deny them this right would be, according to these courts, a deprivation of fredom of religion.   Typically, the Kentucky Court has said:

> The salaries paid these Sisters are theirs and they may do therewith as they choose.   One employed by the state or any of its subdivisions is not forbidden under section 189 from contributing any part, or all, of the salary earned to a religious body of which he or she is a member.   To deny such a right of contribution would be a denial of religious liberty.[49]

The North Dakota Court has agreed that to deny nuns the right to contribute their salaries to their religious order "would in itself constitute a denial of that right of religious liberty which the constitution guarantees." [50]   The Pennsylvania Court adds that "It is none of our business, nor that of these appellants, to inquire into this matter." [51]

There is, however, some authority that religious cannot teach in public schools. Thus, the Missouri Court has said that "Because of the character of their obligations . . . nuns are disqualified from teaching in any public school in the State of Missouri." [52]

Wearing of Religious Garb by Public School Teachers

The cases are divided on whether the wearing of religious garb by public school teachers can be prohibited. Although New Mexico's Constitution reads: "No religious test shall ever be required as a condition of admission into the public schools or any educational institution of this state, either as a teacher or a student . . .," [53] the State Supreme Court has sustained a legislative ban upon the wearing of religious garb in the public schools. [54]

The Pennsylvania Court has similarly sustained such a prohibition, [55] notwithstanding the existence of state constitutional clauses guaranteeing religious liberty [56] and providing that no one is to be disqualified from public office because of religious belief. [57] There is also a New York decision to the effect that religious garb can be outlawed in the public schools. [58] The Iowa Attorney General in 1936 gave his opinion that religious garb cannot be worn in the public schools. [59] However, note should be taken of the language of the Iowa Supreme Court which stated in 1918: "The law does not prescribe the fashion on dress of man or woman; it demands no religious test for admission into the teacher's profession." [60] There are statutes in some other states banning the wearing of religious garb by public school teachers but they are as yet untested. [61]

An attempt to proscribe the wearing of religious garb in public schools was struck down by the Kentucky Court which stated:

> While the dress and the emblems worn by these Sisters proclaim them to be members of certain organizations of the Roman Caitholic Church and that they have taken certain religious vows, these facts do not deprive them of their right to teach in public schools, so long as they do not inject religion or the dogma of their church. The garb does not teach. It is the woman within who teaches. The dress of the Sisters denotes modesty, unworldliness and an unselfish life. No mere significance or insignificance of garb would conceal a teacher's character. [62]

The North Dakota Court refused to find that the wearing of religious garb made the public school a "sectarian" institution and sustained the practice. [63] However, the electorate of North Dakota thereafter voted 93,000 to 83,000 to ban the wearing of religious garb in the public schools. [64] The Indiana Court has agreed with the Kentucky and North Dakota Courts that the wearing of religious garb by public school teachers is permissible. Said the Indiana Court: "Nor does the fact that these teachers in question, while teaching, wore the robes of various orders to which they belonged constitute sectarian teaching or make it illegal for them to be paid their salaries as teachers." [65]

Holy Day Services

Traditionally there has been a significant amount of celebrations of Christian holy days in the public schools.[66] Thus, a 1958-59 Texas study showed that Christmas was observed in 1,655 schools in the state, with Christmas trees in 1,373 schools, an exchange of Christmas gifts in 1,331 schools, the singing of Christmas carols in 1,634 schools and nativity scenes were present in 1,264 schools. Additionally, Easter holidays were given in 1,587 schools with pagents in 627 schools at Easter time. The report further notes that Jewish holy days were celebrated in eighty-five public schools in that State.[67]

A New York court has refused to enjoin a local board of education from authorizing or permitting the erection, display, or installation on school property of a creche or similar depiction of the nativity scene. The school authorities agreed not to assemble or install the creche until after school had recessed for the Christmas vacation and to remove the display before students returned after the new year.[68] More recently, the Florida Court enjoined the religious observance in the public schools of Christmas, Easter and Hanukkah holy days.[69] Although the judgment of the Florida Court was vacated by the United States Supreme Court and remanded in the light of *Murray v. Curlett*,[70] this aspect of the Florida decision probably remains effective.

Christmas, Easter and Hanukkah celebrations are thought to be religious and sectarian activities if they are of a devotional nature and by some are therefore deemed to be unconstitutional.[71] However, there appears to be a recognition that such public school ceremonies are valid if they are but occasions for noting "the common human meanings" embodied in our cultural heritage.[72]

Baccalaureate and Other Graduation Exercises at Churches

Public schools have frequently held baccalaureate and other graduation exercises at churches. This practice has ben held constitutional by the New Mexico Supreme Court. Nothing that in many communities the churches are the only buildings with sufficient seating capacity for such ceremonies, this Court stated:

> We are firmly committed to the doctrine of separation of Church and State . . . but we do not feel it requires us to prohibit the holding of these time honored programs in a building where all who desire to attend may be accommodated. Neither are we fearful that those conducting these services or exercises will fail to observe the proprieties of the occasion and thus give offense to anyone attending.[73]

The Wisconsin Supreme Court has agreed that the holding of public school graduation exercises in churches is constitutional, so long as there are no religious services.[74] Recently, too, the Florida Court has found nothing violative of the state constitution in public schools using churches for baccalaureate services.[75] The United States Supreme Court, however, vacated this judgment and remanded it to the Florida Supreme Court in the light of *Murray v. Curlett*.[76] On remand, the Florida Court affirmed its prior decision,[77] but the Supreme Court of the United States has since reversed.[78] While the issue of the permissibility of baccalaureate exercises was held not to have been properly raised, three justices noted that they would uphold the Florida Court on the merits in this matter.

Where baccalaureate services of a public school were held not in a church, but in the school itself, the New York education authorities have handed down a ruling to the effect that "baccalaureate services are religious services and consequently under the State constitution may not be held in schools."[79] The Massachusetts Attorney General has ruled that prayers may be said at both graduation and baccalaureate services.[80]

Patriotic Exercises

Another religious freedom controversy involving practices in the public schools, came strongly to the fore in the 1930's. A great number of the public school districts in the country had enacted regulations which required that children attending the public schools in these districts each day salute the flag of the United States by reciting the pledge of allegiance. One religious sect—the Jehovah's Witnesses—believed that saluting the flag in this fashion was a form of idolatry and was therefore opposed to the practice. Many members of the sect forbade their children to participate in the salute and pledge. When school authorities sought to compel their conformance, they withdrew their children from the schools. Those who were unable to find other schools for their children were subject to prosecution under the truancy laws of the various states and municipalities.

The Jehovah's Witnesses responded to their dilemma by initiating and waging a number of unsuccessful legal battles in the courts, arguing that the compulsory flag salute violated their religious rights under both state and federal constitutions. The state Supreme Courts uniformly held that since "saluting the flag is nothing more than a symbolic expression ... of one's loyalty for his country," and "does not approach a religious rite," these persons have nothing of which to constitutionally complain. Consequently the courts refused to enjoin the application of the compulsory flag salute laws to the Jehovah's Witnesses. A number of these state court decisions were appealed to the Supreme Court of the United States, but were dismissed without review.[81]

The Jehovah's Witnesses did not give up their struggle and in 1938 they met with some limited success. In the case of *Gobitis v. Minersville*

District, a District Court in Pennsylvania enjoined the school authorities in the district from requiring as a condition of attendance the flag salute.[82] The court observed that Pennsylvania guaranteed these individuals religious liberty. Secondly, the justice pointed out that the individual is the judge of his own religious beliefs, and emphasized that when he acts on those beliefs, he may be interfered with only in the interest of public safety. The court concluded that the plaintiff's refusal to have his children salute the flag can in no way be construed as dangerous to the public safety. The Circuit Court of Appeals affirmed the District Court's holding.[83] The school district appealed to the Supreme Court of the United States.

Because this decision ran counter to several per curiam dismissals in similar cases, the Supreme Court decided it would review this ruling, and granted certiorari.[84] The victory in the lower courts was short lived. The Supreme Court failed to find that the religious rights of the parents and the children were violated by the compulsory flag salute law.[85] In their opinion, rendered in 1940, they deferred to the right of the school district authorities to prescribe programs for the inculcation of patriotism in the students, and affirmed the right of the same authorities to decide, in the interest of maintaining order and discipline in the system, whether the dissidents were entitled to immunity from the laws.

The Jehovah's Witnesses did enjoy one victory in a state court just two years after the *Gobitis* reversal. The Supreme Court of Kansas, in interpreting their own state constitution, declared that members of the Jehovah's Witnesses who were parents of children in the public school could not be convicted under the truancy laws for withdrawing their children from the school to avoid their being compelled to salute the flag. The Court held that the law was not to be construed as justifying the expulsion of the children or the prosecution of the parents, and if so construed, "to that extent it would be void as being in violation of section 7 of our Bill of Rights."[86] Aside from this solitary decision, the state courts followed *Gobitis*.

Within three years after the Supreme Court decision in *Gobitis*, a three judge Federal District Court in West Virginia, upheld, in the case of *Barnette* v. *West Virginia State Board of Education*,[87] the right of the Jehovah's Witnesses to be immune from compliance to that state's compulsory flag salute law.[87] The Board of Education took an immediate direct appeal to the Supreme Court of the United States. The Board made the same arguments so successful in the *Gobitis* case, but this time to no avail. In a landmark opinion, the Supreme Court methodically demolished the holding in *Gobitis*, and ruled that the enforcement against these individuals of a compulsory flag salute law was an unnecessary and unconstitutional infringement on their religious liberties.[88] Said the Court:

> We think the action of the local authorities in compelling the flag
> salute and pledge transcends constitutional limitations on their
> power and invades the sphere of intellect and spirit which it is
> the purpose of the First Amendment to our Constitution to reserve
> from all official control.[89]

Additionally, the Court emphasized that the refusal of persons to participate in this form of patriotic exercise "does not turn on one's possession of particular religious views or the sincerity with which they are
held."[90] Put another way, a child in the public school or his parents
need not be a member of any religious sect or espouse the beliefs of
any sect. It is sufficient if such a compulsion infringes upon the
individual's personal liberty. The rulings in a number of similar cases
then pending before the supreme courts of a few of the states were
foreclosed by the Supreme Court's decision in the *Barnette* case.[91]

Shortly after the *Barnette* decision, the Supreme Court also overruled a number of decisions of the Mississippi Supreme Court which
involved a related problem. Mississippi had a statute during World War II
which made it an offense to disseminate any theory calculated to
encourage disloyalty to the state and federal governments or create an
attitude of stubborn refusal to salute the flag. The conviction of a number
of Jehovah's Witnesses for refusing to salute the flag and teaching that
it was improper were reversed by the Supreme Court. The Court held
that the law as applied to the members of this sect was unconstitutional
under the Fourteenth Amendment.[92]

It may safely be concluded that any attempt by the states or their
localities to impose upon school children a compulsory flag salute is
unconstitutional, if not under the state constitutions, at least under the
federal fundamental law. Although the decisions, in most instances,
involved matters of religious liberty, it is equally likely that *any* compulsory patriotic practice of this type may be found constitutionally
wanting, even in the absence of religious objections.

Right To Educate

The reasonable right of the state to compel and supervise the
education of children in the state is well established.[93] The parent,
of course, has the right to select the kind of environment in which his
child shall be raised and a forcible interest in the suitability of his
formal training. The right (and responsibility) of the state, however,
extends beyond the mere shielding of the child from the consequences
of ignorance. It goes further to the protection of the community from
the dangers consequent upon the failure of the child to have inculcated
the tenets of good and useful citizenship. In short, the state has a
primary interest in the proper behavior of citizens, and may take
reasonable preventive measures to ensure that the child is taught proper

modes of civil conduct. The states have discharged their responsibility
in this area by the establishment of public school systems, provisions for
the accrediting of private institutions, enactment of compulsory attendance laws, and the supervision of the curriculum.

On occasion, the right of the state to educate has come into conflict
with the constitutional rights of parents in this regard. In 1923, the
Supreme Court of the United States struck down an attempt by the
State of Nebraska to prohibit the teaching of any language but English
in the schools of the state. This statute, said the Court, was an infringement both on the right of the parents to have their children instructed in
foreign languages, and of the teachers to render this instruction.[94] Two
years later, the same Supreme Court invalidated an Oregon statute which
required all children in the state to attend the public school. By striking
down this law, the Court vindicated the right of the private schools to
function and the right of the parents to educate their children in them.[95]
In neither instance did these laws bear any reasonable relationship to
the need of the state to provide for the safety and well-being of the
community. There was absolutely nothing to show that the learning of
foreign language was in any way injurious to the health or morals of
the ordinary child, nor is there anything inherently harmful in educating
children in private institutions which adhere to recognized standards of
education.

One major conflict in this area has come about as a result of the
prosecution under compulsory school attendance laws of individuals who
refuse to comply with the laws because of religious scruples. Compulsory school attendance laws have been enacted in all but two of the
states.[96] Essentially, they require that all children in the state be in
attendance at an accredited institution until they arrive at a certain
age limit. The courts of most states have recognized the power of the
state to pass and enforce such laws. Where they have been constitutionally questioned, however, has been in their applicability to persons
whose purposeful non-compliance is the result of religious motivation.
The Amish sects in Pennsylvania and other states, for example, have
forcibly complained against the laws on this ground. They made it a
practice to withdraw their children from school once it was determined
that they were able to begin their life's work—farming. Their religion
teaches them that this attachment to the soil is the means by which
they are to work out their salvation. To delay the process of teaching
the children to identify themselves with the soil and farming is considered
sinful waste. Consequently, they argue that to force them to comply
with the law forces them to violate their beliefs and is unconstitutional.
With the exception of one lower court decision which did hold this
to be an unconstitutional infringement on freedom of conscience,[97] the
Pennsylvania Appellate Courts have come to contrary conclusions.[98]
Affirmed also in the same state was the conviction of Mohammedan

parents who out of religious motivation kept their children home from school on Fridays.[99]   The basis for the Court's reasoning in the latter case was that once the defendants had elected to use the public school, they were bound to comply with *all* its regulations.

A variation of the same problem is the refusal of parents to send their children to an *accredited* institution. While the state has no right, as we have heretofore seen, to require attendance at a state school, it does have the right to establish certain minimum reasonable standards regarding what is to be taught in all schools, teacher qualifications, and physical plants, and to demand that private as well as public schools adhere to them. In New York, for example, an individual was convicted of violating the compulsory school laws by sending his children to a small religious school maintained by the Jewish faith wherein the only instruction was in the Bible, the Talmud, and in elementary Jewish law.   Said the trial judge:

> Recognizing that the religious convictions of some parents require them to advise, and where practicable to compel their children to receive their secular education under the same auspices as their religious education, the Supreme Court in the Pierce case accorded constitutional protection to this conviction. It did not, however, hold that sectarian education could be substituted in whole or in part for statutorily required secular education.[100]

On appeal the conviction was unanimously affirmed without an opinion.[101] In a companion case, a New York Court also ruled that a father who was educating his son, the product of a broken home, in a non-approved Jewish school wherein he was receiving primarily religious education, was not entitled to retain custody of the child as against the claim of the mother unless he complied with the state education law by sending the boy to an accredited school.   The father was given two weeks to comply with the court's order.[102]

In a very recent Nebraska case, a group of parents employed an unqualified teacher to instruct their children in religious and other secular subjects in a small school.   The state demanded that the children be sent to other accredited schools on the ground that they were not complying with the law.   The parents complained that the provisions of the compulsory school laws violated their religious rights under the constitution. The lower court found them in violation of the laws and denied relief.   The Nebraska high Court upheld the lower court and reaffirmed the right of the state to set teacher qualifications, as well as compel attendance at properly accredited schools in the state.[103]

It must be concluded from these decisions that religion is seldom any defense to a failure to comply with the education laws. The state has the right to see that children are educated, that the schools are equipped to provide this education, and that teachers are qualified to instruct. The obligation of the state in this area is great, and reasonable regulations are essential to its discharge. At many points, the wishes of parents must give way and allow the state a free hand with which to operate. Nonetheless, the power of the state in this area is not absolute. Parents do retain important prerogatives and the right to oversee the religious training of their children is one that is essential.

Whenever the official conduct of the state amounts to a limitation of a constitutionally guaranteed right of the individual, it must be subject to the closest scrutiny. If the state possesses a reasonable alternative method of accomplishing its legitimate ends, it has no choice but to employ it. This is true even if the other method or route is inconvenient, administratively more complicated, or perhaps more expensive. There would be complications, for example, in permitting children to be released from classes on the feast days of their faith. Present schedules would be disrupted and new ones devised. Make-up time would have to be scheduled. Teachers would have to be paid for the extra time, and perhaps additional personnel employed. Costs would naturally be increased. However, the right of the parents to have their children participate in important religious activities must not turn on mere inconvenience. Unless the state is able to show that some serious injury will result, it should not interfere.

The same is true with respect to the Amish, and others like them. Most compulsory attendance statutes require that a child remain in school until a certain arbitrary age. This provides no absolute guarantee that the child has learned what he is expected to know—he may have learned it before the required age limit, or he may not have learned it at all. It is suggested that the state possesses a reasonable alternative in this respect, which will protect its interests as well as the freedoms of these religious people. The child could be examined and the extent of his knowledge ascertained. Those failing the examination could be kept in school and those successful could be released. Such a solution preserves the religious rights of the child and parent while at the same time ensuring that the community will be protected from any lack of training in good and useful citizenship. With some effort and concern in this area, the state could find other solutions, probably more satisfactory than those profferred here. It is suggested that at least in these two areas, the states should re-examine their position. The courts have been reluctant, quite naturally, to move in this direction; the initiative lies with the legislatures.

In conclusion, it may be fairly stated that there exists a clearly recognizable trend in the direction of invalidating any form of religious practice in the public schools which is required by state law or school regulations. The result will likely be the same if the court is able to find that the particular practice is carried on under color of official approval or encouragement. At the same time, there is evidence to indicate that the courts are becoming increasingly appreciative of the rights of parents to refuse to have their children participate in exercises or comply with school requirements that they consider offensive to their beliefs, even though the practices are not commonly thought of as religious in themselves.

In this chapter we have discussed the concept of religious freedom as it affects the public educational process. In the following chapter, we will look at this same concept in the broader context of the state's power to limit this right in the interests of citizens generally.

Chapter Four

Limitations Imposed Upon the Free Exercise of Religion

It is fundamental that the states may not establish a church nor deny to their citizens freedom of religion, as these prohibitions have been explained by the Supreme Court of the United States.[1] It is equally fundamental that the states are also charged with the primary responsibility of promoting and safeguarding the general health and well-being of their people. In discharging this responsibility, the states have often enacted legislation which, though legitimate in purpose, has on numerous occasions conflicted with the religious freedoms guaranteed by both federal and state constitutions.

Since the states have the burden of protecting the welfare of their citizenry, they must also have the concommitant power with which to accomplish their task. Commonly denoted the "police power," it allows the states to limit personal liberties in the interests of the public good. Under the general police power doctrine, the states have acted to protect their public by limiting the performance of religious practices physically injurious to the public health. They have not permitted persons to stand on religious scruples in refusing to submit to general health programs. The practice of medicine by unlicensed spiritual healers has been effectively banned and the Sunday closing laws, found in the majority of states, have been consistently upheld as necessary measures to safeguard both the mental and physical health of the populace.

In the interests of preserving the public morality, polygamy and other pluralistic marital practices have been prohibited. In a few states, there is express constitutional language proscribing such practices. Also on the books of many states are statutes providing penalties for blasphemy.

Additionally, the free exercise of religion has been limited in the interests of the public safety and good order of the society. As a result, all kinds of practices which stem from religious motivation have been the subject of some regulation. The use of alcohol in religious

65

ceremonies has been subject to controls. Dangerous instrumentalities employed in religious rites have been outlawed. The solicitation of funds and distribution of literature by religious and charitable organizations have been made subject to much the same regulations as secular and commercial operations, in the interests of fraud prevention and traffic control. Also in the interests of traffic control and general good order, the states and their municipalities have regulated the use of the public thoroughfares for religious parades and other demonstrations. Orderly community organization requires also that churches and other religious institutions conform to proper zoning regulations. On the other hand, state and local courts as well as legislative bodies are normally prohibited from interfering with the internal affairs of churches and church groups.

All of the states of the Union constitutionally guarantee religious liberty, often in language which parallels that of the federal constitution. In addition to the usual freedom of religion clauses, over one-half of the states have inserted into their fundamental law companion language expressly limiting the free exercise of religion. For example, the constitution of Arizona provides:

> The liberty of conscience secured by the provisions of this Constitution shall not be so construed as to excuse acts of licentiousness, or justify practices inconsistent with the peace and safety of the State.[2]

In Maryland, the constitution guarantees all citizens religious liberty except when

> . . . under the color of religion, he shall disturb the good order, peace or safety of the state, or shall infringe the laws of morality, or injure others in their natural, civil or religious rights.[3]

In New Hampshire, a person may enjoy full religious liberty "Provided he doth not disturb the public peace or disturb others in their religious worship."[4]

Reflecting what at one time in the history of the State was a conspicuous local problem, Idaho enacted into its constitution the following clause:

> But that the liberty of conscience hereby secured shall not be construed to . . . excuse acts of licentiousness or justify polygamy or other pernicious practices, inconsistent with the morality or the peace or safety of the State.[5]

The constitutions of Montana,[6] Utah,[7] and Oklahoma[8] also expressly prohibit polygamous or plural marriages even though they may have been entered into from religious motives.

All of these state constitutional prohibitions simply reflect the proposition set to words by Mr. Justice Roberts in the celebrated decision in the case of *Cantwell v. Connecticut* in 1939. There the Justice re-stated the rule:

> Thus the [First] Amendment embraces two concepts—freedom to believe and freedom to act. The first is absolute but, in the nature of things, the second cannot be. Conduct remains subject to regulation for the protection of society.[9]

A person may believe or not believe as his conscience allows; but when he acts he must subject himself to the state's paramount concern for the safety and health of his neighbors.

This constitutional language is probably no more than precatory in nature. Many of the states have not thought it necessary to include it in their constitutions. Yet the great majority in one fashion or another have made positive efforts to restrict certain religious practices. When such attempts at regulation go beyond the restrictions handed down by the Supreme Court of the United States, they will of course be nullified, even though they may not be found violative of the particular state constitutional religion clause. Where problems arise, however, is in the areas of state constitutional interpretation of their own freedom of religion clauses. The primary object of this chapter is to investigate the different ways in which the states have attempted to saddle free exercise by limiting or outlawing certain religious practices and to chronicle their validity.

Limitations Imposed in the Interest of Public Health

The states may, and frequently do, legislate to protect what may be termed "the Public Health". While the end of such legislation is usually legitimate, there is frequently conflict with equally legitimate purposes, ceremonies, or scruples of various religious groups. In contesting state legislation of this type, these religious groups have frequently relied on Freedom of Religion clauses in state constitutions. Thus, courts in these states are confronted with policy decisions as to whether the interest of the society as a whole in legislation designed to insure the public health "justifies" what are certainly interferences with the religious liberty of various sectarian groups. That there is interference cannot be doubted; the problem is whether the social interest protected by the legislation in question should be paramount.

Conflicts between state legislation for the benefit of the public's health and state constitutional clauses relating to religion (usually the typical Freedom of Religion clause) arise in numerous areas, the following of which are considered herein: vaccination against communicable disease, the practice of medicine, fluoridation of the water supply, contraception, transfusions and other medical care, and Sunday closing laws.

1. *Vaccination Against Communicable Disease*

State laws relating to vaccinations, or other comparable health measures, have frequently been attacked as being violative of religious liberty. It is interesting to note that the United States Supreme Court has held constitutional a state law permitting local boards to require, under penalty of a fine, the vaccination of all residents against smallpox.[10] While there is no indication that the defendant's refusal to be vaccinated was based on religious grounds, the case has been cited as authority for the proposition that one cannot refuse to be vaccinated for religious reasons.[11] From a holding that vaccination of all persons may constitutionally be compelled, it would follow that vaccination may be made a condition for admission to public schools. Thus, the typical case in this area arises where a state prosecutes a defendant for failure to follow compulsory vaccination laws, and the defense of religious liberty is raised; or where a person is excluded from a public school for failure to observe a vaccination statute, and gives as his reason religious scruples against such medication.

Thus, parents have been convicted for failure to have their children vaccinated, or, under truancy laws, for failing to send their children to school when they have not complied with vaccination requirements, in the following states: Georgia,[12] Massachusetts,[13] New Hampshire,[14] and Tennessee.[15] Reliance of the defendant on the state constitutional guarantee of freedom of religion[16] in these cases was to no avail. Similarly, courts in Indiana,[17] Kentucky,[18] New Jersey,[19] New York,[20] Ohio,[21] and Texas [22] have held that children may be excluded from attendance at public schools if they have not been vaccinated, despite the fact that such vaccinations are not permitted by their parents' religion. Here, too, claims that compulsory vaccination violates the parents' constitutionally protected freedom of religion [23] have not been upheld.

In a related Florida case, it was held that a statute compelling isolation and hospitalization of tubercular patients was not unconstitutional[24] as discriminatory against all persons other than those of a certain religious belief and faith. While there is no indication in the opinion as to the petitioner's faith, the court does note that "Religious freedom cannot be used as a cloak for any person with a contagious or infectious disease to spread such disease because of his religion."[25] Similarly, the Supreme Court of Washington, noting that tuberculosis is slow, progressive, and infectious, refused to invalidate a regulation of the Board of Regents of the University of Washington which required a chest X-Ray as a condition of admission to that institution.[26] The plaintiff's claim that her religious freedom[27] as a Christian Scientist was infringed by the regulation was overruled in light of what the Court termed a clear, present, grave, and immediate danger to the health of all the students and employees of the University. The dissent characterizes the action as arbitrary, and questions whether a "clear and present" danger was factually established.[28]

In an analogous situation, the Wisconsin Court held constitutional a requirement that all males get a certificate indicating that they were free from venereal disease as a condition to the issuance of a marriage license. The Court, in holding that this requirement did not violate the petitioner's freedom of religion,[29] observed that "We know of no church which desires its ministers to profane the marriage tie by uniting a man afflicted with a loathesome disease to an innocent woman." [30]

2. The Practice of Medicine

Religious groups, or individual members of such groups, are, of course, entitled to use prayer for healing the sick at any time. It is only where such religious means are used commercially that there is a conflict with state licensing requirements, and a church-state problem arises. Not surprisingly, the defense of the practice of religion has been of little avail in prosecutions for the unlicensed practice of medicine.

Thus, Courts in Alabama,[31] Colorado,[32] Washington[33] and Wisconsin[34] have upheld convictions under statutes prescribing criminal penalties for the unlicensed practice of medicine, as against claims that such application of these statutes violated the defendant's religious liberty as guaranteed by the Constitutions[35] of those states.

New York originally held that attendance of a Christian Scientist was not sufficient compliance with a statute making it a misdemeanor not to supply medical care to a minor,[36] despite the objection that such a holding was violative of the free exercise provision[37] of the New York constitution. Thirteen years later, however, the New York Court held Christian Scientists within the exception to the prohibition against the unlicensed practice of medicine granted in the case of the practice of the religious tenets of any church. The court listed Maine, New Hampshire, Massachusetts, Connecticut, North Carolina, North and South Dakota, Kentucky, Tennessee, and Wisconsin as *specifically* exempting Christian Scientists from medical practice acts.[38] While arguments might well be raised by other denominations that the specific exemption of Christian Scientists violates equal protection or establishes religion, the question does not seem to have been litigated.

Two early Pennsylvania cases[39] affirmed the constitutionality[40] of the denial of corporate charters to Christian Scientists on the ground that they practiced "metaphysical healing" which is prohibited without a license, but this is apparently no longer the law in that state.[41]

3. Fluoridation of the Water Supply

Findings by public health authorities that the incidence of tooth decay is lessened by fluoridation of the water supply has raised the issue of whether such action constitutionally justifies the interference with freedom of religion. Here the issue is not as clear cut as in the case of vaccination against smallpox where the danger to the health of the community is much more serious and immediate. Few of the numerous cases[42] decided on fluoridation involve determinations under state constitutional religion clauses. In most cases where the issue of violation of religious freedom was raised, without reference to a particular state constitutional clause, state courts have held against the person seeking to halt contemplated fluoridation on these grounds.[43]

In holding that the fluoridation of water to be used in the City of Bend did not violate Constitutional guarantees of religious liberty, the Supreme Court of Oregon noted that

> ... the measure bears only remotely, if at all, upon the religious practices of any individual . . . it was adopted for the accomplishment of an end, concededly legitimate . . . It is, therefore, a valid exercise of the City's police power.[44]

While there is apparently no authority holding that fluoridation would violate any religious rights guaranteed by state constitutions, the North Dakota Court has held that a cause of action was stated where, amongst other allegations, the plaintiff claimed that such action by a municipality would be in derogation of the freedom of religion[45] guaranteed by the Constitution of that state.[46]

4. Contraception

There has been very little litigation on the subject of contraception in a state *constitutional* context.[47] Apparently only Connecticut and Massachusetts still bar even physicians from giving any information regarding birth control.[48] While numerous attempts have been made to allow the prescription of contraceptives by physicians to married persons under limited circumstances, the only conflict with a state constitutional provision came in 1941 when the Justices of the Supreme Court of Massachusetts were asked to rule on the constitutionality of a proposal that the statutory provision relating to the prevention of pregnancy or conception be amended so as not to apply to certain medical treatment or prescription, nor to teaching in a chartered medical school, nor to the publication or sale of medical treatises or journals. The Justices held that such a proposal did not come within the constitutional provision[49] that "No measure that relates to religion, religious practices or religious institutions . . . shall be proposed by an initiative petition . . ."[50]

On the surface, then, these laws relating to contraception are not "related to religion." Attempts to have them struck down have therefore been based, not on conflicts with freedom of religion, but on arguments that these states deprive patients and/or doctors of life without due process.[51]   While no religion commands the practice of contraception, it is not inconceivable that arguments might be raised that the freedom of religion of an individual is abridged by state statutes denying him access to information on birth control.   Thus, if a religious tenet held by the individual dictated that he limit the size of his family, he might well argue that a statute forbidding doctors to prescribe contraceptive devices was an unreasonable interference with the practice of his religion. Thus far, however, the issue does not seem to have been raised, and criticism of these statutes on religious grounds has been limited to arguments that they amounted to an establishment or preference.[52]

5. *Transfusions and Other Medical Care*

There is a substantial body of state case law dealing with the power of the state to compel medical treatment—transfusions and the like—for those whose religious beliefs do not permit such treatment.[53]   The typical case involves an operation or transfusion necessary to the life of a child, and refusal to allow such treatment because of the religious scruples of the parent.   The courts are generally agreed that such treatment may be compelled in the case of a child, but there is doubt as to whether this rule would be applied in the case of an adult.

Many state cases nowhere discuss or decide these issues under their specific constitutional provisions, but ground their decisions on a more general basis.   For example, a New York court ordered the removal of a child's infected eye, despite the fact that the mother claimed that God had given the child and could do what He wanted with it;[54] a Texas Court ordered orthopedic treatment despite a mother's decision to rely on prayer, the fact that treatment was contrary to the mother's religious belief being held immaterial;[55] and the Missouri Court declared a child with anemia "dependent" and ordered a transfusion despite religious objections of the parents.[56]   A New Jersey Court ordered blood transfusions for a child not yet born despite the objection of Jehovah's Witness parents;[57] and an Ohio Court, in holding similarly under the due process clause of the Fourteenth Amendment, noted that " . . .When a child's right to live and his parents' religious belief collide, the former is paramount and the religious doctrine must give way".[58]

There are but three cases in point which are decided under, or specifically refer to, state Freedom of Religion Clauses.   In a 1903 New York criminal prosecution,[59] a statute making it a crime to neglect to provide medical attention for one's child was held constitutional, despite application to a parent who claimed interference with his constitutionally protected freedom of religion[60] in that his religious beliefs precluded medical aid.   Refusal of the Jehovah's Witness parents to allow a transfusion for a child born with an RH negative factor was held to be sufficient basis for declaring the child "dependent" and ordering a transfusion in a 1952 Ohio case.[61]   The Ohio Court, affirming despite the fact that the child's recovery rendered the point moot, observed that the right of the state as parens patriae outweighed the parents' constitutional freedom of religion.[62]   A recent New Jersey case upheld the declaration of a child as "neglected" where the parents refused to allow a blood transfusion,[63] despite objections that this infringed upon the freedom of religion guaranteed by the New Jersey Constitution.[64]

The problem of whether compelling transfusions or other medical treatment violates the religious freedom guaranteed by a state constitution becomes much more acute where an adult, rather than a child, is involved.   The problem resolves itself into a choice between the interests of the state (for example, in preventing suicide) and the interests of the individual in religious freedom.   There has been little litigation in a church-state posture in this area,[65] and authority under state constitutional clauses protecting freedom of religion is scant.   In a 1955 New York case the Court of Appeals of that state affirmed a lower court holding that an operation to correct a harelip and a cleft-palate in a twelve year old child was not precluded by the father's belief in "forces in the universe", but where the child believed the same thing, the final decision as to the operation should be left to him.[66]   The age of the child and the lack of immediate necessity for the operation would seem to have influenced the Court's decision.   There is dictum in the concurring opinion in an earlier New York case to the effect that "As to an adult . . . I think that there is no power to prescribe the medical treatment he shall receive."[67]

A recent New Jersey case [68] involved ordering transfusions for a pregnant woman.   The court sidestepped the issue, noting that ". . . it is unnecessary to decide that question in broad terms because the welfare of the child and the mother are so intertwined and inseparable . . ."

It is difficult to generalize on the basis of this meager authority, but it may certainly be concluded that different policy reasons will have to be used in compelling medical care for adults who do not desire it than in the case of children whose parents will not allow it.   Whether the freedom of religion clauses of the state constitutions will be evaded in forcing medical treatment upon adults whose religion forbids it, as was the case with reference to children, remain to be fully litigated.

6. Sunday Laws

Our concern with Sunday laws is primarily this: To what extent may the states or their local municipalities be permitted to regulate secular activity on Sunday compatible with federal and state constitutional guarantees of religious freedom? State and municipal statutes which compel the observance of Sunday as a day of rest have been a constant source of litigation throughout our history. Although in recent times they have been attacked as arbitrary, unreasonable, and unnecessary, traditionally they have been assailed on religious grounds. Generally opposed to such laws are those religious sects which hold sacred some other day of the week. They argue that the laws favor those creeds which observe Sunday as a religious holiday and discriminate against those who hold sacred some other day. Thus, it is claimed that the laws invade the minorities' religious freedom and violate the state and federal constitutional bans on aid to churches.

The historical basis for the Sunday laws is to be found in the desire of the people to preserve that day solely for religion. The practice finds its origin in the command given on Mount Sinai that the first day of the week is to be kept "holy to the Lord."[69] Later, in 321 A.D., the Emperor Constantine ordered that the first day of the week be set aside to honor the Lord.[70] The monarchs of England traditionally decreed and strictly enforced the observance of Sunday by penalizing anyone working on that day.[71] Until the American colonies acted to formulate their own regulations, the Sunday laws of England applied in equal force to them.

Virginia in 1610 was the first colony to enact a law banning work on Sunday.[72] This was followed by similar prohibitions in the other colonies.[73] Throughout the colonial period, the observance of Sunday was strictly policed. Further, it has been reported that even as late as 1825—long after independence—regulations in large eastern cities such as New York and Philadelphia still permitted the churches to place chains across the streets in front of their buildings to prevent traffic from passing during service hours.[74] The strict observance of Sunday was characteristic, also, of many of the mid-west regions such as the Ohio valley where strongly entrenched colonial traditions had been carried over by the settlers. By contrast, however, there was little attempt to enforce the observance of Sunday in the raw and busy frontier areas.

Although it is true that the colonies favored the compulsory observance of Sunday as the Lord's Day, no provision for its observance was made in the United States Constitution. Only one remote reference to Sunday is to be found in that document. Article 1, Section 7 provides that Sundays are to be excepted when counting the ten day period during which the President must act on legislation before it automatically becomes law without his signature or veto. This exception simply reflects the desire of the people to relieve the president from the compulsory tasks of his office on a day when all formal business of government is suspended. Apart from this solitary reference to Sunday in the federal constitution, all regulations regarding activity on this day are made by the states.

Throughout the nineteenth century, there is little doubt that Sunday laws were passed for just one reason—to preserve the day for religious worship. They were upheld as such. The courts were certainly aware of their purpose and in most instances saw no real objection to it. Consider, for example, this language of the Arkansas Supreme Court in 1850:

Sunday or the sabbath is properly and emphatically called the Lord's Day, and is one amongst the first and most sacred institutions of the Christian religion. This system of religion is recognized as constituting a part and parcel of the common law, and as such all of the institutions growing out of it, or in any way connected with it, in case they shall not be found to interfere with the rights of conscience, are entitled to the most profound respect, and can rightfully claim the protection of the law-making power of the State.[75]

Said a New York court in 1877: "The Christian religion may be protected from desecration by such laws as the legislature in its wisdom may deem necessary.[76] And a Maryland Court in 1894:

If the Christian religion is, incidentally or otherwise, benefited or fostered by having this day of rest, as it undoubtedly is, there is all the more reason for the enforcement of laws that help to preserve it. Whilst courts have generally sustained Sunday laws as "civil regulations," their decisions will have no less weight if they are shown to be in accordance with divine law as well as human.[77]

Even well into the twentieth century in some places the Sunday laws were recognized as primarily religious in nature and object, and upheld as such, even though the trend was definitely to find them valid only upon humanitarian grounds. As late as 1923, a Virginia court commented:

While the provisions of the statute . . . cannot be enforced as a religious observance, the great moral force that is back of it will make itself felt in its enforcement in conformity with the views of that force.[78]

It was clear to all by this time, however, that these laws could no longer be enforced from any religious motivation. If they were to be upheld, it would have to be because they were necessary to the health and well-being of the community.

At the present time, a large majority of the states do regulate Sunday activity to some extent.[79] However, none of them have attempted to accomplish this by means of constitutional language. Two states— Vermont and Delaware—do have constitutional clauses which "urge" the people to respect the day by refraining from normal workday pursuits. The Vermont constitution provides:

Nevertheless, every sect or denomination of Christians ought to observe the Sabbath or Lord's Day, and keep up some sort of religious worship, which to them shall seem most agreeable to the revealed will of God.[80]

The Delaware constitution simply says that it is "the duty of all men frequently to assemble together for the public worship of Almighty God," in order that the "piety and morality, on which the prosperity of communities depends are hereby promoted."[81]

Neither of these clauses in any way compel such observance. In all instances, Sunday prohibitions take the form of statutes and local ordinances. Presently, these laws range all the way from California's lone prohibition of boxing on Sunday to the very complex and stringent legislation passed by New Jersey.[82]

Generally, the Sunday laws operate in one of two ways. They may be laws which are enacted in detail by the state legislature and which are applicable to all persons in the state or they may be local option statutes which authorize the communities to determine, within certain prescribed limits, their own regulatory scheme. The typical Sunday law, whether it be a state-wide statute or only a local ordinance, usually prohibits three kinds of activity: (1) employers from requiring their employees to work on Sunday; (2) amusements; (3) the sales of goods and some services. In their coverage, these laws vary considerably from state to state. Most of the states are in the first and third category, with exceptions made in most cases for essential manufacturing and for the sale of necessities. Many regulate all three activities, while a few states prohibit only boxing and wrestling,[83] and in some instances barbering.[84] Today amusements are banned only during certain hours of Sunday in many of the states,[85] but in some places hunting and fishing are specifically outlawed entirely on that day.[86]

The great bulk of Sunday legislation enacted in recent times has been directed chiefly at the sale and distribution of goods on Sunday. New legislation in this area has been generated mainly by the spectacular increase in discount merchandising by large chain operations in the retail field. In order to achieve the high volume of sales necessary to make this type of selling profitable, outlets must remain open seven days a week. This has put the non-discount merchants in a less favorable competitive position. Their reaction has been to join with the churches and exert strong pressures for new laws. As a result, many localities which never before had any need for stringent Sunday laws have written new ones and stepped up enforcement.

A second consequence of the development of discount merchandising has been the acquisition by the traditional opponents of the Sunday laws of a new and powerful ally in their battle to eliminate them. The traditional religious arguments against the laws have been supplemented— in some cases overridden—by arguments attacking the necessity for such laws, and claims that they are unfair, unreasonable, and lacking in proper standards of application. In most instances this route is the more effective since the demand for speed in the passage of the new legislation has often resulted in laws riddled with arbitrary exceptions, inconsistencies, and lacking in standards. Without these minimum due process requirements, such laws and ordinances usually meet defeat in the courts. However, where the laws are properly drawn and applied, they will be upheld. Consequently, this is not always the answer to the church-state problem.

Some jurisdictions, sensitive to the plight of the minority sects, make allowances for them by exempting them from the operation of the laws.[87] Normally a person must make known his intention to close on another day of the week, and manifest it usually by affidavit to an officer of the court or some other agency.[88] Some states, however, do not extend the exemption to the ban on Sunday sales.[89]

A few areas have adopted "one-in-seven laws". These laws permit a person to elect the day on which he will refrain from working or selling—again filing some notice of his intention to observe that day with the proper authorities. Coupled with a public nuisance provision, the one-in-seven laws may provide an effective answer to the religion question. A Jewish merchant, for example, could open for business on Sunday without violating any law unless his activity disturbed the peaceful worship of others. This arrangement permits the merchant to defend himself within the context of the common law. And if convicted and ordered to close, he could hardly claim that his religious rights were being violated or that any one sect was being favored by the law. Courts could then accept the religious basis for the Sunday laws and scrap the questionable health and welfare rationale.[90] Three states at present have this type of arrangement.[91]

A third solution to this dilemma is to do away with the Sunday laws entirely. As of this writing, only three states—Iowa, New Mexico, and Wyoming—have no Sunday laws. A few states retain only minor prohibitions such as boxing, wrestling, and in some cases, barbering.[92] Despite the allowances made in some states for minority sects, the introduction of the one-in-seven laws, or even the total abandonment of the Sunday laws altogether, there is still every indication that the Sunday laws will remain for some time to come.

In the first place the number of states which have repealed their Sunday laws is very small compared to the large majority which still retain them. Even those laws which exempt minority sects from their operation sometimes do not extend the exemption to the bans on the sales of certain goods. Secondly, the one-in-seven formula does not appear to have spread to any significant extent. Thirdly, in the last ten years, a significant number of jurisdictions have taken steps to revise, amend, and up-date their Sunday laws to provide greater coverage, stricter enforcement, and to ensure that they meet the strict requirements of equal protection and due process of law.[93] It is true that in some cases, states or municipalities have failed miserably in attempting to accomplish these objectives and the consequence has been confusion and disenchantment. Heavy pressure to make exemptions to the laws has often resulted in very arbitrary classifications, especially as regards the bans on Sunday sales.   Nevertheless, the fact that so many states have gone to the trouble to amend their laws is considerable evidence that the people still strongly favor them.   Fourthly, the proposition that the Sunday laws are favored by the majority of the population is strongly buttressed by the decisions of the state courts, in a great majority of which the laws have been found constitutional.[94]

Although litigation in this area of church and state is considerable it is impossible to discover more than a few instances where Sunday laws were struck down because it was recognized that their character and purpose was obviously religious.

In 1858, the Supreme Court of California was the author of one of these rare decisions.[95]   In reversing the conviction of a Jewish merchant for selling clothing on Sunday, the Court nullified the state's Sunday laws, characterizing such acts as intending to do nothing more than to "enforce as a religious institution, the observance of a day held sacred by the followers of one faith."   Of this particular law the court said:

> The whole scope of the act is expressive of an intention on the part of the legislature to require a periodical cessation from ordinary pursuits, not as a civil duty, necessary for the repression of any existing evil, but in furtherance of the interests, and in aid of . . . the Christian religion.[96]

The tenuity of this decision was decidedly apparent when the same Court overruled it at the next opportunity.[97]   Thereafter, each time the laws were presented for consideration, they were upheld with the Court being scrupulously careful on each occasion to stress their non-religious character.[98]   The re-instatement of that unique decision has perhaps been achieved by California's repeal of its Sunday laws.   At the present time, only boxing is forbidden in the state on Sunday.[99]

A second such instance occurred recently in Massachusetts.[100]   A Jewish meat seller had been charged along with a rabbi with violating the law by selling meat on Sunday.   The defendant, a purveyor of kosher prepared meats, operated what was apparently one of a few such markets in his area.   The rabbi was present in the shop to ensure that the meat was properly prepared.   In keeping with the tenets of his faith, the defendant closed his shop on Saturday, his sabbath, and opened for business on Sunday.   The defendant argued that this law as applied to him was unfair because it obliged him to remain closed two days of the week while those who observed Sunday as the Sabbath were closed only one day in the week. Secondly, he contended that the law was unfair to many of his customers whose week-day pursuits prevented them from shopping any other time than on the week-end and since he was closed on Saturday, this left only Sunday. Thus, the defendant concluded that this law was unconstitutional; first, because it denied him equal economic opportunity because of his religious beliefs, and second, because it violated the religious rights of his customers by making it almost impossible for them to purchase kosher meats, and thirdly, because it violated the constitutional ban against any aid to religion by favoring those sects which observed Sunday as the sabbath.

The District Court in Massachusetts agreed with the defendant and ruled that the Sunday law was unconstitutional. Said the Justices:

> What Massachusetts has done in this statute is to furnish special protection to the dominant Christian sects which celebrate Sunday as the Lord's Day, without furnishing such protection in their religious acts, to those Christian sects and to Orthodox and Conservative Jews who observe Saturday as the sabbath, and to the prejudice of the latter.[101]

This decision, however, was even shorter lived than the early California ruling referred to above. In 1961, just two years after this decision was handed down, it was reversed by the Supreme Court of the United States.[102]

There have been other instances in which these laws have been found invalid, but not on the ground that they violated religious freedom or bans on aid to religious sects. In Florida a Sunday law was ruled unconstitutional because it exempted from its operation a whole battery of services more or less connected with recreational activities on Sunday. Other services, such as automobile garages, repair shops, and the like were not included within the exemption. The Florida Court found that the distinctions were arbitrary, and without any reasonable basis for the exercise of the police power.[103] A similar conclusion was reached by the Missouri Court which struck down a law prohibiting only barbering on Sunday. The court said that this measure was a "special law" enacted in the areas where "a general law can be made applicable," and thus an unwarranted classification.[104] Both states have since corrected these defects and enforce Sunday laws today.

Finally, from Idaho comes a decision which serves as one example of where these laws may not be applied at all. In that state, members of the sect known as the Jehovah's Witnesses were convicted for employing a moving picture machine on Sunday to illustrate a series of religious lectures. Their conviction was quickly reversed by the Supreme Court of Idaho which declared that any construction of the Sunday law to preclude this type of activity would bring it into direct conflict with the religious freedom guarantee of the state's constitution.[105]

Lastly, the belief that the Sunday laws are constitutional and quite likely to remain on the books of most states is most strongly supported by references to a number of recent United States Supreme Court decisions upholding such laws. In a series of cases involving the Sunday laws of Maryland and Pennsylvania decided by that Court in 1961, forceful arguments that the laws offend against the First Amendment religion clauses were rejected in favor of a showing that such measures are within the power of the states to enact, and that they are necessary to the secular interests of the people of those states.[106]

In upholding the laws, the Supreme Court has taken the position that there is nothing unconstitutional about a law which provides all the members of the community a day of rest after the strain and toil of the week's labor. From such legislation, the health and well-being of the inhabitants can only profit. Indeed, the complexities of modern living make such respites a most necessary requirement. Such laws then serve a valid and very vital public purpose. The fact that the day of rest traditionally falls on Sunday, a religious day for a great number of Americans, says the Court, does not serve to negate the public purpose. Because it operates to further some religions does not make it violative of the First Amendment. In the words of Mr. Justice Frankfurter, it is the "primary end" which is determinative of the regulation's purpose, and therefore its constitutionality.[107]

The Supreme Court has held that denial of unemployment insurance benefits by a state to a person who lost her employment because she refused to work on Saturday for religious reasons, constitutes a violation of that person's constitutional right to free exercise of religion.[108]

The answer to the query posed at the outset of this section, at least today, must therefore be that as long as these statutes remain more temporal than ecclesiastical and are properly drafted and applied, it is unlikely that the states will be found to have exceeded their authority or the limits set by the Supreme Court of the United States.

Limitations Imposed In the Interest of Public Morality

No less important than the preservation of the public health is the recognized need to maintain the level of morality in the community. As a consequence, the states have enacted laws making certain practices considered inimical to the public illegal even though motivated by religious considerations. Two outstanding instances of this are the bans upon the practice of polygamy, and the laws on the books of many states punishing blasphemy.

1. Polygamy, Celestial Marriage, etc.

In the interests of protecting the moral values of the people, all states have made illegal the practice of polygamy, celestial marriage, and other pluralistic practices, even when professed as a tenet of one's faith.[109] Four states—Montana, Oklahoma, Idaho, and Utah, while proclaiming in their constitutions complete freedom of religion, expressly prohibit such practices.[110] In all states, persons practicing polygamy may be subject to conviction under the bigamy statutes which punish such actions as crimes. The fact that the wrong was committed for religious reasons does not serve to remove the necessary criminal intent.[111]

The Supreme Court of the United States has ruled long ago that the states do not violate the federal constitution by their prohibitions on polygamy even when practiced as a matter of religious belief.[112] Also, one state has upheld its right to deny the privilege of voting to anyone convicted of the crime of bigamy.[113]

In Utah it is possible to be convicted of the crime of bigamy simply by encouraging others to adhere to the practice of plural marriage.[114] Noting that polygamy statutes regulate conduct and not beliefs, the Utah Supreme Court upheld the conviction of one urging others both verbally and in print to practice polygamy noting that this was conduct injurious to the public morals, and therefore could be regulated. The defendant was convicted under a conspiracy statute.[115] It has also been held that parents who, because of religious beliefs, enter into illegal polygamous marriages could be deprived of the right to the custody and control of their children. In the particular instance, a man had twenty-six children in three families, all located in different areas.[116]

Today a discussion of polygamy, celestial marriage, and other such practices, is of little more than academic interest. The only major sect to advocate polygamy as a religious tenet was the Church of the Latter Day Saints. However, not long after the series of Supreme Court decisions upholding the right of the state to punish persons practicing this kind of marriage, the Mormon faith, under pressure of forfeiting their property, officially proclaimed that the practice was no longer recognized as a tenet of their faith. Finally, as of the present time, the Courts have found no difficulty in adhering to the principles set forth in these early decisions.[117]

2. Blasphemy Laws

At early common law, any attack upon God or religion was punished as the crime of blasphemy. A Pennsylvania law of 1700 provided, for example, that:

> ... whosoever shall wilfully, premeditately and despitefully blaspheme, and speak too loosely and profanely of Almighty God, Christ Jesus, and the Holy Spirit, or the Scripture of Truth, and is legally convicted thereof, shall forfeit and pay the sum of ten pounds.[118]

A high moral standard was considered of prime necessity to the maintenance of sound and successful government. Since the moral behavior of the people was posited upon espoused principles of Christianity, any attempt to undermine the Christian religion in this manner resulted in the rather severe punishment of the offender. In the words of one jurist, blasphemies are "crimes injurious to, and having a malignant influence on society..." [119]

Blasphemy laws were not revoked by the later formation of the state constitutions. Each of the state constitutions clearly and eloquently guaranteed freedom of conscience and religious worship, and found very little problem reconciling these guarantees with the blasphemy laws. In general, there were three main varieties of the offense: (1) denying the being and providence of God, (2) contumacious reproaches of Christ and the scoffing at the Scriptures, (3) immorality tending to subvert all religions. In the early years of our Republic, these laws were much more rigorously enforced than they are at present.

For example, in New York in 1811, an individual was convicted of blasphemy because he uttered "the false, scandalous, malicious, wicked and blasphemous words, 'Jesus Christ was a bastard, and his mother must have been a whore.'" The trial court found him in contempt of the Christian religion and the laws of the state and fined him five hundred dollars. The severity of the fine is indicative of the zeal of the people in safeguarding the integrity of their faith. On appeal of the conviction, the defendant's attorney, in an apparently forceful manner, contended that the state constitution guaranteed a free toleration of all religions and kinds of worship, and that the only exception was to "licentiousness" and not "opinions". He contended that the defendant, according to the indictment, was charged only with attacks upon the divinity of Christ and not religion in general. These, said counsel, were his religious opinions and consequently he had a constitutional right to declare them. [120]

The Appeals Court refused to find that the defendant's remarks amounted to any "serious discussion upon any controverted point in religion," but were "malicious and wanton." Responding to the constitutional argument, the justices wrote:

> The free, equal and undisturbed enjoyment of religious opinion, whatever it may be, and free and decent discussion on any subject is granted and secured; but to revile, with malicious and blasphemous contempt, the religion professed by the whole community, is an abuse of that right. [121]

It is probable that the court was not as much concerned with the specific utterance as it was with the defendant's purpose in making it. It is likely, also, that the Court would refuse to find any satisfactory excuse for the defendant's statements at this time in New York's history.

A comparable result was reached by the Pennsylvania Court about a dozen years later in 1824. There the defendant was indicted for saying that "the Holy Scriptures were a mere fable . . . a contradiction . . . contained a great many lies." The indictment was eventually dismissed for defectiveness. However, in dismissing, the Court took the opportunity to say that

... while our own free constitution secures liberty of conscience and freedom of religious worship to all, it is not necessary to maintain that any man should have the right publicity to vilify the religion of his neighbors and of the country; these two privileges are directly opposed.[122]

Finally, the most important decision involving a blasphemy law in recent times was rendered in Massachusetts in 1921. On the trial of the case, the defendant was found guilty of the offense as a result of his ridiculing the Virgin Birth, the death of Christ, the Trinity, and religion in general. When the defendant appealed claiming constitutional protection, the Court unanimously rejected his position. The law under which the defendant was tried, they said, has stood for over a century. Its basis, they added, is found in the colonial government as far back as 1646 without ever before having been challenged. "We have no hesitation in saying," they concluded, "that the statute . . . in no manner conflicts with our state constitution guarantee of religious freedom ... or speech." [123]

Blasphemy laws are still found in a great many states today. However, it is perhaps unlikely that, given the same or similar sets of facts outlined in the foregoing decisions, any conviction today would survive appeal. Once again it would depend on the circumstances in which the alleged blasphemies occurred and perhaps most importantly, the purpose for which the statements, oral or written, were made. No law may today prohibit any valid criticism of a religious belief in general. Nor may any person be punished for completely disavowing a belief in a Supreme Being, or any religion altogether. What is still forbidden, however, is the use of profane or obscene language tending to disparage religion in general. Those who cherish and respect their beliefs do have a right not to see it consciously maligned or publicly profaned. Laws which punish this kind of activity do not offend against either guarantees of religious freedom or freedom of speech.

Limitations Imposed in the Interest of Public Safety

In the previous sections we have been concerned with regulatory measures designed to safeguard the physical health of the community, and the preservation of the level of moral behavior. In this final section under the general heading of the Police Power, we are interested, primarily, in those controls placed on free exercise of religion for the purpose of forestalling injury to individuals, and preventing disorder and disruption of community life in general. The authors have included in this area the problem of the use of alcohol and the use of dangerous instrumentalities in religious rites, including the right of the state to prohibit the exercise of religious freedom to certain persons in the interests of maintaining discipline and order. Covered also are bans upon fraudulent practices and rites performed under the guise of religion, the solicitation of funds and distribution of literature by religious and charitable groups, and the problems arising from restraints upon religious demonstrations and parades. Lastly, the problems of religious freedom and the application of zoning laws, and the regulation of the internal affairs of churches will be discussed.

1. *Prohibition of Alcoholic Beverages*

While state prohibition laws are certainly much less prevalent today than thirty years ago, the approach taken by courts in this area is indicative of a general philosophy relating to alleged conflicts between freedom of religion and governmental legislation with reference to public health and safety. Laws regulating the use of intoxicating liquors have frequently exempted sacramental wine used by religious sects, and have been attacked, usually as being violative of the guarantees of religious liberty, but with little success.

Thus, the defendant in an Illinois prosecution for violation of the state's prohibition laws claimed that the exemption given wines used for sacramental purposes violated the Illinois constitutional ban upon giving any preference to religion.[124] The defendant argued that, since some religious organizations use wine in religious services, while others do not, the exemption gave a preference to certain religious groups. The Supreme Court of Illinois, in affirming the defendant's conviction, observed that "The right to use intoxicating liquors for such purposes exists in all. It is not a special privilege in those exercising the right because others do not exercise it." [125] In a South Dakota case,[126] it was held that there was no violation of religious liberty in requiring an Orthodox Jew to procure wine for sacramental purposes in the manner provided by law, and a conviction for unlawful possession of liquor was upheld. The Texas prohibition law exempted the use of wines for "sacramental purposes," and Orthodox Jews were not included since their use of wine was as a beverage rather than sacramental. The Supreme Court of that State upheld the prohibition law[127] against an attack alleging that it violated religious liberty under the Texas Constitution.[128]

The regulation of the consumption of alcoholic beverages is clearly within the police power of the state. It would appear from the cases that the majority, and better, rule would exempt from such prohibition alcohol used as part of a "legitimate" religious service. While careful checks may obviously be established by the state to see that the exemption is in fact limited to such services, the result of the Texas case above described would seem harsh. The purpose and intent of prohibition laws would not seem to be evaded by liberal construction of what constitutes a "legitimate" religious service. A holding that the use of wine by the Jewish in private religious ceremonies would certainly appear to be warranted by the spirit if not the letter of the exemptions.

2. The Use of "Dangerous Instrumentalities" in Religious Ceremonies.

State Courts have apparently unanimously held that prosecution of members of various sects using "dangerous instrumentalities" in their religious rituals was not unconstitutional.   Thus, courts in Alabama,[129] Kentucky,[130] North Carolina,[131] Tennessee,[132] and Virginia[133] have upheld the constitutionality of state statutes forbidding the handling of poisonous reptiles in a manner such as to endanger the public health, welfare, and safety, despite defenses that such prohibitions violated the defendant's religious liberty,[134] in that such practices were a part of sects' religious service or that the only people endangered were other members of the sect voluntarily engaged in the same practice.

The Kentucky Court observed that such statutes were not repugnant to constitutional guarantees of religious freedom, for the laws punish acts which have a tendency to disturb the public peace, notwithstanding the fact that these acts conformed to what was believed to be religious duty.[135] The Tennessee Court was more explicit in citing the hazards involved in such practices in noting that the ". . . danger is grave and immediate when and wherever the practice is being indulged." [136]

In a comparable case,[137] the Montana Court affirmed the constitutionality of a statute under which a member of the Crow Indian tribe was convicted for the use of peyote, a narcotic root, in a religious ceremony. Despite the fact that the defendant claimed that his faith dictated such action, the statute was held not to be violative of the freedom of religion clause [138] of the Montana constitution. The California Supreme Court has held contra under the Federal Constitution.[139]

In an 1845 case decided under Louisiana's freedom of religion provision, the Supreme Court of the United States refused to accept jurisdiction over a criminal prosecution in which a Catholic priest was convicted of a violation of a municipal ordinance making it illegal for corpses to be displayed in churches during funeral services.[140] The United States Supreme Court held that it had no jurisdiction over such a question in light of the fact that the religious liberties of the citizens of Louisiana were to be protected by the laws and constitution [141] of that state. Since 1940, however, the religious liberty of a person is within the protection of the United States constitution.

Thus, the type of "dangerous instrumentality"—snake, narcotic, or corpse—is immaterial; if the thing used in a religious ceremony is truly dangerous it is no infringement upon the religious liberty of a member of the sect involved to attach a criminal penalty to such use.

3. Fortune Telling and Spiritualism.

The states have frequently legislated to prevent the commission of fraud, with a resultant conflict with constitutional guarantees of freedom of religion when the alleged fraudulent conduct is done in pursuance of religious belief. The typical case is that of prosecution for fortune telling, with the defendant contending that state statutes prohibiting such conduct violate his religious liberty as guaranteed by the constitution of the state. The initial inquiry, then, is whether such statutes are constitutional. Most courts have held that they are, but the liberal exceptions present in most state statutes mitigate these holdings. A second inquiry, sometimes inextricably interwoven with the first, is whether the practice which the state seeks to prohibit is fraud or religion. There are few cases turning on this point, but it would appear that most states take a rather facile approach, deeming fortune telling done for compensation, fraud, and that done without remuneration, religion.

The Missouri Court in 1922 upheld a city ordinance prohibiting fortune telling (there was apparently no exemption in the case of religion and no distinction between prophecy for profit or gratis) noting that the state's constitutional guarantee of freedom of religion [142] was not abridged by prohibitory acts not inconsistent with good order, peace, health, and safety.[143]

Four states resolving the issue of whether statutes or ordinances prohibiting fortune-telling violated guarantees of religious freedom have upheld the constitutionality of such statutes where the conduct forbidden was that done for compensation. Noting that the Nebraska act did not prohibit spiritualistic seances unless public, open, and for gain, the Supreme Court of that state held that "The making of a public exhibition of religious worship in the form of a seance for gain . . . is not a religious liberty guaranteed by the Constitution." [144] In a 1918 case, a New York court affirmed the constitutionality [145] of a conviction under a statute making persons pretending to tell fortunes "disorderly persons." Noting that the defendant received $1 for her prophecy, the court observed that:

> . . . [T]he defendant was telling fortunes for money. This modern attempt to excuse violations of lawful salutary police regulations, enacted for the protection of the community, by appeals to constitutional rights and religious beliefs, does not find favor with the courts. The state may not interfere with the religious beliefs and opinions of a citizen, but it may prohibit acts and practices which · are deemed to be detrimental to the community.[146]

In 1942, another New York court affirmed a comparable conviction, holding that the defendant, who made predictions regarding death and the like, outside the tenets of her church, did not fall within the exemption in the statute:

> . . . [B]ut this subdivision shall not be construed to interfere with the belief, practices or usages of an incorporated ecclesiastical governing body or the duly licensed teachers or ministers thereof acting in good faith and without personal fee.

The court noted that "it is the duty of every Court to guard . . . [the] . . . free exercise and enjoyment of religious profession and worship without discrimination or preference . . . but no person should be permitted to use the right as a cloak for acts of licentiousness or as a justification of practices inconsistent with the peace or safety of the state." [147]

Under a similar Oklahoma statute, making it unlawful to tell fortunes for money, the defendant medium, who had communicated with the spirit of Minnehaha for $1, argued that the prohibition interfered with the free exercise of her religion. In affirming the conviction and upholding the constitutionality of the statute, the Oklahoma Court observed that "fantastic philosophers and religious zealots, like other people, must conform to wholesome police regulation." [148] A conviction for vagrancy for "fortune telling for compensation" was affirmed by the Supreme Court of Washington, despite the fact that the defendant was a regular and ordained minister of the National Astrological Society, which organization's practices include reading horoscopes. Noting that the defendant received $1 for such a reading, the Court upheld the constitutionality of the statute,[149] observing that ". . . while religious beliefs and opinions may not be interfered with harmful 'practices' may be prohibited." [150]

A California statute prohibiting advertisements of fortune telling by means of psychic powers was held constitutional [151] by the Supreme Court of that state in view of the following section, exempting persons doing acts prohibited thereby in the practice of their religion.[152] The New Jersey Court reversed the conviction of a medium for fortune telling, because the act complained of was part of a religious service, in which freedom to participate is guaranteed by the state's constitution.[153]

The second inquiry, that of whether the practice forbidden is fraud or religion has received little treatment in the state courts. In applying their statutes, and determining their constitutionality, the courts have looked to whether the statute exempted practices done in the pursuance of religious beliefs and/or whether the statute made compensation a test for prohibition, rather than to the merits of the question. The opinion of the Supreme Court of the United States in *United States* v. *Ballard* [154] gives three possible approaches to the problem of actually determining whether the action in question is religion or fraud: the jury is not to decide whether the opinions expressed by the medium are literally true, but rather whether the defendant honestly believed them to be true;[155] the jury should determine the truth or falsity of the representations;[156] and the jury should decide neither truth nor belief in the truth, but the case should be thrown out of court.[157]

4. *Distribution of Religious Literature, Solicitation, Demonstrations.*

Another important area where religious liberty has been obliged to yield to restrictions essential to an orderly and safe civil society is in the matter of religious proselytizing. It is axiomatic that the freedom to disseminate one's beliefs is an integral part of the freedom of religion guaranteed by the federal and state constitutions. Consequently, the problem is to determine the extent to which the proselytizing activities of persons and religious groups can be restricted consonant with that guarantee.

The methods of religious propagation are well-known. Most common are open-air preaching, religious parades and processions, and the sale and distribution of religious literature in all forms (books, pamphlets, newspapers, etc.) either upon the public streets or via door to door peddling. Related to this is the public solicitation of funds by both charitable and religious organizations.

When carried on for purely commercial purposes, such activities are necessarily subject to regulation and control in the public interest. Use of the streets, parks, and other areas, is supervised in the interests of traffic safety and control. Sales of literature and other items either on the street or to the people in their homes and places of business must be supervised also for the purpose of containing fraudulent practices and providing some degree of legitimate privacy. The need to prevent fraudulent practices is especially important as regards charitable solicitation for funds, an activity which provides a wide margin for sharp practices.

Since many religious groups and sects consider such activities to form an important ingredient of their religious worship, itself expressly guaranteed by constitutional clauses, conflicts naturally arise when these groups find themselves subject to these regulations. A number of them have taken the position that while such laws are valid as regards purely commercial activities, they cannot be constitutionally applied to the same activities when they are motivated by religious considerations. A survey of the litigation in the state courts indicates, however, that in the majority of instances such regulations will be upheld as proper exercises of the police power. Nevertheless, when the statutes or ordinances are themselves defective they will be voided. If the Court finds that the restriction imposed is either unnecessary, unreasonable, or discriminatory, it will be invalidated as an unconstitutional infringement on constitutional freedom of religion.

Perhaps most often the subject of regulation, usually on the municipal level, is the distribution of religious literature. In Georgia, a member of the Jehovah's Witnesses sect was convicted of violating a local ordinance of the city of Griffin which required written permission from the city manager before engaging in the distribution of circulars, handbooks, advertising, or literature of any kind, whether given away free or sold. The defendant refused to comply with the ordinance, and gave as a justification for his refusal the absence of any right in the authorities to apply this law to him. He claimed that he was an appointed servant of Jehovah, sent to spread his word and to do his work. Therefore, he asserted, "No external authority should be allowed to place between the finite being and the Infinite when the former is seeking to render homage that is due . . ." He contended that he had chosen the "mode which commands itself to his conscience and judgment as being suitable for him to render . . ." and was constitutionally protected. The Georgia Supreme Court rejected the defendant's contention, and criticized his attack as emphasizing only the religious objections to the measure and not striking at the arbitrary and uncontrolled discretion placed in the hands of the city manager to grant or deny him a permit.[158] Appeal was dismissed by the United States Supreme Court.[159]

One year later, another member of the same religious sect was convicted of violating the same ordinance. Once again, the defendant failed to test the law on the basis of due process, relying only on religious contention. Here, too, the Supreme Court of Georgia could find no basis for review and affirmed the conviction.[160] This time, however, on appeal to the Supreme Court of the United States, the conviction was reversed. The Supreme Court found that the ordinance was invalid on its face as violating the First and Fourteenth Amendments to the Federal Constitution.[161]

The New Jersey, New York and Massachusetts high courts have held valid local ordinances regulating the distribution of religious literature against claims that any kind of restriction offends both against freedom of religion, as well as freedom of speech. The Massachusetts and New Jersey decisions[162] both evolved from the refusal on the part of an individual to obtain a permit or license from the proper civil authority before proceeding to distribute. The New York case involved a provision which simply prohibited all *non-residents* from distributing literature entirely.[163]

Typical of the kind of ordinance which would be found unconstitutional was one enacted by the city of Worcester, Massachusetts. This ordinance flatly prohibited the distribution of handbills or advertising anywhere within the city limits. The Massachusetts high court refused to find this law invalid as applied to the distribution of religious literature citing its soundness in the need of reasonable rules and regulations in the use of the public streets and parks.[164] The Supreme Court of the United States, however, did not agree that the city's need to police its streets was so strong as to eliminate all religious activity, and ruled the provision invalid.[165]

Normally, local ordinances respecting such activities only require that some sort of permission be obtained from the municipality before proceeding. However, when this permission also requires that the applicants pay a fee or tax, the ordinance may be found unconstitutional. In Kentucky, for example, a municipal ordinance provided that itinerant merchants could not peddle merchandise or literature without first applying for a license. The cost of the license was $7.50 by the day, $30.00 by the week and $100.00 by the year. A subsequent attempt to apply this license tax to a minister of the Jehovah's Witnesses was held unconstitutional.[166]

A similar case arose in Florida. It involved an attempt by the city authorities in Tampa to impose a $50.00 license tax on a member of the Jehovah's Witnesses for soliciting subscriptions to the publications of the Watchtower Bible and Tract Society on the streets of the city. In ruling that this requirement was invalid as to this individual, the Florida Supreme Court said:

> To confer a free exercise of religious profession charged with an obligation like this and then lay a heavy tax on the performance of the obligation when no question of morals, safety, and convenience is involved is contrary to the letter and spirit of the Declaration of Right.[167]

This Court also struck down an ordinance which gave to the same city manager the power to withhold permits for this purpose, having no specific standards to which he would be obliged to adhere in making his decision.[168]

A further example of uncontrolled discretion in one individual or council coupled also with totally unnecessary and unreasonable prerequisite for the issuance of a license to distribute religious literature was an ordinance of the city of Moscow, Idaho. This law prohibited the distribution of *any* printed matter along *any* street, alley, sidewalk or park, within the city limits without first obtaining a permit. This permit could only be gotten from a police officer, providing the applicant saluted, in the presence of the officer, the flag of the United States by reciting the pledge of allegiance, and furnishing additional "sufficient" information of identity. The court had no difficulty in finding that such a law violated the state constitution when attacked by a member of the Jehovah's Witnesses who had refused to meet the law's requirements on religious grounds.[169]

Finally, the Oklahoma, New Jersey, South Carolina, and Texas Courts have held such restrictions on the distribution of religious literature unconstitutional either because they unnecessarily infringed upon religious freedom, or because the statutes were themselves defective for lack of fair and adequate standards.[170]

Another characteristic subject of municipal regulation has been the public solicitation of funds by religious and charitable organizations. The primary justification behind this regulation is the protection of the people from fraudulent practices. The regulation of charities having no religious affiliation does not raise too much of a problem. However, when similar restrictions are applied to groups doing this as a part of a religious program, constitutional difficulties may be posed.

In 1916, the California Supreme Court struck down a law which governed the solicitation activities of all religious and charitable organizations in the state. No collections were permitted unless prior approval was obtained from the State Charities Commission, and the proper credentials were issued to the organization. The court found the regulations were unwarranted. It ruled that the authorities had been given a power to designate who may or may not be permitted to engage in such valued work which has too arbitrary. The good to be obtained from unrestrained charitable activity outweighed the risk that some fraud might be perpetrated. The court found further that there was a great possibility that the enforcement of such a law against religious groups raised doubts of its constitutionality and that "In accordance with the dictate of the constitution itself the doubt will be resolved in favor of religious liberty." [171]

This decision must be contrasted, however, with two decisions handed down by the same tribunal a considerable number of years later. Both cases involved a municipal ordinance of the City of Los Angeles regulating charitable solicitations which were made as part of a religious program. Religious organizations were excluded from it by the specific language of the ordinance. Nonetheless, the Court upheld the application of the ordinance to all religious, missionary, and evangelical organizations on the rationale that the intent of the statute was to regulate *all* charitable solicitation even though made as a religious exercise.[172] The court in both cases split five to four. Both were subsequently dismissed on appeal to the United States Supreme Court. The dissents in both cases held that the ordinance as applied violated not only the state constitution, but the federal constitution. The Texas Court on the contrary, found a similar ordinance unconstitutional.[173]

A third major subject for restrictive regulation of this sort is the holding of religious demonstrations in public areas. Proselytizing by this means is a traditional practice among a number of our religious groups. Public prayer meetings, sermons, exhortations, and religious processions are, in many parts of the country, as much a part of the religious scene as the presence of our numerous churches and cathedrals. At the same time, however, these activities also often have the concomitant effect of disrupting the orderly and free flow of traffic, of disturbing the peace and quiet of the community, or in some instances, cause disorderly gatherings. For this reason, they are usually regulated.[174]

Musical instruments, loudspeakers, and other devices even when used in connection with a religious purpose are commonly controlled. A New Hampshire court in 1886 upheld the conviction of an individual for beating a drum in the middle of a town in violation of an ordinance designed to preserve the quiet of the community. The court ruled that the conviction was constitutional even though the man was able to defend his acts on the ground that they were part of his religious worship.[175] A similar result was reached in Pennsylvania where the individual refused to first obtain a permit to use a drum in connection with his public worship;[176] and, in Massachusetts lack of a permit resulted in the successful prosecution of a member of the Salvation Army for playing his cornet on the streets.[177] Loudspeakers fell under the same proscription. The Colorado Supreme Court upheld the arrest of a preacher for employing a speaker within hearing of the business community. One Justice dissented strongly, protesting that the ruling infringed both upon the individual's freedom of religion and speech.[178] The City of Gainsville in Georgia had an even stricter prohibition on loudspeakers, making their use illegal on any of the thoroughfares of the city. When an individual was convicted of broadcasting sermons over such speakers, he immediately appealed what he contended was a denial of his religious freedom, but the Georgia court held it was a valid exercise of the police power.[179]

New York City in 1932 had an ordinance which required all persons to obtain prior approval from the authorities before performing any public worship or exhortation. Under this ordinance an individual was convicted for preaching atheism on the street without a permit. This was reversed on appeal on the ground that the defendant was not within the operation of the law because he was not "conducting worship," but on the contrary, doing just the reverse—denouncing worship.[180] A short time later, the ordinance was amended to require a permit to espouse atheism on the streets. The same individual was again arrested, and this time his conviction was upheld. Their reasoning:

> The passion, rancor and malice sometimes aroused by sectarian religious controversies and attacks on religion seem to justify especial supervision over those who would conduct such meetings on public streets. . . . Practical exigencies and common experience may permit the recognition of degrees of harm and the limitation of regulation to classes where the need is deemed to be clearest.[181]

The fact that disorderliness may "sometimes" occur seemed enough for the court to uphold the law.

This case should be contrasted to one other decision of the New York Court of Appeals rendered in 1940. A group of Jehovah's Witnesses were parading along the streets carrying placards and disseminating information and literature attacking the Catholic Church. An angry and threatening crowd began to form around them which was dispersed by the police who arrested the marchers. They were subsequently convicted of disorderly conduct. On appeal, however, the Court refused to abide by the previous decisions in this area and instead reversed the conviction. The Court noted that only religious preachers were required to have permits, not political speakers because it was believed that attacks upon religion would most inevitably lead to disorder. The court concluded that perhaps this was no longer necessarily the case. Said the Justices:

> In spite of expression of opinion . . . as to the reasonableness of legislative classification which would require permits to hold street meetings for or against religion, but not for the discussion of other subjects, because street speaking on religion would be more likely to lead to disorder and hence require police protection, I doubt if that can be said to hold true today.[182]

The court seemed to feel that the risk of public disorder was not sufficiently great to deny this form of religious exercise.

In most instances public religious demonstrations are only restricted in some degree. However, in some instances they have been totally prohibited. As an example, the city of Moultrie, Georgia had an ordinance which prohibited all such activity on the streets on Saturdays. A large army base was located near the town, and on Saturday the streets were clogged with servicemen and shopping farmers. The Jehovah's Witnesses sought to enjoin the enforcement of the ordinance against their marches and distributions on that day. It was denied and the Georgia Supreme Court upheld the denial as a clear instance of the proper exercise of the police power in the interests of traffic control.[183]

Total prohibitions have always been upheld in the use of children 12-14 years of age in such activity. It is well settled since the United States Supreme Court's decision in *Prince* v. *Massachusetts*[184] that a state can forbid children to sell newspapers and other literature on the busy streets of a city even when such literature is of a religious character. The theory employed by the courts is that the states have rights of *parens patriae* over children which supersede even the rights of the parents in certain circumstances. Thus, shortly after the *Prince* decision, Oregon and Michigan found no difficulty in successfully applying child labor statutes to forbid the distribution against contentions that the religious rights of the parents were being violated.[185] As a rule, however, direct prohibitions are questionable in terms of the validity of their application to religious activities unless they are patently necessary and reasonable. Consequently, most localities restrict themselves to requiring only prior consent for such activity.

Although the majority of restrictive ordinances require only prior approval, the requirements for it must still be minimal and reasonable. The arbitrary power in one person to grant or deny the permit will generally make the law invalid.[186] It must be further noted, however, that the wrongful refusal of the civil authority to grant permission to hold such meetings does not give the citizen the right to go ahead without the license or permit. He must first go to the courts for his relief—at least where the ordinance is valid on its face.[187]

Another area in which states have acted to restrict religious liberties has been in the prisons. In 1957, the New Jersey Superior Court upheld the right of the prison authorities to prevent the attendance at Mass on Sundays and holy days of prisoners incarcerated in the segregation wing of the prison. The court found no violation of constitutional rights since it was reasonably necessary to keep these prisoners apart from the others in order to maintain order and discipline of the prison population.[188] Most recently, in 1961, the California Supreme Court denied a writ of habeus corpus brought to secure the removal of restrictions on the religious activities of prisoners belonging to the Black Muslim sect. The court held that the prisoners are not protected by constitutional guarantees of religious freedom and that refusal to allow these activities did not afford any application of whatever "federal constitutional guarantees may exist for protection of inmates of state prisons."[189]

Finally, persons and organizations cannot be permitted to insulate themselves from the consequences of their unlawful conduct by cloaking it within a religious context. In a number of states, the members of the sect of Jehovah's Witnesses have been convicted of trespassing and disturbing the privacy of people in their homes by making unwanted visits upon them, proferring unwanted literature, and asking to play records for them. In one instance, a member of this sect was convicted for playing a phonograph in the hallway of a ten-family apartment building to the annoyance of the superintendent. However, since the prosecution was unable to show that the tenants were annoyed, the Supreme Court of New York reversed—but not before stating that but for the defective prosecution of the case, the conviction would be upheld.[190] The constitutional freedoms do not sanction the use of private property.[191] Nor do they prevent prosecutions for contempt of court.[192] Lastly, it must be mentioned that the states will use their police power to punish anyone who unlawfully interferes with the freedom of religious exercise regardless of his motivation.[193]

5. Zoning Laws.

Under general rules requiring that zoning ordinances be reasonable, such ordinances which completely ban churches and church-related schools from an entire community will almost certainly be deemed arbitrary, unreasonable, and therefore invalid.[194]

Recently, a number of municipal corporations have endeavored to create exclusively industrial zones, banning therefrom commercial, residential, and other uses. Such zoning can be reasonable,[195] and it is likely that churches and church-related schools can be excluded from such zones.

The cases are divided as to whether municipal corporations can exclude churches and synagogues from residential zones. The majority of state courts hold that under state freedom of religion constitutional clauses churches and synagogues cannot be excluded from these areas. By way of illustration, the New York Court of Appeals has stated:

> It is well established in this country that a zoning ordinance may not wholly exclude a church or a synagogue from any residential district. Such a provision is stricken on the ground that it bears no substantial relation to the public health, safety, morals, peace or general welfare of the community.[196]

There are a few cases holding contrary.[197] Without coming to constitutional freedom of religion clauses, some courts have reversed municipal exclusion of churches from residential zones as (a) beyond municipal power,[198] or, (b) as arbitrary under the facts.[199] In an interesting Pennsylvania case, it was held that it would be a violation of the freedom of religion clause of that state's constitution[200] to hold that it was not permissible within the zoning law (as a valid "accessory use") for a church located in a residential area to use a portion of its property as sleeping quarters for retreatants.[201] In a recent Louisiana case[202] the refusal of residents of a community to waive restrictions to the construction of a Jehovah's Witness Kingdom Hall, although they had made a waiver in the case of a Catholic Church, was upheld. The approval by the Zoning Board of the waiver in the instance of the Catholic Church did not, said the Court, violate the "no preference" provision of the Louisiana Constitution.[203]

Some municipal corporations permit churches in residential zones, but require permits as a condition for such permission. There is authority to the effect that such permits can be denied if the church would occasion traffic hazards and congestion in the surrounding neighborhoods.[204] There has been some willingness on the part of courts to sustain the denial of such permits where the presence of a church would result in substantial depreciation in the value of surrounding property.[205] However, denial of these permits will be reversed whenever the municipal action is deemed arbitrary.[206]

Where all schools are excluded from certain areas, such as industrial or even residential zones, it is likely that a court will conclude that exclusion of church-related schools from such an area is reasonable. However, where public schools are permitted in a residential area, the exclusion of church-related schools will generally be deemed invalid.[207] Thus, the New York Court of Appeals noted that "An ordinance will also be stricken if it attempts to exclude private or parochial schools from any residential area where public schools are permitted."[208] There is little authority contra.[209] Subject, of course, to the customary rule that denials not be arbitrary, municipal corporations have been sustained in requiring permits from church-related schools desiring to build in residential zones.[210]

Municipal corporations have, on a few occasions, been able to exclude from residential zones church-related institutions such as colleges, seminaries, orphanages and hospitals,[211] although there is a good deal of authority to the contrary.[212]

6. Internal Affairs of Churches.

American courts will generally not interfere in ecclesiastical disputes.[213] Such interference is deemed an invasion of the precincts of religious conscience in violation of state constitutional guarantees of freedom of worship.[214] Typically, the North Carolina Court has said:

> The legal or temporal tribunals of the State have no jurisdiction over and no concern with, purely ecclesiastical questions and controversies, for there is a constitutional guarantee of freedom of religious profession and worship, as well as an equally firmly established separation of church and state . . . [215]

A Missouri Court adds: "Freedom of religious profession and worship cannot be maintained if the civil courts exercise jurisdiction over ecclesiastical affairs."[216] The Connecticut Court has ruled that even the state legislature could not divide the property of a religious society over objections of some of the members. This, ruled the Court, violated the state constitution's religious liberty clause.[217]

The general unwillingness of American courts to participate in ecclesiastical disputes is illustrated by their attitude in matters of excommunication. When churches excommunicate members for misconduct or doctrinal deviation, the courts remove themselves entirely from any interference with the decision of the church authorities.[218] Nor will they give their aid to individuals allegedly denied communion by action of the church authorities.[219] The excommunication or other disciplining of priests or ministers is also not reviewed by the civil courts[220] In addition, when churches remove a clergyman for offenses against the church, the courts will customarily hold that the decisions of the ecclesiastical courts are final as to what constitutes an offense against the discipline of the particular church.[221]

In disputes involving pastorates, American courts will normally rule that they will not compel one to receive a certain person as his pastor or restrain individuals from assuming the duties of a pastor.[222] However, some courts hold that the office of pastor is a property right that equity will protect.[223] Furthermore, on the theory that the right to use property is involved, courts have ruled that priests excommunicated by the Roman Catholic Church could not use property of the Church even though a majority of the local congregation or trustees sided with the cleric.[224]

Courts in the states are, if anything, even more unwilling to enter into a dispute as to who is the proper bishop or archbishop of a church. The typical attitude was expressed by the Massachusetts Court which stated:

> Courts do not inquire into questions exclusively ecclesiastical for the reason that religious freedom is the constitutional right of all citizens under our government; and for the further reason that, if the courts should deal with litigation of that nature, the whole subject of doctrinal theology, the customs, canonical laws both written and unwritten, and the fundamental organization of the various religious denominations would need to be examined with care for the purpose of reaching authoritative conclusions. Such a course by the courts would in the end deprive the denominations themselves of interpretations of their own body of church polity, and would establish the courts as the final arbiter in every religious controversy. The ills intendant upon such a practice have been thought far to outweigh the incidental advantage that might flow from its adoption.[225]

The above rules have been applied to fraternal benefit societies limited to members of particular religious faiths. There, too, the courts sustain membership ejection of those who violate the duties of that faith.[226]

Although the courts profess not to interfere in ecclesiastical matters, they have interfered in church matters of a doctrinal nature at times on the theory that civil rights were involved. For example, where the tenets of a faith permitted no musical instruments to be used in religious services, the Kansas Court enjoined minority members and officers from using an organ which they had installed. This was on the theory that it was necessary "for protection of civil rights, and preservation of religious freedom guaranteed by the constitution," [227] which the majority were entitled to enjoy.

Also, when property or contract rights are involved, american courts will ordinarily participate in ecclesiastical disputes.[228] As a rule, however, they have customarily waited until the underlying decision on doctrinal matters has been rendered by the ecclesiastical authorities.[229] Thus, the courts demand that the injured parties exhaust all remedies available to them in the church tribunals before coming into the civil courts.[230] Once the ecclesiastical tribunal has determined the religious nature of the dispute, its decision will be respected by the civil court in which the property rights are being litigated.[231] Indeed, the United States Supreme Court holds that the civil courts are bound to respect the decisions of the church courts under the Fourteenth Amendment to the United States Constitution. The Supreme Court has stated:

> Even in those cases when the property right follows as an incident from decision of the church custom or law on ecclesiastical issues, the church rule controls. This under the Constitution, necessarily follows, in order that there may be free exercise of religion.[232]

When courts adjudicate property rights involved in such a religious controversy, they scrupulously attempt to avoid settling the religious dispute that occasioned the litigation.[233]

Where property has been given in trust to a church for the promulgation of a certain religious doctrine, equity has exerted its powers to prevent abuse of the religious trust where the change was a substantial departure from the tenets of the church at the time the trust was settled.[234]   In Delaware for example, the Court has stated:

> Where the subject of controversy is property which, by deed, will, or other instrument, has been in express terms devoted to the teaching, support and spread of some specific form of religious doctrine or belief, and the doctrine to be taught, or for worship to be used, has been definitely and clearly laid down, it will, in a proper case, be the duty of the civil court to attempt the delicate task of determining whether the one accused of violating the trust is holding or teaching a different doctrine or using a form of worship which is so far variant as to defeat the declared objects of the trust.[235]

In hierarchical churches, courts follow the decision of the supreme church judiciary.[236]   Thus, the South Carolina Court states:

> When a division occurs in a church congregation . . . the question as to which faction is entitled to the church property is answered by determining which of the factions is the representative and successor to the church as it existed prior to the division or schism, and it is determined which of the two factions adhere to or is sanctioned by the appropriate governing body of the denomination.[237]

Consequently, where the local congregation belongs to a large religious discipline, such as Orthodox Jewry, a momentary majority of the local congregation will not be awarded the property when they change their religious practices in a way not conformable with the origin and historic character of the faith of the church of which the local congregation is only one member, as against the minority who faithfully adhere to the characteristic doctrine of the church.[238]   Furthermore, where a particular church congregation is in association with a larger ecclesiastical system, even though there is a unanimous secession or withdrawal of the local congregation from the larger discipline, with a change of belief materially differing from that accepted by the system, it cannot take with it the church property.[239]

The United States Supreme Court has now made a constitutional doctrine of the principle that property disputes of churches belonging to a hierarchical organization are to be resolved in accordance with the decisions of the ecclesiastical rulers.   In the *Kedroff* case, the Supreme Court ruled that the Fourteenth Amendment does not permit a state legislature to decree that others will be entitled to the church property.[240]

When courts take jurisdiction of property disputes between factions of a congregational church, they will customarily award the property to the majority group, so long as it remains true to the fundamentals of the church, as accepted by both factions before the dispute arose.[241] Otherwise stated, if a minority withdraws, it cannot take with it the property dedicated to the worship of the God under the disciplines of the larger and older religious body.[242]

Where, on the other hand, congregational church minorities are the ones remaining true to the fundamentals of the church, they will be awarded the property.[243] Typically, the Pennsylvania Court has stated: "Before civil authority the question is, not which party has the majority, but which is right according to the law by which the body has hitherto consented to be governed." [244] Such a change of doctrine by the majority, however, must be fundamental and substantial before it can be stripped of its right to retain the church property.[245] Courts do not, however, deny the majority of a congregational church all power to change doctrine. Therefore, so long as the changes are minor or "reasonable," the legitimate majority will be continued in its possession of the property by the civil courts.[246]

Finally, for the same reason that courts will not interfere with liberty of conscience and freedom of religion, they will not give judicial aid to a dissenter who attempts to recover back any contributions he may have made to the church. Neither does the court's failure to act deprive these persons of their constitutional right to worship, since they are entirely free to go wherever they wish. They may not take their property with them, however.[247]

Thus, to recapitulate, whenever the state or municipal legislatures or the courts enter the religious arena, extreme care and caution must be observed. In passing legislation which has the purpose or effect of limiting a person's religious liberty, the lawmakers must take a great deal of care in drafting such measures. Their laws and ordinances must meet the strictest standards of due process. In addition, when such regulatory schemes are sought to be applied to limit religious activity, the courts must meticulously scrutinize the laws to see that they do conform therewith. The Supreme Court of the United States has been quick to strike down state statutes and ordinances which seek to limit religious activity where due process requirements have not been met or where the state has attempted to go beyond limits set by the Court.

To pass muster in the Supreme Court of the United States any limitation of religious activity must be reasonably related to some purpose which is within the state's power to effect. Secondly, the statute or ordinance must contain standards which are neither unfair, unreasonable, nor discriminatory. Concededly, actions which are recognized as being inimical to the well-being of the society, although done out of religious beliefs and motives, are not protected either by the federal constitution or by the state constitutions. At the same time, it is axiomatic that any infringement upon religious liberty will be, and should be, examined most closely to ensure protection of the right.

Chapter Five

Bans Upon
Denial of Civil Rights
Because of Religious Beliefs

Generally

With varying degrees of liberality every state by one means or another has taken pains to ensure that the exercise of civil and political rights is not dependent upon a person's religious beliefs. In many of the states such rights are protected under general rights clauses which expressly prohibit any denial of them on religious grounds. Others have included clauses specifically banning any religious test in the exercise of a particular right, e.g., voting or holding public office. Still others preclude such tests under the general freedom of religion sections of their constitutions. It should not be assumed that because a state lacks a specific constitutional reference to the protection of a particular right it is not thus protected. For example, if a state has no clause specifically precluding any religious test in order to serve as a witness or a juror, it is likely that such a test will be found to violate a general rights clause or perhaps the freedom clause.

The purpose of this chapter is to show in what ways the states achieve this objective by constitutional language and the manner in which their courts have interpreted it. The more general clauses will be dealt with first followed thereafter by a discussion of specific clauses in the states which have them.

In the American colonies there was ample evidence that individuals, because of their religious beliefs, were denied not only the rights of holding office and voting (which might more properly be thought of as "political rights"), but also rights of employment, of serving as jurors and qualifying as witnesses.[1] Many of the Colonies had established churches, all different sects of Protestantism. The acquisition of civil rights was conditioned in many cases on membership in one of these churches or sects.[2]

100

The first state constitutional safeguard of civil rights in general against such discriminations because of religious faith was that of New Jersey. As far back as 1776 New Jersey was at least willing to protect all Protestants from such denials. The constitution of that year provided that "no Protestant of this colony shall be denied the enjoyment of any civil right merely on account of his religious principles." [3] It was not until 1844 that this constitutional guarantee was extended to all citizens of New Jersey.[4]

It is to Vermont that the credit must be given for being the first state to ban all religious discrimination in the exercise of general civil and political rights. As early as 1777 a Vermont constitution contained the clause: "nor can any man be justly deprived or abridged of any civil right as a citizen, on account of his religious sentiments." [5] Georgia followed with a similar guarantee. In the 1798 Georgia constitution is found the clause: ". . . nor shall any person be denied the enjoyment of any civil right merely on account of his religious principles." [6] Kentucky was not far behind: in 1799 a Kentucky constitution was drafted including an elaborate clause which provided that "the civil rights, privileges or capacities of no person shall be taken away, or in any wise diminished or enlarged, on account of his belief or disbelief of any religious tenet, dogma or teaching." [7]

During the nineteenth century a general constitutional clause prohibiting discrimination on religious grounds in the exercise of civil rights appeared first in Alabama in the year 1819.[8] Virginia constitutionally particularized such a ban in 1830.[9] The citizens of Virginia, immediately following Independence, very likely may have intended to ban any religious test for the exercise of civil liberties by the memorable Declaration of Rights adopted in 1776.[10] However, this famous document never specifically spoke of such a guarantee.

Arkansas in 1816 was next to constitutionally exclude a religious test for the enjoyment of these general rights.[11] Rhode Island adopted such a provision in 1842 [12] followed by Iowa [13] and Kansas [14] in 1857, Illinois in 1870 [15] West Virginia in 1872,[16] Colorado in 1876,[17] South Dakota and Montana in 1889 [18] and Idaho in 1890.[19] Comparable clauses were not adopted in the older states of Michigan until 1908,[20] Louisiana until 1921,[21] and New York until 1938.[22] New Mexico adopted such a clause in its initial constitutional framework in 1911,[23] and Alaska and Hawaii included such clauses in 1959.[24]

These broadly worded clauses were likely intended to guarantee against any religious tests as qualifications for the exercise of any particular right in states having no companion clause specifically respecting that right. For example, they have been used in Illinois, Kentucky, and New Jersey to occasion judicial rulings that an individual cannot be denied an opportunity to serve as a witness because of his religious beliefs.[25] The same would probably apply to the right of one to sit as a juror, although there are no cases so holding in those states without specific clauses.

Whether this broader type ban would be applied in public office—holding cases is probably no longer critically important since the ruling of the United States Supreme Court in *Torcaso* v. *Watkins*,[26] effectively bans such tests under the federal constitution. Consequently, state constitutional clauses requiring a belief in a supreme diety as a requisite to holding public office may well be nugatory.

It is very likely also that any such tests for the exercise of rights in a state with or without either type of clause, will be held to conflict with the general freedom of religion clauses found in all of the state constitutions.

Public Office Holding

In colonial America many citizens, especially non-Protestants, were ineligible to hold any public office. One notable exception was Rhode Island which never officially disqualified any person because of his religious beliefs or the lack of them. Many of these disqualifications, or more limited versions of them, continued to exist in a number of areas long after Independence.

In 1776, the year of Independence, the people of Maryland adopted a new constitution. In it the right to hold a public office was guaranteed to all who subscribed to "a declaration of a belief in the Christian religion."[27] A companion clause provided that those of the Christian religion, but opposed to making declaration or oaths, were permitted to make a "solemn affirmation". . . by attestation of the Divine Being.[28] This right was not extended to Jews and other non-Christians until 1851. In that year a declaration of belief in the Christian faith was still constitutionally required, but "if the party shall profess to be a Jew, the declaration shall be of his belief in a future state of rewards and punishments."[29] Atheists and agnostics were still denied this right, the requirement being alien to their thinking on such matters.

At the time of the adoption of the United States constitution in 1787, not a single state had specifically prohibited all religious tests as qualifications for public office. The presence of the provision in article 6 of the Federal Constitution that "no religious test shall ever be required as a qualification to any office or public trust under the United States," along with the debates on this clause in the various state ratifying conventions, should have stimulated the citizens in at least some of the states to incorporate comparable prohibitions in their own constitutions. Nonetheless, though a majority of the delegates to the ratifying conventions agreed there should be no religious test for the holding of any federal office, many of them obviously thought it not improper during this period to bar Catholics, Jews, and other non-Protestants from state and local posts.

Thus, changes in the general pattern of discrimination were awhile in coming in many states.

To Delaware belongs the credit for being the first state government to adopt a constitutional clause specifically banning religious tests for the holding of public office. The Delaware constitution of June, 1792 provided thus: "No religious test shall be required as a qualification to any office, or public trust, under this state."[30]   Although South Carolina adopted a constitution in 1790, two years earlier than Delaware, it simply eliminated the "Protestant only" clause present in the previous constiution of 1778.[31] The citizens of South Carolina may well have intended to extend the right of holding public office to all regardless of religious persuasion, but the 1790 document contained no positive clause similar to that langauge found in the Delaware constitution.

Following the course set by Delaware, Ohio established a constitutional ban on religious tests for public office in 1802.[32]   Thereafter, such prohibitions appeared in Indiana in 1816,[33] Mississippi in 1817,[34] Illinois in 1818,[35] and Alabama and Maine in 1819.[36] Tennessee inserted such a provision in 1834,[37] followed by Michigan in 1835.[38]

Somewhat restrictively, Pennsylvania provided in its constitution of 1838 that political and civil rights would be available to any person provided he at least avow a belief in a Supreme Being.[39] Pennsylvania's constiution continues to retain this requirement.[40]

The broader Delaware-type clause was adopted by Rhode Island in 1842,[41] New Jersey in 1844,[42] Iowa in 1846,[43] and in Wisconsin in 1848.[44] Similar clauses are found in the constitutions of Kansas of 1857,[45] Minnesota of 1857,[46] and West Virginia of 1861.[47]

Georgia had no such prohibition until 1865.[48] However, the citizens of Georgia may well have intended to provide equality of right in public office holding as early as 1798. In their constitution of that year they included a provision to the effect that no person shall be denied the enjoyment of "any right merely on account of his religious principles.[49]

Other states which have adopted constitutional provisions specifically banning any religious qualification for public office holding are Nebraska in 1866,[50] Louisiana,[51] Colorado in 1876,[52] Montana,[53] and Washington[54] in 1889 and Wyoming,[55] and Idaho[56] in 1890. Utah inserted such a clause in its constitution of 1896 [57] followed by Oklahoma in 1907 [58] and New Mexico in 1911.[59] When Alaska [60] and Hawaii [61] drafted their first state constitutions in 1959, both states included clauses guaranteeing to all citizens, regardless of religious belief, equal opportunity to serve in public office.

To date there has not been a great deal of litigation involving the meaning of the state constitutional clauses prohibiting religious tests for public office. In interesting decisions from Georgia and Missouri, both courts have ruled that a guardian occupies a public office and this clause prohibits his disqualification or removal on grounds that his religion differed from that of his ward's.[62]

The most noteworthy litigation involving the right to hold public office regardless of one's religious beliefs arose in Maryland. Maryland, as previously observed, had in past years limited office holding to Christians and those non-christians who at least declared a belief in a future state of rewards and punishments. In 1900 the Maryland Court reaffirmed that the state constitutional clause "prohibits any religious test as a qualification for any office of profit and trust other than a declaration of belief in the existence of God. . . ." [63]   In 1922 the Attorney General of Maryland ruled that it was necessary that every official of the state should be "required in some definite way" to declare his belief in the existence of God.[64]   Then in 1959, the Maryland Supreme Court attempted to uphold this requirement by ruling in the case of *Torcaso* v. *Watkins* that one who refused to take an oath of belief in the existence of a God was ineligible to hold the position of Notary Public in the State.[65]   Two years later this decision was reversed by the United States Supreme Court.[66] "This Maryland religious test for public office," declared the Court, "unconstitutionally invades the appellant's freedom of belief and religion and therefore cannot be enforced against him."   On the basis of this holding, it may be proper to assume that provisions like those found in the Arkansas constitution to the effect that: "No person who denies the being of God shall hold any office in the civil departments of this state . . ." [67] are no longer enforceable.   Pennsylvania,[68] Texas,[69] Tennessee,[70] North Carolina [71] and South Carolina [72] have constitutional provisions which limit office holding to those who "acknowledge the being of God and a future state of rewards and punishments" or acknowledge the "existence of a Supreme Being."

There have been no significant federal or state decisions involving the right to hold public office regardless of religious persuasion since the Maryland case.   Indeed, as observed earlier, there were few such rulings prior to 1959.   In 1948 the California Supreme Court had suggested by way of dictum that in investigating the loyalty of public servants the investigations could "not touch on the political or religious opinions or affiliations of an employee." [73]   On another occasion the Texas Court of Civil Appeals, also by way of dictum, remarked in 1940 that the judges did "not think the Legislature may make eligibility to office dependent on religious, social, industrial or economic views." [74]

Clergymen and Public Office Holding

At one time or other in their history, a considerable number of states had constitutional clauses specifically banning clergymen from holding public office.[75]   Illustratively, one early South Carolina constitution elaborately provided:

> And whereas the ministers of the Gospel are by their professions dedicated to the service of God and the care of souls, and ought not to be diverted from the great duties of their function, therefore

no minister of the Gospel or public preacher of any religious persuasion, while he continues in the exercise of his pastoral function, and for two years after, shall be eligible either as Governor, lieutenant-Governor, or member of the Senate, House of representatives, or privy council in this state.[76]

Other states once achieved substantially the same purpose by similar, though less wordy, clauses. Currently such constitutional bars exist only in Maryland and Tennessee.

The present Maryland constitution very simply and unequivocally provides thus: "No minister or preacher of the Gospel, or of any religious creed or denomination . . . shall be eligible as a senator or delegate."[77] The Tennessee clause resembles more closely the clauses found in the earlier constitutions of other states. The first section of the ninth article states:

> Whereas Ministers of the Gospel are by their profession, dedicated to God and the care of souls, and ought not to be diverted from the great duties of their functions; therefore, no Minister of the Gospel, or priest of any denomination whatever, shall be eligible to a seat in either House of the Legislature.[78]

In Tennessee the disqualification goes back to that state's constitution of 1796,[79] while the clause first appears in Maryland in the constitution of 1851.[80] It should be noted that the disqualifications in both states affect only the elective offices of the legislatures.

Traditionally, the underlying justifications for such bans were primarily twofold. It is said, first, that they were prompted by adherence to the principle of the separation of church and state. There existed at one time, according to Stokes, a substantial fear on the part of many that if the clergy were permitted to secure public offices certain denominations would be unduly favored as a result of having prominent members of their faith in positions of power.[81] Concededly, this was the case in some states where a particular denomination e.g., Congregationalists in the New England states was in an influential majority. Secondly such bans were rationalized on the basis that clergymen could not adequately serve two masters. This latter point is well taken, as is evidenced by the conduct of many of our churches which expressly forbid this type of participation in public affairs. Nonetheless, appealing though these arguments may appear, it is at least questionable whether they have weight sufficient enough to justify any denial by the state of the right of such persons to hold any public office.

In the first place, the promotion of efficiency among the members of the clergy of the different denominations is not the formal responsibility of the government. This is and must be the sole concern of the individual church with which the clergyman is associated. The role of the state in this regard is simply to ensure against any improper interference with the efforts of the priest or minister in the performance of his duties. From the viewpoint of the individual churches themselves it is to their continued credit that a great many of them expressly forbid their clergy from seeking and holding public office at least of the elective type. In so doing they effectively uphold the principle of separation of church and state while at the same time accepting the realization that the role of the clergyman is an occupation which cannot be adequately performed on a part-time basis.

Secondly, there is certainly little basis for the argument that the separation principle will be violated by permitting the clergy to hold such positions. There is no evidence that the subsequent removal of such bans by the majority of states which had them has resulted in any significant numbers of clergy being elected to office. Further there exists almost no basis for the charge that, where such persons have held or do hold public office, one faith is the beneficiary of any favoritism. Even assuming that clergy of all faiths were permitted freely by their churches to campaign for office, it is probably quite unlikely that enough of a particular faith or denomination could be elected to have any detrimental effect. In any event the conflict of interest, if such there be, should not be cognizable by the state. Further, such bans may be constitutionally unsound. It is very doubtful if any state could today ban clergymen from such offices under the First and Fourteenth Amendments to the United States Constitution.

Recently the United States Supreme Court struck down an attempt by the state of Maryland to enforce its religious test oath against an office seeker who refused to declare his belief or disbelief in the existence of God.[82] Consistent with this holding, it may well be argued that to deny the right to hold public office to one because he chooses to *live* his religion in the role of a clergyman also violates religious freedom. Such an individual is discriminated against not because he is *religious*, but because he is *a religious*. If he were only religious he would be eligible. It is no answer to say that he was compelled neither to assume this profession nor compelled to hold office. The Supreme Court has said that lack of compulsion "cannot possibly be an excuse." To this extent the disqualification clauses in the Maryland and Tennessee constitutions may well be invalid.

One final point might be raised in conclusion. As earlier noted, the constitutions of both Maryland and Tennessee also contain clauses which prohibit any religious test as a prerequisite to holding public office.[83] If the view is taken that this disqualification is tantamount to a religious test, then the clauses in each constitution are irreconcilable. If, on the other hand, the position is taken that the disqualification is based on other than religious grounds conflict would seem to disappear. Probably the only acceptable reason today would be the feeling that such an individual would not be in a position to adequately perform his official duties in the manner expected. It is suggested, however, that this justification could in certain circumstances present considerable problems.

It follows logically and naturally from the above reasoning that the mere fact of ordination should not preclude one from running for public office. It may, however, raise a rebuttable presumption of ineligibility under the constitution. The question which now arises is this: To what extent consistent with the freedom of religion clause of both state and federal constitutions may election officials or the courts require this individual to establish his eligibility? There are no recent discoverable instances in these states where this precise question has been decided. However, it is clear that a court would have room to maneuver in either direction. In the other states this disqualification would be precluded by constitutional clauses which specifically prohibit any religious test for public office, or perhaps under general clauses precluding a religious test for the enjoyment of any civil rights. In states with neither clause, such tests would probably be found to violate the general freedom of religious clauses in the state constitutions.

Witnesses

The early American common law demanded a belief in God and a future state of rewards and punishments as a qualification for witnesses. An 1809 Connecticut case is representative.[84] There the Court said:

> Every person who does not believe in the obligation of an oath, and a future state of rewards and punishments, or any accountability after death for his conduct, is by law excluded from being a witness; for to such a person the law presumes no credit is to be given. Testimony is not to be received from any person in a court of justice, but under the sanction of an oath. It would therefore be idle to administer an oath to a man who disregards its obligation.
>
> *   *   *   *   *   *
>
> There can be no doubt but that the law intended, that the fear of offending God should have its influence upon a witness to induce him to speak the truth. But no such influence can be expected from the man who disregards an oath. He is, therefore, excluded from being a witness.[85]

Eleven years later the New York Court ruled a disbeliever in God and a future state of rewards and punishments could not be a witness in court.[86] Said this tribunal:

> Religion is a subject on which every man has a right to think according to the dictates of his understanding. It is a solemn concern between his conscience and his God, with which no human tribunal has a right to meddle. But in the development of facts, and the ascertainment of truth, human tribunals have a right to interfere . . . no testimony is entitled to credit, unless delivered

under the solemnity of an oath, which comes home to the conscience of the witness, and will create a lie arising from his belief that false swearing would expose him to punishment in the life to come.[87]

A minority of jurisdictions still retain the old common law. However, changes in the other states have been effectuated by constitutional clauses, by statutes and by court decisions.

In 1846 New York adopted a constitution which provided that "no person shall be rendered incompetent to be a witness on account of his opinions on matters of religious belief." [88] In that same year the Iowa constitution included a more elaborately worded clause intended to accomplish the same purpose.[89] Thereafter, clauses worded similarly to the one first adopted in the New York constitution were inserted in the constitutions of Wisconsin in 1848,[90] California in 1849,[91] Indiana in 1851,[92] and Ohio [93] in the same year. The Ohio clause contained the additional proviso that "nothing herein shall be construed to dispense with oaths and affirmations." [94] The impact of this language was left a number of years later when the Ohio Supreme Court ruled in 1877 that one who did not believe in God could not subscribe to the oath, and hence he could not be competent as a witness.[95] Also in 1851, Maryland provided that only a person "Who believes in the existence of a God and that under his dispensation such person will be morally accountable for his acts, and be rewarded or punished therefor, either in this world or the world to come" shall be competent as a witness in the state.[96] In 1905 the Maryland Court rejected the proposition that a belief in a God and a future state of rewards and punishments required a belief in the Truths of the Scriptures.[97]

New York type clauses were adopted in Kansas in 1855,[98] Minnesota in 1857,[99] Oregon in 1859,[100] Nevada in 1864,[101] Missouri in 1865,[102] and Nebraska in 1866.[103] In 1900, the Kansas Court ruled that this provision prohibited any showing of belief or disbelief in the existence of a God either for determining competency or affecting credibility.[104] Said the Court:

> Our view of the provision . . . is that the people of the state . . . intended that every person should stand upon an exact equality before the law, without regard to what they believed or disbelieved. To permit the question to be asked would assume that a stigma was cast upon a person who disbelieved in the existence of a God in accordance with the doctrines of the Christian church or churches, such as felons suffer by reason of the conviction of a crime.[105]

A similar test was rejected by Minnesota [106] and such a test for credibilty was denied by the Missouri Supreme Court.[107] However, Arkansas's constitution, adopted in 1874, still provides that: "No person who denies the being of a God shall . . . be competent to testify as a witness in any court." [108]   It has been ruled in Arkansas that one's declarations written or verbal are proper evidence bearing on his belief.[109]

Clauses comparable to that of New York's are found also in the constitutions of Texas of 1876,[110] Florida of 1887,[111] North Dakota [112] and Washington [113] of 1889, Wyoming of 1890,[114] Utah of 1896,[115] Michigan in 1909,[116] and Arizona of 1912.[117]   It is worthy of note that Arizona, Oregon and Washington actually specify that the *weight* of any witnesses' testimony *shall not* be affected by his religious opinions.

Although some variation does exist, judicial evidence indicates that the general prohibition against references to religion in the selecting or examining of witnesses is enforced in all states today.[118]   All that is necessary in Texas, according to a Court of the state, is that the prospective witness believe it is wrong to lie.[119]   In Arizona the prospective witness is not allowed to be questioned as to his religious beliefs even though his church may be a party in interest.[120]   Such clauses have also thwarted attempts to exclude children from giving evidence on the ground that they are too young to appreciate religion or have an awareness of any divine punishment.[121]

A number of states which have constitutional clauses specifically banning religious tests for witnesses at times interpret them as indicating that dying declarations are admissible to show that the declarant did not believe in a Supreme Being.   In Oregon, just two years after it adopted its constitution in 1859 inserting such a clause, the Supreme Court of the state ruled that a convicted defendant was entitled to a new trial where he might be permitted to show that statements made of a deceased witness as dying declarations were questionable since the declarant did not believe in a future state of rewards and punishments.[122] Similar opinions have been rendered by the high courts of California [123] and Missouri.[124]   The majority of states apparently apply the rule, that no man shall be incompetent as a witness on account of his religious beliefs, to dying declarations in the same way they do to living witnesses. Most of the jurisdictions with these specific clauses also apply them to prohibit reference to religious belief upon cross examination where counsel is attempting to show credibility.[125]

A minority of states which constitutionally preclude any religious test for determining the competency of witnesses do however permit to a varied extent questions as to religious belief for purposes of impeachment. Ohio has held this to be proper.[126]   Indiana, at least by statute, also seems to authorize such impeachments, although the sole case permitting the practice precedes the adoption of its constitutional clause in 1851.[127]   The Iowa Supreme Court held in 1881 that although a witness' religious beliefs could not affect his competency, lack of belief as affecting his credibility could be shown without violating this clause of the constitution.   However, the witness could not be forced to divulge his beliefs on the stand. They could be shown only by previous voluntary statements if at all.[128]   The same court ruled also that partial tesimony as to his religious beliefs does not operate as a waiver of his constitutional immunity.[129]   Both Nevada and Nebraska may authorize the practice by statute, but there are not cases in either state that can be alluded to for any judicial confirmation.   Mississippi has allowed the practice.[130] In a recent case, the Arizona Court permitted such questioning on cross-examination, but did not decide the religion question squarely, ruling instead that the prosecution's questioning as to church attendance was not prejudicial because the defendant had introduced the subject, and, secondly, because his attorney had failed to object at trial.[131]

Many states lack a specific constitutional clause banning religious tests as qualification for serving as witnesses or determining the admissibility and weight of testimony.   At times, however, a reading together of the state constitutional freedom of religion clauses with the oft-found clause to the effect that the civil rights of no person shall in any way be diminished on account of his religion produces similar judicial decisions, i.e., to the effect that persons can appear as witnesses without regard to religious belief or disbelief.   Indeed, Alabama, with no specific clause, has held in 1901 that dying declarations are admissible from persons who may have believed in no God.   This was accomplished under a general clause which provided that "the civil rights, privileges, and capacities of any citizen shall not be in any manner affected by his religious principles." [132]   However, a judicial question still exists in Alabama as to whether the common law pertaining to the religious beliefs of witnesses is still applicable.   The decision mentioned above had been rendered on re-hearing.[133]   The initial opinion had gone the other way, with all judges concurring.   On the rehearing all but one justice [134] had changed his mind.

In a similar Alabama case decided some years later, the court chose to avoid the issue of whether questioning a person as to his religious beliefs was in violation of the general constitutional prohibition on denial of civil rights because of religion.[135]   It merely affirmed the trial court, which sustained an objection to a question as to whether a person who made a dying declaration was an infidel, on the ground that the *mere* fact one was an infidel could not disqualify him under the common law.

Illinois affords another example, where, since 1890 under the constitution of 1870, the Court has held that there is no longer any test of qualification in respect to religious belief or want thereof as affects the competency of witnesses.   This was accomplished by a general religious freedom and enjoyment of civil rights clause.[136]   A similar guarantee was the source for the ruling of the Virginia Court in 1846 that no person is incapacitated as a witness on account of his religious persuasions.[137]   It is true also that some of these states without specific constitutional bans upon religious tests for witnesses disallow questioning on cross examination relative to the witness' faith or lack of it for impeachment purposes. Thus, the Kentucky Court has said:

> We think this provision of the constitution (religious liberty/civil rights) not only permits persons to testify without regard to religious belief or disbelief, but that it was intended to prevent any inquiry into that purpose for the purpose of effecting credibility.[138]

As early as 1879 the New Hampshire Court also ruled that it would be improper on cross-examination to ask the witness his views regarding religion. Said the Court: "This is not because the inquiry might tend to disgrace him, but because it would be a personal scrutiny into the state of his faith and conscience contrary to the spirit of our institutions."[139] Finally, in New Jersey, the Court held as far back as 1889 that a person who did not believe that God would punish his perjury was at least competent to testify in his own behalf. Such a denial on religious grounds would seriously offend the civil right of one to speak in his own behalf guaranteed in the New Jersey constitution.[140]

A number of other states lacking any specific constitutional bans upon religious tests as qualifications for serving as witnesses have effected a similar result by statute. Many statutes passed in these states abrogate in part, at least, the earlier common law. However, as late as 1932 it was still apparently required that one believe in a Supreme Being and a state of future punishments and rewards in New Jersey. A New Jersey statute excused a person from taking an oath before testifying if he would affirm that he was "conscientiously scrupulous of taking an oath." However, in order for one to come within the purview of that statute he had to believe in God, for according to the court in 1932, the words "conscientiously scrupulous" in the statute were "applicable only to those who had scruples conscientiously founded on religious belief and whose religious beliefs embraced a belief in a Deity and in the power of that Deity to accomplish punishment."[141] This was an extremely limited abrogation of the common law. Under the most recent New Jersey constitution such a test would probably no longer be permissible.[142]

Lastly, a few states by statute specifically permit impeachment of witnesses because of their lack of religious beliefs. These statutes and the decisional law in the states not having any specific constitutional clauses are adequately reported elsewhere.[143]

Jurors

In our early history it was commonplace to exclude from jury service persons not having what was regarded as the necessary religious beliefs. In many areas, during the colonial period especially, this right was limited to those of a particular sect or denomination. Other areas extended the right to all persons who expressed a belief in the Christian religion. In the more liberal era following Independence, and more especially after the adoption of the United States Constitution, it became generally true that any one believing in a Supreme Being and a future state of rewards and punishments was eligible to sit on a jury. Today in almost every state in the Union, an atheist or agnostic is deemed competent for jury service providing that he at least realizes that his actions are binding upon his conscience. An affirmation to that effect is all that is usually necessary.

Maryland made provisions for the untrammeled right of jury duty in 1851. Its constitution adopted that year provided: ". . . nor shall any person be deemed incompetent as a . . . juror who believes in the existence of God, and that under his dispensation such person will be held morally accountable for his acts, and be rewarded or punished therefore, either in this world or in the world to come." [144] Inasmuch as a juror is required to believe in God and punishment, the Maryland clause reflects the earlier practice.

Oregon appears to deserve recognition for being the first state to constitutionally ban all religious disqualifications for jury services. In 1857 the framers inserted this clause: "No person shall be rendered incompetent as a . . . juror in consequence of his opinions on matters of religion." [145] In the years that followed many other states followed Oregon's lead. Similar clauses were subsequently adopted in Missouri in 1865,[146] Tennessee in 1870,[147] West Virginia in 1872,[148] California in 1879,[149] North Dakota [150] and Washington in 1889,[151] Wyoming in 1890,[152] Utah in 1896,[153] and Arizona in 1912.[154] Just what these provisions do and do not allow has been the subject of interesting litigation.

In California, the general rule seems to be that no questions of a religious nature may be asked of a prospective juror when religion is not at all in issue in the case.[155] However, in a recent decision in this same jurisdiction, a defendant in appealing from a conviction for grand theft claimed prejudicial misconduct on the part of the trial court in permitting the prosecution to ask prospective jurors if they were members of the Seventh-Day Adventist Church. Six members of this faith eventually served on the jury that convicted him. The Court held there was no error, and one of the reasons it gave was that, "no religious issue was involved in this case." [156] Apparently, this Court felt that the defendant was not prejudiced by the prosecution's actions, and therefore, the defendant was not entitled to relief even though the prosecution may have technically violated the constitutional clause. California permits exceptions to the general rule in instances where "religious belief plays a large part in the pleaded defense," or may have a substantial effect on the decisions in particular types of litigation. For example, in an action to recover under a property settlement agreement prior to divorce proceedings, the Court held it no error to interrogate prospective jurors as to

their religious beliefs and affiliations.[157]   The rationale of the Court was
that while "no person shall be rendered incompetent to be a juror on
account of his opinions on matters of religious belief," this belief may
result in a "state of mind which would be a ground for challenge for
cause." According to the Court: "Both parties had the right to secure
jurors who were unbiased . . .   One of the causes for challenge for
cause is the 'existence of a state of mind in the juror evincing enmity or
bias to either party (Code of Civil Procedure).' "[158]   On another occasion,
involving a will contest, the Court framed its rule thus:

> It is not to be doubted that the state of mind of a prospective
> juror, resulting from religious belief, or any other cause might dis-
> qualify such person from acting as a juror in a particular case,
> regardless of the question of general competency to act as a juror.
> But in such cases it is the state of mind which is material and
> which disqualifies and such state of mind is material only in the
> event it entitles a party to a challenge for cause.[159]

In Tennessee, it was held very early that an atheist may serve as a
juror.[160]   But this same jurisdiction has found no problem with permitting removal of one for his membership or affiliation with a church
if it is possible that the juror will directly benefit from the litigation.[161]
Similarly a Maryland court has indicated that the questioning of prospective
jurors as to their general feelings toward a particular church would be
permissible in a suit for damages wherein the church was alleged to have
been negligent.[162]   On the other hand, the high court of that same state
has upheld the refusal of a trial court to allow questioning of jurors as to
religious belief by defense attorneys in a prosecution for abortion.[163]
Utah has refused to permit the exclusion for cause of Mormons in
the trial of a polygamy case,[164] and in Missouri, the Court refused to grant
a Catholic defendant in a civil assault case a new trial on the ground
that the constitution was violated because counsel for the plaintiff was
allowed to ask prospective jurors whether they were members of a
church and then whether it was the Catholic or Protestant church.[165]
Texas has held that asking prospective jurors whether or not they or
any members of their family were Jehovah's Witnesses, in the prosecution of a Jehovah Witness for murder, was at least not error sufficient
to warrant appellate relief.[166]   Lastly, both California and Washington
high courts have ruled that persons having conscientious scruples against
the death penalty stemming from religious or other beliefs, may for
that reason be excused from juries trying cases where capital punishment
is involved.[167]
All of the above decisions are exceptions to the general doctrine
codified by specific constitutional clauses.   They seem to fall into
three general categories.   First, exception will probably always be
allowed where it can be shown that a person because of his beliefs is
incapable of deciding a cause in accordance with the laws and the facts.

Secondly, since bias is always ground for removal for cause, questions touching on matters of religion, belief, church membership or affiliation will be allowed if they might reasonably divulge bias against or in favor of a party. Third, exclusion for cause probably might be permitted where it can be shown that a particular juror is in a position to benefit directly from the outcome of the litigation in some material way.

Most of the decisions in this particular area appear to uphold the trial court in permitting religion to enter into the picture. This is largely attributable to the deference paid by appellate courts to the wide discretion of trial court judges on matters of jury selection. Secondly, the appellate courts tend to find that the error, if any, was not prejudicial even though the constitution may be technically violated.

There appears to be no discernible difference in result in those states which lack a specific clause prohibiting any religious tests for jury service. Although a person may be excluded for conscientious scruples from any cause whatever,[168] he may not be denied the right merely because he holds a belief in a certain faith or membership in a certain church. New York has said mere religious "bigotry" is not sufficient ground for disqualification.[169] Nevertheless, some jurisdictions without specific bans on religious tests have, at times, refused to permit atheists to sit in on juries. Said the North Carolina Court in 1924: "If he be an atheist, or deny the existence of a God, he is presumed to be insensible to the obligations of an oath."[170]

While a number of the "non-clause" states seem to permit questioning into religious matters on *voir dire*, the tendency is not to permit exclusion for cause even though the juror's church membership may be the same as one of the litigants,[171] or for that matter opposed to a defendant's creed as, for example, in an abortion prosecution.[172] Mississippi, not long ago, even refused to exclude a juror who was a member of the same church and lodge as one of the parties to the cause.[173] Conceivably, the court may exclude for cause if membership coincides, for example, in the same parish or congregation, but almost certainly may not where one of the jurors is found to be of the same general faith as one of the parties. Again, the competency of jurors to sit in a given situation is left to the judge, whose decision, while frequently challenged, is rarely overturned.

In a recent Minnesota case,[174] the Supreme Court of that state reversed a contempt proceeding wherein a woman had refused to serve on a jury because of religious convictions. Reconsidering the case in light of *Sherbert v. Verner*,[175] the Minnesota Court held that, in the absence of a present or prospective showing that the effectiveness of the jury system would be seriously jeopardized by excusing from duty jurors whose religious convictions prohibit them from so serving, such persons should be exempt.

Voting

Early in the colonial history of America, the limitation of the right to vote to only those members of a recognized sect was quite commonplace. Even in those colonies where it was decreed that "all Christians" were entitled to vote, Catholics were sometimes especially excepted.[176] Later, with growth of religious liberty and the subsequent adoption of the federal constitution, voting qualifications based on religious belief disappeared from most of the states.

In many states the religious test for voting was prohibited by the adoption of constitutional clauses to the effect that no civil or political rights were to be abridged on account of religious belief. Others outlawed the practice by finding it in violation of the general freedom of religion clauses passed by almost all states in the manner of the federal constitution. Today, the constitutions of seven states have separate language which specifically prohibits any religious qualification in the exercise of the general franchise. The Kansas clause is illustrative. Section seven of the Bill of rights provides: "No religious test . . . shall be required . . . for any voter at any election. . . ."[177] Similar clauses are found in the present fundamental law of New Mexico,[178] West Virginia,[179] Arkansas,[180] Michigan,[171] Minnesota,[182] and Utah[183].

Throughout the Nineteenth Century and up to the present time there are almost no discoverable instances of judicial decisions dealing with attempts to impose religious qualifications on the voters of a state. In only one instance has it been significantly argued that the right to vote was denied because of religious beliefs. Idaho and Nevada passed laws making it a crime to practice or advocate polygamous marriage, a practice embraced by the Mormon religion. Idaho passed its first law while it still had territorial status. The law was immediately attacked as violative of the First Amendment. The territorial court upheld the measure on the ground that while the federal constitution precluded any religious test for the right to vote in the territory, Idaho was free to disenfranchise those who were found guilty of a crime.[184] Appeal to the Supreme Court of the United States was dismissed.[185]

Upon achieving statehood in 1890, Idaho gave the prohibition constitutional status. Inserted within that document was a clause specifically prohibiting polygamists from voting in any election in the state.[186] Pursuant to this clause, the legislature passed an oath statute which required the voter to swear that he belonged to no sect which preached polygamy or celestial marriage nor encouraged such practices in any way.[187] In early test of this law, the Idaho Court declared that the oath did not violate the religious freedom clause of the new constitution[188] as the oath was merely a voting qualification which the legislature in a companion clause of the same constitutional document had been given authority to require.[189] This companion clause was apparently the saving feature in this instance, since an identical Nevada law was struck down by its Supreme Court.[190]   The reason given there was that the legislature of Nevada had been given no constitutional authority to set any other qualifications for voting in the state over and above those already specified by the constitution.

It has been long since settled that the practice of polygamy may be forbidden even though it may be sanctioned by religious belief.[191] The Mormon Church has itself rejected the practice as part of its doctrine. Therefore, these problems will likely not arise again.

Probably no state today would find it constitutionally valid to require any religious test for voting in any election.   Any attempt to do so would almost certainly be found violative of the equal protection doctrine of the Fourteenth Amendment to the United States Constitution as well.

Conscientious Objectors

The right of conscientious objectors to be exempted from military service has long been recognized in the United States.   There was a tradition of exempting Quakers from military service in Rhode Island dating back to 1672,[192] and the people of Pennsylvania, in drafting their Constitution of 1776, stated: "Nor can any man who is conscientiously scrupulous of bearing arms, be justly compelled thereto, if he will pay such equivalent..."[193]   In that same year the Delaware Constitution was adopted with virtually identical language.[194]   Other Eighteenth Century constitutions exempted Quakers, and some exempted all conscientious objectors, from serving in the military.   The New York Constitution of 1777,[195] the New Hampshire Constitution of 1784,[196] and the Vermont Constitution of 1794,[197] were the forerunners of numerous such constitutional provisions.[198]   Virginia and North Carolina were illustrative of a different solution to the problem: they had no constitutional provisions but provided for exemption of conscientious objectors by statute.[199]

Under either approach, the type of exemption—at all times or only during peace; those exempted—only certain denominations or all conscientious objectors; and the conditions of exemption—ranging from none to payment of a commutation fee; varied, but there was a general recognition of exemptions for conscientious objectors.

The state courts, however, were much less clear in their recognition of this right, establishing criteria which limited, or frequently eliminated, these exemptions.   In two Massachusetts cases[200] conscientious objectors were denied exemptions because the certificates which they filed mentioned that they were members of a sect (Quakers), but did not certify that they were scrupulous of bearing arms, or, on the other hand, mentioned scrupulosity, but did not certify to being a member of a particular sect.   A more liberal Maine court permitted exemption on the basis of the petitioner's "measurably conforming" to the tenets of the Quaker Church.[201]

Twenty-two state constitutions[202] still excuse conscientious objectors from militia duty in varying degrees and under various circumstances. Some exempt conscientious objectors without imposing any conditions,[203] others require payment of an "equivalent".[204]   Some limit the exemption to peacetime,[205] while others have no such limitation.[206]   Most exempt by constitutional language, others direct the legislature to do so.[207]   All save one excuse a broad class of objectors, whether this be defined in terms of members of religious sects opposed to war,[208] or merely in terms of individual scruples.[209]   Maine, however, excludes only Quakers and Shakers.[210]

With the enactment of federal conscription laws and a one hundred year lapse in drafting for militias by states, the problem of service in the military by conscientious objectors has become a Federal rather than state issue. While the broad provisions for exempting conscientious objectors under Federal law are beyond the scope of this section, the treatment of the issues raised by conscientious objectors under the Federal Constitution, although not binding on State courts deciding cases arising under their constitutions, gives valuable insight into the manner in which these same issues might well be resolved should they arise on a state level.

Historically, the problem began on a federal level when James Madison introduced in Congress his proposed amendments which were to become the Bill of Rights. The original draft stated that ". . . no person religiously scrupulous of bearing arms shall be compelled to render military service in person."[211]   Rhode Island, Pennslyvania, and North Carolina also gave indication of a desire for an amendment on the subject,[212] and, while the select Committee chosen by the House of Representatives to weigh a bill of rights recommended adoption of an amendment providing that "no person religiously scrupulous shall be compelled to bear arms", the proposal died in conference with the Senate.[213]

The United States Supreme Court in 1904 stated that an individual

> . . . may be compelled by force if need be, against his will and without regard to his personal wishes or his pecuniary interests, or even his religious or political convictions, to take his place in the ranks of the army of his country, and risk the chance of being shot in its defense . . .[214]

The Court was more explicit in 1931 when it remarked that "The privilege of the native born conscientious objector to avoid bearing arms comes, not from the Constitution, but from the Acts of Congress."[215]

These statements would seem to clearly indicate that the conscientious objector, in the absence of specific constitutional language, would have to seek his relief, if any, on legislative rather than constitutional grounds.

The problem of the conscientious objectors has also cropped up in two rather diverse areas under the Federal Constitution. The Supreme Court has passed on the claims of students at a state supported University to the privilege of attending such an institution without submitting to its requirement of military training. The Court held that there

> . . . is no ground for the contention that the regents order, requiring able-bodied male students . . . to take the prescribed instruction in military science and tactics, transgresses any constitutional right asserted by these appellants.[216]

Thus, conscientious objectors cannot claim that compulsory ROTC infringes upon any constitutionally protected religious freedom.

In *Re Summers*,[217] the U.S. Supreme Court, by a 5-4 vote, held that the refusal of an application for admission to the practice of law in Illinois, on the ground that the applicant would be unable in good faith to take the required oath to support the constitution of the State, because of conscientious scruples resulting in unwillingness to serve in the state militia in time of war, was not a denial of any right of the applicant under the First and 14th Amendments. Justice Black, speaking for the minority, said that:

> It may be, as many people think, that Christ's Gospel of love and submission is not suited to a world in which men still fight and kill one another. But I am not ready to say that a mere profession of belief in that Gospel is a sufficient reason to keep otherwise well qualified men out of the legal profession, or to drive law abiding lawyers of that belief out of the profession, which would be the next logical development.[218]

It is difficult to imagine any other areas in which the problem of exemptions for conscientious objectors might appear, but the guiding principle: a legislative, rather than constitutional right, almost universally granted in some areas, and somewhat inconsistently denied in others, retains its vitality.

Clearly, the state may, in the exercise of its war power, demand military service from *all* its citizens in time of emergency. Equally clearly, as a matter of policy, conscientious objectors have been exempted from such service. It seems to be stretching this rationale, however, and a bit inconsistent, to grant such exemption during war, and yet, during peace, penalize conscientious objectors who are applicants for the bar, or college students unwilling to train in the ROTC.

In conclusion, it may be safely stated that there exists little danger today that any individual will be denied the right to hold a public office, to vote, to hold employment, or serve as a witness or a juror on account of his religious persuasion or lack thereof. The evidence thus gleaned indicates that the state constitutional clauses have been effective in defeating any attempts to discriminate in this area. It is true that at one time a number of states continued to make belief in a God or Supreme Being a requirement for the exercise of some of these rights; but since the Supreme Court's ruling in the *Torcaso* case, such a test can no longer be validly imposed upon persons seeking to hold a public office or public employment.

Witnesses and jurors pose slighlty different problems, but the same prohibitions still apply. No individual may be denied the right to serve as a witness or sit as a juror merely because he embraces a particular religious belief or philosophy. However, like all other rights possessed by an individual, they can only be exercised in concert with the rights of other persons. Consequently, the rights of a party to the litigation may override the right of a witness or a juror to remain silent as to his beliefs. The presumption however, appears to be clearly in favor of right of the witness or juror not to testify or answer questions regarding his religion. As on all matters relating to evidence, the court in its discretion must decide. In deciding, the court must take the utmost care to avoid any unnecessary infringement of religious freedom.

Conscientious objectors present still another dilemma. Their traditional exemption from military service has been, for the great part, constitutionally guaranteed; conversely, as the "constitutionalization" of the exemption has grown, its scope has narrowed. Thus, today, the right of conscientious objectors to be exempted from military service is everywhere recognized, while comparable exemptions in peacetime, non-military situations, are severely limited.

Chapter Six

State Constitutional Clauses
Providing for Tax Exemptions
To Churches and Church-Related Institutions

Introductory

"The right to make exemptions," says Cooley, "is involved in the right to select the subjects of taxation and apportion the public burdens among them, and must be understood to exist in the law making power where it has not in terms been taken away."[1] The power to levy income and other taxes is derived from the constitutions of the federal and state governments and the authority to make exceptions from the lists is part of this power.[2] This power is limited in that it is not to be exercised in an arbitrary and discriminatory manner.[3]

In the United States, tax exemptions are universally accorded to churches, and to the schools, charitable organizations, and other institutions commonly supported by them. The great majority of the states extend this privilege by express constitutional language. Others have done so by statute. In either event the result is merely a codification, as we shall discover, of a tradition and practice long prevalent in this country both before and after the adoption of the federal constitution. Unquestionably, these exemptions represent the greatest single example of government recognition of religion in this country today.

With the recent intensification of the church-state controversy, notably in the area of aid to denominational schools and religious practices in the public schools, attention has been focused on this practice of exempting the churches. A number of legal scholars have taken the position that such exemptions as are presently allowed to the churches are in violation of the First Amendment to the federal constitution in that they contravene its ban on the establishment of religion.[4] They argue in the main that, regardless of past practice, tax benefits can no longer be justified in the light of the decisions of the United States Supreme Court in the

120

Everson and *McCollum* cases,[5] if indeed they could have been justified on any other grounds. They contend that the holdings in these cases must be read as proscribing such exemptions whether they are granted by the states or by the Federal Government. Indeed one litigant, recently victorious in her attempt to outlaw the practice of prayer reading in the public schools, has already indicated her intention to litigate the constitutionality of exemptions to churches in the courts.[6] Other knowledgeable persons have from time to time called for a review of the practice on policy as well as legal grounds.[7] For instance, the Assembly of the Presbyterian Church of the United States has gone on record as having grave doubts whether churches should be entitled to tax exemptions. In addition a study of the practice is under way by the National Council of Churches.

The traditional positions on the question of separation will, of course, be taken in the controversy, arguments proffered; and, it is hoped, an enlightened dialogue established. This will require a good deal of serious and honest investigation of the whole question of exemptions to the churches. The subject must be dealt with and discussed in the best informed and most intelligent atmosphere. To accomplish this, a scholarly and organized gathering of evidence is necesary so that any conclusions arrived at will most truly reflect the purpose of and need for the practice.

The purpose of this chapter is to investigate the way in which the states have granted or denied tax exemptions to churches under their respective constitutions. Specifically, it is an effort to discover how the courts of the individual states construe and interpret the language of the tax exemption clauses in their constitutions, and to obtain some idea of the type of property which the states privilege. However, before delving into the constitutions themselves, it might be well to consider some of the historical origins of the practice.

The Exemptions Historically

The practice of exempting the churches is by no means peculiar to the American experience. One author writes that "a perusal of the history of tax exemption indicates that the granting of tax immunity to ecclesiastical property . . . is probably as old as the institution of taxation."[8] The Pharaohs are known to have exempted the priests from exactments levied on their subjects, as did the rulers of Judah, as recorded for us in the Talmud.[9] The early Romans reasoned that property devoted to the Gods lost all qualities of human ownership, and to tax such property would be inconsistent with their belief. Constantine has been said to have granted the privilege in the early Christian era. Saladin, the great opponent of the crusaders, in order to raise funds imposed what was known as the "Saladin tithe," said to be the first occasion when movable property was regularly taxed; from this tithe the books and apparatus of clergymen were exempted.

In medieval times the taxes were collected by the manor lords who in return afforded the taxpayers protection. The role of the church in this period was to provide both with spiritual guidance. In England, writes Stimson, the first instance of a direct tax levied by the state was the "danegeld", imposed for the purpose of buying off the Danish pirates. From this levy the church was exempt since its duty was to pray for the defense rather than to furnish material assistance.[10]   It has also been pointed out that there are many recorded instances in which the lords spiritual were called upon to contribute to the support of the temporal authority.[11]   Owing to the unsystematic collection of taxes and the relative material wealth possessed by the spiritual leaders of this period, it is suggested that the exaction was probably more properly termed a "tribute" than a tax. The great majority of churches were, of course, establishments. Historically they claimed realms equal to, but theoretically independent from, the secular government. Nonetheless most of them were supported by the state.

The practice of exempting the churches was carried over into the American colonies, as was the practice of maintaining establishments. No justification for either was ever sought; and since the practice was so in accord with the sentiment of the colonists, none was ever needed. A Connecticut court reported that the principle of exempting the property of religious institutions "has been inseparably interwoven with the structure of government and the habits of our people, since 1638 . . . . "[12]

Tax Exemptions and the Federal Government

While the adoption of the First Amendment struck the death knell for federal establishments, it had no effect on the practice of granting tax exemptions in favor of religions. The First Amendment to the Constitution provides: "Congress shall make no law respecting an establishment of religion, or prohibiting the free exercise thereof." This has been interpreted to mean that the federal government is forbidden to foster the establishment of a national church, and further, to directly aid any one church in preference to another.

There is nothing in the Constitution or the First Amendment expressly forbidding tax exemptions to the churches. As far as anyone has been able to discover, the topic was never mentioned in the debates which took place prior to the adoption of the First Amendment. In the years directly following the adoption of that Amendment, church property in the District of Columbia was never assessed for taxes even though there was no statute expressly providing for their exemption until 1871. The founding fathers on the whole were extraordinary men—characteristically strong-willed men of great sagacity. As the authors of our fundamental law, they could certainly be counted upon to denounce in the strongest terms the practices they felt to be in violation of the will of the nation as reflected by its constitution. Nonetheless, it continued to be generally accepted that the exemptions made to the churches were not only quite desirable, but constitutional as well. Professor Paulsen, in his treatment of the subject, remarks that the "tax exemption for religious institutions has been the American practice since the disestablishment of churches."[13]

Of course, in the early period of the United States, the means used by the federal government to raise what relatively little revenue it required had slight impact on the populace. For the most part the national treasury was kept up by the excises and tariff revenues. However, with the development of the national government came the need for more and more money, which inevitably resulted in numerous revenue laws taxing almost every conceivable type of income.[14] From these taxes the property and income of churches and religious groups, as well as other charitable and benevolent organizations are generally exempted.

A singular attempt by the Federal Government to outlaw the practice was made by President Grant, who recommended in his seventh annual State of the Union Address to Congress on December 7, 1875 the removal of tax immunity from all church property.[15] He urged the Congress to declare church and state "forever separate and distinct . . . and that all church property . . . bear its own proportion of taxes."[16] Although a number of other proposals made by Grant formed the basis for a proposed constitutional amendment submitted to Congress one week later by Representative Blaine of Maine, this particular measure was not included. It has been properly commented that this "omission" probably reflected the mind of an astute politician acutely aware that to insert such a proposal in his amendment would doom its passage.[17]

Each time new tax measures were proposed or legislated the American people moved quickly, stubbornly insisting that their country's churches and religious tradition should not be made to suffer as a result of each new burden. Thus, today, even with our immense and all-encompassing federal revenue structure, the churches and their related institutions remain free from assessment on their holdings and their income.[18]

To date no cases involving the constitutionality of federal tax exemptions to the churches and church related institutions have come before the Supreme Court of the United States. In the main, this is due to the Court's practice of denying standing to sue to taxpayers who attempt to contest the taxing policies of the Congress. One prominent authority doubts that there will ever be any test of the federal exemption statutes, and is of further opinion that if one should occur, the Court will employ a fiction in upholding its validity.[19]

Tax Exemptions and the States

The states, however, present a considerably different picture. In general, the states borrowed quite freely from the federal constitution in writing their own fundamental law. Each of them provided essentially the same guarantees and limitations upon the government in regard to religious freedom and establishment. Over one half today are forbidden by constitutional language to contribute to the support of any mode of worship, place of worship, or denominational institution. Yet nearly all the states, many of which adopted new constitutions shortly following the ratification of the first amendment to the federal constitution, included within their fundamental law clauses providing for the exemption of churches from taxation. It must be noted also that many of the men instrumental in the passage of the first amendment and its subsequent ratification by the legislatures of the states were very often instrumental in the framing of their own constitutional clauses. Therefore, while it is firmly established today that the founding fathers clearly intended at least to ban establishments on the national level, it seems proper to conclude that they never intended to prohibit the traditional practice of exempting the churches from taxation. This is borne out by their legislative and judicial conduct.

The Charter States

A number of the early colonial constitutions contained no language relative to tax exemptions for churches. Of the original thirteen, only Pennsylvania, Massachusetts, and New Hampshire had colonial constitutions containing any language which related to the exemption of churches and religious institutions from taxation. Both South Carolina and Georgia had a number of early colonial constitutions, but exemption language did not appear in a constitution of either state until after the adoption of the United States Constitution. North Carolina did not have such a clause until 1868, and Virginia was silent until 1870. Clauses exempting churches do not appear in a Delaware constitution until 1897, while New York and New Jersey waited until 1938 and 1947, respectively, before adopting any specific exemption clauses in their fundamental law. Of the thirteen original states, Rhode Island, Maryland and Connecticut still today fail to exempt churches, schools, and charitable institutions from the assessment and payment of property and other taxes by constitutional fiat.

Pennsylvania

Pennsylvania appears to have been the first of the original states to incorporate in a constitution language exempting churches and other institutions and organizations. They were protected by a clause in the constitution of 1776 which provided that religious societies and educational institutions should be "encouraged and protected," in the enjoyment of their "immunities and estates" to which they have been accustomed under the former laws of this state.[20] This language merely assured the continuance of a practice long in being and is nearly identical to language found in the colonial constitutions of Massachusetts, New Hampshire, South Carolina, and in Georgia.

In 1790, shortly after the adoption of the Federal Constitution, Pennsylvania drafted a new document reaffirming the exempt status of the churches by providing that all the "rights, privileges and immunities and estates of religious societies . . . shall remain as if the constitution of this state had not been altered."[21] The same clause reappears unchanged in the constitution of 1838.[22] No decisions appear under any of these earlier clauses and they continued unchanged as the basis for the exemptions during the next forty-five years.

The present constitution, adopted in 1873, continues to exempt the churches, but the phrasing has undergone considerable change. Instead of the general terminology found in the earlier constitutions, the framers circumscribed the exemption, placing a limitation upon the power of the legislature to act. Section 1 of Article 9 provides that ". . . the General Assembly may, by general laws, exempt . . . actual places of religious worship . . . institutions of purely public charity.[23] The limiting nature of the clause is readily apparent, especially as regards the phrase "actual places of worship." Conceivably, no church property, except the chapel area itself, could be exempt and the decisions of the Pennsylvania courts reflect the narrowness of this language. For example, at the present time, parsonages and rectories are not exempt, even though they are contiguous to a church auditorium;[24] nor are church parking lots.[25] The living quarters of custodians, although they may be located on the church property or in the building itself used for worship, are not exempt.[26] It appears also well settled in Pennsylvania that churches in the course of construction are not exempt.[27]

One further observation is worth making at this point. The Pennsylvania Supreme Court has consistently refused to extend the exemption of "places of religious worship" to property which is used only periodically or "incidentally" for religious purposes, but was not constructed or conceived to that end.[28] For example, the periodic use of a rectory or parsonage for Sunday School classes or marriage instruction and other activities of like kind or, indeed, even occasional services, probably will not bring the property so used within the exemption as a place of "actual worship," so long as the property is substantially used as a parsonage;[29] nor apparently are such properties exempt as "public" charities.

Perhaps to compensate for the strictness of the phrase "actual places of religious worship," the courts have relied on the phrase "purely public charity" in order to exempt a great deal of property, religious in nature and purpose, but not actually used for worship. Consequently, the construction of this phrase has been very broad indeed. In one illustration, the Pennsylvania Supreme Court held that an orphanage giving preference to those of the Presbyterian faith was exempt as a "purely public charity."[30]   A similar result was achieved some years later involving a school which preferred those of the Episcopalian religion.[31]   A training camp for missionaries was found to be a "public charity," [32] as was a convent annexed to a religiously affiliated school[33]—although neither would qualify as "places of religious worship."   Even the dissemination of literature of a religious nature was exempted on this ground.[34]   The property of Y.M.C.A.'s is exempt as a "public charity," even though they may rent lodging to persons or operate cafeterias, shops, and the like.[35]

It seems difficult to conceive of convents, denominational schools and institutions which prefer those of a particular faith as being "purely public" in nature.   Such a liberal interpretation of this phrase can be explained perhaps only by the court's solicitude for the public policy underlying the practice, and a disinclination to be restricted by the narrow language in which the church exemption is couched.   While the courts are always conscious of their duty to interpret the language within the meaning and purpose intended by the framers, the result of attempting to balance the two objectives is often characterized by striking inconsistencies.   For example, a school for the training of ministerial candidates is exempt in Pennsylvania;[36] yet the houses and rectories to which the young ministers and priests are asigned upon graduation are not.[37] This result, perhaps, may well be dictated by the language of the clause, but it is nonetheless inconsistent with its spirit.   In addition, where property is used both as a place of public charity and for private use, the property may be split, and the portions used as a public charity be exempt.[38]   This does not apply, as we have seen, in the case of parsonages or to places of worship.   If a portion of a church or other place of actual worship is used for non-exempt purposes, the entire property could lose its exempt status.

Massachusetts

Massachusetts was next in the point of time to embody a tax exemption for churches within its constitution.   It did so in 1780.   Although this constitution was adopted during the colonial period, it is still the fundamental law of the state today.   Throughout the decades it has been amended quite frequently and in 1919 was almost completely rearranged. The clause which granted the exemption of churches in the colonial period, however, has been retained in its original wording.   By its terms the legislature is directed "in all future periods" of the Commonwealth "to cherish literature, sciences, and other forms of learning and all seminaries of them."   The lawmakers in the future were further implored to "encourage" both private societies and public institutions which had as their objectives an inculcation of the virtues of "humanity and general benevolence . . . charity, industry, and frugality, honesty, and generous sentiments among the people."[39]   One means the framers of this language obviously had in mind by way of achieving these lofty aims was to *excuse* them, whenever possible, from the burden of taxation.

Pursuant to the policy expressed in this rather antiquated phraseology, the legislature of Massachusetts has provided that certain types of property used by churches, schools, and charity be exempt from the tax rolls. "Houses of worship" are of course exempt, along with the pews and other furnishings.[40] The scope of this exemption has also been held to a reasonable extent to include the surrounding property.[41] However, it has not been found sufficiently broad to include vacant property owned by a religious group upon which it intends in the future to erect a church,[42] as we have seen was also the case in Pennsylvania.[43]

However, unlike Pennsylvania, the Massachusetts exemption law at present *does* encompass parsonages and rectories,[44] although previously such property was not exempt.[45] In addition, the exemption had been originally limited to a value of $5,000, but this was increased to the more realistic figure of $10,000 assessed value in 1953.[46] In 1954, this exemption was also amended to include the official residence of the district superintendent of the Methodist Church.[47]

Denominational schools and institutions in Massachusetts enjoy equal immunity with public and non-sectarian institutions,[48] and seminaries for the training of men and women for church work are included.[49] Additionally, by statute the state provides that all personal property owned or held in trust for any exempt organization is also exempt as long as the income is used for religious, educational, or benevolent purposes.[50]

New Hampshire

The experience and practice in New Hampshire resembles that of Massachusetts and Pennsylvania in the area of tax exemptions to churches. Exemption language quite similar to that found in the early constitutions of those two states was introduced into a constitution of New Hampshire in 1784,[51] and renewed in a new constitution adopted in 1792.[52] The clause was incorporated in the amended constitution of 1902 without any change in the wording[53] and has not been altered under the present form of the constitution as amended in 1955.[54]

Each of these successive constitutions, in addition to containing this exemption clause, also provided that *all* persons were free to worship as they chose, and that all sects of religion were to be tolerated in New Hampshire. However, the sects were not all equal in the eyes of the government. As late as 1875, the constitution continued to provide that the Protestant faith was to be favored.[55]

In New Hampshire in the latter part of the Nineteenth Century, the question eventually arose as to whether or not tax exemptions, by virtue of this preference, could be limited only to Protestant institutions. The Supreme Court of New Hampshire said, decidedly, that they were not in the case of *Ward* v. *Manchester* (1876).[56] This case involved the question of whether an academy operated by the Roman Catholic Church for the purpose of training and educating young girls was exempt from taxation. In language that has been characterized by one authority as "magnanimous for that state at that year," the court removed all doubt as to the coverage of this clause, at least as regards the schools and institutions owned and operated by religious groups not adhering to the Protestant faith.[57]   After first affirming that "every denomination of Christians is declared to be *equal* (emphasis added) under the protection of the law," the Court reasoned thus:

> Protection and action are reciprocal. Our Constitution prescribes the duty of the legislators and magistrates . . . to cherish . . . all seminaries and public schools; to encourage private and public institutions for the promotion of . . . arts and sciences, etc., . . . inculcate the principles of humanity and general benevolence . . . . . . It is none of our business . . . whether the lady superior of the sisters of mercy (sic) upholds the dogma of the Romish Church, or inculcates the doctrine of universal salvation after the most liberal sort of protestantism. It would be a reproach to us if it were otherwise . . . .[58]

As a consequence of this decision, the Constitution of New Hampshire was amended in 1877 to prohibit the support of *any* sect by the state, at the expense of the taxpayers of other faiths.

In 1955, the New Hampshire high court, in upholding the exemption of a hospital operated by a religious group, made it clear that what was intended by this amendment was the final elimination of favoritism toward a single sect, and not the total elimination of benefits such as tax exemptions, traditionaly enjoyed by all sects.[59] Said the Justices:

> What was intended to be forbidden by the amendment of 1877 was support of a sect or denomination by the state, at the expense of the taxpayers of other denominations or of no denomination, It was not intended that the members of denominations should be deprived of public benefit because of their beliefs.[60]

In 1910 the Supreme Court of New Hampshire held further that it was not improper to exempt parsonages, even though the statute at that time spoke only of . . . "House of Worship." [61] In addition, the court ruled that incidental secular use of churches or other exempt properties would not result in the loss of their exempt status. In construing the statute passed in 1842 pursuant to the constitutional policy of encouraging learning and religion, the court commented:

> Argument is unnecessary to show that the purpose was to promote religious worship, and not to discourage it by limiting the exemp- tion to a very small number of church buildings in the state in

which no secular entertainments were permitted. Indeed, it is probable that there were none of that exclusive character . . . . [N]o one ever supposed that such use made the meeting house liable to taxation.[62]

Today parsonages as well as convents, monasteries, and seminaries, are by statute exempt.[63]

South Carolina

South Carolina first codified its long standing exemption policy in the constitution of 1790. It simply provided that all the "rights, privileges, and immunities" enjoyed by the churches, religious societies, and educational institutions in the past will be continued as if this constitution had not been altered."[64] The wording is almost identical with the exemption clause of the Pennsylvania constitution adopted in the same year.[65] It is significant that the adoption of the Federal Constitution just a short time earlier had no effect on the practice. Both states reformed their constitutions to conform with their new status as sovereign members of a federal union, but took pains to ensure that practices such as excusing the church from taxes would continue. This same guarantee found its way into the post Civil War constitution of 1865.[66]

Three years later, the Constitution of South Carolina was once again reformed. At that time the framers established a clear constitutional basis for the exemptions in place of the simple "guarantee" of the earlier constitution. Article 9, Section 1 of the 1868 Constitution of South Carolina provides that the legislature in its discretion may "by law exempt property used for educational, literary, religious, or charitable purposes."[67] This clause remained the basis for exempting the churches until 1895. There is no judicial evidence of just how the clause was applied and interpreted but the breadth of the language indicates that just about all property which could be said to be devoted to one of the enumerated "purposes" would be exempt—probably with little question.

In 1895, the present South Carolina constitution was adopted. It embodied some significant changes in the tax exemption clause.[68] The ultimate effect of the change was to narrow the scope of the exemption and restrict its coverage. The general word "purpose" was eliminated and the names of each particular type of institution entitled to the exemption were substituted.[69] As a result of this modification, many kinds of property, even though devoted to and used for religious or charitable purposes, might have difficulty obtaining an exemption if not within any of the enunciated categories. It is likely that they will be denied it. The constitution further limits the exemption to the property "actually occupied by them," thereby eliminating property under construction.

Another significant change is that the exemption, instead of being discretionary with the legislature, is now made mandatory. The law-making body may enumerate the particulars of the exemption; but it may not add to or subtract from that set forth in the Constitution.

Unfortunately, there is little litigation regarding this clause. As a consequence we are denied the opportunity of discovering how the Supreme Court of South Carolina would construe and interpret it. It has been settled, however, as it has been in the majority of states, that the property of exempt institutions and organizations is not exempt from special assessments for municipal improvement. Such assessments are not considered a "tax" within the meaning of the exemption clause.[70]

In addition to the types of exemptions mentioned in the constitution itself, the South Carolina code further provides that property employed in the publication of a religious newspaper is exempt.[71] Also exempt are benevolent and science organizations, notably Young Mens Christian Associations, Boy Scout Camps, and the like.[72]

While the legislature may not limit the *categories* of exempt property, it may and has limited the *amount* of property which a church may exempt.[73] This is indicative of a general fear on the part of a number of states that without such limitation, the churches will acquire too much power through the acquisition of property.

Georgia

In a number of respects the experience in Georgia differs from that of the states heretofore discussed. The framers of the constitutions were busy throughout the years, having written no less than eight documents —the latest one adopted in 1945. Two of the documents framed during the colonial period were silent on tax exemptions.[74] However, a clause in the post-colonial constitution of 1798 provided that "one or more seminaries of learning should be promoted," with a direction to the legislature to grant them "further donations and privileges." In addition, this clause declared that it "should be the duty of the legislature . . . to provide effectual measures for . . . permanent security of funds and endowments of such institutions.[75] Georgia was the first state to provide for direct "donations" in a constitution, as well as being the first of the early states to constitutionally ensure the security of endowment funds as well as the other property of such institutions.

This early clause centered on schools and learning and made no express provision for the churches. In this respect it differs from the early exemption clauses in those states already discussed. Nonetheless, the failure to include the property of churches within the early clause did not operate as a bar to the exemption of such property. For example, during the period in which this constitution was in force, the legislature passed an act exempting certain property from levy and sale for debts, generally upon the theory that it must be preserved for the benefit of the debtor's family. In an early decision (1851), the Georgia Supreme Court held that a "family bible" was a clear example of one of the types of property the legislature intended to preserve.[76] Of major importance to us in this case is the language of Nesbie, J., which is indicative of the uncodified policy of exempting the churches during this and later periods. Said the Justice:

> . . . This state is bound, although not named by an Act of the legislature, for the maintenance of religion, the advancement of learning or the support of the poor. If not bound, such acts might be defective in their operations. The whole public being interested, they must be so construed as to be effectual—that is, they must be so construed as to protect the rights of the public under them. . . .[77]

Two later constitutions, adopted in 1865 and 1868 respectively, were also silent on tax exemptions for churches. But in 1877 the framers of another Georgia Constitution for the first time embodied within such a document specific language authorizing the legislature to exempt from taxation "places of public worship" and institutions of "purely public charity."[78] The clause is unchanged in the present constitution adopted in 1945 except to the extent that it now also includes "all intangible personal property owned by or . . . held in trust" for the benefit of the exempt organizations,[79] and is similar to the guarantee found in the earlier Georgia Constitutions regarding "endowment funds."

As stated above, the inclusion of church property within the exemption clause by no means signaled innovation. It merely gave the traditional practice of exempting the churches constitutional backing. Ten years after the constitution of 1877 became the fundamental law of Georgia, its high court explained the purpose of exempting the churches, indicating the necessity of their being exempted along with the schools.[80] "Every government," said the court, "to carry out its obligations to the people . . . is bound to adopt measures to promote these great objects [of religion and learning]."[81] Further:

> The public recognition of religious worship . . . is not based entirely, perhaps not even mainly, upon a sense of what is due to the Supreme Being himself as the authority of all good and of all law; but the same reasons of state policy, which include the government to aid institutions of charity and seminaries of instruction will include it also to foster religious worship and religious institutions, as the conservators of public morals and valuable, if not indispensable assistants in the preservation of public order.[82]

In the instant case, it was ruled that a tax in the guise of an assessment for local improvements could not be imposed upon the property of exempt institutions, but the decision was overruled some years later and it was settled that churches and other exempt properties were not exempt from such assessment because, again, it was not considered a "tax" within the meaning of the exemption clause.[83]   In its opinion the court conceded that the services of religion were of "untold value" to the community, but countered that it is the "glory of religion in this country that it serves as a volunteer without money and without price."[84]

The form of the exemption, phrased as it is in terms of "religious worship", excludes, as it does in most of the states, a large amount of property, religious in nature, but not used for worship—parsonages and other such residences being one such example.[85]

By statute, Georgia also provides for the exemption of corporations, funds, or foundations organized and operated exclusively for religious purposes.[86]

Of the original charter states, then, only Pennsylvania, Massachusetts, New Hampshire, South Carolina and Georgia saw any need to provide for or limit tax exemptions for churches and church-related institutions by clauses in their earlier constitutions.   They continue to do so today.   Of those remaining, North Carolina, Virginia, and Delaware provided exemptions only by statute or, absent a statute, merely refrained, as a matter of custom, from assessing church property.   New York and New Jersey did not incorporate the exemption into their fundamental law until the turn of the century.   Finally three of the charter states—Rhode Island, Maryland, and Connecticut, even today make no constitutional provision for exempting churches.

North Carolina

Exemption language first appeared in a North Carolina Constitution in 1868.   The clause provided generally for the "encouragement of religion, morality, [and] knowledge," as "necessary for good government." [87]   To this end the general assembly was authorized to exempt "property held for . . . religious purposes." [88]   This exemption, without any change in the wording, forms a part of the present constitution in force since 1876.[89]

One significant change, however, must be noted.   The language of the clause itself speaks in terms of "permitting" the legislature to provide for these exemptions, but it has now been settled that the exemption is *mandatory*, relieving the assembly of any of the discretion it once had.[90]

The constitutional clause broadly permits the exemption for religious "purposes," instead of limiting to places of "worship."   No decisions have been found whereby some clue might be obtained as to the scope of the exemption.   It appears that by continued employment of the much broader term, the exemption at least would not be limited to the church building itself, but would also include parsonage, parking lots, and recreational facilities connected with churches and charitable institutions, monasteries and convents, camp meeting grounds, retreat houses, and similar institutions.

This appears to be borne out by the state assembly's elaboration on the exemption. By statute, the property of "churches, religious societies, charitable, education, literary and benevolent institutions and orders," are free from taxation in North Carolina.[91]

Virginia

This briefly worded exemption clause found in the North Carolina Constitution stands in marked contrast to the elaborate language of the Virginia Constitution. Both states seem, however, to cover the same ground, merely employing different legislative techniques. Whereas North Carolina has chosen to have the extent of the exemption determined by interpretation, Virginia, instead, has attempted to cover everything within the clause itself.

In spite of the fact that the Commonwealth of Virginia had numerous earlier constitutions[92] it was not until 1870 that a clause exempting property devoted to religion was included in the fundamental law of the state. That constitution gave the legislature the power for the first time to exempt from taxation "all property used exclusively for . . . benevolent, charitable, educational, and religious purposes.[93] The clause was permissive only, yet liberal in that it employed the broad term "purposes."

This clause was scrapped and replaced by a *mandatory*, self-executing type exemption in the present constitution, adopted in 1902.[94] A second significant change was the substitution of the words "religious worship" for "purposes," serving now to limit the scope of the exemption. Nonetheless, the exemption is still quite broad. In addition to the buildings and the land which they actually occupy, the furnishings and endowments held by the churches or religious bodies are exempt. Residences of ministers are exempt under this clause, as is the property and funds belonging to Young Men's Christian Associations and like religious and benevolent organizations. The exemption clause also exempts the *surrounding* land "reasonably necessary for the convenient use of these buildings" by the exempt groups.

In addition, Virginia constitutionally provides that when such property is used only *partly* for any of the enunciated purposes, the exemption may be allocated to the portion so used—only the remainder being liable to taxation. The Virginia exemption statute is similarly worded.[95]

To reiterate, the exemption is fixed by the constitution itself, and the legislature no longer has the power to subtract from or add to its terms. The Supreme Court of Virginia had occasion to construe this section in a case involving the validity of an exemption for a Y.M.C.A. organization.[96] The court held that a building for housing persons for a small charge was not run for profit, but was operated primarily for the furtherance of the religious purpose of the organization. Not only were bible classes available to the occupants, but a good and moral atmosphere was provided in the interests of their spiritual welfare. In declining to give this section a particular construction demanded by the common-wealth, the court said:

> It is insisted by the Commonwealth that the provision of Section 183 of the Constitution must receive a strict construction. The general rule is that Provisions exempting property of individuals or private corporations from taxation must be strictly construed, taxation of such property being the rule and exemption from taxation being the exception. One of the reasons for this is that all such persons should bear their fair share of the burdens of taxation, and that lessening the burden of one increases the burden of others. But as the policy of the State has always been to exempt property of the character mentioned and described in Section 183 of the Constitution it should not be construed with the same degree of strictness that applies to provisions making exemptions contrary to the policy of the state, since as to such property exemption is the rule and taxation the exception.[97]

The "policy" of the state to "always exempt property of the character mentioned . . ." in Section 183 undoubtedly serves to explain why the numerous earlier constitutions failed to have such clauses. The practice was so deeply embedded in the tradition of the people of the state that none were ever thought needed.

Delaware

Like Virginia, Delaware has had a number of earlier constitutions, but also like Virginia, none contained clauses exempting church prop-erty.[98]

Article 8, Section 1 of the present constitution in force since 1897 provides that the general assembly "may . . . exempt . . . such property as in the opinion of the General Assembly will best promote the public welfare."

Pursuant to this very broad authority from the constitution, the assembly has enacted a very extensive list of the organizations whose property is exempted from taxation. Among these are churches, schools, private hospitals, Young Men's Christian Associations, the Salvation Army, and numerous others, including many operated by religious or-ganizations.[99]

Under statutes passed pursuant to this clause, the Delaware Court held that a residence for teachers teaching in a free religious school, and of a group peculiarly identified with their religion whose rules required them to live together in a community arrangement, was exempt.[100] Simi-larly, a Quaker school, charging tuition of its students was found exempt.[101]   In a rather recent decision, the high court of the state held that a rectory building, owned and used by a church for church and religious purposes, was within the exemption permitted by the constitution and created by a general tax exemption statute.   Consequently, it was not subject to a city tax, notwithstanding the fact that the building was not specifically exempted from taxation by the city's charter.[102]

New Jersey-New York

It has only been in relatively recent times that New York and New Jersey have provided in their constitutions for the exemption of property devoted to religion.[103]   Both states had exempted church property solely by statute by authority of the legislature's general power of taxation.[104] Nonetheless, prior to the enactment of formal exemption laws, the consensus was that such property was immune.   As one court in New Jersey had occasion to remark:

> Meeting houses and school houses, although not formally exempted by the tax laws prior to 1851, were seldom assessed. . . . This omission was so obviously proper, and so entirely in accordance with public sentiment, that it universally prevailed and was in fact a contemporaneous construction of the laws, which this court would probably have sanctioned had the question been formally raised.[105]

New York gave constitutional recognition to this type of exemption in 1938,[106] and New Jersey in 1947.[107]   The clauses are identical.   Instead of directing that the exemption be granted, or authorizing the legislators to grant them, the clauses prohibit the legislators from interfering with the exemptions hitherto enjoyed by the churches.   The New York constitutional clause will serve to illustrate.   Article 16, section 1 states:

> Exemption from taxation may be granted only by general laws. Exemptions may be altered or repealed *except* (emphasis added) those exempting real or personal property used exclusively for religious, educational, or charitable purposes as defined by law and owned by any corporation or association organized or conducted exclusively for one or more of such purposes and not operating for profit.

The New Jersey constitution adds that "exemptions . . . now in existence should be continued."[108]

Both states have rather elaborate statutory provisions exempting property of the churches and charitable groups.   The New York tax law, quite liberally, exempts the real property of organizations dedicated to the mental and moral improvement of the people of the state, including among others the property devoted to religious, bible, tract, missionary, hospital, and educational purposes.[109]   Moreover, dwelling houses of clergymen held by a religious organization and actually used by the clergy are exempt.[110] Even part of the real property owned by the minister himself is exempt.[111] Finally, a relatively recent limitation imposed upon the exemption of cemetery property is not applicable to cemeteries operated by religious societies.[112]

The New Jersey statute provides exemption for about the same categories of property.[113] However, the statute requires *ownership* as well as *use* of the property in order for it to qualify.

The exemption statutes in both states are liberally inclusive of many types of church property. However, the courts have indicated a tendency throughout the years towards stricter interpretation. For instance, in New Jersey, property of an exempt institution employed in the raising of farm produce to be consumed by the residents was exempt as being necessary for the fair enjoyment of the building.[114] Later, in 1907, this same exemption was held improper. The exemption of property necessary for the fair enjoyment of the buildings, themselves exempt, said the Supreme Court of New Jersey, "did not encompass such things as lands under cultivation for the benefit of the residents of the building."[115] Also, in 1955, the New Jersey Supreme Court refused to enjoin the collection of a tax on the dwellings of clergymen serving as faculty members of a Bible Institute—even though parsonages, in general, are exempt.[116]

Rhode Island-Connecticut-Maryland

As previously stated, Rhode Island, Connecticut, and Maryland have never given explicit constitutional fiat to the practice of exempting church property. In these jurisdictions, the exemption has traditionally been accomplished by statute and this continues to be so today.

Rhode Island did not adopt a constitution until 1842. Up to that time it continued to operate under its original colonial charter. Present practice in this state provides the exemption, by statute, of buildings used exclusively for worship,[117] parsonages,[118] intangible personal property owned or held in trust for a religious society, and bibles from property tax.[119] The exemption does not extend to assessments for local improvements.[120]

Quite recently, the exemption of religious societies from property and other taxes was judicially attacked in Rhode Island.[121] It was contended that the practice was violative of the constitutional ban upon aid to religion, and infringed upon its guarantee of freedom of worship. In refusing to find that the exemption violated the constitution, Justice Powers, who spoke for the high court of the state, underscored the precedent back of the practice. Said the Justice:

> In this state, exemptions to churches were common prior to as well as after the adoption of our constitution in 1842. Indeed in Pfeffer on *Church, State and Freedom* at page 184, it was stated: "The universality of the exemption from taxes in the United States

is hardly open to doubt; constitutional or statutory provision for such exemption exists today in all states as well as in the District of Columbia. Churches, other houses of worship, and the land on which they stand are everywhere freed from tax levies, as is personal property devoted to religious uses." [122]

The Justice then went on to reiterate the Rhode Island experience:

It is not without significance, we think, that exemptions such as these here assailed were quite common in this state when the people adopted their constitution in 1842, including the provisions of Art. I, Sec. 3, as they now exist.[123]

In Connecticut from very early times, the exemption of church and school property was accomplished by statutes. The most famous of these was passed in 1702. It provided:

All lands, tenements and hereditaments and other estates . . . granted by the General Assembly, colony or by any town and village to the ministry of the gospel or school of learning . . . be exempted out of the general lists of estates, and free from the payment of rates.

In 1826, the Supreme Court of Connecticut held that a tax on a fund granted to a religious society and loaned by that society at interest was illegal.[124] The contention was made that subsequent revision of this statute in 1821 had precluded the exemption. The court, however, concluded that the grant, having been made to the society previous to 1821, was not affected by any revision. The conclusion was grounded on the novel theory that under the statute, the government made a contract with those persons who "might be disposed to give their property [for] . . . religious purposes and charitable uses." Thus they had a vested right in the clause which "no subsequent legislature could divest." [125]

At the present time, Connecticut, by statute, exempts the personal property of religious organizations, houses of worship with their furnishings, hospitals, schools, camps, orphan homes, infirmaries, and reformatories operated by religious sects.[126] It further exempts clergymen's dwellings,[127] but not houses used by them for retreats.[128] Connecticut denies exemption to the property of institutions such as Masonic lodges, ruling that they do not come within the scope of the phrase "houses of worship." [129]

Article 15 of the Maryland Declaration of Rights requires uniformity of taxation. The courts have held, however, that this constitutional requirement "does not forbid the creation of reasonable exemptions in furtherance of the public good." [130] Present practice in Maryland is to exempt by statute the property of churches, including the parsonages.[131]

Retreat houses are also exempt, in contrast to Connecticut where the exemption is denied them.[132]

Vermont

Vermont, the last state to have had a colonial constitution, embodied within that early document, drawn and adopted in 1777, language purporting to "encourage" religion, charity and learning by giving "rewards and immunities" to institutions promoting these ends.[133]   The clause is similar to those found in the early constitutions of states already discussed.   It was also found in the constitution of 1786,[134] and in the constitution of 1793;[135] and has survived numerous revisions of that constitution, the most recent being in 1954.[136]

The clause is not self-executing inasmuch as the exemptions may be granted only by general law.   It is mandatory, however, to the extent that it imposes a duty on the legislature to encourage religion, charity, and learning by the giving of "rewards and immunities" which "in justice they should enjoy."   In pursuance of this duty, Vermont today exempts by statute the real and personal property *used* for religious and charitable purposes.[137]   Apparently there is no need for the church or charity to *own* the property, because the statute also provides that "lands leased by towns for the support of the gospel" are exempt.[138] However, in order for a religious society or a church to be eligible for an exemption for a rectory or parsonage, it must be *owned* by them, as well as *used* for that purpose.[139]   The property of the Y.M.C.A.'s is also specifically exempted.[140]

The Supreme Court of Vermont, in determining the legal efficacy of the exemptions, has applied the traditional rule of strict construction to tax exemptions of this sort, indicating that "this is not affected by Chapter 2, Section 64 of our state constitution."[141]   However, it has also applied the countervailing rule of construction which requires that such exemptions *not* be given a construction which would undermine the purpose for which they were granted.[142]

Kentucky

Kentucky, one of the last states to join the union before 1800, had no exemption clauses in its early constitutions.[143]   This state, however, has had considerable contemporary experience in this area.

The present constitution of Kentucky, adopted in 1890, contains a lengthy, elaborately worded clause which mandatorily provides for an exemption to all places "actually used for public worship," and the surrounding grounds.   It further exempts all places of "purely public charity," educational institutions, parsonages and rectories.   The exemption for churches, parsonages, and rectories is limited to one half of an acre in cities and towns and two acres in the rural areas.[144]

Since the exemption is itself elaborated in the constitution, there was little left for the legislature to enact. The only significant statute is one exempting transfers to religious and charitable institutions from the inheritance tax.[145]

While the clause is comprehensive, and the exemption generous, the Kentucky court has been careful not to depart from its intended purpose. It cautioned:

> When the framers of the constitution undertook to define in exact terms what should be exempt we are not at liberty to add to the terms which they selected with so much care and precision. . . . If we depart from the narrow limits of exemption which they have set we insofar destroy that quality of taxation which they so laboriously aimed to attain.[146]

On another occasion, the Supreme Court of the state underscored the policy of the state toward this matter: "Religious societies are deemed to be public benefactors. . . . Hence, they are regarded with favor." [147]

Some examples of where Kentucky has denied the exemption include the case of a trust fund set up for the purpose of fostering the principles of a certain religious sect by means of employing an evangelist.[148] Further, property adjacent to a church purchased by the church for the purpose of preventing any possible construction which it claimed would cut off light and air to the building was denied exemption.[149] In the opinion of the court the property was not being used for any of the purposes specified in the constitution.

By contrast, the Kentucky Supreme Court *has* allowed exemptions for property owned by a school, but leased for commercial use. The income was used to support a school operated under the auspices of a religious sect.[150] The school was open to all, but gave preference to ministerial candidates. In addition, all students were obliged to attend chapel once each day. From this and other decisions of the Kentucky court, it is clear that exemptions to educational institutions are not confined to the buildings themselves, but include any property owned by them no matter how invested so long as the income is used for educational purposes.

At one time, there existed some doubt as to whether sectarian schools were to enjoy immunity on the same level as the non-sectarian institutions. In 1918, however, the Supreme Court of Kentucky handed down a ruling to the effect that the exemption applies to *all* property of educational institutions, stating that "this is true whether the school be sectarian or not." [151]

Charities received the same treatment. The Kentucky court ruled that charitable projects undertaken by religious sects were entitled to the same privileges as those non-church affiliated.

> The fact that a charity is run by a sect does not mean it may not classify as a public charity. This is the manner in which much

charitable work is done, via sectarian organizations pledged to charity and good works.[152]

States Admitted to the Union: 1800-1820

During the first twenty years of the 19th Century, seven new states joined the Union.   These were Ohio, Indiana, Illinois, Louisiana, Alabama, Maine, and Mississippi.

Ohio

Ohio's early constitution exempted the property of churches in about the same language as some of the states already discussed—namely, that religion, morality and knowledge are essential to good government and should be encouraged.[153]   In 1851 this language was replaced by a clause which provided in part that the legislature is free to exempt from taxation all houses "used exclusively for public worship" and institutions of "purely public charity."[154]   The duty to exempt such property is not mandatory on the legislature which is at liberty to alter or repeal the exemptions as it chooses.

The legislature has made statutory provision for the exemption and, in addition, has amplified the constitutional exemption by including within its scope all property "necessary for the proper occupancy or use and enjoyment" of the exempt buildings or property.[155]   The authority to do this has been held to be implied from the constitutional language.

This language has captured the attention of the Ohio courts on various occasions.[156]   First, with reference to the doctrine of "exclusive use," it has been held that a non-religious or non-charitable use of such property which can be honestly said to be no more than reasonably "incidental" to the major purpose of the property has no effect on its exempt status.   In one instance a tax was assessed against property housing a Hebrew school.[157]   The property consisted of a one and a half story building, the main portion of which was used for religious training and services. A part-time caretaker with his wife and child occupied three rooms on the second floor.   He attended to his custodial duties only in the evenings and was employed elsewhere during the day time.   As compensation, he received the use of the rooms rent-free and was paid $30 a month.   As a result of this arrangement the property was taxed.   The school asserted that the tax was improper and finally prevailed in the Ohio Supreme Court.   Justice Taft, author of the opinion, made this observation:

> The Attorney General argues, and the Board of Tax Appeals has apparently held, that the words "used exclusively for public worship," should be interpreted literally to exclude any other use whatsoever.   Such a literal construction could prevent any exemption being given under these words of the constitution. . . .   Such a literal construction would not be a reasonable construction.   The

people certainly intended that the words they used in the constitution should be given a reasonable meaning. . ..[158]

By way of illustration he cited a number of activities of churches used to encourage the people to worship, which in themselves could not constitute worship. Among those he listed were rooms used to entertain young children so that their parents may attend services in a spirit of contemplative meditation. Another was the use of rooms and facilities in the preparation and consumption of church suppers. "Certainly," he concluded, "it was not the intention of the people that their words 'used exclusively for public worship' should be so literally construed that any such uses would prevent tax exemption of a church building." [159] It is likely the Justice had in mind an earlier decision which found that a church does not lose its religious character just because it sells certain goods for a commercial profit following and in connection with religious services.[160]

Second, the Ohio courts addressed themselves to the problem of how much additional property was necessary to the enjoyment of the exempt property. It was contended by one plaintiff that the exemption was limited to only so much additional property as was necessary to afford light and air, as well as passage to the church building.[161] The Justices rejected this contention. "We do not think," they wrote, "[that] the constitution requires a construction so rigid." They continued:

> The express authority given in the Constitution to exempt buildings of the description named, carried with it *impliedly* (emphasis added) authority to exempt such grounds as may be reasonably necessary for their use.[162]

"Reasonably necessary," they declared meant, "reasonably appropriate." "If the ground is no more than is reasonably appropriate to the purpose . . . it comes fairly within the limits prescribed by the constitution."[163] Quite inconsistent with this interpretation of the exemption is the refusal of Ohio to extend the exemption to parsonages and church parking lots as being appropriate to the purpose of the church.[164]

Thirdly, in addition to the determination that the property is being used for worship or for charitable purposes, there must be an additional finding that the worship is "public" or that the charity is one "purely public." At one time in Ohio this was interpreted to deny any exemption to institutions which limited entry to persons subscribing to a particular belief. Accordingly, institutions for the training of ministers and priests were not exempt.[165] The reason offered was that there was no direct educational benefit to the community at large. Similarly, the residences of ministers and teachers in conjunction with a church or a school where they discharged their duties were denied the exemption.[166] The reasons given were that these properties were not used for worship, for charitable purposes; or they were not open to the public generally if they were so used.[167]

Relatively recently, however, Ohio has somewhat modified its position in this regard. In the late 1940's, a controversy arose over the attempted taxation of a Bible College operated by the Society of Friends.[168] It was found that the college was open to persons of all faiths. It was further disclosed that the student body was in fact representative of a number of denominations, as well as some who listed no affiliation. The Department of Theology, however, was limited to those preparing for the ministry. On these facts, the court found that the institution was open to the public generally, and permitted the exemption. More significant, perhaps, is the language of Justice Taft who concurred in a separate opinion. He took the position that since 1912 it was no longer required that an institution be open to the public generally in order for it to be exempt. He concluded thusly:

> The fact, that such institution restricts admission to the followers of the Christian or any other lawful religion, will not prevent it from having tax exemption of its property used exclusively for lawful educational or religious purposes.[169]

The author was joined in his opinion by one other jurist.[170] It appears, then, from Justice Taft's reading of the constitution and statute that all institutions of learning, regardless of whether they are limited to persons of one faith or another, are exempt.

In cases where portions of property are devoted to different purposes, some are tax exempt and some not. The present rule is that the property may be split for tax purposes. This often occurs when floors of the same building are devoted to diverse purposes.[171]

Finally, in Ohio, the general rule is that land purchased by an exempt organization upon which there is only an intention to construct an exempt structure is not itself exempt.[172] However, if the intention to build has progressed to the point that plans have been drawn and funds are available, the exemption will be permitted.[173]

Louisiana

Louisiana joined the Union in 1812, ten years after Ohio, but unlike Ohio, did not initially provide a tax exemption for churches.[174] It was not until 1864 that the General Assembly was constitutionally provided with the power to exempt property "actually used for school, church, and charitable purposes."[175] In 1879 this was re-written to read that all "places of religious worship . . . charitable institution . . . all buildings used exclusively for colleges or other school property . . ." were to be exempt.[176] It differs from the previous clause in two important ways. First, the exemption was made mandatory; secondly the scope of the exemption is narrowed by the substitution of the phrase "religious worship" for the phrase "religious purposes." The literal impact of the latter change is to deny the exemption to any religious property not actually a church. Apparently, however, the Louisiana Supreme Court did not think that such was intended by the legislature because in 1889 it ruled the residence of a bishop exempt.[177] The question was settled in 1898 by drafting the exempting clause to include parsonages and rectories.[178] The same exemption clause was found in the constitutions of 1913 and 1921.[179]

The exemption clause of the Louisiana constitution is drafted in considerable detail. The extensive drafting has apparently made it unnecessary for the legislature to improve on it by statute, and has undoubtedly contributed to the scantiness of litigation in this area. The Attorney General of Louisiana has ruled that the exceptions are not dependent on *ownership*.[180] That is, it need *only* be *used* for any of the enumerated purposes. One other discoverable point concerns property purchased with a view to future construction. It is not entirely clear just what the status of such property is. In one early instance such property was denied the exemption.[181] The court at that time, however, placed considerable emphasis on the fact that the property had lain fallow for ten years with no decision ever made as to precisely what was to be erected thereon. A different result might have been reached if some positive steps had been taken by the owners.

Finally, Louisiana, quite unlike many of the other jurisdictions, constitutionally exempts clergymen from license taxes.[182] In addition, it exempts religious, educational, and charitable property from inheritance and gift taxes.[183]

Indiana

The early Indiana constitution of 1816, like many of the earlier constitutions in other states, provided in a general way for the encouragement of scientific and intellectual pursuits, giving "rewards and immunities" to promote honesty and morality.[184] The present constitution of 1851 directs the legislature to provide for taxation "exempting such only for . . . educational, literary, scientific, religious, or charitable purposes, as may be exempted by law."[185] Note that the exemption is phrased in the liberal terms "religious purposes" rather than the more restrictive phraseology of "religious worship." Note also that "exclusiveness" is not made a *constitutional* requirement in this state. By statute, however, the exemption is limited to buildings used for "religious worship," including parsonages, with the exemptions extended to fifteen acres of surrounding land.[186] In addition, the statute exempts Y.M.C.A. buildings and those of similar organizations.[187] Property purchased with the present intention to build structures to be devoted to religious, educational and charitable purposes is also exempt.[188]   Not exempt in Indiana, however, are properties used for the publishing, printing and distributing of religious books.[189]

Mississippi

Mississippi by contrast is one of the few states today that does not provide for the exemption of the churches in its fundamental law.   Both the constitutions of 1817 and 1832 provided for general encouragement of religion and educational institutions,[190] but the Constitution of 1868 restricts any government encouragement to the public schools only.[191]

The exemption today is granted by statute.[192]   It exempts all property belonging to any religious society, ecclesiastical bodies or their congregations, as well as property of charitable organizations.   In addition, it privileges all hospitals, *providing* they maintain charity wards.   It should be noted here that the property, when owned by a church group, probably need not be *used* for worship.   On the other hand, property must be put to *some* use because it has been held in Mississippi that vacant lots are not exempt.[193]   Mississippi law also allows the property to be used or rented out for commercial purposes so long as the proceeds are devoted to one or another of the enumerated purposes.[194]

Illinois

The first constitution of the state of Illinois had no constitutional provision for exempting churches and church-related institutions.[195]   In 1848, however, a new constitution authorized the general assembly of the state to exempt any property it thought necessary for school, religious and charitable purposes.[196]   The same clause was inserted in the present constitution adopted in 1870, amended only to the extent that the terms "real and personal" were inserted to modify the class of property to which the exemption should apply.[197]

Although the exemption is framed in a broad fashion, i.e., the use of the term "purposes," the Illinois court has held that term to mean "religious worship," thereby judicially narrowing the scope of the privilege.[198]   As a result, camp meeting grounds, parsonages, rectories, and other religious houses are not exempt because they are not used strictly for worship.[199] According to this doctrine, it was of no moment that activities of a general religious nature were held in these places.[200]   This doctrine has been modified recently by a statute which exempts parsonages and rectories.[201] The exemption statute also adds the requirement of *exclusive* use.[202] However, other *occasional* (or even regular) use of the property will not result in denial of the exemption.[203]   This means, according to the Illinois courts, that if property is devoted *primarily* to religious purposes, it does not matter that it is *incidentally* used for some secular purpose.[204] This appears to be the rule applicable at least where the activities are designed to advance the welfare and general purposes of the religious group.

When a particular use cannot be categorized as "incidental" in this sense, Illinois permits the property to be divided for taxation purposes. That portion not found to be used for *worship* will be separately assessed.[205]

Earlier Illinois law required that in addition to property being used exclusively for public worship, it had to be *owned* by the institutions claiming the exemption.[206] Present law permits the exemptions regardless of ownership.[207]

As in the great majority of states, the general doctrine underlying all exemptions of this nature is that they must benefit the public at large. In Illinois, however, it is not at all necessary that the institutions be accessible to the public at large, or even that the benefit be of a direct nature, as is required by the laws of many states. Illustrative of this are the seminaries for the training of young men for the ministry which are exempt.[208] Their calling and training are recognized as a sufficient benefit to the community to justify the privilege. On the other hand, an exemption was denied to a cloister of nuns who spent all their time in prayer and meditation for the world.[209] To the Illinois Supreme Court, at least, the benefit was not sufficient to merit the exemption. Said Mr. Justice Cartwright in denying the exemption:

> The use of property for religious purposes tends to conditions affording compensation for the exemption, which is not a mere gift to religion but for a public purpose. In every case the exemption rests upon a general public benefit.[210]

Schools of all kinds provide the most common illustration in support of the public benefit theory. Nonetheless, despite the long tradition of excluding denominational schools and organizations from the purview of the exemption privilege, the practice has occasionally been attacked. The issue was definitely decided in favor of the religious schools and organizations in the celebrated case of *Garrett Biblical Institute v. Elmhurst State Bank*, decided by the Illinois Supreme Court in 1928.[211] In this case the high court held that a charter granted to this institution by the state, which exempted it from taxation, violated neither the state constitution of 1848 nor the federal constitution, notwithstanding the provision in the charter itself that no doctrines in conflict with the Methodist Episcopal Church or its articles of faith shall be taught, and that its students are necessarily restricted to those who adhere to this religion. Mr. Justice Farmer, in this important decision, made it very clear that denominational institutions were entitled to the exemption on the same terms as those of a seculiar nature:

> It is practically universally recognized that in a Christian nation such as ours it is important to the public that there should be

schools not devoted entirely to the training of stimulating the brain or intellect, but that such teaching may also be supplemented by training and building up the moral character and better impulses of the heart. The State cannot, under the constitution, prefer one religious denomination or its teachings and require the public to contribute to its support, but it is not a violation of the constitution, either in spirit or letter, to authorize religious denominations to establish and conduct at their own expense, without cost to the public, schools for the development of moral improvement as well as the intellectual betterment of its students. Pursuing this policy in establishing institutions of learning, the State granted the right to religious denominations, without discrimination, to establish and maintain such institutions.[212]

Before leaving this discussion of the Illinois practice, two other points should be noted. Statutes, charters, etc. which attempt to exempt religious institutions from assessments for local improvements are generally unconstitutional.[213] Secondly, religious publishing societies are exempt from personal property taxes on their stocks so long as any profit realized is devoted to a religious purpose.[214]

Alabama-Maine

The last states to enter the Union during this period were Alabama and Maine. Alabama, although it had a number of previous constitutions,[215] did not make such a constitutional grant until 1875. Article 10, section 6 of the constitution of 1875 provided:

> Property of private corporations, associations, and individuals shall forever be taxed at the same rate: *Provided,* this section shall not apply to institutions or enterprises devoted exclusively to religion, education, or charitable purposes.[216]

In the constitution of 1901, this exemption was limited to lots of one acre in cities and towns, and five acres in the country.[217] Similar acreage limitations, it will be recalled, were required by the Kentucky constitution. Note also that the exemption once again is directed to the general end and "purposes," rather than the more restricted category "worship." The statutory exemption is framed in the language "public worship" but its coverage is broadened to include property owned by any religion, educational, or charitable organization.[218]

Like Illinois, the test applied to these types of exemptions in Alabama is the use to which it is put. In an opinion delivered in *Anniston Land Co. v. State of Alabama,*[219] the Court declared:

> . . . it is manifest that Section 91 of the constitution makes use of the property, irrespective of ownership, the test of the right of exemption from taxation. . . .
> If the framers . . . had intended to exempt all property belonging

to literary and charitable institutions from taxation, the language would have been different.[220]

The Court further stated that ownership was not evidence of *use*. Following the rule of construction handed down in *Anniston,* the Court has consistently denied any exemption to property owned by an exempt group which is rented out for commercial purposes, even though the rents and profits are used for a religious purpose.[221] Nor will property be split up for tax purposes into exempt and non-exempt portions. If the property is used for any other purpose, then apparently it will not be exempt.[222] It is not clear whether or not the doctrine of "incidental" use may be applied as in Illinois.

The constitution of Maine adopted in 1819 and amended as of 1955 does not provide a tax exemption. The exemption is permitted solely by statute. It excludes from taxation houses of worship and parsonages, the latter up to a limit of $6,000 with personal property exempted to the same extent.[223] Litigation in this area is almost non-existent. One case has held, however, that the exemption does not encompass property devoted to missionary work.[224] Schools, benevolent and charitable institutions, of course, are beneficiaries of various exemptions.[225]

States Admitted to the Union: 1820-1850

During the period of the next thirty years, eight new states became members of the Union. With a single exception—Wisconsin—all today constitutionally grant tax privileges to religious, educational, and charitable institutions.

Missouri

To qualify for an exemption under Missouri's constitution, property must be used exclusively for church, school, or charitable purposes.[226] Earlier judicial precedent indicates that Missouri required a strict adherence to this requirement. In a series of decisions involving a St. Louis Y.M.C.A. organization, the courts uniformly refused to grant any exemption when it devoted any of its property to a use not religious or benevolent. In 1914, all property of the organization was held taxable because fifteen per cent had been sub-let for commercial purposes, notwithstanding the fact that the rentals were used for religious purposes.[227] To avoid this result, the Y.M.C.A. decided to operate its own cafeterias, barber shops, and the like. In 1928 the court again found that the property was not being used exclusively for religious or charitable purposes and again held all property taxable.[228] In 1932, the Y.M.C.A. argued that although its property was not now being used for religious or charitable purposes, it was at least available for them. This was also held insufficient. It was not enough, according to the court, that the property "may be used" for religious purposes; it must *actually* be so used.[229] In all of these cases the rule of strict construction was consistently applied. The result was to destroy rather than promote the purposes for which the exemption was intended. The courts in Missouri recognized this gradually, and began to temper their attitude. A greater emphasis was placed on *reasonableness,* and in 1945 the Supreme Court of Missouri finally ruled that the exemption was construed much too strictly.[230] In overruling the previous Y.M.C.A. cases, the Court wrote that charitable (and religious) purposes now included:

> . . . all humanitarian activities, though rendered at cost or less, which are intended to improve the physical, mental and moral condition of the recipients, and make it less likely that they will become burdens on society. . . .[231]

The exemptions should be construed strictly, but not unreasonably.

It seems apparently well settled in Missouri that faculty residences on school grounds do not detract from the property's exclusive use as a school.[232] However, religious publishing houses and other similar enterprises are considered commercially competitive and are declared subject to taxation.[233]

Finally, although the exemption is framed in terms of "religious worship," an exemption is permitted for premises maintained as a residence (in St. Louis) for the use and occupancy of bishops of the Methodist Episcopal Church, who may from time to time be stationed there.[234]

Arkansas

Arkansas, like Missouri, felt no need to insert provisions exempting religious property in its earlier constitution.[235] Such a clause is not found in a constitution of this state until 1868. Article 10, Section 2 of that document provided mandatorily that "public school houses, houses used exclusively for public worship, institutions of purely public charity . . . shall *never* (emphasis added) be taxed." This clause was replaced by the more explicit, exhaustive language found in the present Arkansas constitution. Article 16, Section 5 reads thusly:

> The following property shall be exempt from taxation: . . . churches used as such, cemeteries used exclusively as such, school buildings and apparatus, libraries and grounds used exclusively for school purposes, and buildings and grounds and materials used exclusively for public charity.

Both of these clauses are mandatory. The exemptions may be changed only by amendment of the constitution.

The primary test for determining whether property is exempt or not is *use*. One authority is of the opinion that some degree of ownership is also necessary.[236] However, it has yet to be adjudged so. At any rate, ownership notwithstanding, the property must be *used* for an exempt purpose.

The interesting case of *Pulaski County v. First Baptist Church* (1908) [237] is illustrative. It involved a congregation which owned two adjoining lots. A church was erected upon one of the lots. On the other was a well for drinking water and an outhouse, both used by the worshippers. The court was of the opinion that the latter property was not *necessary* to the use of the church and denied an exemption. Chief Justice Hill thought the construction given the constitutional clause was too strict and not warranted by its purpose. He dissented:

> If the Constitution be taken literally, only the church-house would be exempt; but it has not been construed with such literalness, and should not be. It was not the mere walls and roof, but the place of the religious meeting that was exempted. The legislature meeting within less than ten years after the Constitution was framed [1875] placed that construction upon it by the enactment of [the statute of 1883.] If the Constitution be taken literally this act would be unconstitutional, for it exempts the grounds attached to the building necessary for the proper use and enjoyment of same . . . while the Constitution only exempts *eo nomine* the church. This was giving a reasonable interpretation to the constitutional exemption.[238]

Later courts agreed with the dissenter and in 1948 it was held that an entire twenty acre tract of land was exempt simply because a single church was located on a portion of it.[239]

Assuming then, that the property is *reasonably necessary* to the church or other exempt property, what kind of *use* must it be put to in order to qualify? According to one authority, it seems clear that property sub-let for a commercial purpose will not be exempt even though the profits are used for religious or charitable purposes.[240] A greater problem arises when the property is used for both exempt and non-exempt purposes. There are no decisions to guide us to an answer to this question in Arkansas, but it is likely that the courts today will apply the "primary purpose" test used by most of the other states. This is to say that if the non-exempt use is merely "incidental" to the primary use, the whole of the property will probably be exempt. Where the exempt use is only "incidental," none of the property will be exempt. Should the latter be the case, there is still no indication that the property would be divided for this purpose. This particular approach has the advantage of fairness and seems best suited to carrying out the purpose of the exemption, and would apply across the board to educational and charitable exemptions as well as to churches.

At a very early point, doubt was also expressed in this jurisdiction that the exemption was to encompass private and church-related schools as well as public schools. The Supreme Court of Arkansas in 1844 declared that the exemption applied to *all* schools regardless of their affiliation.[241] The question was never again raised.

Parsonages, as such, are not mentioned either in the constitution or statute and, no decisions were discovered involving them in Arkansas. However, from related decisions, it is apparent that they are presently exempt.[242] The constitution exempts "churches as such" and the statute says "houses of worship" with necessary surrounding property. We have seen from the experience of other states that the use of this restrictive language oftentimes has resulted in the exclusion of rectories and parsonages from the exemption. Since they appear to be exempt in Arkansas, it might not be incorrect to conclude that the exemption is being construed to mean for "religious purposes," giving it a greater flexibility.

Finally, as in most other states, there is no exemption of church and charitable property from assessment taxes.[243]

Michigan

From its earliest history, Michigan has constitutionally sanctioned the exemption of educational property. The legislators were exhorted to encourage "by all suitable means" the promotion of learning in all its forms.[244] Until 1908 the constitution made no reference to the exemption of property used for religious purposes. In the document adopted that year the legislature was only urged to "encourage" religion and morality as well as knowledge because of the feeling that they were necessary to good and successful government.[245]

Thus, at the present time, Michigan, by statute enacted in 1961 exempts "houses of worship" and parsonages owned by a religious society and used as such, as well as making similar provisions for charitable and educational institutions.[246] "Houses of worship" is not a flexible phrase and Michigan courts have rarely attempted to bend it. The exemption clearly does not embrace houses used for social activities or janitor's quarters.[247] Vacant lots upon which there is an intention to build are not exempt, nor are retreat houses and the like.[248] In one instance involving a retreat house, only the chapel and "stations of the Cross" were exempt.[249] Ownership in Michigan is not sufficient (probably not even evidence of) grounds for an exemption.[250] *Use* is practically the only criterion.

Parsonages, first exempted in 1869, are still exempt today.[251] It is very important, however, that they be used *only* as parsonages. That is, they must be occupied by a priest or minister on a full time basis.[252] None of these institutions are exempt from local assessments of any kind.[253]

In a new constitution effective on January 1, 1964, a change has been introduced. Replacing the general language which has served as the past authority for these exemptions is a new, more explicit clause.[254] It says that all property owned and occupied by non-profit religious or educational organizations and used exclusively for religious or educational purposes shall be exempt; making the exemption mandatory where previously it was only discretionary.   Secondly, it appears to clear up the ambiguity regarding the exemption of lots upon which churches are constructed.   Thirdly, it also seems to indicate that ownership and occupancy must coincide.   In general, it appears that this clause is intended to liberalize the exemption and may result in the exemption of property of religious organizations which today do not enjoy that status.   This conjecture is based on the use of the broader term "purposes."

Florida

In Florida the first constitutional exemption was adopted in 1868.[255] The effect of the clause was to give the legislature general authority to exempt from taxation the property of all religious as well as all educational institutions.   This provision is unchanged in the present constitution adopted in 1885.   Article 9, Section 1 presently provides that all property must be taxed at a uniform rate, except that "as may be exempt by law for . . . educational . . . religious or charitable purposes."[256]

The earlier constitution of 1868 had a companion clause which provided that all corporate property be taxed *except* the property of religious corporations.[257] This clause was amended in 1875,[258] and Article 16, Section 16 now provides that all corporate property shall be taxed "unless such property be held and used exclusively for religious . . . educational . . . or charitable purposes."[259] This section applies only to institutions which are incorporated.   Unincorporated institutions must qualify under Article 9, Section 1.

The two sections are alike in some respects, dissimilar in others. Primarily, it should be noted the former clause is permissive,[260] in that it requires action on the part of the legislature, while the latter is self-operative.[261]   Secondly, both clauses employ the term "purposes" indicating that the framers, at least, desired the greatest flexibility in granting the immunity.   In the first clause, however, the legislature has by statute limited the exemption to places where worship *actually* takes place.[262]   Thirdly, the clause exempting corporate property requires that it be used "exclusively" for religious or other purposes, while the general clause omits that qualifying term.   Constitutionally at least, the property of incorporated religious institutions even though used partly for other purposes could still be exempt under this provision.

The exemptions are alike in that to qualify under either the property must in fact be *owned* and *used* for religious purposes.[263]   It will be recalled that in a number of the other states, the test was more often *use* than *ownership*.   In Florida, neither alone is sufficient.

The Constitution appears to favor the incorporated institutions over those not incorporated.[264] Conjecture is that perhaps the state is willing to permit a larger bounty to these institutions in return for a greater degree of control over them.

Parsonages are exempt under one or the other of these provisions depending, of course, on whether or not they are incorporated. This has been extended to include homes for retired ministers or other religious.[265]

Texas

From 1848 to 1876, Texas constitutions simply gave the legislative bodies carte blanche to exempt whatever property they thought "proper to except" with no mention of religion.[266] In 1876 Texas removed most of the legislature's discretion in this field by inserting a mandatory and extensively worded exemption clause within its present constitutional framework. Article 8, section 2 provides for exemption of:

> actual places [of] religious worship, also any property owned by a church or by a strictly religious society for the exclusive use as a dwelling place for the ministry of such church or religious society, and which yields no revenue whatever for such church or religious society, . . . [limited to one acre] . . . all buildings . . . and necessary furniture of all schools and property used exclusively and reasonably necessary in conducting any association engaged in promoting the religious . . . development . . . ; also the endowment funds of such institutions of learning and religion not used with a view to profit. . . .[267]

The phrase "actual places of religious worship" was narrowly construed and eliminated practically everything but the church building and the lot on which it stood. Parsonages and rectories clearly were not exempt.[268] This situation was neither satisfactory nor in keeping with the overall object of the exemption, and eventually the clause was amended in 1928 to specifically include such residences.[269] They are now exempt provided they are *owned* by a religious society as well as *used* for their intended purposes;[270] ownership must be coincidental with use. On the other hand, in recent times it is constitutionally proper to exempt church yards if their use was in some way *connected* with church activities.[271] In spite of this, however, a building used for preparing religious broadcasts was denied exemption because it was not a place of "actual religious worship."[272]

An earlier problem arose in Texas with regard to Y.M.C.A.'s and other similar service organizations. In 1913, the Texas legislature passed a statute exempting the property of such organizations.[273] In 1926, this statute was held unconstitutional.[274] The court ruled that under the constitution, the legislature could exempt only "places of actual worship" and that Y.M.C.A.'s were not such places. In 1928, Article 8, section 2 of the Constitution was amended to permit the exemption.[275] This was accomplished by language to the effect that "property used exclusively and reasonably necessary in conducting any association engaged in promoting . . . religious . . . development" was now exempt.

The Texas legislature is not at liberty to alter or repeal the exemption granted in the constitution, but it may set the terms upon which it will be granted or denied. With regard to the Y.M.C.A. organizations, the Texas lawmakers have determined that the language of the constitution exempting their property means that they must *all* provide religious, educational *and* physical development simultaneously.[276]

The constitution also exempts "all buildings and necessary furniture of all schools." A question soon arose as to the scope of this language, especially as regards denominational schools. This was the issue in the important case of *Cassiano v. Ursuline Academy*.[277] *Cassiano* involved an attempt by the tax collector to sell for non-payment of taxes the property of a girls academy operated by a group of nuns. The tax collector contended that the particular property sought to be sold did not fall within the constitutional exemption because it did not *directly* contribute to the operation of the school. The Supreme Court of Texas rejected the contention. The word "building," said the Court, "has its broader signification consonant with the purpose of the exemption and the settled policy of the state." Even though it was not directly involved in the operation of the school, the Court agreed with the defendants that the property in question was "necessary and used for the proper and economical conduct of the school." "Authority is not wanting," concluded the court, "to extend the exemption to land much less directly employed to forward the interest of the school."[278] The additional argument was made that perhaps a different result should have been achieved since it was a private school which was involved. In blunt fashion, the court answered that there were no grounds to warrant any inference that the framers of the constitution, in using the word "building" intended any discrimination against private schools. Despite the liberality which characterized the holding in this case, the same court a few short years later refused to extend the exemption to college farm property employed to provide food for the students.[279]

One final point regarding exempt property—it must be at the same time *owned* and *used* by the institution in order to qualify for the exemption under either the constitution or statute.[280]

Iowa

Iowa's initial constitution contained no clause exempting church and other property.[281] However, the present document, adopted in 1857, does so provide.[282] The constitution states that the "General Assembly shall encourage by all suitable means, intellectual, moral, scientific . . . pursuits." A short time after the adoption of this clause, the legislature responded with a statute exempting from general taxation all property of literary institutions, places of worship, and the dwellings of clergymen, provided the properties are used *solely* for their appropriate objects.[283] In 1877, this statute was attacked as being unconstitutional on the ground that it violated the ban on the use of public funds in aid of religion. The Supreme Court of Iowa held in *Griswold College v. State of Iowa* that the statute did not conflict with the constitution and permitted the exemption.[284] Said the court:

> The argument is, that exemption from taxation of church property is the same thing as compelling contribution to churches to the extent of the exemption. We think the constitutional prohibition extends to the levying of tithes, taxes, or other rates for church purposes, and that it does not include the exemption from taxation of such church property as the legislature may think proper.[285]

The issue has not been raised since that decision.

In order for property to be exempt, it must be used *solely* for its *appropriate* object. The *Griswold* case also stands for the proposition that the proper test of *use* is whether it is "appropriate to effectuate the objects of the institution" and *not* whether it is actually necessary. In *Griswold,* the argument arose over whether a faculty residence built and owned by a college, and a parsonage owned by a religious society, should be exempt under this statute since they were "not devoted solely to the object of the institutions." The Court refused to accept the contention, and commented thus:

> It seems to us that it is not a question as to whether the land and buildings are used solely for literary or religious purposes. . . . . We do not believe that the statute is susceptible of any such narrow and restricted construction.[286]

One justice, however, dissented in these words:

> In my judgment if the property is owned and used for the purpose and object of paying or reducing salaries, the same is used for pecuniary profit.[287]

The statute precludes any exemption to property used in any way for pecuniary profit without regard as to how the profits themselves are employed. The only test, then, is *use.*[288]

Wisconsin

In Wisconsin the exemption of church property is by statute only.[289] The first exemption law was passed back in 1849.[290] Its modern counterpart specifically exempts the property of churches, religious, benevolent, and educational societies used by them for the appropriate purposes for which they exist. In 1955, the statute was amended to require that the property also be *owned* as well as *used* by the exempt institutions.[291]   In 1949, the same privilege was extended to parsonages,[292] and in 1955 to the residences maintained for members of religious orders and communities and ordained teachers when permanently occupied by them.[293] The latter properties are not required to be contiguous to the institution which they serve. Additional statutes provide a similar exemption from state income and inheritance taxes.[294]

The statutes have never been judicially attacked as being in derogation of the constitutional prohibition banning aid to religion. However, in a recent decision dealing with the topic of bus transportation there is dicta indicating that such exemptions would be found proper. The Court stated in delivering its opinion that the exemption of religious organizations or parochial school property does not "transcend the religious classification prohibition in the constitution."[295]   Finally, Y.M.C.A. and Y.W.C.A. organizations and Bible Camps are specifically exempted from taxation under Wisconsin law.[296]

The California Experience

In the great majority of states, the practice of exempting the property of churches and other institutions from taxation, at least in the past, has rarely become a major controversy. Most of the judicial decisions in this area deal mainly with the construction of the language in which the clause or statute is drafted. Where courts have been urged to outlaw the practice because it violates the principle of no-establishment, it has been a rare instance when they actually did so. However, in one respect —the exemption of private and church-related schools—California once represented the minority position.

California's initial constitution was drafted without any clause exempting religious, charitable, or educational property.[297] Instead, exemption of such property was accomplished by statute alone. In 1879, a new constitution was adopted. One clause in that constitution directed that "the legislature shall encourage by all suitable means the promotion of intellectual, scientific, moral, and agricultural improvement,[298] and is part of the general article dealing with education. Under article 13, section 1 of the same constitution, entitled "Revenue and Taxation," an exemption is given for "property used exclusively for public schools."[299] As late as 1876, however, there was still no constitutional provision for the exemption of church property; nor was there *any* exemption for the property of private and church-related schools. Apparently the only learning and morality the framers were willing to encourage was the kind taught in the public schools. It was another quarter century before the constitution was amended at all in this regard.

In 1900 an amendment to Article 13, section 1 (Title 2, Section 1½) was adopted which exempted "all buildings" and that amount of real property necessary for the "convenient use and occupation" of the buildings when used "solely and exclusively for religious worship." [300]   The reader will appreciate at a glance the rather restrictive nature of the exemption. Its impact is to deny any exemption to property which may be serving religion in a multitude of ways, by confining its coverage to buildings (and the land upon which they are situated) which are used only for worship.

In 1944 the exemption clause was again amended, introducing changes which had a significant effect.[301] In place of the term "building" was substituted the term "property." Instead of confining the exemption to property used for "religious worship," the clause exempted property when it was used "exclusively for religious . . . purposes." The effect of these changes was to increase the kinds of property which could be free from taxation. In addition, the constitutional exemption was extended to cover the various funds and foundations established to support the exempt organizations.[302] Another amendment passed in 1952 extended the exemption to buildings in the course of construction and the equipment they housed.[303] Finally in 1956, the clause was extended one step further to exempt property of churches utilized for the parking of worshippers' automobiles.[304]

The California courts have said a good deal regarding the constitutional tax exemption to the schools and churches. In affirming the exemption of a retreat house, including the portions used by the priests and brothers as residences, the California Supreme Court clearly acknowledged that the rule of strict construction was to be applied to the exemptions.[305] Nonetheless, it also cautioned that "adherence to this rule does not require so rigid and narrow an interpretation of the exempting language as to defeat the apparent design of the lawmakers."[306] On another occasion the Court said it would not "disturb" such an exemption so long as it has a "reasonable basis." [307] At still another time: "Our interpretation of the tax exemption must be as broad as is reasonably necessary to uphold it."[308] Accordingly, the Supreme Court of California has enunciated the general test that the exemption of property "used exclusively for religious . . . purposes" should be held to include *any* property of the religious or charitable entity which is used exclusively for *any* facility which is *incidental* to and reasonably necessary for the accomplishment of religious or charitable *purposes*. The whole of the integrated activities must be examined in determining the tax status of property.[309]

Examples of property to which the exemption has been permitted in California include, among others, student parking lots at schools, housing provided by schools to faculty members, and residences for married students and their families.[310] In addition, missionary rest homes have been exempt,[311] as have retreat houses,[312] and the property of humanitarian societies.[313] Examples of types of property to which the exemption has been denied under this constitutional clause include quantities of religious literature stored in tax exempt buildings;[314] and a school of nursing conducted incident to a hospital plant.[315] In the past both the legislatures and the courts in California have dealt favorably with tax exemptions benefiting churches and charitable groups. All indications are that they will do so in the future. However, with regard to similar benefits for private and church-related *schools* California's record was otherwise.

Throughout the years California has been quite liberal in extending tax exemption privileges to churches and religious organizations. It has, however, acted in quite the reverse manner regarding the same status for private schools. The constitution of 1879 gave the legislature the power generally to exempt from taxation institutions devoted to the "advancement of science."[316] This was interpreted by that body as intended to apply to *public* institutions of learning. In 1894 this interpretation was sanctioned by amendment, which, by its specific terms, only exempted school property which was "used exclusively for *public schools*." [317] Thus, before 1901 the property of all private institutions of learning in California was taxed.

The first institution to break through the barrier separating public and private schools in this regard was Stanford University. In 1901, the property of the university was declared exempt by a special act of the legislature.[318] Fourteen years later the property of *all* institutions of *higher* learning was removed from the tax rolls. This is as far as the legislature went. Until 1951, the property of all private primary and secondary schools continued to be taxed.

In 1951, the California state legislature amended the state Revenue and Taxation Code to exempt "[p]roperty used exclusively for school purposes of less than college grade." [319] In 1944, when the lawmakers had enacted this section of the Code,[320] they specifically provided that an exemption was *not* to be given to any schools "of less than college grade." [321] Since the public schools were already exempt under the Constitution, this was directed only toward the private schools. The purpose of the 1951 amendment to this section, then, was to put the private schools on a par with the public schools. Although the measure met with the unanimous approval of the legislators and was agreeably signed by the Governor,[322] the issue was by no means eliminated.

After passage of the measure, the forces opposed countered swiftly. During the 1952 interim elections, they succeeded in placing the measure before the electorate on a referendum ballot.[323] The people of the state were urged to ratify a proposition designed to prohibit the exemption of private and church-related school property from taxation by means of an amendment to the constitution. The authors of this extreme measure conducted a vigorous, well-run, and well financed campaign. Their appeal was mainly to bigotry. The campaign was characterized by extremely vicious attacks directed primarily at the Catholic Church as operator of the largest private school system in the state and the faith having the most to gain from the defeat of the proposition. The church and its hierarchy were denounced in the most spurious terms and no stone was left unturned to discredit both. Other churches and groups were also maliciously maligned. Bitter hatreds and prejudices long since banished from the political scene were dredged up, dusted off, and paraded before the people of the state. The reaction was disgust, and many citizens who might have voted for the proposition registered this disgust by joining with the great majority in defeating the measure by the sound plurality of 75,000 votes.[324]

The opposition forces then went into the court. A citizen, Alfred J. Lundberg, commenced a class suit in California Superior Court, alleging that the exemption violated both the state and federal constitutions. The efforts of this faction were temporarily rewarded by a favorable ruling on their position. The decision, however, was not unanimous. Two justices agreed that the statute violated the state constitution, but declined to pass on the federal question. A third justice dissented on the ground that neither constitution was violated.

In 1956 this decision was appealed to the California Supreme Court. The Supreme Court reversed by a four to three vote.[325] The justices ruled that the statute was clearly authorized by the 1944 amendment to the exemption clause of the constitution; that it violated no other provision; and at least as applied to schools, did no evil to the Federal Constitution. Rehearing was denied.

Mr. Lundberg died shortly after the denial of the rehearing and a Mr. Heisey was substituted as party plaintiff. He was purportedly a member of the class represented by Mr. Lundberg. Appeal was made to the Supreme Court of the United States that same year. It was dismissed for want of any "Federal question" [326] and the exemption remained valid.

In 1958 an attempt was again made to remove the exemption by an amendment to the constitution. The proposed amendment was once again put to a referendum vote.[327] The character of the campaign differed from the previous campaign in 1962 only in its intensity and degree of viciousness.[328] The attack upon the Catholic Church and other allied groups reached such proportions that the Vice-President of the United States, Mr. Nixon, was moved to denounce the tactics of the these forces as bigotry at its worst."[329] The people of California registered their disapproval of this strategy of hate at the polls. This time the measure was defeated by an even larger plurality than before.

The appeal of those favoring the exemption of private school property had been to common justice, the appeal of those against to bigotry and injustice. In accepting the wisdom of the former, the electorate clearly rejected the unreasonableness of the latter.

States Admitted to the Union: 1850-1875

During the period 1850-1875 seven additional states became members of the Union. All seven have adopted constitutions with clauses either exempting the property of religious, educational, and charitable institutions from taxation or authorizing the legislatures to do so. Three of these states—Minnesota, Colorado, and Kansas are in the former group. The others—West Virginia, Nevada, Oregon and Nebraska—make up the latter category. It is interesting to observe that at least five of the seven states grant the exemption in terms of religious "purpose" rather than restricting it to building or property used for "worship" alone. Minnesota and Colorado are the exceptions.

Colorado

In its constitution, Colorado exempts all real and personal property "used solely and exclusively for religious worship, for schools or for strictly charitable purposes . . . unless otherwise provided by law." [330] This clause is, in some respects, unique and merits some discussion. Note that in its literal terms, the scope of the clause is quite narrow. Taken literally it only exempts property used regularly for worship. It is limited also to school buildings, presmably only when they are used regularly as such. Charitable "purposes" must be "strictly" so. Nothing is said about property which may be "convenient or necessary" to the occupancy of the schools or churches, or of property used for religious activity other than purely worship. This rather inflexible clause would seem to eliminate the possibility of an exemption for such property. The exemption statute is of little help as it simply reaffirms the constitutional exemption. [331] The legislature has the power to alter or repeal the exemption but it has not as yet felt any need to do so.

Since the exemption language of this constitutional clause and its accompanying statute is so restrictive, it is not at all surprising that the Supreme Court of Colorado has tended to be lenient in its interpretation. In 1901 a controversy arose regarding the tax status of a theological school operated by the Episcopal Diocese of Colorado. [332] The school building had been devised to the diocese on the following terms: the bishop of the Diocese should head the school; he should reside in the building with his family, paying no rent; and he should discharge his diocesan duties from the school. No students lived at the school. Further, the entirety of the building was considered to be "family" quarters. It was contended that the exemption of the school was unconstitutional. The Supreme Court of Colorado held the exemption proper. Said the justices:

> The fundamental object of the law was to exempt property used
> for school purposes from taxation. To carry out this design, the
> uses permissible must necessarily embrace all which are proper and
> appropriate to effect the objects of the institution claiming the
> benefits of the exemption.[333]

The bishop's use of the school as a residence, said the Court, was
"incidental" to his duties as a bishop, but the Court remarked that it
was "closely allied with his duties as an instructor." The Court outlined the test it would apply in all future tax exemption cases under this
section of the constitution accordingly:

> In determining these questions it must be borne in mind that
> whether in any given case property is or is not exempt, must be
> determined by considering all of the facts and circumstances, and
> the intentions and purposes of those in charge of the institution
> to which the property belongs respecting the use and occupation
> of such property.[334]

Both this rule of construction and this test of the exemption formed the
basis for subsequent decisions in this area.

Analogous language is found in another important decision handed
down thirty-two years later (1933).[335] The particular issue here was
whether property, used to raise livestock, and located adjacent to the
campus of a non-sectarian college operated by a religious organization,
was exempt from taxation where the products of the farm were consumed
by the students, although a portion of them were also sold commercially.
In upholding the exemption, the Court said:

> Applying the same broad, liberal rule of construction adopted by
> the court in cases of this character, we conclude that the property
> in question is exempt. To confine the exemption to the building
> and the campus would seriously cripple the institution in
> carrying out its laudable purpose. The entire property constitutes
> a unit. It is reasonably necessary to effect the objects of the
> institution, and it is used solely for that purpose.[336]

Both the above instances involved schools. Nonetheless, it is apparent
that the rule was also intended to apply to other types of property
in cases arising under this clause.

In 1936 another case arose under this clause involving church property.[337] The First Baptist Church of Denver had purchased property for
a new church. Demolition and preparation of the land for construction
had just begun when the depression caused the work to be halted. The
property was taxed and the church instituted an action to have it
declared exempt. In declaring the property exempt, the Court reviewed
its earlier decisions:

The statute with reference to exemptions is practically in the same words as the constitutional provision. It has not been materially changed over a course of many years, from which fact it seems logical to conclude that the people of the state have approved the liberal rule of construction adopted by the courts; otherwise they would have taken action through the legislature to further limit the conditions under which property of religious, charitable and educational institutions may be exempt.[338]

The application in this instance of the liberal rule of construction probably surprised no one. However, it is unlikely that either side was prepared for the bounteous fashion in which the Court applied the test in this case. Said the Court:

> The rule of construction . . . is substantially this: When an admittedly charitable institution undertakes in good faith to extend its plant and facilities for charitable work and evidences this fact by the expenditure of money and the doing of work as part of a program looking toward the erection of a building to be used when completed for charitable purposes, this is within the spirit of the constitutional and statutory tax exemption provisions. . . . In effect we held that the requirements of the Constitution and statutes are met if there is a bonafide continuing intention to construct a building to be devoted to the specified uses, evidenced by work and the expediture of money toward that end.[339]

Further:

> The church organization having no objectives other than religious, charitable and educational, under the rule we have applied (above) is entitled to the benefit of the presumption that when the building is completed it will be used exclusively for religious purposes.[340]

The effect of this language is certainly far-reaching. Unfortunately, there are no later decisions to indicate which way the court might go in the future. It is likely that the hardship factor had a considerable influence on the outcome. On the other hand, it must be pointed out that the same result could have been accomplished without the enunciation of such a broad rule.

Minnesota

The Constitution of Minnesota exempts from taxation "all churches, church property and houses of worship" as well as "academies, colleges, universities, and all seminaries of learning."[341] The wording of the present constitutional clause dates from the adoption of an amendment in 1906. Prior to the amendment the constitution exempted "all churches, church property *used for religious purposes* and houses of worship."[342] While this latter clause was very broad with reference to the exemption for institutions of learning, it was more restrictive with regard to some properties of the church. For example, faculty residences of schools and colleges were generally exempt [343] while parsonages and rectories were not.[344] An exemption for the latter was usually denied on the ground that such property was used for a *secular* rather than a religious purpose.

By the amendment, this prohibtion has been eradicated. The phrase "used for religious purposes" was eliminated and, according to the Minnesota Court, "the intent undoubtedly was to extend the benefits of tax exemption to a larger classification of church property." [345] The exemption was now made as broad as that regarding colleges and other institutions of learning as well as hospitals and charitable institutions.[346] At present, parsonages are exempt as well as other types of semi-religious property.[347]

In Minnesota, even before its organization as a territory, there has always been a policy of the state to assist as much as is possible the practice of religion and the maintenance of schools. This policy is manifest in both state and territorial legislation and judicial decisions. It was in this historic light that the Supreme Court of Minnesota declared:

> In construing the section of the Constitution under consideration, the spirit of the times when it was adopted, as shown by the attitude of the territorial legislature and the people, should be infused into it, and reasons of practicability and effectiveness, so far as consistent with the usual canons of construction, applied in determining its purpose and meaning.[348]

The canon of construction applicable to a tax exemption, of course, is that it be strictly construed against the one claiming the exemption. However, the court in Minnesota has repeatedly shown a keen awareness of the dangers of too literal an enforcement of this maxim. Queried one Court:

> [S]hould strict rules of construction be applied to the tax exemption of private institutions doing the very work the state deems so imperative, but wherein it realizes that with all its efforts the desired measure of success has not been fully achieved? We think not.[349]

In a more recent decision,[350] the Minnesota Supreme Court set forth in precise language the way in which exemptions of this type should be approached. The Court first characterized the exemption as one given "in the interest of the public welfare" and not just to a church building or a parsonage. It was given, according to the Court, "to the church as a living institution for the advancement of religion or a way of life." Thus:

> Although it is a general rule that constitutional provisions exempting property from taxation are to be strictly construed, such provisions, though not subject to extension by construction or implication,

are to be given a reasonable, natural and practical interpretation to effectuate the purpose for which the exemption is granted.[351] At the time this rule was enunciated the *only* test was the *use* to which the property was devoted.[352] It was not necessary that the organization claiming the exemption also be the owner. In 1955, however, the Attorney General ruled that from that date there had to be a *concurrence of use and ownership* in order for the property to be exempt.[353]

The exemption statute[354] is framed in the same terms as the constitutional clause, which is itself self-executing.[355] The statute merely reflects the constitutional exemption. There is no exemption under either the constitution or statute from special assessment taxes for local improvement.[356] Minnesota follows the majority of states in this respect.

Oregon, Nevada, West Virginia

The constitutions of Oregon, Nevada, and West Virginia all authorize the immunity of church, charitable, and educational property from taxation.[357] The clauses, however, are not self operative. Instead, the exemption of such property requires a separate legislative enactment.

The exemption statutes in these three states do not differ radically.[358] All three generally exempt churches, chapels, schools, property of charitable institutions, along with the land necessary to their use and occupation. In Oregon and Nevada the test of the exemption is both use *and* ownership. The test in West Virginia is "purposes",[359] but it is unclear whether the "use" or "purpose" must be coincidental to ownership. From the available precedent, the tax collector in West Virginia seems only to be concerned with the use of the property.

Probably none of these states will deny an exemption to property which is occasionally used for something other than a pure religious, educational or charitable purpose. A portion of the Nevada statute nevertheless does provide that if property is used exclusively *or in part,* for any other purpose, and a rent or *other consideration* is given, then the property will not be exempt.[360] There are no discoverable decisions interpreting this phrase, but it is unlikely that it would be interpreted to preclude an exemption for church property which is used "incidentally" for a non-religious or charitable purpose, so long as it is not leased or rented to any third parties.

Nevada and West Virginia statutes expressly exempt parsonages and rectories. When it was contended in West Virginia that the exemption violated the constitutional ban against state aid to religion, the State Supreme Court disagreed. Use of such property as a parsonage, said the court, fell clearly within the meaning of "religious purposes."[361] Although not expressly mentioned, such exemptions are most probably within the scope of Oregon's exemption statute which, in addition to "houses of public worship" liberally exempts buildings used for recreation or entertainment by religious organizations. It further extends its coverage to include parking lots used regularly by those in attendance at the exempt buildings.

Finally, in Oregon it was contended that the grant of an exemption to a hospital run by nuns violated a number of constitutional bans upon state aid to or interference with religion. The Supreme Court of Oregon found that the hospital fell within the meaning of the constitutional clause and exemption statute, and that it was fully compatible with the rest of the constitution.[362]

Nebraska

Nebraska exempts church property in the same manner as those states just discussed.[363] The only test in Nebraska is *use*.[364] Ownership is not relevant except perhaps as evidence of the use. In this connection the Nebraska High Court, upholding an exemption for a school operated by the Seventh Day Adventist Church, pointed out that

> [I]t [the school] is not sectarian but is a religious school . . . . The Academy is an accredited school and it graduates students who meet its requirements . . . .

And:

> This state is committed to the doctrine that in determining whether or not property is within a tax exemption provision, the *use* of the property and not the status or character of the owner of the property controls.[365]

Like the great majority of states this *use must be exclusive*. The exclusiveness, however, is not destroyed by an incidental non-religious use of the property.[366] The property may be divided for purposes of the exemption.[367] In the event of a non-exclusive use, the entire property does not suffer the loss of the exemption—only the portion used for other purposes.

In a case involving the Society of the Scottish Rite, it was urged that since no recognized religion was preached by the society nor practiced by any of the members, the society's property was not exempt. The Nebraska Supreme Court disdained such formal requirements:

> [N]either the profession of a sectarian creed, nor the formal dedication or occupation of property to promote the objects and purposes of a faith thus expressed, is an essential element of a 'religious use' nor a necessary prerequisite to and of an 'exclusive religious purpose'.[368]

No exemption is permitted from special assessments.[369]

Kansas

The constitution of Kansas exempts from taxation "all property used exclusively for . . . religious . . . purposes."[370] Previous constitutions had set a limit on the amount of property which a religious institution could exempt. The present constitution sets no limit.[371] However, the present exemption *statute* restricts the amount of exempt church property to ten acres and parsonage property to one half acre.[372]

Prior to the adoption of the present constitution, the exemption was restricted to "houses of public worship" and "school houses".[373] Although the present constitution exempts in broad terms of "religious purposes", its scope is narrowed by the statute. The statute exempts parsonages, but the extension of the exemption to the residence of the Episcopal Bishop was held to be improper.[374] The test of the exemption statute in Kansas is use and not mere ownership.[375] Noteworthy also is a separate statute which specifically exempts the property of denominational schools and colleges.[376] Most states exempt such property under their general exemption statute. Finally, it has been held in Kansas that stores of religious materials and supplies are not immune from payment thereon of personal property taxes.[377]

States Admitted to Union: 1875-1900

Of the states which achieved their statehood during the last twenty-five years of the nineteenth century, a number made constitutional provision for the exemption of religious, educational, and charitable property from taxation. However, Washington and Idaho prefer to grant this immunity solely by statute. In general, all allow the exemption of church buildings, school property, and the property of charitable institutions. The exemptions differ only in the amount of property which a particular organization may hold exempt.

Washington, Idaho

Both Washington and Idaho by statute alone exempt school and church buildings as well as those housing charitable institutions.[378] In Washington, land adjacent to exempt structures is itself exempt up to five acres provided a great majority of it is utilized in the same manner.[379] Both states expressly exempt parsonages and rectories. Idaho, in addition, also exempts halls and buildings used by the organizations for recreational and social purposes. The test in Idaho apparently is *ownership* as well as *exclusive use*. Although there are no discoverable decisions indicating this, the statute itself exempts property "belonging" to any religious corporation. In Washington the only test is "exclusive use."[380]

North Dakota

North Dakota's Constitution, adopted in 1889, provides that property "used exclusively for school, religious, cemetery, charitable . . . purposes is exempt.[381] This clause is self-executing, and the exemption is mandatory. Although the clause exempts for "religious purposes," this has been interpreted by the legislature to mean "religious worship."[382]   The statute further limits the amount of surrounding property which may be exempt, along with the building, to two acres.   Parsonages are exempt as well as the residences of bishops and other church dignitaries.[383]   All of the personal property of any of these exempt organizations is also expressly exempted from taxation.   In North Dakota it seems that the property must be *owned* as well as *used exclusively* for an exempt purpose in order to qualify for exempt status.   There are no decisions on this point involving religious institutions or schools, but in one case involving a purely charitable institution the court cited *ownership* as determinative of the exemption.[384]

South Dakota

South Dakota constitutionally exempts church property in language closely resembling that of its sister state directly to the north.   However, unlike North Dakota's clause, it is not self-executing or mandatory, but merely *authorizes* the state legislature to exempt property "used exclusively for . . . school, religious, . . . and charitable purposes."[385]   Pursuant to this authorization, the legislature has exempted "all property belonging to any charitable, benevolent, or religious society and used exclusively for [these] purposes."[386]   The statute retains the use of the general term "purposes", but adds the requirement that the property also "belong" to the institution.   Except on this point, the scope of the statute is the same as the constitutional clause.   The legislature also took pains to specify that the phrase "charitable society" as it is used in the statute includes the charitable operations of any church, school, or lodge.[387]

There exists some question as to precisely what constitutes the actual test of the exemption in this jurisdiction.   Consider this language extracted from an opinion handed down by the Supreme Court of South Dakota in 1925:

> The case has been given most careful and thorough consideration . . . and we are of the opinion that under our present constitution and existing statute all property that is owned by religious, educational, or charitable or benevolent societies *regardless of its character, extent, location or the purposes for which it is used, and all property, regardless of its character or extent, that is used exclusively* for charitable, benevolent, religious or educational purposes, is exempt from taxation.[388]

According to this interpretation, it might be fairly said that *ownership* alone of property by a religious or charitable organzation would be sufficient to declare it exempt.   However, in a later decision it was held that at least as regards an exemption for property of religious institutions "the *purpose* of the *use* . . . controls."[389]

In construing these provisions, the North Dakota Supreme Court has to a consderable degree relaxed the traditional rule of strict construction. Consider this dicta from a case decided in 1921:

> We question whether the rule of strict construction should have any place in determining the intention of those who framed and who adopted those provisions of our Constitution relating to exemptions of property used for religious or educational purposes; it would almost seem to us that . . . it might well be held that a liberal rather than a strict construction would be applied to our constitutional and statutory provisions in relation to exemption from taxation of property used for school and religious purposes.[390]

Most recently, the same court adopted the view that "constitutional and statutory provisions are to be given a reasonable, natural and practical construction to effectuate the purpose for which an exemption is created."[391] As in the great majority of states, South Dakota refuses to have what they deem to be a desirable public policy undermined by inflexibly worded provisions or stringent rules of judicial construction.

Montana

In Montana the constitution exempts "places of actual worship", and "places of purely public charity".[392] The clause is permissive only; however, the statute directly reflects its wording.[393] The particular wording of clause and statute requires that a church or other religious meeting or charity hall must be presently used, and precludes any exemption for buildings or other property which is acquired, but not as yet put into use.[394]

Wyoming, Utah

The Wyoming constitution mandatorily exempts "lots with buildings thereon used exclusively for religious worship. . . ."[395] Utah's clause is identical.[396] The exemption statutes of both states mirror the constitutional clauses.[397] Neither state has had much judicial experience with such exemptions. It was ruled in Utah, however, that if part of the property should be used for some other purpose, the whole of the exemption is not lost. Only that portion so used is liable to the tax.[398]

States Admitted Since 1900

All but one of the states which have come into the union since the turn of the century provide for the exemption of church and school property in their constitutions. The exception is Hawaii which grants the exemption only by statute. Since the history of statehood for each is relatively short—a few years for Alaska and Hawaii—there is little in the way of judicial precedent in this area. The exemptions do not differ radically from those of a great number of other states. For these reasons, this particular group of states can be dealt with briefly.

Hawaii

Hawaii, as was already mentioned, exempts only by statute.[399] The statute presently on the books is perhaps the most extensive of all the states. The main exemption provision is broken down into no less than sixty-nine sub-items. Generally, it exempts "all non-profit private schools and the property of religious societies when used for religious, educational, hospital, community . . . or character building purposes". It then proceeds to specify precisely the organizations to be exempted. These include parsonages, YMCA's and numerous private schools as well as other types of institutions too numerous to mention. The Hawaiian reports reveal, however, no important litigation of these exemptions in the last thirty-five years.

Oklahoma, New Mexico, Arizona, Alaska

The four remaining states of Oklahoma, New Mexico, Arizona and Alaska mandatorily provide similar exemptions in their respective constitutions. In Oklahoma both constitutional clause and exemption statute exempt property "used for religious, etc. purposes." [400] One unique feature of the Oklahoma tax exemption statute is worthy of note. Most states provide that no exemption shall be given if any of the property is not used for an exempt purpose regardless of how the proceeds are used. In Oklahoma, however, such an institution may exempt even revenue producing property up to a limit of twenty-five hundred dollars. Otherwise, the sole test of the exemption in Oklahoma is use.[401] Oklahoma has also permitted an exemption to property upon which there is a "bonafide" intent to build—simply a matter of proof.

New Mexico simply exempts "all church property".[402] Such property, however, must be used for church purposes. If it is used to raise revenue it is taxable even though the revenue is devoted to church purposes.[403] Further, property acquired by a church upon which there is only an intent to build in the future is not exempt.[404]

The Arizona constitution exempts "all property of religious associations or institutions not used or held for profit." [405] The statute, however, exempts churches and other buildings "used for religious worship." [406] The statute has considerably narrowed the scope of the constitutional clause Shortly after this constitution was adopted the question arose as to whether the exemption given for educational institutions included private schools.[407] The court promptly held that they were indeed covered. Said Udall, J.:

> But it is also true that it has always been the policy of this State to encourage the establishment of private educational institutions.

And the principle of strict construction of exempting statutes should not be used to subvert that policy.[408]

The fact that the students paid tuition was, according to the Justice, contemplated by the legislators. Secondly, he declared that no restriction was intended simply because some of the students came from substantial income families or, for that matter, out-of-state.

Finally, Alaska's exemption provisions resemble in detail those just discussed.[409] There is perhaps only one significant difference in the clause itself. Unlike the others, it specifically provides that all of the property used exclusively for religious purposes *or any* portion *of it* is exempt. This phrase evidences a clear intention on the part of the framers to permit property to be divided for exemption purposes.

Conclusion

It is evident from the foregoing survey of tax exemptions that all of the states in the union today grant, either by constitutional clause or by statute, some measure of tax relief to religious societies and the organizations and institutions which they support. Despite the current emphasis on the doctrine of strict separation of church and state, it is abundantly clear that as a matter of principle and practice, the states have not denied tax exemptions on the grounds that they violated this doctrine.

Consistent and widespread throughout the country is the firm belief that the practice of granting tax exemptions to religious societies is justified not only on the basis of a long unbroken tradition, but also on grounds of present public policy. Professor Cooley, in his celebrated and authoritative treatise on taxation concludes that tax benefits of this kind to churches and religious societies are entirely valid providing "some principle of public policy can support a presumption that the public interests will be subserved by the exemptions allowed."[410] There is ample evidence to support just such a presumption.

The role played by religion in the phenomenal success of this nation was, and is still today, decisive. Religion has provided this society with the moral guides by which our individual and public conduct is measured. As a practical matter, the religious societies provide our communities with extremely vital services in a manner many times more efficient and less costly than would be provision of comparable services by the state. The majority of churches operate well organized educational, charitable, recreational, and welfare agencies which would otherwise have to be underwritten by the taxpayers at considerable expense.

The contributions of the churches and religious societies have not gone unrecognized by the courts, legislatures or the people of the states. In 1831, the Connecticut legislature enacted a law which made it easier for religious societies in the state to purchase property. In the preamble to the statute, the lawmakers stated their reason for passing the law by declaring that it was "their duty to countenance and encourage virtue and religion by every means in their power.[411] The high Court of the same state had occasion at a later time to construe the exemption statute. In its opinion the Court commented that the statute "is not merely an act of grace on the part of the State. It stands squarely on State interest."[412]

A declaration by a New York Court serves as an excellent example of the general attitude towards religion, and why it ought to be encouraged. Said the justices:

> The policy of the law has been, in this state from the early days, to encourage, foster and protect corporate institutions of religious and literary character, because the religious, moral, and intellectual culture afforded by them were deemed, as they are in fact, beneficial to the public, necessary to the advancement of civilization, and the promotion of the welfare of society.[413]

On another occasion, the Court of that same state aired the economic justification for the tax immunity.

> The purely monetary benefit which accrues to the city through this exemption by the legislature far exceeds the amount of the taxes cancelled.[414]

The Nebraska Court has also reminded us that the churches are "bearing burdens that would otherwise be imposed upon the public."[415]

Carl Zollman, the well-known legal scholar, states the case for tax exemptions for church-run schools most eloquently. Says Professor Zollman:

> . . . Since private schools relieve the congestion that exists in public schools, particularly in the cities, it is obvious that the burden of taxation is considerably lightened by those private institutions even though they go beyond the work ordinarily done by the State. The State, therefore, is making a very good bargain in having part of its work performed by them in consideration of this tax exemption. It would be decisively the loser if all these institutions were abolished, their property taxed, and the work done by them transferred to the State. The public nature of the work voluntarily shouldered by these private institutions, is, therefore, a full and sufficient justification for the exemption extended to them. . . . [416]

Society is indeed repaid manifold by the churches for the privilege of not being taxed on their property.

Nonetheless, it has been suggested by some that regardless of the humanitarian contributions made by religious societies, in actuality they have no official status, perform no official functions, and consequently, are not entitled to any support through tax immunities. Such an argument is without substantial merit. It is based on the entirely false as-

sumption that an organization must be an instrument of the government
before it can act in the interests of the community. It was never intended
by the American people that the government should be the only dis-
penser of public welfare.

It is also commonly contended that the exemptions are inequitable
because they discriminate in favor of part of the community to the detri-
ment of others. This argument tends to favor only the strict logic of
the proposition and deny its reality. Professor Cooley makes this point
very well when he writes:

> The discrimination is opposed by some persons but whether or not
> it is proper or politic, it cannot be declared unwarranted by the
> general principles of government. . . . the question of what taxes
> shall be levied, and upon what classes of persons or property, is
> always one of public policy which the legislature must solve. But
> another view is not entirely without plausibility. Whoever con-
> tributes to support of churches also contributes to pay the taxes,
> if any, imposed upon them. But as most persons who pay taxes, as
> all do, in some form, and with some regard to their ability, contri-
> bute to the support of churches, it is of little importance to the
> general public whether taxes are levied on church property
> or not, as whatever is collected from church property, while it
> goes to diminish what will be collected from individual property,
> will at the same time increase to the same extent what the individ-
> uals pay for the support of religious instruction, so that the burden
> in the one case will be substantially the same as in the other. We
> do not say that this view is strictly correct, but it is perhaps safe
> to say that the inequality occasioned by the exception of church
> property from taxation is not so great as without reflection one
> would be likely to suspect.[417]

In a sense, those who support the churches bear a double burden. This
burden would be made even heavier if the tax exemptions were with-
drawn. Services would inevitably have to be curtailed and smaller
churches which do not enjoy a strong financial status would suffer greatly
—possibly to the point of having to cease operations.

Loss of revenue is often cited as a practical argument against the
practice of exempting the property of religious societies. In communities
where the need for revenue is a very real problem, such a position may
find considerable favor with the authorities. On the other hand, the
potential loss of the services of the religious societies may in the long
run prove that the raising of needed revenue by taxing the property of
churches is an unwise fiscal policy. In order to be logically consistent,
this policy could not be limited only to the religious institutions. On the
contrary, all manner of institutions which presently enjoy the tax advantages would then be subject to the taxes. Included would be private
charities of a non-denominational nature, non-denominational hospitals,

orphanages, and the like, for their exemption too results, in some measure, in the loss of public revenues. Professor Paulsen, in his scholarly study of exemptions is one who objects to the practice on this and other grounds. However, he does come to the conclusion that, insofar as the available statistical information shows, the loss of revenue through tax exemptions and deductions for contributions does not seem to be "the most important segment of the problem."[418] "As a practical matter," he continues, "aid by tax exemptions puts a very real limit on the total amount of support given religious institutions." Such aid is "never more than the sum saved . . ."[419]

Two arguments of a rather secondary nature might be mentioned. First, it has been charged that a religious society which receives tax benefits from the government would always be reluctant to criticize its benefactor for fear that it might lose the exemption. Critics are quick to point to instances where churches entirely supported by the state in turn do the bidding of the state. One must hesitate to include the United States in this category. Tax exemptions have continued to be the practice in this country since the adoption of the federal union and there is no evidence that the churches have been unwilling to criticize authority. On the contrary, the churches have been extremely vocal on most matters of general public concern as well as their own particular interests.

Secondly, it has been alleged that the exemptions breed an excessive number of churches. Without going into the merits of such an argument, suffice it to say that any official attempt to define what is meant by "excessive" in this context might well raise grave questions with respect to religious freedom. Under our system, the smallest sect or group is protected in its beliefs and mode of worship so long as its activities do not endanger the public health and safety.

It is apparent that none of these arguments have been sufficient to sway the courts in the various states. The gain to be realized by exempting the churches is obviously considered to outweigh any loss of revenue or other disadvantage, real or imagined. It is this concept of the overriding benefit to society as a whole which has most influenced the states in their present policies. Those who advocate change in this area must thus weigh most carefully the consequences of such a move.

APPENDIX

SELECTED STATE CONSTITUTIONAL CLAUSES DEALING WITH RELIGION

NOTE: The state constitutional clauses dealing with religion, or which might control litigation relating to religion, are numerous. Only those clauses which, in the opinion of the authors, have been, or are likely to be, most frequently litigated have been included. Clauses most germane to actual litigation, but only peripherally related to this study—state constitutional clauses exempting non-profit educational and charitable institutions from taxation, for example—have been omitted.

With the exception of Michigan (which has a new Constitution effective January 1, 1964), prior constitutions have not been extracted. The reader is directed to Thorpe, *The Federal and State Constitutions* (Washington, D.C., 1909), an excellent seven volume work containing all the constitutions of the states prior to 1908. The complete texts of the current constitutions of the fifty states can be found in *Constitutions of the United States, National and State* (New York: Oceana Publications, Inc., 1962).

CONSTITUTION OF ALABAMA
1901
PREAMBLE

We, the people of the State of Alabama, . . . invoking the favor and guidance of Almighty God, . . .

ARTICLE I. DECLARATION OF RIGHTS

Sec. 3. Religious freedom. That no religion shall be established by law; that no preference shall be given by law to any religious sect, society, denomination or mode of worship; that no one shall be compelled by law to attend any place of worship; nor to pay any tithes, taxes, or other rate for building or repairing any place of worship, or for maintaining any minister or ministry; that no religious test shall be required as a qualification to any office or public trust under this state; and that the civil rights, privileges, and capacities of any citizen shall not be in any manner affected by his religious principles.

ARTICLE IV. LEGISLATIVE DEPARTMENT

Sec. 73. Aid to charitable or educational institutions. No appropriation shall be made to any charitable or educational institution not under the absolute control of the state, other than normal schools established by law for the professional training of teachers for the public schools of the state, except by a vote of two-thirds of all the members elected to each house.

Sec. 91. Exemptions from taxation. The legislature shall not tax the property, real or personal, of . . . lots in incorporated cities and towns, or within one mile of any city or town to the extent of one acre, nor lots one mile or more distant from such cities or towns to the extent of five acres, with the buildings thereon, when same are used exclusively for religious worship, for schools, or for purposes purely charitable.

ARTICLE XI. TAXATION

Sec. 217. Uniform taxation. The property of private corporations, associations, and individuals of this state shall forever be taxed at the same rate, provided, this section shall not apply to institutions devoted exclusively to religious, educational, or charitable purposes.

ARTICLE XII. CORPORATIONS

Sec. 229. General corporate law . . . The legislature shall, by general law, provide for the payment to the State of Alabama of a franchise tax by corporations organized under the laws of this state, which shall be in proportion to the amount of capital stock; but strictly benevolent, educational, or religious corporations shall not be required to pay such a tax...

ARTICLE XIV. EDUCATION

Sec. 263. Support of sectarian schools. No money raised for the support of the public shall be appropriated to or used for the support of any sectarian or denominational school.

CONSTITUTION OF ALASKA
1959
PREAMBLE

We, the people of Alaska, grateful to God...in order to secure and transmit to succeeding generations our heritage of...religious liberty...

ARTICLE I. DECLARATION OF RIGHTS

Sec. 3. Civil rights. No person is to be denied the enjoyment of any civil or political right because of race, color, creed, or national origin. The legislature shall implement this section.

Sec. 4. Freedom of religion. No law shall be made respecting an establishment of religion, or prohibiting the free exercise thereof.

ARTICLE VII. HEALTH, EDUCATION, AND WELFARE

Sec. 1. Public education. The legislature shall by general law establish and maintain a system of public schools open to all children of the State, and may provide for other public educational institutions. Schools and institutions so established shall be free from sectarian control. No money shall be paid from funds for the direct benefit of any religious or other private educational institution.

ARTICLE IX. FINANCE AND TAXATION

Sec. 4. Exemptions...All, or any portion of, property used exclusively for non-profit religious, charitable, cemetery, or educational purposes as defined by law, shall be exempt from taxation. Other exemptions of like or different kind may be granted by general law. All valid existing exemptions shall be retained until otherwise provided by law.

Sec. 6. Public Purpose. No tax shall be levied, or appropriation of public money made, or public property transferred, nor shall the public credit be used, except for a public purpose.

CONSTITUTION OF ARIZONA
1912
PREAMBLE

We, the people of the State of Arizona, grateful to Almighty God for our liberties...

ARTICLE II. DECLARATION OF RIGHTS

Sec. 7. Oaths and affirmations. The mode of administering an oath, or affirmation, shall be such as shall be most consistent with and binding upon the conscience of the person to whom such oath, or affirmation, may be administered.

Sec. 12. Liberty of conscience; appropriations for religious purposes prohibited; religious freedom. The liberty of conscience secured by the provisions of this Constitution shall not be so construed as to excuse acts of licentiousness, or justify practices inconsistent with the peace and safety of the State. No public money or property shall be appropriated for or applied to any religious worship, exercise or instruction, or to the support of any religious establishment. No religious qualification shall be required for any public office or employment, nor shall any person be incompetent as a witness or juror in consequence of his opinion on matters of religion, nor be questioned touching his religious belief in any court of justice to affect the weight of his testimony.

ARTICLE IX. PUBLIC DEBT, REVENUE AND TAXATION

Sec. 2. There shall be exempt from taxation all federal, state, county and municipal property. Property of educational, charitable and religious associations or institutions not used or held for profit may be exempt from taxation by law...

Sec. 10. Aid of church, private or sectarian school, or public service corporation. No tax shall be laid or appropriation of public money made in aid of any church, or private or sectarian school, or any public service corporation.

ARTICLE XI. EDUCATION

Sec. 7. Sectarian instruction; religious or political test or qualification. No sectarian instruction shall be imparted in any school or State educational institution that may be established under this Constitution, and no religious or political test or qualification shall ever be required as a condition of admission into any public educational institution of the State, as teacher, student, or pupil; but the liberty of conscience hereby secured shall not be so construed as to justify practices or conduct inconsistent with the good order, peace, morality, or safety of the State, or with the rights of others.

ARTICLE XX. ORDINANCE

First. Toleration of religious sentiment. Perfect toleration of religious sentiment shall be secured to every inhabitant of this State, and no inhabitant of this State shall be molested in person or property on account of his or her mode of religious worship, or lack of the same.

Second. Polygamy. Polygamous or plural marriages, or polygamous cohabitation are forever prohibited within this State.

Seventh. Public school system; suffrage. Provisions shall be made by law for the establishment and maintenance of a system of public schools which shall be open to all the children of the State and be free from sectarian control, and said schools shall always be conducted in English. . . .

CONSTITUTION OF ARKANSAS
1874
PREAMBLE

We, the people of the State of Arkansas, grateful to Almighty God for the privilege of choosing our own form of government, for our civil and religious liberty...

ARTICLE II. DECLARATION OF RIGHTS

Sec. 24. Religious liberty. All men have a natural and indefeasible right to worship Almighty God according to the dictates of their own consciences; no man can, of right, be compelled to attend, erect or support any place of worship; or to maintain any ministry against his consent. No human authority can, in any case or manner whatsoever, control or interfere with the right of conscience; and no preference shall ever be given, by law, to any religious establishment, denomination or mode of worship above any other.

Sec. 25. Protection of religion. Religion, morality and knowledge being essential to good government, the General Assembly shall enact suitable laws to protect every religious denomination in the peaceable enjoyment of its own mode of public worship.

Sec. 26. Religious tests. No religious test shall ever be required of any person as a qualification to vote or hold office, nor shall any person be rendered incompetent to be a witness on account of his religious belief; but nothing herein shall be construed to dispense with oaths or affirmations.

ARTICLE XVI.   FINANCE AND TAXATION

Sec. 5. Tax exemptions. ...Provided, further, that the following property shall be exempt from taxation; Public property used exclusively for public purposes; churches used as such; cemeteries used exclusively as such; school buildings and apparatus; libraries and grounds used exclusively for school purposes, and building and grounds and materials used exclusively for public charity.

ARTICLE XIX.   MISCELLANEOUS PROVISIONS

Sec. 1. Atheists disqualified from holding office or testifying as witness. No person who denies the being of a God shall hold any office in the civil departments of this State nor be competent to testify as a witness in any court.

CONSTITUTION OF CALIFORNIA
1879
PREAMBLE

We, the People of the State of California, grateful to Almighty God...

ARTICLE I.   DECLARATION OF RIGHTS

Sec. 4. Liberty of conscience. The free exercise and enjoyment of religious profession and worship, without discrimination or preference, shall forever be guaranteed in this State; and no person shall be rendered incompetent to be a witness or juror on account of his opinions on matters of religious belief; but the liberty of conscience hereby secured shall not be so construed as to excuse acts of licentiousness, or justify practices inconsistent with the peace or safety of this State.

ARTICLE IV.　LEGISLATIVE DEPARTMENT

Sec. 22. Appropriations...no state aid for private institutions; exceptions. ...no money shall ever be appropriated or drawn from the State Treasury for the purpose or benefit of any corporation, association, asylum, hospital, or any other institution not under the exclusive management and control of the State as a state institution, nor shall any grant or donation of property ever be made thereto by the State except that notwithstanding anything contained in this or any other section of the Constitution

(1) Federal-state funds for hospital construction...
(2) Aid to institutions for support and maintenance of orphans, half-orphans, abandoned children, and children of needy parents. . . .
(3) Aid to needy blind persons. . . .
(4) Aid to needy physically handicapped persons. . . .
(5) State's right to inquire into management of institutions. . . .

Sec. 30. Public aid for sectarian purposes prohibited. Neither the Legislature, nor any county, city and county, township, school district, or other municipal corporation, shall ever make any appropriation, or pay from any public fund whatever, or grant anything to or in aid of any religious sect, church, creed, or sectarian purpose, or help to support or sustain any school, college, university, hospital, or other institution controlled by any religious creed, church, or sectarian denomination whatever; nor shall any grant or donation of personal property or real estate ever be made by the State, or any city, city and county, town, or other municipal corporation for any religious creed, church, or sectarian purpose whatever; provided that nothing in this section shall prevent the Legislature granting aid pursuant to Section 22 of this article.

ARTICLE IX.　EDUCATION

Sec. 8. No public money for sectarian schools. No public money shall ever be appropriated for the support of any sectarian or denominational school, or any school not under the exclusive control of the officers of the public schools; nor shall any sectarian or denominational doctrine be taught, or instruction thereon be permitted, directly or indirectly, in any of the common schools of this State.

Sec. 9. University of California. . . . The university shall be entirely independent of all political or sectarian influence and kept free therefrom in the appointment of its regents and in the administration of its affairs. . . .

ARTICLE XIII.   REVENUE AND TAXATION

Sec. 1½. Exemption of church property; church buildings under construction; parking lots.   All buildings and equipment, and so much of the real property on which they are situated as may be required for the convenient use and occupation of said buildings, when the same are used solely and exclusively for religious worship, and any building and its equipment in the course of erection, together with the land on which it is located as may be required for the convenient use and occupation of the building, if such building, equipment and land are intended to be used solely and exclusively for religious worship, and, until the Legislature shall otherwise provide by law, that real property owned by the owner of the building which the owner is required by law to make available for, and which is necessarily and reasonably required and exclusively used for the parking of the automobiles of persons while attending or engaged in religious worship in said building whether or not said real property is contiguous to land on which said building is located, and which real property has not been rented or used for any commercial purpose at any other time during the preceding year, shall be free from taxation; provided that no building so used or, in the course of erection, intended to be so used, its equipment or the land on which it is located, which may be rented for religious purposes and rent received by the owner therefor, shall be exempt from taxation.

CONSTITUTION OF COLORADO
1876
PREAMBLE

We the people of Colorado with profound reverence for the Supreme Ruler of the Universe...

ARTICLE II.   BILL OF RIGHTS

Sec. 4. Religious freedom.   The free exercise and enjoyment of religious profession and worship, without discrimination, shall forever hereafter be guaranteed; and no person shall be denied any civil or political right, privilege or capacity, on account of his opinions concerning religion; but the liberty of conscience hereby secured shall not be construed to dispense with oaths or affirmations, excuse acts of licentiousness or justify practices inconsistent with the good order, peace or safety of the state. No person shall be required to attend or support any ministry or place of worship, religious sect or denomination against his consent.   Nor shall any preference be given by law to any religious denomination or mode of worship.

ARTICLE V. LEGISLATIVE DEPARTMENT

Sec. 34. Appropriations to Private Institutions Forbidden. No appropriation shall be made for charitable, industrial, educational or benevolent purposes to any person, corporation or community not under the absolute control of the state, nor to any denominational or sectarian institution or association.

ARTICLE IX. EDUCATION

Sec. 7. Aid to private schools, churches, sectarian purposes, for-bidden. Neither the general assembly, nor any county, city, town, town-ship, school district or other public corporation, shall ever make any appropriation, or pay from any public fund or moneys whatever, any-thing in aid of any church or sectarian society, or for any sectarian purpose, or to help support or sustain any school, academy, seminary, college, university or other literary or scientific institution, controlled by any church or sectarian denomination whatsoever; nor shall any grant or donation of land, money or other personal property, ever be made by the state, or any such public corporation to any church, or for any sectarian purpose.

Sec. 8. Religious test and race discrimination forbidden; sectarian tenets. No religious test or qualification shall ever be required of any person as a condition of admission into any public education institution of the state, either as a teacher or student; and no teacher or student of any such institution shall ever be required to attend or participate in any religious service whatever. No sectarian tenets or doctrines shall ever be taught in the public schools, nor shall any distinction or classification of pupils be made on account of race or color.

ARTICLE X. REVENUE

Sec. 5. Property used for religious worship, schools and charitable purposes exempt. Property real and personal, that is used solely and exclusively for religious worship, for schools or for strictly charitable purposes, also cemeteries not used or held for private or corporate profit, shall be exempt from taxation, unless otherwise provided by general law.

ARTICLE XVII. MILITIA

Sec. 5. Exemptions in time of peace. No person having con-scientious scruples against bearing arms, shall be compelled to do militia duty in time of peace; provided, such person shall pay an equivalent for such exemption.

CONSTITUTION OF CONNECTICUT
1818
PREAMBLE

The people of Connecticut acknowledging with gratitude, the good providence of God, in having permitted them to enjoy a free government...

ARTICLE FIRST. DECLARATION OF RIGHTS

Sec. 3. Religious liberty. The exercise and enjoyment of religious profession and worship, without discrimination, shall forever be free to all persons in this state; provided, that the right hereby declared and established, shall not be so construed as to excuse acts of licentiousness, or to justify practices inconsistent with the peace and safety of the state.

Sec. 4. No preferences in Christian sects or modes of worship. No preference shall be given by law to any Christian sect or mode of worship.

ARTICLE SEVENTH.   OF RELIGION

Sec. 1. Compulsory support of religion prohibited; all denominations of Christians to have equal rights. It being the duty of all men to worship the Supreme Being, the Great Creator and Preserver of the Universe, and their right to render that worship, in the mode most consistent with the dictates of their consciences; no person shall by law be compelled to join or support, nor be classed with, or associated to, any congregation, church or religious association. But every person now belonging to such congregation, church, or religious association shall remain a member thereof until he shall have separated himself therefrom, in the manner hereinafter provided. And each and every society or denomination of Christians in this state, shall have and enjoy the same and equal powers, rights and privileges; and shall have power and authority to support and maintain the ministers or teachers of their respective denominations, and to build and repair houses for public worship, by a tax on the members of any such society only, to be laid by a major vote of the legal voters assembled at any society meeting, warned and held according to law, or in any other manner.

Sec. 2. Right to separate from Christian societies or denominations. If any person shall choose to separate himself from the society or denomination of Christians to which he may belong, and shall leave a written notice thereof with the clerk of such society, he shall thereupon be no longer liable for any future expenses which may be incurred by said society.

ARTICLE EIGHTH. OF EDUCATION

Sec. 2.   The school fund shall remain a perpetual fund.   The fund, called the SCHOOL FUND, shall remain a perpetual fund, the interest of which shall be inviolably appropriated to the support and encouragement of the public, or common schools throughout the state, and for the equal benefit of all the people thereof...and no law shall ever be made, authorizing said fund to be diverted to any other use than the encouragement and support of public, or common schools, among the several school societies, as justice and equity shall require.

CONSTITUTION OF DELAWARE
1897
PREAMBLE

Through Divine goodness, all men have by nature the rights of worshipping and serving their Creator according to the dictates of their consciences...

ARTICLE I.   BILL OF RIGHTS

Sec. 1.   Freedom of religion.   Although it is the duty of all men frequently to assemble together for the public worship of Almighty God; and piety and morality, on which the prosperity of communities depend are hereby promoted; yet no man shall or ought to be compelled to attend any religious worship, to contribute to the erection or support of any place of worship, or to the maintenance of any ministry, against his own free will and consent; and no power shall or ought to be vested in or assumed by any magistrate that shall in any case interfere with, or in any manner control the rights of conscience, in the free exercise of religious worship, nor a preference given by law to any religious societies, denominations, or modes of worship.

Sec. 2.   Religious test for office not required.   No religious test shall be required as a qualification to any office, or public trust, under this State.

ARTICLE VIII.   REVENUE AND TAXATION

Sec. 1.   ...Exemption for public welfare purposes...the General Assembly may by general laws exempt from taxation such property as in the opinion of the General Assembly will best promote the public welfare.

ARTICLE IX.   CORPORATIONS

Sec. 4.   Rights, privileges, immunities and estates.   The rights, privileges, immunities and estates of religious societies and corporate bodies, except as herein otherwise provided, shall remain as if the Constitution of this State had not been altered.

ARTICLE X. EDUCATION

Sec. 3. Use of educational funds by religious schools; exemption of school property from taxation. No portion of any fund now existing, or which may hereafter be appropriated, or raised by tax, for educational purposes, shall be appropriated to, or used by, or in aid of any sectarian, church or denominational school; provided, that all real or personal property used for school purposes, where the tuition is free, shall be exempt from taxation and assessment for public purposes.

Sec. 4. Use of public school fund. No part of the principal or income of the Public School Fund, now or hereafter existing, shall be used for any other purpose than the support of free public schools.

CONSTITUTION OF FLORIDA
1887
PREAMBLE

We, the people of the State of Florida, grateful to Almighty God...

DECLARATION OF RIGHTS

Sec. 5. Religious freedom; liberty of conscience, etc. The free exercise and enjoyment of religious profession and worship shall forever be allowed in this State, and no person shall be rendered incompetent as a witness on account of his religious opinions; but the liberty of conscience hereby secured shall not be so construed as to justify licentiousness or practices subversive of, or inconsistent with, the peace or moral safety of the State or society.

Sec. 6. Religious preferences; public aid, etc. No preference shall be given by law to any church, sect or mode of worship and no money shall ever be taken from the public treasury directly or indirectly in aid of any church, sect or religious denomination or in aid of any sectarian institution.

ARTICLE IX. TAXATION AND FINANCE

Sec. 1. Uniform and equal rate of taxation; special rates. The Legislature shall provide for a uniform and equal rate of taxation...and shall prescribe such regulations as shall secure a just valuation of all property, both real and personal, excepting such property as may be exempted by law for municipal, educational, literary, scientific, religious or charitable purposes.

ARTICLE XII.   EDUCATION

Sec. 13.   Restriction on use of county or district school funds.   No law shall be enacted authorizing the diversion or the lending of any County or District School Funds, or the appropriation of any part of the permanent or available school Fund to any other than school purposes; nor shall the same, or any part thereof, be appropriated to or used for the support of any sectarian school.

ARTICLE XIV.   MILITIA

Sec. 1.   Composition of state militia.   All able bodied male inhabitants of the State between the ages of eighteen and forty-five years, that are citizens of the United States . . . shall constitute the militia of the State, but no male citizen of whatever religious creed or opinion shall be exempt from military duty except upon such conditions as may be prescribed by law.

CONSTITUTION OF GEORGIA
1945
PREAMBLE

...we the people of Georgia relying upon the protection and guidance of Almighty God...

ARTICLE I.   BILL OF RIGHTS

Paragraph XII.   Freedom of conscience.   All men have the natural and inalienable right to worship God, each according to the dictates of his own conscience, and no human authority should, in any case, control or interfere with such right of conscience.

Paragraph XIII.   Religious opinions; liberty of conscience.   No inhabitant of this State shall be molested in person or property, or prohibited from holding any public office, or trust, on account of his religious opinions; but the right of liberty of conscience shall not be so construed as to excuse acts of licentiousness, or justify practices inconsistent with the peace and safety of the State.

Paragraph XIV.   Appropriations to churches, sects, etc., forbidden. No money shall ever be taken from the public Treasury, directly or indirectly, in aid of any church, sect, or denomination of religionists, or of any sectarian institution.

ARTICLE VII.   FINANCE, TAXATION AND PUBLIC DEBT
SECTION I

Paragraph IV.   Exemptions from taxation.   The General Assembly may, by law, exempt from taxation all public property; places of religious worship or burial and all property owned by religious groups used ony for residential purposes and from which no income is derived; all institutions of purely public charity; all intangible personal property owned by or irrevocably held in trust for the exclusive benefit of, religious, educational and charitable institutions, no part of the net profit from the operation of which can inure to the benefit of any private person; all buildings erected for, and used as, a college, incorporated academy or other seminary of learning, and also all funds or property held or used as endowment by such colleges, incorporated academies or seminaries of learning, provided the same is not invested in real estate; and provided, further that said exemptions shall only apply to such colleges, incorporated academies or other seminaries of learning as are open to the general public;...

CONSTITUTION OF HAWII
1959
PREAMBLE

We, the people of the State of Hawii, grateful for Divine Guidance...

ARTICLE I.   BILL OF RIGHTS

Sec. 3.   Freedom of religion, speech, press, assembly and petition. No law shall be enacted respecting an establishment of religion or prohibiting the free exercise thereof, or abridging the freedom of speech or of the press, or the right of the people peaceably to assemble and to petition the government for a redress of grievances.

Sec. 4.   Due process and equal protection.   No person shall be deprived of life, liberty or property without due process of law, nor be denied the equal protection of the laws, nor be denied the enjoyment of his civil rights or be discriminated against in the exercise thereof because of race, religion, sex or ancestry.

Sec. 7.   Enlistment, segregation.   No citizen shall be denied enlistment in any military organization of this State nor be segregated therein because of race, religious principles or ancestry.

ARTICLE VI.   TAXATION AND FINANCE

Sec. 6.   Appropriations for private purposes prohibited.   No tax shall be levied or appropriation of public money or property made, nor shall the public credit be used, directly or indirectly, except for a public purpose.   No grant shall be made in violation of Section 3 of Article I of this constitution.

ARTICLE IX. EDUCATION

Sec. 1. Public education. The State shall provide for the establishment, support and control of a statewide system of public schools free from sectarian control, a state university, public libraries and such other educational institutions as may be deemed desirable, including physical facilities therefor. There shall be no segregation in public educational institutions, because of race, religion or ancestry; nor shall public funds be appropriated for the support or benefit of any sectarian or private educational institution.

CONSTITUTION OF IDAHO
1890
PREAMBLE

We, the people of the state of Idaho, grateful to Almighty God...

ARTICLE I. DECLARATION OF RIGHTS

Sec. 4. Guaranty of religious liberty. The exercise and enjoyment of religious faith and worship shall forever be guaranteed; and no person shall be denied any civil or political right, privilege, or capacity on account of his religious opinions; but the liberty of conscience hereby secured shall not be construed to dispense with oaths or affirmations, or excuse acts of licentiousness or justify polygamous or other pernicious practices, inconsistent with morality or the peace or safety of the state; nor to permit any person, organization, or association to directly or indirectly aid or abet, counsel or advise any person to commit the crime of bigamy or polygamy, or any other crime. No person shall be required to attend or support any ministry or place of worship, religious sect or denomination, or any tithes against his consent; nor shall any preference be given by law to any religious denomination or mode of worship. Bigamy and polygamy are forever prohibited in the state, and the legislature shall provide by law for the punishment of such crimes.

ARTICLE VI. SUFFRAGE AND ELECTIONS

Sec. 3. Disqualification of certain persons. No person is permitted to vote, serve as a juror, or hold any civil office...who is a bigamist or polygamist, or is living in what is known as patriarchal, plural or celestial marriage, or in violation of any law of this state, or of the United States, forbidding any such crime; or who in any manner, teaches, advises, counsels, aids, or encourages any person to enter into bigamy, polygamy, or such patriarchal, plural, or celestial marriage, or to live in violation of any such law, or to commit any such crime; or who is a member of, or contributes to the support, aid, or encouragement of, any order, organization, association, corporation, or society, which teaches, advises, counsels, encourages, or aids any person to enter into bigamy, polygamy or such patriarchal or plural marriage, or which teaches or advises that the laws of this state prescribing rules of civil conduct, are not the supreme law of the state;...

ARTICLE IX.   EDUCATION AND SCHOOL LANDS

Sec. 5. Sectarian appropriations prohibited. Neither the legislature nor any county, city, town, township, school district, or other public corporation, shall ever make any appropriation, or pay from any public fund or moneys whatever, anything in aid of any church or sectarian or religious society, or for any sectarian or religious purpose, or to help support or sustain any school, academy, seminary, college, university or other literary or scientific institution, controlled by any church, sectarian or religious denomination whatsoever; nor shall any grant or donation of land, money or other personal property ever be made by the state, or any such public corporation, to any church, or for any sectarian or religious purpose.

Sec. 6. Religious test and teaching in school prohibited. No religious test or qualification shall ever be required of any person as a condition of admission into any public educational institution of the state, either as teacher or student; and no teacher or student of any such institution shall ever be required to attend or participate in any religious service whatever. No sectarian or religious tenets or doctrines shall ever be taught in the public schools, nor shall any distinction or classification of pupils be made on account of race or color. No books, papers, tracts, or documents of a political, sectarian or denominational character shall be used or introduced in any schools established under the provisions of this article, nor shall any teacher or any district receive any of the public school moneys in which the schools have not been taught in accordance with the provisions of this article.

ARTICLE XIV.   MILITIA

Sec. 1. Persons subject to military duty. All able-bodied male persons, residents of this state, between the ages of eighteen and forty-five years, shall be enrolled in the militia, and perform such military duty as may be required by law; but no person having conscientious scruples against bearing arms, shall be compelled to perform such duty in time of peace. Every person claiming such exemption from service, shall, in lieu thereof, pay into the school fund of the county of which he may be a resident, an equivalent in money, the amount and manner of payment to be fixed by law.

ARTICLE XXI.   SCHEDULE AND ORDINANCE

Sec. 19. Religious freedom guaranteed...It is ordained by the

State of Idaho that perfect toleration of religious sentiment shall be secured, and no inhabitant of said state shall ever be molested in person or property on account of his or her mode of religious worship. . . .

CONSTITUTION OF ILLINOIS
1870
PREAMBLE

We, the people of the State of Illinois—grateful to Almighty God for the civil, political and religious liberty which He hath so long permitted us to enjoy, and looking to Him for a blessing upon our endeavors to secure and transmit the same unimpaired to succeeding generations, . . .

ARTICLE II. BILL OF RIGHTS

Sec. 3. Religious freedom. The free exercise and enjoyment of religious profession and worship, without discrimination, shall forever be guaranteed; and no person shall be denied any civil or political right, privilege or capacity, on account of his religious opinions; but the liberty of conscience hereby secured shall not be construed to dispense with oaths or affirmations, excuse acts of licentiousness, or justify practices inconsistent with the peace or safety of the State. No person shall be required to attend or support any ministry or place of worship against his consent nor shall any preference be given by law to any religious denomination or mode of worship.

ARTICLE VII. EDUCATION

Sec. 3. Public funds for sectarian purposes forbidden. Neither the General Assembly nor any county, city, town, township, school district, or other public corporation, shall ever make any appropriation or pay from any public fund whatever, anything in aid of any church or sectarian purpose, or to help support or sustain any school, academy, seminary, college, university, or other literary or scientific institution, controlled by any church or sectarian denomination whatever; nor shall any grant or donation of land, money, or other personal property ever be made by the State, or any such public corporation, to any church, or for any sectarian purpose.

ARTICLE IX. REVENUE

Sec. 3. Tax exemptions. The property of the State, counties, and other municipal corporations, both real and personal, and such other property, as may be used exclusively for agricultural and horticultural societies, for school, religious, cemetery and charitable purposes, may be exempted from taxation; but such exemption shall be only by general law. . . .

ARTICLE XII.   MILITIA

Sec. 6. Conscientious objectors. No person having conscientious scruples against bearing arms, shall be compelled to do militia duty in time of peace: Provided, such person shall pay an equivalent for such exemption.

CONSTITUTION OF INDIANA
1851
PREAMBLE

We, the People of the State of Indiana, grateful to Almighty God . . .

ARTICLE I.   BILL OF RIGHTS

right to worship Almighty God, according to the dictates of their own
Sec. 2. Right to worship. All men shall be secured in the natural consciences.

Sec. 3. Freedom of religion. No law shall, in any case whatever, control the free exercise and enjoyment of religious opinions, or interfere with the rights of conscience.

Sec. 4. Creedal preference. No preference shall be given, by law, to any creed, religious society, or mode of worship; and no man shall be compelled to attend, erect, or support, any place of worship, or to maintain any ministry, against his consent.

Sec. 5. Religious test for office. No religious test shall be required, as a qualification for any office of trust or profit.

Sec. 6. No state aid for religious institutions. No money shall be drawn from the treasury, for the benefit of any religious or theological institution.

Sec. 7. Religion no bar to competency of witnesses. No person shall be rendered incompetent as a witness, in consequence of his opinions on matters of religion.

ARTICLE 10.   FINANCE

Sec. 1. Assessment and taxation. The General Assembly shall provide, by law, for a uniform and equal rate of assessment and taxation; and shall prescribe such regulations as shall secure a just valuation for taxation of all property, both real and personal, excepting such only for municipal, educational, literary, scientific, religious or charitable purpose, as may be specifically exempted by law.

ARTICLE 12.   MILITIA

Sec. 6. Conscientious objectors. No person, conscientiously opposed to bearing arms, shall be compelled to do militia duty; but such person shall pay an equivalent for exemption; the amount to be prescribed by law.

CONSTITUTION OF IOWA
1857
PREAMBLE

We, the People of the State of Iowa, grateful to the Supreme Being for the blessings hitherto enjoyed, and feeling our dependence on Him for a continuation of those blessings, . . .

ARTICLE I. BILL OF RIGHTS

Sec. 3. Religion. The General Assembly shall make no law respecting an establishment of religion, or prohibiting the free exercise thereof; nor shall any person be compelled to attend any place of worship, pay tithes, taxes or other rates for building or repairing places of worship, or the maintenance of any minister, or ministry.

Sec. 4. Religious test; witnesses. No religious test shall be required as a qualification for any office, or public trust, and no person shall be deprived of any of his rights, privileges, or capacities, or disqualified from the performance of any of his public or private duties, or rendered incompetent to give evidence in any court of law or equity, in consequence of his opinions on the subject of religion; and any party to any judicial proceeding shall have the right to use as a witness, or take the testimony of, any other person not disqualified on account of interest, who may be cognizant of any fact material to the case; and parties to suits may be witnesses as provided by law.

ARTICLE VI. MILITIA

Sec. 2. Exemption. No person or persons conscientiously scrupulous of bearing arms shall be compelled to do military duty in time of peace; Provided that such person or persons shall pay an equivalent for such exemption in the same manner as other citizens.

CONSTITUTION OF KANSAS
1861
PREAMBLE

We, the people of Kansas, grateful to Almighty God . . .

BILL OF RIGHTS

Sec. 7. Religious liberty. The right to worship God according to the dictates of conscience shall never be infringed; nor shall any person be compelled to attend or support any form of worship; nor shall any control of or interference with the rights of conscience be permitted, nor any preference be given by law to any religious establishment or mode of worship. No religious test or property qualification shall be required for any office of public trust, nor for any vote at any election, nor shall any person be incompetent to testify on account of religious belief.

ARTICLE 6.   EDUCATION

Sec. 8. Nonsectarianism. No religious sect or sects shall ever control any part of the common-school or university funds of the state.

ARTICLE 8.   MILITIA

Sec. 1. Composition; exemption. The militia shall be composed of all able-bodied male citizens between the ages of twenty-one and forty-five years, except such as are exempted by the laws of the United States or of this state; but all citizens of any religious denomination whatever who from scruples of conscience may be averse to bearing arms shall be exempted therefrom, upon such conditions as may be prescribed by law.

ARTICLE 11.   FINANCE AND TAXATION

Sec. 1. Exemption. All property used exclusively for state, county, municipal, literary, educational, scientific, religious, benevolent and charitable purposes, . . . shall be exempted from taxation.

ARTICLE 12.   CORPORATIONS

Sec. 2. Liability of stockholders. Dues from corporations shall be secured by the individual liability of the stockholders to the amount of stock owned by each stockholder, and such other means as shall be provided by law; but such individual liability shall not apply to railroad corporations nor corporations for religious or charitable purposes.

Sec. 3. Religious corporations. The title to all property of religious corporations, shall vest in trustees, whose election shall be by the members of such corporations.

CONSTITUTION OF KENTUCKY
1891
PREAMBLE

We, the people of the Commonwealth of Kentucky, grateful to Almighty God, . . .

BILL OF RIGHTS

Sec. 1. Rights of life, liberty, worship, pursuit of safety and happiness, free speech, acquiring and protecting property, peaceable assembly, redress of grievances, bearing arms. All men are, by nature, free and equal, and have certain inherent and inalienable rights, among which may be reckoned:

. . .

Second. The right of worshipping Almighty God according to the dictates of their consciences.

Sec. 5. Right of Religious Freedom. No preference shall ever be given by law to any religious sect, society or denomination; nor to any particular creed, mode of worship or system of ecclesiastical policy; nor shall any person be compelled to attend any place of worship, to contribute to the erection or maintenance of any such place, or to the salary or support of any minister or religion; nor shall any man be compelled to send his child to any school to which he may be conscientiously opposed; and the civil rights, privileges or capacities of no person shall be taken away, or in anywise diminished or enlarged, on account of his belief or disbelief of any religious tenet, dogma or teaching. No human authority shall, in any case whatever, control or interfere with the rights of conscience.

REVENUE AND TAXATION

Sec. 170. Property exempt from taxation. There shall be exempt from taxation public property used for public purposes; places actually used for religious worship, with the grounds attached thereto and used and appurtenant to the house of worship, not exceeding one-half acre in cities or towns, and not exceeding two acres in the country; places of burial not held for private or corporate profit, institutions of purely public charity, and institutions of education not used or employed for gain by any person or corporation, and the income of which is devoted solely to the cause of education, public libraries, their endowments, and the income of such property as is used exclusively for their maintenance; all parsonages or residences owned by any religious society, and occupied as a home, and for no other purpose, by the minister of any religion, with not exceeding one-half acres of ground in towns and cities and two acres of ground in the country appurtenant thereto; . . .

EDUCATION

Sec. 189. School money not to be used for church, sectarian or denominational school. No portion of any fund or tax now existing, or that may hereafter be raised or levied for educational purposes, shall be appropriated to, or used by, or in aid of any church, sectarian or denominational school.

THE MILITIA

Sec. 220. General assembly to provide for militia; exemption from service. The General Assembly shall provide for maintaining an organized militia, and may exempt from military service persons having conscientious scruples against bearing arms; but such persons shall pay an equivalent for such exemption.

CONSTITUTION OF LOUISIANA
1921
PREAMBLE

We, the people of the State of Louisiana, grateful to Almighty God; . . .

ARTICLE I.   BILL OF RIGHTS

Sec. 4. Freedom of religion. Every person has the natural right to worship God according to the dictates of his own conscience. No law shall be passed respecting an establishment of religion, nor prohibiting the free exercise thereof; nor shall any preference ever be given to, nor any discrimination made against, any church, sect or creed of religion, or any form of religious faith or worship.

ARTICLE IV.   LIMITATIONS

Sec. 8. Public funds; prohibited expenditure for sectarian, private, charitable or benevolent purposes; state charities; religious discrimination. No money shall ever be taken from the public treasury, directly or indirectly, in aid of any church, sect or denomination or religion, or in aid of any priest, preacher, minister or teacher thereof, as such, and no preference shall ever be given to, nor any discrimination made against any church, sect or creed of religion, or any form of religious faith or worship. No appropriation from the State treasury shall be made for private, charitable or benevolent purposes to any person or community; provided, this shall not apply to the State Asylums for the Insane, and the State Schools for the Deaf and Dumb and the Blind, and the Charity Hospitals, and public charitable institutions conducted under State authority.

Sec. 16. Forced heirship; abolition prohibited; adopted children; fidei commissa or trust estates; restrictions. . . . and provided that this prohibition as to trust estates or fidei commissas shall not apply to donations strictly for educational, charitable, religious purposes or trusts created by employers for the benefit of their employees . . .

ARTICLE X.   REVENUE AND TAXATION

Sec. 4. Tax exemptions. The following property, and no other, shall be exempt from taxation.

1. Public property. All public property.

2. Religious, charitable and educational property. Places of religious worship, rectories and parsonages belonging to religious denominations and used as places of residence for ministers; places of burial; places devoted to charitable undertakings, including that of such organizations as lodges and clubs, schools, and colleges; but the exemption shall extend only to property, and grounds thereunto appurtenant, used for the above mentioned purposes, and not leased for profit or income. . . .

Sec. 8. License taxes; restrictions. License taxes may be levied on such classes of persons, association of persons and corporations pursuing any trade, business, occupation, vocation or profession, as the Legislature may deem proper, except . . . ministers of religion, . . .

ARTICLE XII.   PUBLIC EDUCATION

Sec. 13. Public funds for private or sectarian schools; cooperative regional education. No public funds shall be used for the support of any private or sectarian school. Provided, that the Legislature may enact appropriate legislation to permit institutions of higher learning which receive all or part of their support from the State of Louisiana to engage in interstate and intrastate education agreements with other state governments, agencies of other state governments, institutions of higher learning of other state governments and private institutions of higher learning within or outside state boundaries.

ARTICLE XIV.   PAROCHIAL AND MUNICIPAL AFFAIRS

Sec. 15. Civil service system; state; cities.

(A) (1) Appointments and promotions; examinations; discrimination. . . . no person in the State or City Classified Service shall be discriminated against or subjected to any disciplinary action for political or religious reasons, and all such persons shall have the right of appeal from such actions. . . .

CONSTITUTION OF MAINE
1820
PREAMBLE

Objects of government. We the people of Maine, . . . acknowledging with grateful hearts the goodness of the Sovereign Ruler of the Universe in affording us an opportunity, so favorable to the design; and imploring His aid and direction in its accomplishment, . . .

ARTICLE I.   DECLARATION OF RIGHTS

Sec. 3. Religious freedom; proviso; sects equal; religious tests prohibited; religious teachers. All men have a natural and unalienable right to worship Almighty God according to the dicates of their own consciences, and no one shall be hurt, molested or restrained in his person, liberty or estate for worshipping God in the manner and season most agreeable to the dictates of his own conscience, nor for his religious professions or sentiments, provided he does not disturb the public peace, nor obstruct others in their religious worship;—and all persons demeaning themselves peaceably, as good members of the state, shall be equally under the protection of the laws, and no subordination nor preference of any one sect or denomination to another shall ever be established by law, nor shall any religious test be required as a qualification for any office or trust, under this state; and all religious societies in this state, whether incorporate or unincorporate, shall at all times have the exclusive right of electing their public teachers, and contracting with them for their support and maintenance.

ARTICLE VII. MILITARY

Sec. 5. Persons exempt from military duty. Persons of the denominations of Quakersand Shakers, justices of the supreme judicial court, ministers of the gospel and persons exempted by the laws of the United States may be exempted from military duty, but no other able-bodied person of the age of eighteen and under the age of forty-five years, excepting officers of the militia who have been honorably discharged shall be so exempted unless he shall pay an equivalent to be fixed by law.

ARTICLE IX. GENERAL PROVISIONS

Sec. 1. Oaths and subscriptions; proviso; before whom to be taken. Every person elected or appointed to either of the places or offices provided in this constitution, and every person elected, appointed, or commissioned to any judicial, executive, military or other office under this state, shall before he enter on the discharge of the duties of his place or office, take and subscribe the following oath or affirmation: "I.............................. do swear, that I will support the Constitution of the United States and of this State, so long as I shall continue a citizen thereof. So help me God."

"I........................... do swear, that I will faithfully discharge, to the best of my abilities, the duties incumbent on me as .... according to the Constitution and laws of the State. So help me God." Provided, that an affirmation in the above forms may be substituted, when the person shall be conscientiously scrupulous of taking and subscribing an oath. . . .

CONSTITUTION OF MARYLAND
1867
DECLARATION OF RIGHTS

We, the People of the State of Maryland, grateful to Almighty God for our civil and religious liberty, . . .

ARTICLE 36. Religious freedom. That as it is the duty of every man to worship God in such manner as he thinks most acceptable to Him, all persons are equally entitled to protection in their religious liberty; wherefore, no person ought by any law to be molested in his person or estate, on account of his religious persuasion, or profession, or for his religious practice, unless, under the color of religion, he shall disturb the good order, peace or safety of the State, or shall infringe the laws of morality, or injure others in their natural, civil or religious rights; nor ought any person to be compelled to frequent, or maintain, or contribute, unless on contract to maintain, any place of worship, or any ministry; nor shall any person otherwise competent, be deemed incompetent as a witness, or juror, on account of his religious belief; provided, he believes in the existence of God, and that under His dispensation such person will be held morally accountable for his acts, and be rewarded or punished therefor either in this world or in the world to come.

ARTICLE 37. Religious test as qualification for office; oath of office. That no religious test ought ever to be required as a qualification for any office of profit or trust in this State, other than a declaration of belief in the existence of God; nor shall the Legislature prescribe any other oath of office than the oath prescribed by this Constitution.

ARTICLE 38. Gifts, etc., for religious purposes. That every gift, sale or devise of land to any Minister, Public Teacher, or Preacher of the Gospel as such, or to any Religious Sect, Order or Denomination, or to, or for the support, use or benefit of, or in trust for, any Minister, Public Teacher, or Preacher of the Gospel, as such, or any Religious Sect, Order or Denomination; and every gift or sale of goods, or chattels to go in succession, or to take place after the death of the Seller or Donor, to or for such support, use or benefit; and also every devise of goods or chattels to or for the support, use or benefit of any Minister, Public Teacher, or Preacher of the Gospel, as such, or any Religious Sect, Order or Denomination, without the prior or subsequent sanction of the Legislature, shall be void; except always, any sale, gift, lease or devise of any quantity of land, not exceeding five acres, for a church, meeting-house, or other house of worship, or parsonage, or for a burying ground, which shall be improved, enjoyed or used only for such purpose; or such sale, gift, lease or devise shall be void. Provided, however, that except in so far as the General Assembly shall hereafter by law otherwise enact, the consent of the Legislature shall not be required to any gift, grant, deed, or conveyance executed after the 2nd day of November, 1948, or to any devise or bequest contained in the will of any person dying after said 2nd day of November, 1948, for any of the purposes hereinabove in this Article mentioned.

ARTICLE 39. Manner of administering oath or affirmation. That the manner of administering an oath or affirmation to any person, ought to be such as those of the religious persuasion, profession, or denomination, of which he is a member, generally esteem the most effectual confirmation by the attestation of the Divine Being.

ARTICLE III. LEGISLATIVE DEPARTMENT

Sec. 11. Ministers and persons holding civil offices under state not eligible as senators or delegates. No Minister of the Gospel, or of any religious creed, or denomination, and no person holding any civil office of profit, or trust, under this State, except Justices of the Peace, shall be eligible as Senator, or Delegate.

CONSTITUTION OF MASSACHUSETTS
1780
PREAMBLE

. . .WE, therefore, the people of Massachusetts, acknowledging, with grateful hearts, the goodness of the Great Legislator of the Universe, in affording us, in the course of his Providence, . . .

PART THE FIRST. A DECLARATION OF THE RIGHTS OF THE INHABITANTS OF THE COMMONWEALTH OF MASSACHUSETTS

ARTICLE II. Right and duty of public religious worship; protection therein. It is the right as well as the Duty of all men in society, publicly, and at stated seasons to worship the Supreme Being, the great Creator and preserver of the Universe. And no Subject shall be hurt, molested, or restrained, in his person, Liberty, or Estate, for worshipping God in the manner and season most agreeable to the Dictates of his own conscience, or for his religious profession or sentiments; provided he doth not Disturb the public peace, or obstruct others in their religious Worship.

ARTICLE III. Legislature empowerd to compel provision for public worship. As the happiness of a people, and the good order and preservation of civil government, essentially depend upon piety, religion and morality; and as these cannot be generally diffused through a Community, but by the institution of the public Worship of God, and of public instructions in piety, religion and morality: Therefore, to promote their happiness and to secure the good order and preservation of their government, the people of this Commonwealth have a right to invest their legislature with power to authorize and require, and the Legislature shall, from time to time, authorize and require the several Towns, Parishes, precincts, and other bodies politic, or religious societies, to make suitable provision, at their own Expense, for the institution of the Public worship of God, and for the support and maintenance of public protestant teachers of piety, religion and morality, in all cases where such provision shall not be made Voluntarily.—And the people of this

Commonwealth have also a right to, and do, invest their legislature with authority to enjoin upon all the Subjects an attendance upon the instructions of the public teachers aforesaid, at stated times and seasons, if there be any on whose instructions they can Conscientiously and conveniently attend—Provided notwithstanding, that the several towns, parishes, precincts, and other bodies politic, or religious societies, shall, at all times, have the exclusive right of electing their public Teachers, and of contracting with them for their support and maintenance.—And all monies, paid by the Subject to the Support of public worship, and of the public teachers aforesaid shall, if he require it, be uniformly applied to the support of the public teachers of his religious sect or denomination, provided there be any on whose instructions he attends; otherwise it may be paid towards the support of the teacher or teachers of the parish or precinct in which the said monies are raised—And every denomination of Christians, demeaning themselves peaceably, and as good Subjects of the Commonwealth, shall be equally under the protection of the Law: And no subordination of any one sect or denomination to another shall ever be established by law.

ARTICLE XVIII. Moral qualifications for office; moral obligations of law-givers and magistrates. A frequent recurrence to the fundamental principles of the constitution and a constant adherence to those of piety, justice, moderation, temperance, industry, and frugality, are absolutely necessary to preserve the advantages of liberty, and to maintain a free government. The people ought, consequently, to have a particular attention to all those principles, in the choice of their Officers and Representatives; and they have a right to require of their law-givers and magistrates an exact and constant observance of them, in the formation and execution of the laws necessary for the good administration of the Commonwealth.

ARTICLES OF AMENDMENT

ARTICLE XI. Religious Freedom Established.

"Instead of the Third Article of the Bill of Rights, the following Modification and Amendment thereof is substituted.

As the public worship of God and instructions in piety, religion and morality, promote the happiness and prosperity of a people and the security of a Republican Government;—Therefore, the several religious societies of this Commonwealth, whether corporate or unincorporate, at any meeting legally warned and holden for that purpose, shall ever have the right to elect their pastors or religious teachers, to contract with them for their support, to raise money for erecting and repairing houses for public worship, for the maintenance of religious instruction, and for the payment of necessary expenses; And all persons belonging to any religious society shall be taken and held to be members, until they shall file with the Clerk of such Society, a written notice, declaring the dissolution of their membership, and thenceforth shall not be liable for any grant or contract, which may be thereafter made, or entered into by such society;—And all religious sects and denominations demeaning themselves peaceably and as good citizens of the Commonwealth, shall be equally under the protection of the law; and no subordination of any one sect or denomination to another shall ever be established by law."

ARTICLE XLVI. Religious Freedom, Public Money not to be appropriated for Founding, Maintaining or aiding Educational, Charitable or Religious Institutions not publicly owned, care or support of public charges in private hospitals; religious services for inmates of certain institutions.

[In place of article XVIII of the articles of amendment of the constitution ratified and adopted April 9, 1821, the following article of amendment, submitted by the constitutional convention, was ratified and adopted November 6, 1917.]

ARTICLE XVIII. Section 1. No law shall be passed prohibiting the free exercise of religion.

Section 2. All moneys raised by taxation in the towns and cities for the support of public schools, and all moneys which may be appropriated by the commonwealth for the support of common schools shall be applied to, and expended in, no other schools than those which are conducted according to law, under the order and superintendence of the authorities of the town or city in which the money is expended; and no grant, appropriation or use of public money or property or loan of public credit shall be made or authorized by the commonwealth or any political division thereof for the purpose of founding, maintaining or aiding any school or institution of learning, whether under public control or otherwise, wherein any denominational doctrine is inculcated or any other school, or any college, infirmary, hospital institution, or educational, charitable or religious undertaking which is not publicly owned and under the exclusive control, order and superintendence of public officers or public agents authorized by the commonwealth, or federal authority or both, except that appropriations may be made for the maintenance and support of the Soldiers' Home in Massachusetts and for free public libraries in any city or town, and to carry out legal obligations, if any, already entered into; and no such grant, appropriation or use of public money or property or loan of public credit shall be made or authorized for the purpose of founding, maintaining or aiding any church, religious denomination or society.

Section 3. Nothing herein contained shall be construed to prevent the commonwealth, or any political division thereof, from paying to privately controlled hospitals, infirmaries, or institutions for the deaf, dumb or blind not more than the ordinary and reasonable compensation for care or support actually rendered or furnished by such hospitals, infirmaries or institutions to such persons as may be in whole or in part unable to support or care for themselves.

Section 4. Nothing herein contained shall be construed to deprive any inmate of a publicly controlled reformatory, panel or charitable institution of the opportunity of religious exercises therein of his own faith; but no inmate of such institution shall be compelled to attend religious services or receive religious instruction against his will, or, if a minor, without the consent of his parent or guardian.

ARTICLE XLVIII.   THE INITIATIVE AND REFERENDUM

Section 2. Excluded Matters.—No measure that relates to religion, religious practices or religious institutions: . . . shall be proposed by an initiative petition. . . .

CONSTITUTION OF MICHIGAN
1963
(Effective January 1, 1964)

Preamble. We, the people of the State of Michigan, grateful to Almighty God . . .

ARTICLE I
DECLARATION OF RIGHTS

Equal protection; discrimination. Sec. 2. No person shall be denied the equal protection of the laws; nor shall any person be denied the enjoyment of his civil or political rights or be discriminated against in the exercise thereof because of religion, race, color or national origin. The legislature shall implement this section by appropriate legislation.

Freedom of worship and religious belief; appropriations. Sec. 4. Every person shall be at liberty to worship God according to the dictates of his own conscience. No person shall be compelled to attend, or, against his consent, to contribute to the erection or support of any place of religious worship, or to pay tithes, taxes or other rates for the support of any minister of the gospel or teacher of religion. No money shall be appropriated or drawn from the treasury for the benefit of any religious sect or society, theological or religious seminary; nor shall property belonging to the state be appropriated for any such purpose. The civil and political rights, privileges and capacities of no person shall be diminished or enlarged on acount of his religious belief.

Witness; competency, religious beliefs. Sec. 18. No person shall be rendered incompetent to be a witness on account of his opinions on matters of religious belief.

ARTICLE IV
LEGISLATIVE BRANCH

Chaplains in state institutions. Sec. 47. The legislature may authorize the employment of chaplains in state institutions of detention or confinement.

ARTICLE VIII
EDUCATION

Encouragement of education. Sec. 1. Religion, morality and knowledge being necessary to good government and the happiness of mankind, schools and the means of education shall forever be encouraged.

ARTICLE IX
FINANCE AND TAXATION

Exemption of religious or educational nonprofit organizations. Sec. 4. Property owned and occupied by non-profit religious or educational organizations and used exclusively for religious or educational purposes, as defined by law, shall be exempt from real and personal property taxes.

CONSTITUTION OF MICHIGAN
1890
PREAMBLE

We, the people of the State of Michigan, grateful to Almighty God . . .

ARTICLE II. DECLARATION OF RIGHTS

Sec. 3. Freedom of worship; disabilities. Every person shall be at liberty to worship God according to the dictates of his own conscience. No person shall be compelled to attend, or, against his consent, to contribute to the erection or support of any place of religious worship, or to pay tithes, taxes or other rates for the support of any minister of the gospel or teacher of religion. No money shall be appropriated or drawn from the treasury for the benefit of any religious sect or society, theological or religious seminary; nor shall property belonging to the state be appropriated for any such purpose. The civil and political rights, privileges and capacities of no person shall be diminished or enlarged on account of his religious belief.

Sec. 17. Competency of witnesses. No person shall be rendered incompetent to be a witness on account of his opinions on matters of religious belief.

ARTICLE V. LEGISLATIVE DEPARTMENT

Sec. 26. Chaplain for prisons; appropriations for religious services. The legislature may authorize the employment of a chaplain for each of the state prisons; but no money shall be appropriated for the payment of any religious services in either house of the legislature.

ARTICLE XI. EDUCATION

Sec. I. Encouragement of education. Religion, morality and knowledge being necessary to good government and the happiness of mankind, schools and the means of education shall forever be encouraged.

ARTICLE XV. MILITIA

Sec. I. Militia; membership. The militia shall be composed of all able-bodied male citizens between the ages of 18 and 45 years, except such as are exempted by the laws of the United States or of this state; but all such citizens of any religious denomination, who, from scruples of conscience, may be averse to bearing arms, shall be excused therefrom upon such conditions as shall be prescribed by law.

CONSTITUTION OF MINNESOTA
1857
PREAMBLE

We, the people of the State of Minnesota, grateful to God...

ARTICLE I. BILL OF RIGHTS

Sec. 16. Freedom of conscience; no preference to be given to any religious establishment or mode of worship. The enumeration of rights in this constitution shall not be construed to deny or impair others retained by and inherent in the people. The right of every man to worship God according to the dictates of his own conscience shall never be infringed, nor shall any man be compelled to attend, erect or support any place of worship, or to maintain any religious or ecclesiastical ministry, against his consent; nor shall any control of or interference with the rights of conscience be permitted, or any preference be given by law to any religious establishment or mode of worship; but the liberty of conscience hereby secured shall not be so construed as to excuse acts of licentiousness, or justify practices inconsistent with the peace or safety of the State, nor shall any money be drawn from the treasury for the benefit of any religious societies, or religious or theological seminaries.

Sec. 17. No religious test or property qualifications to be required. No religious test or amount of property shall ever be required as a qualification for any office of public trust under the State. No religious test or amount of property shall ever be required as a qualification of any voter at any election in this State; nor shall any person be rendered incompetent to give evidence in any court of law or equity in consequence of his opinion upon the subject of religion.

ARTICLE VIII. SCHOOL FUNDS, EDUCATION AND SCIENCE

Sec. 3. Public schools in each township to be established. The legislature shall make such provisions, by taxation or otherwise, as, with the income arising from the school funds, will secure a thorough and efficient system of public schools in each township in the State.

Prohibition as to aiding sectarian school. But in no case shall the moneys derived as aforesaid, or any portion thereof, or any public moneys or property, be appropriated or used for the support of schools wherein the distinctive doctrines, creeds or tenets of any particular Christian or other religious sect are promulgated or taught.

ARTICLE IX. FINANCES OF THE STATE AND BANKS AND BANKING

Sec. I. Power of taxation; legislature may authorize. The power of taxation shall never be surrendered, suspended or contracted away. Taxes shall be uniform upon the same class of subjects, and shall be levied and collected for public purposes, but public burying grounds, public school houses, public hospitals, academies, colleges, universities and all seminaries of learning, all churches, church property and houses of worship, institutions of purely public charity, and public property used exclusively for any public purpose, shall be exempt from taxation...

CONSTITUTION OF MISSISSIPPI
1890
PREAMBLE

We, the people of Mississippi in convention assembled, grateful to Almighty God, and invoking his blessing on our work...

ARTICLE 3. BILL OF RIGHTS

Sec. 18. Freedom of religion. No religious test as a qualification for office shall be required; and no preference shall be given by law to any religious sect or mode of worship; but the free enjoyment of all religious sentiments and the different modes of worship shall be held sacred. The rights hereby secured shall not be construed to justify acts of licentiousness injurious to morals or dangerous to the peace and safety of the state, or to exclude the Holy Bible from use in any public school of this state.

ARTICLE 4. LEGISLATIVE DEPARTMENT

Sec. 66. Donations by legislature. No law granting a donation or gratuity in favor of any person or object shall be enacted except by the concurrence of two-thirds of the members elect of each branch of the legislature, nor by any vote for a sectarian purpose or use.

Sec. 90. Certain local, private or special laws, prohibited. The legislature shall not pass local, private, or special laws in any of the following enumerated cases, but such matters shall be provided for only by general laws, viz: ...

...(p) Providing for the management or support of any private or common school, incorporating the same, or granting such school any privileges; ...

...(u) Granting any lands under control of the state to any person or corporation...

ARTICLE 8.　EDUCATION

Sec. 208. Sectarian instruction. No religious or other sect or sects shall ever control any part of the school or other educational funds of this state; nor shall any funds be appropriated toward the support of any sectarian school, or to any school that at the time of receiving such appropriation is not conducted as a free school.

ARTICLE XIV.　GENERAL PROVISIONS

Sec. 265. Atheists. No person who denies the existence of a Supreme Being shall hold any office in this state.

CONSTITUTION OF MISSOURI
1945
PREAMBLE

We, the people of Missouri with profound reverence for the Supreme Ruler of the Universe, and grateful for His goodness...

ARTICLE I.　BILL OF RIGHTS

Sec. 5. Religious freedom; liberty of conscience and belief; limitations. That all men have a natural and indefeasible right to worship Almighty God according to the dictates of their own consciences; that no human authority can control or interfere with the rights of conscience; that no person shall, on account of his religious persuasion or belief, be rendered ineligible to any public office of trust or profit in this state, be disqualified from testifying or serving as a juror, or be molested in his person or estate; but this section shall not be construed to excuse acts of licentiousness, nor to justify practices inconsistent with the good order, peace or safety of the state, or with the rights of others.

Sec. 6. Practice and support of religion not compulsory; contracts therefor enforcible. That no person can be compelled to erect, support or attend any place or system of worship, or to maintain or support any priest, minister, preacher or teacher of any sect, church, creed or denomination of religion; but if any person shall voluntarily make a contract for any such object, he shall be held to the performance of the same.

Sec. 7.   Public aid for religious purposes; preferences and discriminations on religious grounds.   That no money shall ever be taken from the public treasury, directly or indirectly, in aid of any church, sect or denomination of religion, or in aid of any priest, preacher, minister or teacher thereof, as such; and that no preference shall be given to nor any discrimination made against any church, sect or creed of religion, or any form of religious faith or worship.

ARTICLE III.   LEGISLATIVE DEPARTMENT

Sec. 38(a).   Limitation on use of state funds and credit; exceptions; public calamity; blind pensions; old-age assistance; aid to children; direct relief; adjusted compensation for veterans; rehabilitation; participation in federal aid.   The general assembly shall have no power to grant public money or property, or lend or authorize the lending of public credit, to any private person, association or corporation, excepting aid in public calamity, and general laws providing for pensions for the blind, for old age assistance, for aid to dependent or crippled children or the blind, for direct relief, for adjusted compensation, bonus or rehabilitation for discharged members of the armed services of the United States who were bona fide residents of this state during their service, and for the rehabilitation of other persons...

ARTICLE IX.   EDUCATION

Sec. 8.   Prohibition of public aid for religious purposes and institutions.   Neither the general assembly, nor any county, city, town, township, school district or other municipal corporation, shall ever make an appropriation or pay from any public fund whatever, anything in aid of any religious creed, church or sectarian purpose or to help to support or sustain any private or public school, academy, seminary, college, university, or other institution of learning controlled by any religious creed, church or sectarian denomination whatever; nor shall any grant or donation of personal property or real estate ever be made by the state, or any county, city, town or other municipal corporation, for any religious creed, church, or sectarian purpose whatever.

ARTICLE X.   TAXATION

Sec. 6.   Exemptions from taxation.   All property, real and personal, of the state, counties and other political subdivisions, and non profit cemeteries, shall be exempt from taxation; and all property, real and personal not held for private or corporate profit and used exclusively for religious worship, for schools and colleges, for purposes purely charitable, or for agricultural and horticultural societies may be exempted from taxation by general law. All laws exempting from taxation property other than the property enumerated in this article, shall be void.

CONSTITUTION OF MONTANA
1889
PREAMBLE

We, the people of Montana, grateful to Almighty God...

ARTICLE III. A DECLARATION OF RIGHTS OF THE PEOPLE OF THE STATE OF MONTANA

Sec. 4. Religious freedom. The free exercise and enjoyment of religious profession and worship, without discrimination, shall forever hereafter be guaranteed and no person shall be denied any civil or political right or privilege on account of his opinions concerning religion, but the liberty of conscience hereby shall not be construed to dispense with oaths or affirmations, excuse acts of licentiousness, by bigamous or polygamous marriage, or otherwise, or justify practices inconsistent with the good order, peace, or safety of the state, or opposed to the civil authority thereof, or of the United States. No person shall be required to attend any place of worship or support any ministry, religious sect, or denomination, against his consent; nor shall any preference be given by law to any religious denomination or mode of worship.

ARTICLE V. LEGISLATIVE DEPARTMENT

Sec. 35. Appropriations to private institutions. No appropriation shall be made for charitable, industrial, educational or benevolent purpose to any person, corporation or community not under the absolute control of the state, nor to any denominational or sectarian institution or association.

ARTICLE XI. EDUCATION

Sec. 8. State aid to sectarian schools. Neither the legislative assembly, nor any county, city, town, or school district, or other public corporations, shall ever make directly, or indirectly, any appropriation, or pay from any public fund or moneys whatever, or make any grant of lands or other property in aid of any church, or for any sectarian purpose, or to aid in the support of any school, academy, seminary, college, university, or other literary, scientific institution, controlled in whole or in part by any church, sect or denomination whatever.

Sec. 9. Admission to public schools; religious teaching. No religious or partisan test or qualification shall ever be required of any person as a condition of admission into any public educational institution of the state, either as teacher or student; nor shall attendance be required at any religious service whatever, nor shall any sectarian tenets be taught in any public educational institution of the state; nor shall any person be debarred admission to any of the collegiate departments of the university on account of sex.

ARTICLE XII. REVENUE AND TAXATION

Sec. 2. Property exempt from taxation...and such other property as may be used exclusively for the agricultural and horticultural societies, for educational purposes, places for actual religious worship, hospitals and places of burial not used or held for private or corporate profit, institutions of purely public charity...may be exempt from taxation.

ARTICLE XIII. PUBLIC INDEBTEDNESS

Sec. 1. Prohibition against state and subdivision participation in private enterprises. Neither the state, nor any county, city, town, municipality, nor other subdivisions of the state shall ever give or loan its credit in aid of, or make any donation or grant, by subsidy or otherwise, to any individual, association or corporation, or become a subscriber to, or a share holder in, any company or corporation, or a joint owner with any person, company, or corporation, except as to such ownership as may accrue to the state by operation or provision of law.

ORDINANCE NO. I. FEDERAL RELATIONS

Be It Ordained: First. That perfect toleration of religious sentiment shall be secured and that no inhabitant of the state of Montana shall ever be molested in person or property, on account of his or her mode of religious worship.

Fourth. That provision shall be made for the establishment and maintenance of a uniform system of public schools, which shall be open to all the children of said state of Montana and free from sectarian control.

CONSTITUTION OF NEBRASKA
1875
PREAMBLE

We, the people, grateful to Almighty God...

ARTICLE I. BILL OF RIGHTS

Sec. 4. Religious freedom. All persons have a natural and indefeasible right to worship Almighty God according to the dictates of their own consciences.   No person shall be compelled to attend, erect or support any place of worship against his consent, and no preference shall be given by law to any religious society, nor shall any interference with the rights of conscience be permitted.   No religious test shall be required as a qualification for office, nor shall any person be incompetent to be a witness on account of his religious beliefs; but nothing herein shall be construed to dispense with oaths and affirmations.   Religion, morality, and knowledge, however, being essential to good government, it shall be the duty of the Legislature to pass suitable laws to protect every religious denomination in the peaceable enjoyment of its own mode of public worship, and to encourage schools and the means of instruction.

ARTICLE VII.   EDUCATION

Sec. 11.   Sectarian instruction; religious test of teacher or student. No sectarian instruction shall be allowed in any school or institution supported in whole or in part by the public funds set apart for educational purposes, nor shall the state accept any grant, conveyance, or bequest of money, lands or other property to be used for sectarian purposes. Neither the State Legislature nor any county, city or other public corporation shall ever make any appropriation from any public fund, or grant any public land in aid of any sectarian or denominational school or college, or any educational institution which is not exclusively owned and controlled by the state or a governmental subdivision thereof.   No religious test or qualification shall be required of teacher or student, for admission to or continuance in any public school or educational institution supported in whole or in part by public taxation.

ARTICLE VIII.   REVENUE

Sec. 2.   Exemption of property from taxation.   The property of the state and its governmental subdivisions shall be exempt from taxation. The Legislature by general law may exempt property owned by and used exclusively for agricultural and horticultural societies, and property owned and used exclusively for educational, religious, charitable, or cemetery purposes, when such property is not owned or used for financial gain or profit to either the owner or user...

CONSTITUTION OF NEVADA
1864
ORDINANCE

...freedom of religious worship...lands.
Second.   That perfect toleration of religious sentiment shall be secured, and no inhabitant of said state shall ever be molested, in person or property, on account of his or her mode of religious worship.

PREAMBLE

We the people of the State of Nevada Grateful to Almighty God...

ARTICLE I. DECLARATION OF RIGHTS

Sec. 4. Liberty of conscience. The free exercise and enjoyment of religious profession and worship without discrimination or preference shall forever be allowed in this State, and no person shall be rendered incompetent to be a witness on account of his opinions on matters of his religious belief, but the liberty of consciene (conscience) hereby secured, shall not be so construed, as to excuse acts of licentiousness or justify practices inconsistent with the peace, or safety of this State.

ARTICLE 8. MUNICIPAL AND OTHER CORPORATIONS

Sec. 2. Corporate property subject to taxation; exemptions. All real property, and possessory rights to the same, as well as personal property in this State, belonging to corporations now existing or hereafter created shall be subject to taxation, the same as property of individuals; Provided that the property of corporations formed for Municipal, Charitable, Religious, or Educational purposes may be exempted by law.

ARTICLE II. EDUCATION

Sec. 2 Uniform system of common schools. The legislature shall provide for a uniform system of common schools, by which a school shall be established and maintained in each school district at least six months in every year, and any school district which shall allow instruction of a sectarian character therein may be deprived of its proportion of the interest of the public school fund during such neglect or infraction, and the legislature may pass such laws as will tend to secure a general attendance of the children in each school district upon said public schools.

Sec. 9. Sectarian instruction prohibited in common schools, university. No sectarian instruction shall be imparted or tolerated in any school or University that may be established under this Constitution.

Sec. 10. No public funds to be used for sectarian purposes. No public funds of any kind or character whatever, State, County or Municipal, shall be used for sectarian purpose.

CONSTITUTION OF NEW HAMPSHIRE
1784
PART FIRST. BILL OF RIGHTS

Article 4th. Rights of conscience unalienable. Among the natural rights, some are, in their very nature unalienable, because no equivalent can be given or received for them. Of this kind are the Rights of Conscience.

Article 5th. Religious freedom recognized. Every individual has a natural and unalienable right to worship God according to the dictates of his own conscience, and reason; and no subject shall be hurt, molested, or restrained, in his person, liberty, or estate, for worshipping God in the manner and season most agreeable to the dictates of his own conscience; or for his religious profession, sentiments, or persuasion; provided he doth not disturb the public peace or disturb others in their religious worship.

Article 6th. Public worship of the Deity to be encouraged; right or electing religious teachers; free toleration; existing contracts not affected. As morality and piety, rightly grounded on evangelical principles, will give the best and greatest security to government, and will lay, in the hearts of men, the strongest obligations to the subjection; and as the knowledge of these is most likely to be propagated through a society, by the institution of the public worship of the Deity, and of public instruction in morality and religion; therefore, to promote these important purposes, the people of this state have a right to empower, and do hereby fully empower, the legislature, to authorize, from time to time, the several towns, parishes, bodies, corporate, or religious societies, within this state, to make adequate provision, at their own expense, for the support and maintenance of public Protestant teachers of piety, religion, and morality:

Provided notwithstanding, that the several towns, parishes, bodies corporate or religious societies, shall, at all times have the exclusive right of electing their own public teachers, and of contracting with them for their support and maintenance. And no person, of any one particular religious sect or denomination, shall ever be compelled to pay towards the support of the teacher or teachers of another persuasion, sect, or denomination.

And every denomination of Christians, demeaning themselves quietly, and as good subjects of the state, shall be equally under the protection of the law; And no subordination of any one sect or denomination to another, shall ever be established by law.

And nothing herein shall be understood to affect any former contracts made for the support of the ministry; but all such contracts shall remain, and be in the same state as if this constitution had not been made.

Art. 13th. Conscientiously scrupulous, not compellable to bear arms. No person, who is conscientiously scrupulous about the lawfulness of bearing arms, shall be compelled thereto, provided he will pay an equivalent.

PART SECOND. FORM OF GOVERNMENT
ENCOURAGEMENT OF LITERATURE, TRADES, ETC.

Article 83. Encouragement of literature; control of corporations, monopolies and trusts...Provided, nevertheless, that no money raised by taxation shall ever be granted or applied for the use of the schools or institutions of any religious sect or denomination...

OATHS AND SUBSCRIPTIONS

Article 84. Oath of civil officers. Any person chosen governor, councilor, senator, or representative, military or civil officer, (town officers excepted) accepting the trust, shall, before he proceeds to execute the duties of his office, make and subscribe the following declaration, viz—

I, A.B. do solemnly swear, that I will bear faith and true allegiance to the State of New Hampshire, and will support the constitution thereof. So help me God.

I, A.B. do solemnly and sincerely swear and affirm, that I will faithfully and impartially discharge and perform all the duties incumbent on me as—, according to the best of my abilities, agreeably to the rules and regulations of this constitution and the laws of the state of New Hampshire. So help me God.

Provided always, when any person chosen or appointed as aforesaid, shall be of the denomination called Quakers, or shall be scrupulous of swearing, and shall decline taking the said oaths, such (person) shall take and subscribe them, omitting the word "swear" and likewise the words "So help me God", subjoining instead thereof: "This I do under the pains and penalties of perjury."

CONSTITUTION OF NEW JERSEY
1947

We, the people of the State of New Jersey, grateful to Almighty God for the civil and religious liberty which He hath so long permitted us to enjoy, and looking to Him for a blessing upon our endeavors to secure and transmit the same unimpaired to succeeding generations, do ordain and establish this Constitution.

ARTICLE I. RIGHTS AND PRIVILEGES

3. Rights of conscience; religious freedom. No person shall be deprived of the inestimable privilege of worshipping Almighty God in a manner agreeable to the dictates of his own conscience; nor under any pretense whatever be compelled to attend any place of worship contrary to his faith and judgment; nor shall any person be obliged to pay tithes, taxes, or other rates for building or repairing any church or churches, place or places of worship, or for the maintenance of any minister or ministry, contrary to what he believes to be right or has deliberately and voluntarily engaged to perform.

4. Establishment of religious sect; religious or racial test for public

office. There shall be no establishment of one religious sect in preference to another; no religious or racial test shall be required as a qualification for any office or public trust.

5. Denial of rights; discrimination; segregation. No person shall be denied the enjoyment of any civil or military right, nor be discriminated against in the exercise of any civil or military right, nor be segregated in the militia or in the public schools, because of religious principles, race, color, ancestry or national origin.

ARTICLE IV. LEGISLATIVE
SECTION VII

2. Gambling

B. It shall be lawful for the Legislature to authorize by law, bona fide veterans, charitable, educational, religious or fraternal organizations, civic and service clubs, volunteer fire companies and first-aid or rescue squads to conduct games of chance of, and restricted to, the selling of rights to participate, and the awarding of prizes in the specific kind of games of chance sometimes known as raffles, conducted by the drawing for prizes or by the allotment of prizes by chance, when the entire net proceeds of such games of chance are to be devoted to educational, charitable, patriotic, religious or public-spirited uses, in any municipality, in which such law shall be adopted by a majority of the qualified voters, voting thereon, at a general or special election as the submission thereof shall be prescribed by law and for the Legislature, from time to time, to restrict and control, by law, the conduct of such games of chance.

ARTICLE VIII. TAXATION AND FINANCE
SECTION I

2. Taxation; exemptions, in general. Exemption from taxation may be granted only by general laws. Until otherwise provided by law all exemptions from taxation validly granted and now in existence shall be continued. Exemptions from taxation may be altered or repealed, except those exempting real and personal property used exclusively for religious, educational, charitable or cemetery purposes, as defined by law, and owned by any corporation or association organized and conducted exclusively for one or more of such purposes and not operating for profit.

SECTION III

3. Donations of land and appropriations of money to private agencies. No donation of land or appropriation of money shall be made by the State or any county or municipal corporation to or for the use of any society, association or corporation whatever.

SECTION IV

3. Transportation of school children. The Legislature may, within reasonable limitations as to distance to be prescribed, provide for the transportation of children within the ages of five to eighteen years inclusive, to and from any school.

CONSTITUTION OF NEW MEXICO
1913
PREAMBLE

We, the people of New Mexico, grateful to Almighty God...

ARTICLE II. BILL OF RIGHTS

Sec. 5. Rights under treaty of Guadalupe Hidalgo preserved. The rights, privileges and immunities, civil, political and religious, guaranteed to the people of New Mexico by the treaty of Guadalupe Hidalgo shall be preserved inviolate.

Sec. 11. Freedom of religion. Every man shall be free to worship God according to the dictates of his own conscience, and no person shall ever be molested or denied any civil or political right or privilege on account of his religious opinion or mode of religious worship. No person shall be required to attend any place of worship or support any religious sect or denomination; nor shall any preference be given by law to any religious denomination or mode of worship.

ARTICLE IV. LEGISLATIVE DEPARTMENT

Sec. 31. Aid to charities. No appropriation shall be made for charitable, educational or other benevolent purposes to any person, corporation, association, institution or community, not under the absolute control of the state, but the legislature may, in its discretion, make appropriations for the charitable institutions and hospitals, for the maintenance of which annual appropriations were made by the legislative assembly of nineteen hundred and nine.

ARTICLE VII. ELECTIVE FRANCHISE

Sec. 3. Religious and racial equality protected; restrictions on amendments. The right of any citizen of the state to vote, hold office, or sit upon juries, shall never be restricted, abridged or impaired on account of religion, race, language or color, or inability to speak, read or write the English or Spanish languages except as may be otherwise provided in this Constitution...

ARTICLE VIII. TAXATION AND REVENUE

Sec. 3. Tax exempt property . . . all church property, all property used for educational or charitable purposes, all cemeteries not used or held for private or corporate profit...shall be exempt from taxation.

Provided, however, that any...property acquired by churches, property acquired and used for educational or charitable purposes, where such property was, prior to such transfer, subject to the lien of any tax or assessment for the principal or interest of any bonded indebtedness shall not be exempt from such lien, nor from the payment of such taxes or assessments.

ARTICLE IX. STATE, COUNTY AND MUNICIPAL INDEBTEDNESS

Sec. 14. Aid to private enterprise. Neither the state, nor any county, school district, or municipality, except as otherwise provided in this Constitution, shall directly or indirectly lend or pledge its credit, or make any donation to or in aid of any person, association, or public or private corporation, or in aid of any private enterprise for the construction of any railroad; provided, nothing herein shall be construed to prohibit the State or any county or municipality from making provision for the care and maintenance of sick and indigent persons.

ARTICLE XII. EDUCATION

Sec. 3. Control of educational institutions provided for in constitution; use of state land proceeds. The schools, colleges, universities and other educational institutions provided for by this Constitution shall forever remain under the exclusive control of the State, and no part of the proceeds arising from the sale or disposal of any lands granted to the State by Congress, or any other funds appropriated, levied or collected for educational purposes, shall be used for the support of any sectarian, denominational or private school, college or university.

Sec. 9. Religious tests in schools. No religious test shall ever be required as a condition of admission into the public schools or any educational institution of this State, either as a teacher or student and no teacher or students of such school or institution shall ever be required to attend or participate in any religious service whatsoever.

ARTICLE XX. MISCELLANEOUS

Sec. 13. Sacramental wines. The use of wines solely for sacramental purposes under church authority at any place within the state shall never be prohibited.

ARTICLE XXI. COMPACT WITH THE UNITED STATES

Sec. 1. Religious toleration; polygamy. Perfect toleration of religious sentiment shall be secured, and no inhabitant of this state shall ever be molested in person or property on account of his or her mode of religious worship. Polygamous or plural marriages and polygamous cohabitation are forever prohibited.

Sec. 4. Public Schools. Provision shall be made for the establishment and maintenance of a system of public schools which shall be open to all the children of the State and free from sectarian control, and said schools shall always be conducted in English.

CONSTITUTION OF NEW YORK
1895
PREAMBLE

We, the people of the State of New York, grateful to Almighty God.

ARTICLE I. BILL OF RIGHTS

Sec. 3. Freedom of worship; religious liberty. The free exercise and enjoyment of religious profession and worship, without discrimination or preference, shall forever be allowed in this state to all mankind; and no person shall be rendered incompetent to be a witness on account of his opinions on matters of religious belief; but the liberty of conscience hereby secured shall not be so construed as to excuse acts of licentiousness, or justify practices inconsistent with the peace or safety of this state.

Sec. 11. Equal protection of laws; discrimination in civil rights prohibited. No person shall be denied the equal protection of the laws of this state or any subdivision thereof. No person shall, because of race, color, creed or religion, be subjected to any discrimination in his civil rights by any other person or by any firm, corporation, or institution, or by the state or any agency or subdivision of the state.

ARTICLE VII.   STATE FINANCE

Sec. 8. Gift or loan of state credit or money prohibited; exceptions for enumerated purposes. The money of the state shall not be given or loaned to or in aid of any private corporation or association, or private undertaking; nor shall the credit of the state be given or loaned to or in aid of any individual, or public or private corporation or association, or private undertaking, but the foregoing provisions shall not apply to any fund or property now held or which may hereafter be held by the state for educational purposes.

Subject to the limitations on indebtedness and taxation, nothing in this constitution contained shall prevent the legislature from providing for the aid, care and support of the needy directly or through subdivisions of the state; or for the protection by insurance or otherwise, against the hazards of unemployment, sickness and old age; or for the education and support of the blind, the deaf, the dumb, the physically handicapped and juvenile delinquents as it may deem proper; or for health and welfare services for all children, either directly or through subdivisions of the state, incuding school districts; or for the aid, care and support of neglected and dependent children and of the needy sick through agencies and institutions authorized by the state board of social welfare or other state department having the power of inspection thereof, by payments made on a per capita basis directly or through the subdivisions of the state; or for the increase in the amount of pensions of any member of a retirement system of the state, or of a subdivision of the state. The enumeration of legislative powers in this paragraph shall not be taken to diminish any power of the legislature hitherto existing.

ARTICLE VIII.   LOCAL FINANCES

Sec. 1. Gift or loan of property or credit of local subdivisions prohibited; exceptions for enumerated purposes...

Subject to the limitations on indebtedness and taxation applying to any county, city or town, nothing in this constitution contained shall prevent a county, city or town from making such provision for the aid, care and support of the needy as may be authorized by law, nor prevent any such county, city or town from providing for the care, support, maintenance and secular education of inmates of orphan asylums, homes for dependent children or correctional institutions and of children placed in family homes by authorized agencies, whether under public or private control. . . .

Payments by counties, cities or towns to charitable, eleemosynary, correctional and reformatory institutions and agencies, wholly or partly under private control, for care, support and maintenance may be authorized, but shall not be required by the legislature. . . .

ARTICLE XI.   EDUCATION

Sec. 4. Use of public property or money in aid of denominational schools prohibited; transportation of children authorized. Neither the state nor any subdivision thereof shall use its property or credit or any public money, or authorize or permit either to be used, directly or indirectly, in aid of maintenance, other than for examination or inspection, of any school or institution of learning wholly or in part under the control or direction of any religious denomination, or in which any denominational tenet or doctrine is taught, but the legislature may provide for the transportation of children to and from any school or institution of learning.

ARTICLE XVI.   TAXATION

Sec. 1. . . . exemptions from taxation. . . .

Exemptions from taxation may be granted only by general laws.

Exemptions may be altered or repealed except those exempting real or personal property used exclusively for religious, educational or charitable purposes as defined by law and owned by any corporation or association organized or conducted exclusively for one or more of such purposes and not operating for profit.

CONSTITUTION OF NORTH CAROLINA
1868
PREAMBLE

We, the people of the State of North Carolina, grateful to Almighty God, the Sovereign Ruler of Nations...and acknowledging our dependence upon Him for the continuance of those blessings to us and our posterity...

ARTICLE I.   DECLARATION OF RIGHTS

Sec. 26.   Religious liberty.   All persons have a natural and inalienable right to worship Almighty God according to the dictates of their own consciences, and no human authority should, in any case whatever, control or interfere with the rights of conscience.

ARTICLE V.   REVENUE AND TAXATION

Sec. 5.   Property exempt from taxation.   Property belonging to the State or to municipal corporations, shall be exempt from taxation.   The General Assembly may exempt cemeteries and property held for educational, scientific, literary, charitable, or religious purposes;...

ARTICLE VI.   SUFFRAGE AND ELIGIBILITY TO OFFICE

Sec. 8.   Disqualification for office.   The following classes of persons shall be disqualified for office: first, all persons who shall deny the being of Almighty God...

ARTICLE IX.   EDUCATION

Sec. 1.   Education shall be encouraged. Religion, morality, and knowledge being necessary to good government and the happiness of mankind, schools and the means of education shall forever be encouraged.

ARTICLE XI.   PUNISHMENTS, PENAL INSTITUTIONS, AND PUBLIC CHARITIES

Sec. 7.   Provision for the poor and orphans.   Beneficent provisions for the poor, the unfortunate and orphan, being one of the first duties of a civilized and Christian state, the General Assembly shall, at its first session, appoint and define the duties of a board of public charities, to whom shall be entrusted the supervision of all charitable and penal State institutions, and who shall annually report to the Governor upon their condition, with suggestions for their improvement.

ARTICLE XII.   MILITIA

Sec. 1. Who are liable to militia duty. All able-bodied male citizens of the State of North Carolina, between the ages of twenty-one and forty years, who are citizens of the United States, shall be liable to duty in the militia: Provided, that all persons who may be averse to bearing arms, from religious scruples, shall be exempt therefrom.

CONSTITUTION OF NORTH DAKOTA
1889

We, the people of North Dakota, grateful to Almighty God...

ARTICLE I.   DECLARATION OF RIGHTS

Sec. 4. Religious freedom. The free exercise and enjoyment of religious profession and worship, without discrimination or preference, shall be forever guaranteed in this state, and no person shall be rendered incompetent to be a witness or juror on account of his opinion on matters of religious belief; but the liberty of conscience hereby secured shall not be so construed as to excuse acts of licentiousness, or justify practices inconsistent with the peace or safety of this state.

ARTICLE VIII.   EDUCATION

Sec. 147. Public schools. A high degree of intelligence, patriotism, integrity and morality on the part of every voter in a government by the people being necessary in order to insure the continuance of that government and the prosperity and happiness of the people, the legislative assembly shall make provision for the establishment and maintenance of a system of public schools which shall be open to all children of the state of North Dakota and free from sectarian control. This legislative requirement shall be irrevocable without the consent of the United States and the people of North Dakota.

Sec. 149. Moral instruction. In all schools instruction shall be given as far as practicable in those branches of knowledge that tend to impress upon the mind the vital importance of truthfulness, temperance, purity, public spirit, and respect for honest labor of every kind.

Sec. 152. Support of private schools. All colleges, universities, and other educational institutions, for the support of which lands have been granted to this state, or which are supported by a public tax, shall remain under the absolute and exclusive control of the state. No money raised for the support of the public schools of the state shall be appropriated to or used for the support of any sectarian school.

ARTICLE IX. SCHOOL AND PUBLIC LANDS

Sec. 158. Sale of school lands. . . .

Any said lands that may be required for...school house sites, church sites, cemetery sites, sites for other educational or charitable institutions...or for any of the purposes for which private lands may be taken under the right of eminent domain under the Constitution and laws of this state, may be sold under the provisions of this Article, and shall be paid for in full at the time of sale, or at any time thereafter as herein provided...

ARTICLE XI. REVENUE AND TAXATION

Sec. 176. Exemptions....and property used exclusively for schools, religious, cemetery, charitable or other purposes shall be exempt from taxation. . . .

ARTICLE XII. PUBLIC DEBT AND PUBLIC WORKS

Sec. 185. Internal improvements. . . . neither the state nor any political subdivision thereof shall otherwise loan or give its credit or make donations to or in aid of any individual, association or corporation except for reasonable support of the poor, nor subscribe to or become the owner of capital stock in any association or corporation.

ARTICLE XIII. MILITIA

Sec. 188. Composition. The militia of this state shall consist of all able-bodied male persons residing in the state, between the ages of eighteen and forty-five years, except such as may be exempted by the laws of the United States or of this state. Persons whose religious tenets or conscientious scruples forbid them to bear arms shall not be compelled to do so in times of peace, but shall pay an equivalent for a personal service.

ARTICLE XVI. COMPACT WITH THE UNITED STATES

Sec. 203. First. Religious liberty. Perfect toleration of religious sentiment shall be secured, and no inhabitant of this state shall ever be molested in person or property on account of his or her mode of religious worship. . . .

ARTICLE XVII. MISCELLANEOUS

Sec. 211. Oath of office. Members of the legislative assembly and judicial departments, except of such inferior officers as may be by law exempted shall before they enter on the duties of their respective offices, take and subscribe the following oath or affirmation: "I do solemnly swear (or affirm as the case may be) that I will support the constitution of the United States and the constitution of the state of North Dakota; and that I will faithfully discharge the duties of the office of........ ... according to the best of my ability, so help me God" (if an oath), (under pains and penalties of perjury) if an affirmation, and no other oath, declaration, or test shall be required as a qualification for any office or public trust.

CONSTITUTION OF OHIO
1851
PREAMBLE

We, the people of the State of Ohio, grateful to Almighty God...

ARTICLE I. BILL OF RIGHTS

Sec. 7. Rights of conscience; the necessity of religion and knowledge. All men have a natural and indefeasible right to worship Almighty God according to the dictates of their own conscience. No person shall be compelled to attend, erect, or support any place of worship, or maintain any form of worship, against his consent; and no preference shall be given, by law, to any religious society; nor shall any interference with the rights of conscience be permitted. No religious test shall be required, as a qualification for office, nor shall any person be incompetent to be a witness on account of his religious belief; but nothing herein shall be construed to dispense with oaths and affirmations. Religion, morality, and knowledge, however, being essential to good government, it shall be the duty of the General Assembly to pass suitable laws, to protect every religious denomination in the peaceable enjoyment of its own mode of public worship, and to encourage schools and the means of instruction.

ARTICLE VI. EDUCATION

Sec. 1. Funds for educational and religious purposes. The principal of all funds, arising from the sale, or other disposition of lands, or other property, granted or entrusted to this State for educational and religious purposes, shall forever be preserved inviolate, and undiminished; and, the income arising therefrom, shall be faithfully applied to the specific objects of the original grants, or appropriations.

Sec. 2. Common school fund to be raised; how controlled. The General Assembly shall make such provisions, by taxation, or otherwise, as, with the income arising from the school trust fund, will secure a thorough and efficient system of common schools throughout the State; but, no religious or other sect, or sects, shall ever have any exclusive right to, or control of, any part of the school funds of this State.

ARTICLE VII. FINANCE AND TAXATION

Sec. 2. Taxation by uniform rule; exemption. . . . general laws may be passed to exempt burying grounds, public school houses, houses used exclusively for public worship, institutions used exclusively for charitable purposes and public property used exclusively for any public purpose, but all such laws shall be subject to alteration or repeal;...

CONSTITUTION OF OKLAHOMA
1907
PREAMBLE

Invoking the guidance of Almighty God. . .

ARTICLE I.   FEDERAL RELATIONS

Sec. 2. Religious liberty; polygamous or plural marriages. Perfect toleration of religious sentiment shall be secured, and no inhabitant of the State shall ever be molested in person or property on account of his or her mode of religious worship; and no religious test shall be required for the exercise of civil or political rights. Polygamous or plural marriages are forever prohibited.

Sec. 5. Public schools; separate schools. Provisions shall be made for the establishment and maintenance of a system of public schools, which shall be open to all the children of the State and free from sectarian control; and said schools shall always be conducted in English: Provided, that nothing herein shall preclude the teaching of other languages in said public schools: And Provided, further, that this shall not be construed to prevent the establishment and maintenance of separate schools for white and colored children.

ARTICLE II.   BILL OF RIGHTS

Sec. 5. Public money or property; use for sectarian purposes. No public money or property shall ever be appropriated, applied, donated, or used, directly or indirectly, for the use, benefit, or support of any sect, church, denomination, or system of religion, or for the use, benefit, or support of any priest, preacher, minister, or other religious teacher or dignitary, or sectarian institution as such.

ARTICLE X.   REVENUE AND TAXATION

Sec. 6. Property exempt from taxation; exemptions under territorial laws; exemption of certain property for limited time. All property used for free public libraries, free museums, public cemeteries, property used exclusively for schools, colleges, and all property used exclusively for religious and charitable purposes...shall be exempt from taxation.

Sec. 15. Pledge or loan of credit; donations. The credit of the State shall not be given, pledged, or loaned to any individual, company, corporation, or association, municipality, or political subdivision of the State; nor shall the State become an owner or stockholder in, nor make donation by gift, subscription to stock, by tax, or otherwise, to any company, association, or corporation.

ARTICLE XI. STATE AND SCHOOL LANDS

Sec. 5. University and College lands; control of institutions; diversion of funds. . . . Such educational institutions shall remain under the exclusive control of the State and no part of the proceeds arising from the sale or disposal of any lands granted for educational purposes, or the income or rentals thereof, shall be used for the support of any religious or sectarian school, college, or university, and no portion of the funds arising from the sale of sections thirteen or any indemnity lands in lieu thereof, either principal or interest shall ever be diverted, either temporarily or permanently, from the purpose for which said lands were granted to the State. . . .

CONSTITUTION OF OREGON
1859
ARTICLE I. BILL OF RIGHTS

Sec. 2. Freedom of worship. All men shall be secure in the Natural right, to worship Almighty God according to the dictates of their own consciences.——

Sec. 3. Freedom of religious opinion. No law shall in any case whatever control the free exercise, and enjoyment of religeous (sic) opinions, or interfere with the rights of conscience.——

Sec. 4. No religious qualification for office. No religious test shall be required as a qualification for any office of trust or profit.

Sec. 5. No money to be appropriated for religion. No money shall be drawn from the Treasury for the benefit of any religeous (sic), or theological institution, nor shall any money be appropriated for the payment of any religeous (sic) services in either house of the Legislative Assembly.

Sec. 6. No religious test for witnesses or jurors. No person shall be rendered incompetent as a witness, or juror in consequence of his opinions on matters of religeon (sic); nor be questioned in any Court of Justice touching his religeous (sic) belief to affect the weight of his testimony.——

ARTICLE X. THE MILITIA

Sec. 2. Who exempt. Persons whose religeous (sic) tenets, or conscientious scruples forbid them to bear arms shall not be compelled to do so in time of peace, but shall pay an equivalent for personal service.

CONSTITUTION OF PENNSYLVANIA
1874
PREAMBLE

We, the people of the Commonwealth of Pennsylvania, grateful to Almighty God...and humbly invoking His guidance...

ARTICLE I. DECLARATION OF RIGHTS

Sec. 3. Rights of conscience; freedom of religious worship. All men have a natural and indefeasible right to worship Almighty God according to the dictates of their own consciences; no man can of right be compelled to attend, erect or support any place of worship, or to maintain any ministry against his consent; no human authority can, in any case whatever, control or interfere with the rights of conscience and no preference shall ever be given by law to any religious establishment or modes of worship.

Sec. 4. No disqualification for religious belief. No person who acknowledges the being of a God, and a future state of rewards and punishments shall, on account of his religious sentiments, be disqualified to hold any office or place of trust or profit under this Commonwealth.

ARTICLE III. LEGISLATION

Sec. 17. Appropriations to charitable and educational institutions. No appropriation shall be made to any charitable or educational institution not under the absolute control of the Commonwealth, other than normal schools established by law for the professional training of teachers for the public schools of the State, except by a vote of two-thirds of all the members elected to each House.

Sec. 18. Certain appropriations forbidden. No appropriations shall be made for charitable, educational or benevolent purposes to any person or community nor to any denominational and sectarian institution, corporation or association; Provided, that appropriations may be made for pensions or gratuities for military services, and to blind persons twenty-one years of age and upwards, and for assistance to mothers having dependent children, and to aged persons, without adequate means of support.

ARTICLE IX. TAXATION AND FINANCE

Sec. 1. Taxes to be uniform; exemptions. All taxes shall be uniform, upon the same class of subjects, within the territorial limits of the authority levying the tax, and shall be levied and collected under general laws; but the General Assembly may, by general laws, exempt from taxation public property used for public purposes, actual places of religious worship, places of burial not used or held for private or corporate profit, and institutions of purely public charity. . . .

ARTICLE X. EDUCATION

Sec. 2. Diversion of school moneys to sectarian schools. No money raised for the support of the public schools of the Commonwealth shall be appropriated to or used for the support of any sectarian school.

ARTICLE XI. MILITIA

Sec. 1. Militia to be organized; maintenance; exemption from service. The freeman of this Commonwealth shall be armed, organized and disciplined for its defense when and in such manner as may be directed by law. The General Assembly shall provide for maintaining the militia by appropriations from the Treasury of the Commonwealth, and may exempt from military service persons having conscientious scruples against bearing arms.

CONSTITUTION OF RHODE ISLAND
1843

We, the people of the State of Rhode Island and Providence Plantations, grateful to Almighty God for the civil and religious liberty which He hath so long permitted us to enjoy, and looking to Him for a blessing upon our endeavors...

ARTICLE I. DECLARATION OF CERTAIN CONSTITUTIONAL RIGHTS AND PRINCIPLES

Sec. 3. Religious freedom secured. Whereas Almighty God hath created the mind free; and all attempts to influence it by temporal punishments or burdens, or by civil incapacitations, tend to beget habits of hypocrisy and meanness; and whereas a principal object of our venerable ancestors, in their migration to this country and their settlement of this state, was as they expresed it, to hold forth a lively experiment, that a flourishing civil state may stand and be best maintained with full liberty in religious concernments: We, therefore, declare that no man shall be compelled to frequent or to support any religious worship, place, or ministry whatever, except in fulfillment of his own voluntary contract; nor enforced, restrained, molested, or burdened in his body or goods; nor disqualified from holding any office; nor otherwise suffer on account of his religious belief; and that every man shall be free to worship God according to the dictates of his own conscience, and to profess and by argument to maintain his opinion in matters of religion; and that the same shall in no wise diminish, enlarge or affect his civil capacity.

CONSTITUTION OF SOUTH CAROLINA
1895

We, the people of the State of South Carolina...grateful to God for our liberties...

ARTICLE I.   DECLARATION OF RIGHTS

Sec. 4. Religious worship; freedom of speech; petition. The General Assembly shall make no law respecting an establishment of religion or prohibiting the free exercise thereof, or abridging the freedom of speech or of the press; or the right of the people peaceably to assemble and to petition the Government or any department thereof for a redress of grievances.

ARTICLE X.   FINANCE AND TAXATION

Sec. 1. Taxation and assessment. The General Assembly shall provide by law for a uniform and equal rate of assessment and taxation, and shall prescribe regulations to secure a just valuation for taxation of all property, real, personal and possessory, except mines and mining claims, the products of which alone shall be taxed; and also excepting such property as may be exempted by law for municipal, educational, literary, scientific, religious or charitable purposes:...

Sec. 4. Property exempt from taxation; household goods and furniture. There shall be exempted from taxation all County, township and municipal property used exclusively for public purposes and not for revenue, and the property of all schools, colleges and institutions of learning, all charitable institutions in the nature of asylums for the infirm, deaf and dumb, blind, idiotic and indigent persons, except where the profits of such institutions are applied to private uses; all public libraries, churches, parsonages and burying grounds; but property of associations and societies, although connected with charitable objects, shall not be exempt from State, County or municipal taxation; Provided, that as to real estate this exemption shall not extend beyond the buildings and premises actually occupied by such schools, colleges, institutions of learning, asylums, libraries, churches, parsonages and burial grounds, although connected with charitable objects.

ARTICLE XI.   EDUCATION

Sec. 9. Property or credit of state shall not benefit sectarian institutions. The property or credit of the State of South Carolina, or of any county, city, town, township, school district, or other subdivision of the said State, or any public money, from whatever source derived, shall not, by gift, donation, loan, contract, appropriation, or otherwise, be used, directly or indirectly, in aid or maintenance of any college, school, hospital, orphan house, or other institution, society or organization, of whatever kind, which is wholly or in part under the direction or control of any church or of any religious or sectarian denomination, society or organization.

ARTICLE XIII. MILITIA

Sec. 1. Militia. The militia of this State shall consist of all able-bodied male citizens of the State between the ages of eighteen and forty-five years, except such persons as are now or may be exempted by the laws of the United States or this State, or who from religious scruples may be averse to bearing arms, and shall be organized, officered, armed, equipped and disciplined as the General Assembly may by law direct.

ARTICLE XVII. MISCELLANEOUS MATTERS

Sec. 4. Supreme Being. No person who denies the existence of a Supreme Being shall hold any office under this Constitution.

CONSTITUTION OF SOUTH DAKOTA
1889
PREAMBLE

We, the people of South Dakota, grateful to Almighty God...

ARTICLE VI. BILL OF RIGHTS

Sec. 3. Religious freedom. The right to worship God according to the dictates of conscience shall never be infringed. No person shall be denied any civil or political right, privilege or position on account of his religious opinions; but the liberty of conscience hereby secured shall not be so construed as to excuse licentiousness, the invasion of the rights of others, or justify practices inconsistent with the peace or safety of the state.

No person shall be compelled to attend or support any ministry or place of worship against his consent nor shall any preference be given by law to any religious establishment or mode of worship. No money or property of the state shall be given or appropriated for the benefit of any sectarian or religious society or institution.

ARTICLE VIII. EDUCATION AND SCHOOL LANDS

Sec. 16. Aid to sectarian schools. No appropriation of lands, money or other property or credits to aid any sectarian school shall ever be made by the state, or any county or municipality within the state, nor shall the state or any county or municipality within the state accept any grant, conveyance, gift or bequest of lands, money or other property to be used for sectarian purposes, and no sectarian instruction shall be allowed in any school or institution aided or supported by the state.

ARTICLE XI. REVENUE AND FINANCE

Sec. 6. Exemption of private property. The legislature shall, by general law, exempt from taxation, property used exclusively for agricultural and horticultural societies, for school, religious, cemetery and charitable poses (sic)...

ARTICLE XV. MILITIA

Sec. 7. Conscientious objectors. No person having conscientious scruples against bearing arms shall be compelled to do military duty in time of peace.

ARTICLE XXII. COMPACT WITH THE UNITED STATES

First. That perfect toleration of religious sentiment shall be secured and that no inhabitant of this state shall ever be molested in person or property on account of his or her mode of religious worship.

Fourth. That provision shall be made for the establishment and maintenance of systems of public schools, which shall be open to all the children of this state, and free from sectarian control.

ARTICLE XXVI. SCHEDULE AND ORDINANCE

Sec. 18. First. That perfect toleration of religious sentiment shall be secured, and that no inhabitant of this state shall ever be molested in person or property on account of his or her mode of religious worship.

Fourth. That provision shall be made for the establishment and maintenance of systems of public schools, which shall be open to all the children of this state, and free from sectarian control.

CONSTITUTION OF TENNESSEE
1870
ARTICLE I. DECLARATION OF RIGHTS

Sec. 3. Right of worship free. That all men have a natural and indefeasible right to worship Almighty God according to the dictates of their own conscience; that no man can of right be compelled to attend, erect, or support any place of worship, or to maintain any minister against his consent; that no human authority can, in any case whatever, control or interfere with the rights of conscience; and that no preference shall ever be given, by law, to any religious establishment or mode of worship.

Sec. 4. No religious or political test. That no political or religious test, other than an oath to support the Constitution of the United States and of this State, shall ever be required as a qualification to any office, or public trust under this State.

Sec. 6. Trial by jury. That the right of trial by jury shall remain inviolate, and no religious or political test shall ever be required as a qualification for jurors.

Sec. 28. No one compelled to bear arms. That no citizen of this State shall be compelled to bear arms, provided he will pay an equivalent, to be ascertained by law.

ARTICLE II.   DISTRIBUTION OF POWERS

Sec. 28. Taxation of property . . . All property real, personal or mixed shall be taxed, but the Legislature may except such as may be held by the State, by Counties, Cities or Towns, and used exclusively for public or corporation purposes, and such as may be held and used for purposes purely religious, charitable, scientific, literary or educational. . . .

ARTICLE VIII.   MILITIA

Sec. 3. Exemptions from attending musters. The Legislature shall pass laws exempting citizens belonging to any sect or denomination of religion, the tenets of which are known to be opposed to the bearing of arms, from attending private and general musters.

ARTICLE IX.   DISQUALIFICATIONS

Sec. 1. Ineligibility of ministers and priests to seats in legislatures. Whereas Ministers of the Gospel are by their profession, dedicated to God and the care of souls, and ought not to be diverted from the great duties of their functions; therefore, no Minister of the Gospel, or priest of any denomination whatever, shall be eligible to a seat in either House of the Legislature.

Sec. 2. No atheist or disbeliever shall hold a civil office. No person who denies the being of God, or a future state of rewards and punishments, shall hold any office in the civil department of this State.

ARTICLE XI.   MISCELLANEOUS PROVISIONS

Sec. 15. Religious Holidays. No person shall in time of peace be required to perform any service to the public on any day set apart by his religion as a day of rest.

CONSTITUTION OF TEXAS
1876
PREAMBLE

Humbly invoking the blessing of Almighty God, the people of the State of Texas, do ordain and establish this Constitution.

ARTICLE I. BILL OF RIGHTS

Sec. 4. No religious test for office. No religious test shall ever be required as a qualification to any office, or public trust, in this State; nor shall anyone be excluded from holding office on account of his religious sentiments provided he acknowledge the existence of a Supreme Being.

Sec. 5. How oaths shall be administered. No person shall be disqualified to give evidence in any of the Courts of this State, on account of his religious opinion, or for the want of any religious belief, but all oaths or affirmations shall be administered in the mode most binding upon the conscience, and shall be taken subject to the pains and penalties of perjury.

Sec. 6. Freedom in religious worship guaranteed. All men have a natural and indefeasible right to worship Almighty God according to the dictates of their own consciences. No man shall be compelled to attend, erect or support any place or worship, or to maintain any ministry against his consent. No human authority ought, in any case whatever, to control or interfere with the rights of conscience in matters of religion, and no preference shall ever be given by law to any religious society or mode of worship. But it shall be the duty of the Legislature to pass such laws as may be necessary to protect equally every religious denomination in the peaceable enjoyment of its own mode of public worship.

Sec. 7. No appropriation for sectarian purposes. No money shall be appropriated, or drawn from the Treasury for the benefit of any sect, or religious society, theological or religious seminary; nor shall property belonging to the State be appropriated for any such purposes.

ARTICLE III. LEGISLATIVE DEPARTMENT

Sec. 51-a. Assistance to needy aged, needy blind, and needy children; limitation on annual expenditures for same. The Legislature shall have the power, by General Laws, to provide, subject to limitations and restrictions herein contained, and such other limitations, restrictions and regulations as may by the Legislature be deemed expedient for assistance to, and for the payment of assistance to:

(1) Needy aged persons who are actual bona fide citizens of Texas and who are over the age of sixty-five (65) years: . . .

(2) Needy blind persons who are actual bona fide citizens of Texas and are over the age of twenty-one (21) years; . . .

(3) Needy children who are actual bona fide citizens of Texas and are under the age of sixteen (16) years; . . .

ARTICLE VII. EDUCATION — THE PUBLIC FREE SCHOOLS

Sec. 5. Permanent school fund; interest; alienation; sectarian schools. . . . And no law shall ever be enacted appropriating any part of the permanent or available school fund to any other purpose whatever; nor shall the same, or any part thereof ever be appropriated to or used for the support of any sectarian school; . . .

ARTICLE VIII.   TAXATION AND REVENUE

Sec. 2. . . . exemptions. . . . but the legislature may, by general laws, exempt from taxation, public property used for public purposes; actual places of religious worship, also any property owned by a church or by strictly religious society for the exclusive use as a dwelling place for the ministry of such church or religious society, and which yields no revenue whatever to such church or religious society; provided that such exemption shall not extend to more property than is reasonably necessary for a dwelling place and in no event more than one acre of land; places of burial not held for private or corporate profit; all buildings used exclusively and owned by persons or associations of persons for school purposes and the necessary furniture of all schools and property used exclusively and reasonably necessary in conducting any association engaged in promoting the religious, educational and physical development of boys, girls, young men or young women operating under a State or National organization of like character; also the endowment funds of such institutions of learning and religion not used with a view to profit; . . .

ARTICLE XVI.   GENERAL PROVISIONS

Sec. 47. Scruples against bearing arms. Any person who conscientiously scruples to bear arms, shall not be compelled to do so, but shall pay an equivalent for personal service.

CONSTITUTION OF UTAH
1896
PREAMBLE

Grateful to Almighty God for life and liberty, we, the people of Utah, in order to secure and perpetuate the principles of free government, do ordain and establish this CONSTITUTION.

ARTICLE I.   DECLARATION OF RIGHTS

Sec. 1. Inherent and inalienable rights. All men have the inherent and inalienable right to enjoy and defend their lives and liberties; to acquire, possess and protect property; to worship according to the dictates of their consciences; to assemble peaceably, protest against wrongs, and petition for redress of grievances; to communicate freely their thoughts and opinions, being responsible for the abuse of that right.

Sec. 4. Religious liberty. The rights of conscience shall never be infringed. The State shall make no law respecting an establishment of religion or prohibiting the free exercise thereof; no religious test shall be required as a qualification for any office of public trust or for any vote at any election; nor shall any person be incompetent as a witness or juror on account of religious belief or the absence thereof. There shall be no union of Church and State, nor shall any church dominate the State or interfere with its functions. No public money or property shall be appropriated for or applied to any religious worship, exercise or instruction, or for the support of any ecclesiastical establishment. No property qualification shall be required of any person to vote, or hold office, except as provided in this Constitution.

ARTICLE III. ORDINANCE

First: —Religious toleration; polygamy forbidden. Perfect toleration of religious sentiment is guaranteed. No inhabitant of this State shall ever be molested in person or property on account of his or her mode of religious worship; but polygamous or plural marriages are forever prohibited.

Fourth: —Free, nonsectarian schools. The Legislature shall make laws for the establishment and maintenance of a system of public schools, which shall be open to all the children of the State and be free from sectarian control.

ARTICLE X. EDUCATION

Sec. 1. Free nonsectarian schools. The Legislature shall provide for the establishment of a uniform system of public schools, which shall be open to all children of the State, and be free from sectarian control.

Sec. 12. No religious or partisan tests in schools. Neither religious nor partisan test or qualification shall be required of any person as a condition of admission, as teacher or student, into any public educational institution of the State.

Sec. 13. Public aid to church schools, forbidden. Neither the Legislature nor any county, city, town, school district or other public corporation, shall make any appropriation to aid in the support of any school, seminary, academy, college, university or other institution, controlled in whole, or in part, by any church, sect or denomination whatever.

ARTICLE XIII. REVENUE AND TAXATION

Sec. 2. Tangible property to be taxed; value ascertained; properties exempt; legislature to provide annual tax for state. All tangible property in the state, not exempt under the laws of the United States, or under this constitution, shall be taxed in proporation to its value, to be ascertained as provided by law. The property of the state, counties, cities, towns, school districts, municipal corporations and public libraries, lots with the buildings thereon used exclusively for either religious worship or charitable purposes, and places of burial not held or used for private or corporate benefit, shall be exempt from taxation. . . .

CONSTITUTION OF VERMONT
1793

CHAPTER I.   A DECLARATION OF THE RIGHTS OF THE INHABITANTS OF THE STATE OF VERMONT

Art. 3rd.   Religious freedom and worship.   That all men have a natural and unalienable right, to worship Almighty God, according to the dictates of their own consciences and understandings, as in their opinion shall be regulated by the word of God; and that no man ought to, or of right can be compelled to attend any religious worship, or erect or support any place of worship, or maintain any minister, contrary to the dictates of his conscience, nor can any man be justly deprived or abridged of any civil right as a citizen, on account of his religious sentiments, or peculia(r) mode of religious worship; and that no authority can, or ought to be vested in, or assumed by, any power whatever, that shall in any case interfere with, or in any manner control the rights of conscience, in the free exercise of religious worship.   Nevertheless, every sect or denomination of christians ought to observe the sabbath or Lord's day, and keep up some sort of religious worship, which to them shall seem most agreeable to the revealed will of God.

Art. 9th.   Citizens' rights and duties in the state; bearing arms; taxation.   That every member of society hath a right to be protected in the enjoyment of life, liberty, and property, and therefor is bound to contribute his proportion towards the expense of that protection, and yield his personal service, when necessary, or an equivalent thereto, but no part of any person's property can be justly taken from him, or appiled to public uses, without his own consent, or that of the Representative Body of the freemen, nor can any man who is conscientiously scrupulous of bearing arms, be justly compelled thereto, if he will pay such equivalent; . . .

CHAPTER II.   PLAN OR FRAME OF GOVERNMENT

Sec. 64.   Laws to encourage virtue and prevent vice; schools; religious socities.   Laws for the encouragement of virtue and prevention of vice and immorality, ought to be constantly kept in force, and duly executed; and a competent number of schools ought to be maintained in each town, or by towns jointly with the consent of the General Assembly, for the convenient instruction of youth.   All religious societies, or bodies of men that may be united or incorporated for the advancement of religion and learning, or for other pious and charitable purposes, shall be encouraged and protected in the enjoyment of the privileges, immunities, and estates, which they in justice ought to enjoy, under such regulations as the General Assembly of this State shall direct.

CONSTITUTION OF VIRGINIA
1902

ARTICLE I.   BILL OF RIGHTS

Sec. 16.   Religious freedom.   That religion or the duty which we owe to our Creator, and the manner of discharging it, can be directed only by reason and conviction, not by force or violence; and, therefore, all men are equally entitled to the free exercise of religion, according to the dictates of conscience; and that it is the mutual duty of all to practice Christian forbearance, love and charity towards each other.

ARTICLE IV.   LEGISLATIVE DEPARTMENT

Sec. 58.   Prohibitions on general assembly as to suspension of writ of habeas corpus, and enactment of laws referring to religion and other laws. . . .

No man shall be compelled to frequent or support any religious worship, place or ministry, whatsoever, nor shall be enforced, restrained, molested, or burthened in his body or goods, nor shall otherwise suffer on account of his religious opinions or belief; but all men shall be free to profess and by argument to maintain their opinions in matters of religion, and the same shall in no wise diminish, enlarge, or affect, their civil capacities.   And the General Assembly shall not prescribe any religious test whatever, or confer any peculiar privilege or advantages on any sect or denomination, or pass any law requiring or authorizing any religious society, or the people of any district within this State, to levy on themselves, or others, any tax for the erection or repair of any house of public worship, or for the support of any church or ministry; but it shall be left free to every person to select his religious instructor, and to make for his support such private contract as he shall please.

Sec. 59.   General assembly shall not incorporate churches or religious denominations; may secure church property.   The General Assembly shall not grant a charter of incorporation to any church or religious denomination, but may secure the title to church property to an extent to be limited by law.

Sec. 67.   Limitations on appropriations by general assembly to charitable and other institutions; exceptions.   The General Assembly shall not make any appropriation of public funds, or personal property, or of any real estate, to any church, or sectarian society, association, or institution of any kind whatever, which is entirely or partly, directly or indirectly, controlled by any church or sectarian society; nor shall the General Assembly make any like appropriation to any charitable institution which is not owned or controlled by the State; except that it may, in its discretion, make appropriation to nonsectarian institutions for the reform of youthful criminals; but nothing herein contained shall prohibit the General Assembly from authorizing counties, cities, or towns to make such appropriations to any charitable institution or association.

ARTICLE IX.   EDUCATION AND PUBLIC INSTRUCTION

Sec. 141. State appropriations prohibited to schools or institutions of learning not owned or exclusively controlled by the state or some subdivision thereof; exceptions to rule. No appropriation of public funds shall be made to any school or institution of learning not owned or exclusively controlled by the State or some political subdivision thereof; provided, first that the General Assembly may, and the governing bodies of the several counties, cities and towns, may, subject to such limitations as may be imposed by the General Assembly, appropriate funds for educational purposes which may be expended in furtherance of elementary, secondary, collegiate or graduate education of Virginia students in public and nonsectarian private schools and institutions of learning, in addition to those owned or exclusively controlled by the State or any such county, city or town; second, that the General Assembly may appropriate funds to an agency, or to a school or institution of learning owned or controlled by an agency, created and established by two or more States under a joint agreement to which this State is a party for the purpose of providing educational facilities for the citizens of the several States joining such agreement; third, that counties, cities, towns, and districts may make appropriations to nonsectarian schools of manual, industrial or technical training, and also to any school or institution of learning owned or exclusively controlled by such county, city, town, or school district.

ARTICLE XIII.   TAXATION AND FINANCE

Sec. 183. Property exempt from taxation. Unless otherwise provided in this Constitution, the following property and no other shall be exempt from taxation, State and local, including inheritance taxes: . . .

(b) Buildings with land they actually occupy, and the furniture and furnishings therein and endowment funds lawfully owned and held by churches or religious bodies, and wholly and exclusively used for religious worship, or for the residence of the minister of any such church or religious body, together with the additional adjacent land reasonably necessary for the convenient use of any such building. . . .

(e) Real estate belonging to, actually and exclusively occupied and used by, and personal property, including endowment funds, belonging to Young Men's Christian Associations, and other similar religious associations, orphan or other asylums, reformatories, hospitals and nunneries, conducted not for profit, but exclusively as charities, . . .

CONSTITUTION OF WASHINGTON
1889
PREAMBLE

We the people of the State of Washington, grateful to the Supreme Ruler of the Universe for our liberties, do ordain this constitution.

ARTICLE I.   DECLARATION OF RIGHTS

Sec. 11.   Religious freedom.   Absolute freedom of conscience in all matters of religious sentiment, belief and worship, shall be guaranteed to every individual, and no one shall be molested or disturbed in person or property on account of religion; but the liberty of conscience hereby secured shall not be so construed as to excuse acts of licentiousness or justify practices inconsistent with the peace and safety of the state.   No public money or property shall be appropriated for or applied to any religious worship, exercise or instruction, or the support of any religious establishment; Provided, however, That this article shall not be so construed as to forbid the employment by the state of a chaplain for such of the state custodial, correctional and mental institutions as in the discretion of the legislature may seem justified.   No religious qualification shall be required for any public office or employment, nor shall any person be incompetent as a witness or juror, in consequence of his opinion on matters of religion, nor be questioned in any court of justice touching his religious belief to affect the weight of his testimony.

ARTICLE IX.   EDUCATION

Sec. 4.   Sectarian control or influence prohibited.   All schools maintained or supported wholly or in part by the public funds shall be forever free from sectarian control or influence.

ARTICLE X.   MILITIA

Sec. 6.   Exemption from military duty.   No person or persons, having conscientious scruples against bearing arms, shall be compelled to do militia duty in time of peace, Provided, such person or persons shall pay an equivalent for such exemption.

ARTICLE XXVI.   COMPACT WITH THE UNITED STATES

First: That perfect toleration of religious sentiment shall be secured and that no inhabitant of this state shall ever be molested in person or property on account of his or her mode of religious worship.

Fourth.   Provision shall be made for the establishment and maintenance of systems of public schools free from sectarian control which shall be open to all the children of said state.

CONSTITUTION OF WEST VIRGINIA
1872
PREAMBLE

Since through Divine Providence we enjoy the blessings of civil, political and religious liberty, we the people of West Virginia, in and through the provisions of this Constitution, reaffirm our faith in and constant reliance upon God and seek diligently to promote, preserve and perpetuate good government in the State of West Virginia for the common welfare, freedom and security of ourselves and our posterity.

ARTICLE III.   BILL OF RIGHTS

11.   Political tests condemned.   Political tests, requiring persons, as a prerequisite to the enjoyment of their civil and political rights, to purge themselves by their own oaths, of past alleged offenses, are repugnant to the principles of free government, and are cruel and oppressive.   No religious or political test oath shall be required as a prerequisite or qualification to vote, serve as a juror, sue, plead, appeal, or pursue any profession or employment.   Nor shall any person be deprived by law of any right or privilege, because of any act done prior to the passage of such law.

15.   Religious freedom guaranteed.   No man shall be compelled to frequent or support any religious worship, place or ministry whatsoever, nor shall any man be enforced, restrained, molested or burthened, in his body or goods or otherwise suffer, on account of his religious opinions or belief, but all men shall be free to profess, and, by argument, to maintain their opinions in matters of religion; and the same shall, in no wise, affect, diminish, or enlarge their civil capacities; and the legislature shall not prescribe any religious test whatever, or confer any peculiar privileges or advantages on any sect or denomination, or pass any law requiring or authorizing any religious society, or the people of any district within this State, to levy on themselves, or others any tax for the erection or repair of any house for public worship, or for the support of any church or ministry, but it shall be left free for every person to select his religious instructor, and to make for his support such private contract as he shall please.

ARTICLE VI.   LEGISLATURE

Sec. 47.   Incorporation of religious denominations prohibited.   No charter of incorporation shall be granted to any church or religious denomination.   Provisions may be made by general laws for securing the title to church property, and for the sale and transfer thereof, so that it shall be held, used, or transferred for the purposes of such church, or religious denomination.

ARTICLE X.   TAXATION AND FINANCE

1. Uniform taxation. Subject to the exceptions in this section contained, taxation shall be equal and uniform throughout the State, and all property, both real and personal, shall be taxed in proportion to its value to be ascertained and directed by law. . . . but property used for educational, literary, scientific, religious or charitable purposes, all cemeteries, public property, the personal property, including live stock, employed exclusively in agriculture as above defined and the products of agriculture as so defined while owned by the producers may by law be exempted from taxation; . . .

CONSTITUTION OF WISCONSIN
1848
PREAMBLE

We, the people of Wisconsin, grateful to Almighty God for our freedom, in order to secure its blessings, form a more perfect government, insure domestic tranquillity and promote the general welfare, do establish this constitution.

ARTICLE I.   DECLARATION OF RIGHTS

Sec. 18. Freedom of worship; liberty of conscience; state religion; public funds. The right of every man to worship Almighty God according to the dictates of his own conscience shall never be infringed; nor shall any man be compelled to attend, erect or support any place of worship, or to maintain any ministry, against his consent; nor shall any control of, or interference with, the rights of conscience be permitted, or any preference be given by law to any religious establishments or modes of worship; nor shall any money be drawn from the treasury for the benefit of religious societies, or religious or theological seminaries.

Sec. 19. Religious test prohibited. No religious tests shall ever be required as a qualification for any office of public trust under the state, and no person shall be rendered incompetent to give evidence in any court of law or equity in consequence of his opinions on the subject of religion.

ARTICLE X.   EDUCATION

Sec. 3. District schools; tuition; sectarian instruction. The legislature shall provide by law for the establishment of district schools, which shall be as nearly uniform as practicable; and such schools shall be free and without charge for tuition to all children between the ages of four and twenty years; and no sectarian instruction shall be allowed therein.

Sec. 6. State university; support. Provision shall be made by law for the establishment of a state university at or near the seat of state government, and for connecting with the same, from time to time, such colleges in different parts of the state as the interests of education may require. The proceeds of all lands that have been or may hereafter be granted by the United States to the state for the support of a university shall be and remain a perpetual fund to be called "the university fund," the interest of which shall be appropriated to the support of the state university, and no sectarian instruction shall be allowed in such university.

CONSTITUTION OF WYOMING
1890
PREAMBLE

We, the people of the state of Wyoming, grateful to God for our civil, political and religious liberties, and desiring to secure them to ourselves and perpetuate them to our posterity, do ordain and establish this constitution.

ARTICLE I.   DECLARATION OF RIGHTS

Sec. 18. Religious liberty. The free exercise and enjoyment of religious profession and worship without discrimination or preference shall be forever guaranteed in this state, and no person shall be rendered incompetent to hold any office of trust or profit, or to serve as a witness or juror, because of his opinion on any matter of religious belief whatever; but the liberty of conscience hereby secured shall not be so construed as to excuse acts of licentiousness or justify practices inconsistent with the peace or safety of the state.

Sec. 19. Appropriations for religious societies prohibited. No money of the state shall ever be given or appropriated to any sectarian or religious society or institution.

ARTICLE III.   LEGISLATIVE DEPARTMENT

Sec. 36. Prohibited appropriations. No appropriation shall be made for charitable, industrial, educational or benevolent purposes to any person, corporation or community not under the absolute control of the state, nor to any denominational or sectarian institution or association.

ARTICLE VII.   EDUCATION

Sec. 8. Distribution of school funds. Provisions shall be made by general law for the equitable distribution of such income among the several counties according to the number of children of school age in each; which several counties shall in like manner distribute the proportion of said fund by them received respectively to the several school districts embraced therein. But no appropriation shall be made from said fund to any district for the year in which a school has not been maintained for at least three months; nor shall any portion of any public school fund ever be used to support or assist any private school, or any school, academy, seminary, college or other institution of learning controlled by any church or sectarian organization or religious denomination whatsoever.

Sec. 12. Sectarianism prohibited. No sectarian instruction, qualifications or tests shall be imparted, exacted, applied or in any manner tolerated in the schools of any grade or character controlled by the state, nor shall attendance be required at any religious service therein, nor shall any sectarian tenets or doctrines be taught or favoured in any public school or institution that may be established under this constitution.

ARTICLE XV.   TAXATION AND REVENUE

Sec. 12. Exemptions from taxation. The property of the United States, the State, counties, cities, towns, school districts and municipal corporations, when used primarily for a governmental purpose, and public libraries, lots with the buildings thereon used exclusively for religious worship, church parsonages, church schools and public cemeteries, shall be exempt from taxation, and such other property as the legislature may by general law provide.

ARTICLE XVI.   PUBLIC INDEBTEDNESS

Sec. 6. Loan of credit; internal improvements. Neither the state nor any county, city, township, town, school district, or any other political subdivision shall loan or give its credit or make donations to or in aid of any individual, association or corporation, except for necessary support of the poor, nor subscribe to or become the owner of the capital stock of any association or corporation. . . .

ARTICLE XVII.   STATE MILITIA

Sec. 1. Of whom constituted. The militia of the state shall consist of all able-bodied male citizens of the state, between the ages of eighteen and forty-five years; except such as are exempted by the law of the United States or of the state. But all such citizens having scruples of conscience averse to bearing arms shall be excused therefrom upon such conditions as shall be prescribed by law.

ARTICLE XXI.   SCHEDULE

Sec. 25. Religious liberty. Perfect toleration of religious sentiment shall be secured, and no inhabitant of this state shall ever be molested in person or property on account of his or her mode of religious worship.

Sec. 28. Provision for public schools. The legislature shall make laws for the establishment and maintenance of systems of public schools which shall be open to all the children of the state and free from sectarian control.

FOOTNOTES

Chapter One

1. Cal. Const. art. IV, § 30.
2. 37 Ops. Att'y. Gen. 105.
3. Frohlinger v. Richardson, 63 C.A. 209, 218 P. 497 (1923).
4. Los Angeles County v. Holliginer, 200 C.A. 902, 19 Cal. Rptr. 648 (1962).
5. Ga. Const. art. I, § 1, par. 14.
6. Mayor & Alderman of Savannah v. Richter, 160 Ga. 178, 127 S.E. 148 (1925).
7. Ill. Const. art. VIII, § 3.
8. Stead v. President, etc. of Commons of Kaskaskia, 243 Ill. 239, 90 N.E. 645 (1909).
9. Cf. Annot., 111 A.L.R. 1051 (1937); also, cf. Annot., 94 A.L.R. 2d 1274 (1964). New York Boards of Education, however, are not authorized to lease or rent school property to private organizations. Letter of Board of Education of New York City dated Jan. 29, 1964.
10. Pfeffer, *Church, State and Freedom* (Boston, 1953) p. 181, ". . . the use is gratuitous even though—as is frequently the case—a nominal fee is charged to cover heat or lighting expense." at p. 182.
11. Cf. Annot. 79 A.L.R. 2d 1148 (1961).
12. Most statutes authorizing non-school uses confer upon the local school authorities great discretion, and courts seem inclined to sustain local authorities in granting or denying use of school buildings by religious groups. See, eg., McKnight v. Bd. of Educ. 365 Pa. 422, 72 A. 2d 207, app. dis. 341 U.S. 913 (1950); State ex rel. Greisinger v. Grand Rapids Bd. of Educ. 88 Ohio App. 364, 110 N.E. 2d 294, app. dis 153 Ohio St. 474, 92 N.E. 2d 393, cer. den. 340 U.S. 820, reh. den. 341 U.S. 917 (1951); School Directors v. Toll, 149 Ill. App. 451 (1909); Boyd v. Mitchell, 69 Ark. 202, 62 S.W. 61 (1901); Sheldon v. Centre School Dist., 25 Conn. 224 (1856). See also Greenbanks v. Boutwell, 43 Vt. 207 (1870) holding that a school district may not build a structure larger than needed for school purposes to accommodate religious groups; but the district may allow the use of a hall, once it is constructed, for other than school purposes. There are, of course, decisions stating that local authorities do not have the authority to allow school buildings to be used for religious services during non-school hours. See Bender v. Streabich, 182 Pa. 251, 37 A. 853 (1897); Spencer v. Joint School District, 15 Kan. 259 (1875); Dorton v. Hearn, 67 Mo. 301 (1878); Schofield v. Eighth School Dist., 27 Conn. 499 (1858).
13. McKnight v. Bd. of Public Educ., *Ibid;* Greisinger v. Grand Rapids Bd. of Educ., *Ibid.*
14. Fla. Decl. Rights § 6.
15. Southside Estates Baptist Church v. Board of Trustees, 115 So. 2d 697 (Fla. 1959).
16. Id. at 700.
17. *Ibid.*
18. *Ibid.*
19. Koener v. Borck, 100 So. 2d 398 (Fla. 1958).
20. *Id.* at 401.
21. Spencer v. School District, 15 Kan. 259, 262-63 (1875); Harmon v. Driggers, 116 S.C. 238, 107 S.E. 923 (1921) held that a condition in a deed that premises shall be used as a "school for white children only" was not breached by use of a school building for preaching since the word "only" referred to white children and not the use of the school. See also, Swadley v. Haynes, 41 S.W. 1066 (Tenn. 1897).
22. Spencer v. School District, *Ibid.* at 263.

23. Ill. Const. art. II, § 3.
24. Ill. Const. art. VIII, § 2.
25. Ill. Const. art. VIII, § 3.
25. Ill. Rev. Stat. of 1874, § 39.
27. Nicholas v. School Directors, 93 Ill. 61, 34 Am. Rep. 160 (1879).
28. *Id.* at 64.
29. Hurd v. Walters, 48 Ind. 148 (1874).
30. Baggerly v. Lee, 37 Ind. App. 139, 73 N.E. 921 (1905).
31. Davis v. Boget, 50 Iowa ll (1878), Townsend v. Gagan, 35 Iowa 194 (1872).
32. Davis v. Boget, *ibid.* at 16.
33. Iowa Const. art. I. § 3.
34. Davis v. Boget, *supra.* note 31 at 16.
35. Neb. Const. art I, § 4.
36. State v. Dilley, 95 Neb. 527, 145 N.W. 999 (1914).
37. Lewis v. Bd. of Educ. of City of N.Y., 285 N.Y.S. 164, 157 Misc. 520 (1935), modied on other grounds, 247 App. Div. 106, 286 N.Y.S. 174, rearg. denied, 247 App. Div. 873, 288 N.Y.S. 751, appeal dis, 276 N.Y. 490, 12 N.E. 2d 172.
38. *Id.* at 165-66.
39. N.Y. Const. art. I, § 3.
40. Baer v. Kolmorgen, 14 Misc. 2d 1015, 181 N.Y.S. 2d 230 (1958).
41. Lawrence v. Buchmueller, 40 Misc. 2d 300, 243 N.Y.S. 2d, 87 (1963).
42. Lewis v. Maneville, 201 Misc. 120, 107 N.Y.S. 2d 865 (1950).
43. Bender v. Streabich, 17 Pa. Co. Ct. 609 (1896), affirmed 182 Pa. 251 (1897); See Hysong v. Gallitizin Borough School District, 164 Pa. 629, 30 A. 482 (1894) where a lower court's injunction against the use of a public school for religious instruction was apparently affirmed.
44. Pa. Stat. Ann. tit. 24, § 7.75 (1950).
45. 1 Ops. Att'y. Gen. 161.
46. Calif. Const. art. IV, § 30.
47. La. Const. art. I, § 4.
48. State ex rel. Singlemann v. Morrison, 57 So. 238, 246 (La. 1952).
49. Pfeffer, op. cit., p. 181; Punke, *Community Use of Public School Facilities,* (New York, 1951), p. 36.
50. Pfeffer, op. cit., p. 180: ". . . if the use by the sectarian group is regular and extended in duration, no constitutional distinction can logically be drawn between such use and an outright grant of public funds or property to the sectarian group."
51. Cf. Punke, op. cit., p. 36.
52. Pfeffer, op. cit., p. 181.
53. Stokes, *Church and State in the United States,* (New York, 1950) Vol. II, p. 586 ". . . it is clear that public-school buildings, if used at all for religious purposes outside of school hours, must be made available on the same terms to all responsible groups in the community."
54. Stokes, op. cit., p. 587: ". . . there is serious doubt whether in principle a public-school building should be used, except in rare emergencies, for any purpose of religious education directly connected with one Church."; id. at 589: 'In a word, Church and State may co-operate in the use of buildings to meet emergency needs, but there must be a clear distinction between public and ecclesiastical functions, and no attempt by either party to confuse the distinction."
55. N.M. Const. art. IV, § 31. See Ala. Const. art. IV, § 73, Cal. Const. art. IV, § 22, La. Const. art. IV, § 8, Mass. Const. amend. XLVI, § 2, N.Y. Const. art. VII, § 8, Pa. Const. art. III, § 17, Va. Const. art. IV, § 67.
56. S.C. Const. art. XI, § 9. See Pa. Const. art. III, § 18.
57. Wyo. Const. art. III, § 36. See Colo. Const. art. V, § 34, Mont. Const. art. V, § 35.
58. Mo. Const. art. III, §38a, Tex. Const. art. III, § 51(a).
59. E.g., Ala. Const. art. IV, § 73, N.Y. Const. art. VIII, § 1.
60. Cf. Annot., 22 A.L.R. 1319 (1923), 55 A.L.R. 320 (1928).
61. Pa. Const. art. III, § 18.
62. Collins v. Kephart, 271 Pa. 428, 117 A. 440 (1921).
63. *Id.* at 433, 117 A. at 441.

64. *Id.* at 433-34, 117 A. at 441-42.
65. Constitutional Defense League v. Waters, 308 Pa. 150, 162 A. 216 (1932); Collins v. Martin, 290 Pa. 388, 139 A. 122 (1927).
66. Collins v. Lewis, 276 Pa. 435, 438, 120 A. 389, 390 (1932).
67. N.M. Const. art. IV, § 31. See n. 55 and accompanying text.
68. Ops. Att'y Gen. 147 (1929-30).
69. Ops. Att'y Gen. No. 6426 (1955-56).
70. S.C. Const. art. XI, § 9. See n. 56 and accompanying text.
71. Parker v. Bates, 216 S.C. 52, 63, 56 S.E. 2d 723, 728 (1949).
72. Richter v. Savannah, 160 Ga. 178, 127 S.E. 148 (1925).
73. Ga. Const. art. I, § 1, par. 14.
74. Board of Managers of James Walker Memorial Hosp. v. City of Wilmington, 237 N.C. 179, 74 S.E. 2d 749 (1953). N.C. Const., art. II, § 29.
75. Miss. Const. art. VIII, § 208.
76. Craig v. Mercy Hosp.—Street Memorial, 209 Miss. 490, 47 So. 2d 867, overruling sugg. of error, 209 Miss. 427, 45 So. 2d 809 (1950).
77. *Id.* at 439, 45 So. 2d at 814.
78. *Id.* at 443, 45 So. 2d at 822.
79. N.H. Const. Pt. II, art. 83.
80. Opinion of the Justices, 99 N.H. 519, 113 A. 2d 114 (1955).
81. *Id.* at 522, 113 A. 2d at 116.
82. *Ibid.*
83. Ky. Const. Bill of Rts., § 5.
84. Kentucky Bldg. Comm'n v. Effron, 310 Ky. 355, 220 S.W. 2d 836 (1949).
85. *Id.* at 358-59, 220 S.W. 2d at 838 (emphasis added).
86. *Id.* at 359, 220 S.W. 2d at 838.
87. Abernathy v. City of Irvine, 355 S.W. 2d 159, (Ky. 1961), cer. den. 371 U.S. 831 (1962).
88. Lien v. City of Ketchikan, 383 P. 2d 721 (Alaska. 1963).
89. Ala. Const. art. I, § 4.
90. Lien v. City of Ketchikan, supra. Note 88 at 724.
91. 175 U.S. 291 (1899).
92. *Id.* at 297-98.
93. *Id.* at 298.
94. *Id.* at 298-99.
95. N.Y. Const. art. VII, § 8. In a 1940 case decided hereunder, a New York Court held that construction of chapels with private funds in state prisons was permissible. People v. Lyons, 173 Misc. 821, 21 N.Y.S. 2nd 250 (1940).
96. N.Y. Const. art. VIII, § 1.
97. Shepherd's Fold of Protestant Church v. New York, 96 N.Y. 137 (1884).
98. Sargent v. Board of Educ., 177 N.Y. 317, 69 N.E. 722 (1904).
99. Schade v. Alleghany County, 386 Pa. 507, 126 A. 2d 911 (1956).
100. Pa. Const. art. III, § 18. See n. 61 and accompanying text.
101. Constitutional Defense League v. Waters, Collins v. Martin, *supra.* note 65.
102. Ill. Const. art II. § 3.
103. Ill. Const. art VIII, § 3.
104. McClean County v. Humphreys, 104 Ill. 78 (1882).
105. Cook County v. Chicago Industrial School for Girls, 125 Ill. 540, 18 N.E. 183 (1888).
106. *Id.* at 571, 18 N.E. at 197-198.
107. Dunn v. Chicago Industrial School for Girls, 280 Ill. 613, 117 N.E. 735 (1917).
108. *Id.* at 616, 117 N.E. at 736.
109. *Id.* at 618, 117 N.E. at 737.
110. Dunn v. Addison Manual Training School for Boys, 281 Ill. 352, 117 N.E. 993 (1917).
111. Trost v. Ketteler Manual Training School for Boys, 282 Ill 504, 118 N.E. 743 (1918).
112. St. Hedwig's Industrial School for Girls v. Cook County, 289 Ill. 432, 124 N.E. 629 (1919).
113. *Id.* at 438, 124 N.E. at 635.
114. Md. Decl. Rts. art. 36.
115. St. Mary's Industrial School v. Brown, 45 Md. 317 (1876).

116. *Id.* at 336.
117. *Ibid.*
118. Fla. Decl. Rts. § 6. See n. 14 and accompanying text.
119. Fenske v. Coddington, 57 So. 2d 452 (Fla. 1952).
120. Okla. Const. art. II, § 5.
121. State v. Williamson, 347 P. 2d 204 (Okla. 1959).
122. *Id.* at 207.
123. Murrow Indian Orphans Home v. Childers, 197 Okla. 249, 171 P. 2d 600 (1946).
124. *Id.* at 251, 171 P. 2d at 603.
125. State ex. rel. Nevada Orphan Asylum v. Hallock, 16 Nev. 373 (1882).
126. Nev. Const. art. XI, § 10.
127. Ill. Const. art. II, § 3. See n. 102 and accompanying text.
128. Reichwald v. Catholic Bishop of Chicago, 258 Ill. 44,101 N.E. 266 (1913). See n. 95 for New York case reaching same result.
129. *Id.* at 47-48, 101 N.E. at 267.
130. Annot., 142 A.L.R. 1076 (1943).
131. La. Const. art. IV. § 8.
132. State ex rel. Orr v. City of New Orleans, 50 La. Ann. 880, 24 So. 666 (1898).
133. Ops. Att'y Gen. 837 (1938-40), 2154 (1940-42).
134. Ops. Att'y Gen. 2246 (1940-42).
135. Neb. Const. art. I, § 4.
136. Neb. Const. art. VII, § 11.
137. United Community Services v. Omaha National Bank, 162 Neb. 786, 77 N.W. 2d 576 (1956).
138. *Id.* at 804-05, 77 N.W. 2d at 589.
139. Bennett v. City of La Grange 153 Ga. 428, 112 S.E. 482 (1922).
140. Ga. Const. art. I, § 1, para. 14.
141. Utah Const. art. I, § 4.
142. Thomas v. Daughters of Utah Pioneers, 114 Utah 108, 197 P. 2d 477 (1948).
143. *Id.* at 129, 197 P. 2d at 489.

Chapter Two

1. Alaska Const. art. VII, § 1; Cal. Const. art. IX, § 8 Colo. Const. art. IX, § 7; Conn. Const. art. VIII, § 2; Del. Const. art. X, § 3; Hawaii Const. art. IX, § 1; Idaho Const. art. IX, § 5; Ill. Const, art. VIII, § 3; Kan. Const. art. VI, § 8; Ky. Const. § 189; La. Const. art. XII, § 13; Mass. Const. Amend. XLVI, § 2; Mo. Const. art. IX, § 8; Mont. Const. art. XI, § 8; Neb. Const. art. VII, § 11; N.H. Const. Pt. II, art. 83; N.M. Const. art. XII, § 3; N.Y. Const. art. XI, § 4; Ohio Const. art, VI, § 2; Okla. Const. art. XI, § 5; Pa. Const. art. X, § 2; S.C. Const. art. XI, § 9; S.D. Const. art. VIII, § 16; Utah Const. art. X, § 13; Va. Const. art. IX, § 141; Wyo. Const. art. VII, § 8.
2. Ariz. Const. art. IX, § 10; Ga. Const. art I, § 1, par. 14; Nev. Const. art. XI, § 10; Ore. Const. art. I, § 5; Wash. Const. art. I, § 11; Wyo. Const. art. I, § 19.
3. N.C. Const. art. IX, § 4.
4. E.g., Mont. Const. art. V, § 35.
5. E.g., Mo. Const. art. I, § 6.
6. E.g., Mo. Const. art. X, § 8.
7. E.g., Del. Const. art. X, § 3.
8. E.g., Ariz. Const. art. IX, § 10.
9. E.g., N.Y. Const. art. XI, § 4. See note 34 and accompanying text.
10. Kan. Const. art. VI, § 8.
11. Mass. Const. Art. XVIII (1821).
12. Merrick v. Amherst, 94 Mass. (12 Allen) 500, 508 (1866).
13. Jenkins v. Andover, 103 Mass. 94 (1869).
14. Opinion of the Justices, 214 Mass. 599, 601, 102 N.E. 464, 464-65 (1913).
15. Mass. Const. Amend. art. XLVI, § 2.

16. Neb. Const. art. I, § 4.
17. Neb. Const. art. VII, § 11.
18. State ex rel. Public School District v. Taylor, 122 Neb. 454, 240 N.W. 573 (1932).
19. Mo. Const. art. I, § 5.
20. Mo. Const. art. I, § 6.
21. Mo. Const. art. I, § 7.
22. Mo. Const. art. IX, § 8.
23. Harfst v. Hoegen, 349 Mo. 608, 163 S.W. 2d 609, 141 A.L.R. 1136 (1942).
24. Berghorn v. School Dist., 364 Mo. 121, 260 S.W. 2d 573 (1953).
25. Wright v. School Dist., 151 Kan. 485, 99 P. 2d 737 (1940).
26. Kan. Const. Bill of Rights, § 7.
27. Kan. Const. art. VI, § 8.
28. Atchison, T. & S. F. Ry. v. City of Atchison, 47 Kan. 712, 28 P. 1000 (1892).
29. Collins v. Kephart, 271 Pa. 428, 117 A. 440 (1921). See chapter I, notes 62-64 and accompanying text.
30. Nance v. Johnson, 84 Tex. 712, 19 S.W. 559 (1892).
31. Gerhardt v. Heid, 66 N.D. 444, 267 N.W. 127 (1936).
32. Murrow Indian Orphans Home v. Childers, 197 Okla. 249, 171 P. 2d 600 (1946).
33. Okla. Const. art. X, § 15.
34. N.Y. Const. art. XI, § 4.
35. St. Patrick's Church v. Heerman, 68 Misc. 487, 124 N.Y.S. 705 (1910).
36. Laws passed in Maryland in 1962 and 1963 authorized matching grants of public funds to two Catholic Colleges in that state. The constitutionality of such appropriations remain to be litigated. See Gianella, *Religion and the Public Order* (Chicago, 1964).
37. La. Const. art. I, § 4.
38. La. Const. art. XII, § 13.
39. Bordon v. Louisiana State Bd. of Educ., 168 La. 1005, 1019, 123 So. 655, 660, 67 A.L.R. 1183 (1929).
40. Cochran v. Louisiana State Bd. of Educ., 281 U.S. 370 (1930).
41. Miss. Const. art. III, § 18.
42. Miss. Const. art VIII, § 208.
43. Chance v. Mississippi State Textbook Rating & Purchasing Bd., 190 Miss. 453, 467-68, 200 So. 706, 710 (1940).
44. *Id.* at 474, 200 So. at 713.
45. N.Y. Const. art. XI, § 4. See Footnote 34 and accompanying text.
46. Smith v. Donahue, 195 N.Y. Supp. 715, 719 (1922).
47. N.M. Const. art. XII, § 3.
48. Zellers v. Huff, 55 N.M. 501, 236 P. 2d 949 (1951). See O.A.G. No. 5453, 1951-52.
49. Ore. Const. art. I, § 5.
50. Dickman v. School Dist. 366 P. 2d 533, 544, 93 ALR 2d 969 (Ore.) cert. denied, 371 U.S. 823 (1961). The South Dakota Court has not expressly condemned the practice, but would seem to have done so by implication in refusing to interpret a statute as authorizing the giving of books to parochial school children, relying on the rule than an interpretation upholding the constitutionality of a statute should be chosen over one which would invalidate the statute. Haas v. Independent School District, 69 S.D. 303, 9 N.W. 2d 707 (1943).
51. Letter from the Attorney General of Rhode Island dated April 25, 1964 in the possession of the authors.
52. Everson v. Board of Educ., 330 U.S. 1, rehearing denied, 330 U.S. 855 (1947).
53. The Iowa Court has limited school bus transportation to children attending public schools under the statutes of that state with no constitutional issue being decided. Silver Lake Consolidated School District v. Parker, 238 Iowa 984, 29 N.W. 2d 214 (1947). See O.A.G. 1936, p. 512; 1925-26, p. 417.
54. Judd v. Board of Educ., 278 N.Y. 22, 15 N.E. 2d 576 (1938).
55. N.Y. Const. art. XI, § 4.
56. Board of Education v. Allen, 192 N.Y.S. 2d 186 (1959).
57. N.J. Const. art. VIII, § IV, par. 3.

58. Everson v. Board of Educ., 133 N.J.L. 350, 44 A. 2d 333 (1945).
59. Everson v. Board of Educ., *supra.* note 52.
60. Alaska Const. art. VII, § 1.
61. Matthews v. Quinton, 362 P. 2d 932 (Alaska. 1959).
62. *Id.* at 951-52 (dissenting opinion).
63. Calif. Const. art. IV, § 30.
64. Bowker v. Baker, 73 C.A. 2d 653, 167 P. 2d 256, 261 (1946).
65. Conn. Const. art. VII, § 1.
66. Conn. Const. art. VIII, § 2.
67. Snyder v. Town of Newton, 147 Conn. 374, 382, 161 A. 2d 770 (1960), app. dis., 365 U.S. 299 (1961).
68. *Id.* at 391.
69. Del. Const. art. X, § 3.
70. Delaware ex. rel. Traub v. Brown, 35 Del. 181, 172 A. 835 (1934).
71. Ky. Const. Bill of Rights § 5.
72. Nichols v. Henry, 301 Ky. 434, 191 S.W. 2d 930, 934-35 (1945).
73. Squires v. City of Augusta, 155 Me. 151, 153 A. 2d 80 (1959); Ch. 90-A, § 12 III(e).
74. Md. Const. Declaration of Rights art. 36.
75. Md. Const. art. VIII, § 3.
76. Board of Educ. v. Wheat, 174 Md. 314, 199 A. 628 (1938).
77. Adams v. St. Mary's County, 180 Md. 550, 26 A. 2d 377 (1942).
78. Quinn v. School Committee of Plymouth, 332 Mass. 410, 125 N.E. 2d 410 (1955); See O.A.G. 1963, p. 40.
79. Mo. Const. art. I, § 6.
80. Mo. Const. art I, § 7.
81. Mo. Const. art. IX, § 6.
82. Mo. Const. art. IX, § 7.
83. McVey v. Hawkins, 258 S.W. 2d 927 (Mo. 1953).
84. N.M. Const. art. XII, § 3. See note 47 and accompanying text.
85. Zellers v. Huff, *supra,* note 48. But see N. M. Stats. 73-7-67.
86. Okla. Const. art. II, § 5.
87. Gurney v. Ferguson, 190 Okla. 254, 122 P. 2d 100 (1941), appeal dismissed 371 U.S. 588 (1942); Board of Educ. v. Antone, 384 P. 2d 911 (Okla. 1963).
88. Pa. Const. art. X, § 2.
89. Connel v. Board of School Directors, 365 Pa. 585, 52 A. 2d 645, appeal dismissed 332 U.S. 748 (1947).
90. School Dist. v. Houghton, 387 Pa. 236, 128 A. 2d 58 (1957).
91. Ops. Att'y. Gen. (July 2, 1963), cited in Gianella, *Religion and the Public Order* (Chicago, 1964) [A "memo," rather than an opinion].
92. Wash. Const. art I, § 11.
93. Wash. Const. art. IX, § 4.
94. Visser v. School Dist., 33 Wash. 2d 699, 207 P. 2d 198 (1949).
95. Wis. Const. art. I, § 18.
96. Reynolds v. Nusbaum, 17 Wis. 2d 148, 115 N.W. 2d 761, 765 (1962).
97. Ops. Att'y. Gen. 1946-48, p. 836.
98. Ops. Att'y. Gen. No. 4177 (1963), cited in *Freedom in Education,* Vol. 5, No. 8, p. 3 (published bi-monthly by Citizens for Educational Freedom).
99. Ops. Att'y. Gen. Aug. 18, 1944, 166-A-7.
100. Minn. Const. art. VIII, § 3.
101. 1949-50 A.G.R. 223: 1951-52 A.G.R. 45;; 1957-58 A.G.R. 217.
102. Oklahoma Ry. v. St. Joseph's School, 33 Okla. 755, 127 Pac. 1087 (1912).
103. Millard v. Board of Educ., 121 Ill. 297, 10 N.E. 669 (1887).
104. Ill. Const. art II, § 3.
105. Wis. Const. art. I, § 18.
106. Dorner v. School Dist., 137 Wis. 353, 118 N.W. 353 (1908).
107. Ky. Const. § 189.
108. Crain v. Walker, 222 Ky. 828, 839-40, 2 S.W. 2d 654, 659 (1928).
109. Williams v. School District, 173 Ky. 708, 725, 191 S.W. 507, 513 (1917).
110. Iowa Const. art. I, § 3.
111. Knowlton v. Baumhover, 182 Iowa 691, 166 N.W. 202 (1918).
112. Scripture v. Breuns, 59 Iowa 70, 12 N.W. 760 (1882).

113. Zellers v. Huff, *supra.* note 48.
114. N.M. Const. art XII, § 3.
115. See, e.g., Mo. Const. art. I, § 7; Okla. Const. art. II, § 5.
116. State ex rel Public School Dist. v. Taylor, 122 Neb. 454, 240 N.W. 573 (1932).
117. Zellers v. Huff, *supra.* note 48.
118. Harfst. Hoegen, *supra.* note 23.
119. Mo. Const. art. I, § 7.   See infra. note 134 and accompanying text.
120. Ind. Const. art. I, § 6.
121. State ex rel. Johnson v. Boyd, 217 Ind. 348, 28 N.E. 2d 256, noted in 50 Yale L.J. 917 (1941).
122. Gubler v. Utah State Teachers Retirement Bd., 113 Utah 188, 192 P. 2d 580 (1940).
123. Utah Const., art. I, § 4.
124. Utah Const. art X, § 13.
125. Otken v. Lamkin, 56 Miss. 758 (1879).
126. Miss. Const. art. VIII, § 208.
127. Synod of South Dakota v. State, 2 S.D. 366 (1891).
128. S.D. Const. art. VI, § 3.
129. S.D. Const. art. VIII, § 16.
130. Hlebanja v. Brewe, 58 S.D. 351, 236 N.W. 296 (1931).
131. Almond v. Day, 197 Va. 419, 89 S.E. 2d 851 (1956).   Payment of tuition, by the state, for pupils attending educational institutions was held violative of the Federal Constitution, without a finding of unconstitutionality with reference to the state constitution, in Swart v. South Burlington Town School District, 162 A. 2d 514 (Vt. 1961).
132. Va. Const. art. IV, § 67.
133. State ex rel. Atwood v. Johnson, 170 Wis. 251, 176 N.W. 224 (1920).
134. Mo. Const. art. I, § 7.
135. Kirtzele v. City of St. Louis, (Sup. 1961), 347 S.W. 2d 695.
136. 64th St. Residences, Inc. v. City of New York, 4 N.Y.S. 2d 268, 150 N.E. 2d 396, cert. denied, 357 U.S. 907 (1957).
137. Id. at 276, 150 N.E. 2d at 399.
138. *Id.*
139. N.Y. Const. art. XI, § 4.   See footnote 34 and accompanying text.
140. Cal. Const. art. I, § 4.
141. Gordon v. Board of Educ., 78 C.A. 2d 464, 178 P. 2d 488, 493 (1947).
142. Ill. Const. art. II, § 3.   See footnote 104 and accompanying text.
143. People ex rel. Latimer v. Board of Educ., 394 Ill. 228, 233, 68 N.E. 2d 305, 167 A.L.R. 1467 (1946).
144. Stein v. Brown, 125 Misc. 692, 211 N.Y.S. 822 (Sup. Ct. 1925).
145. People v. Graves, 219 N.Y.S. 189, 196, 219 App. Div. 233 (1927).
146. 303 N.Y. 161, 102 N.Y.S. 2d 27 (1957).
147. *Id.* at 168.
148. *Id.*
149. Zorach v. Clauson, 343 U.S. 306 (1951).
150. Ore. Rev. Stat., § 336.260 (1953).
151. Dilger v. School Dist., 222 Ore. 108, 352 P. 2d 564 (1960).
152. Note, Constitutionality of Utah Released Time Program, 3 Utah L. Rev. 329 (1953).
153. *Id.* at 339.
154. Wash. Const. art. I, § 11.   See footnote 92 and accompanying text.
155. Perry v. School Dist., 54 Wash. 2d 886, 344 P. 2d 1036 (1959).
156. *Id.* at 897.
157. Wis. Const. Art. I, § 18.
158. 15 Ops. Att'y Gen. 483, 488 (1926).
159. 38 Ops. Att'y Gen. 288 (1949).
160. Correspondence from diocesan superintendents of schools in the possession of the authors.
161. See, however, Knowlton v. Baumhover, *supra.* note 111 with accompanying text.

162. "Such use of a public building by a religious group raises no constitutional church-state problem if the group pays a fair rental. . . ." Pfeffer, *Church, State and Freedom,* p. 181 (Boston, 1953).
163. Ops. Att'y. Gen. No. 257, cited in Gianella, *Religion and the Public Order* (Chicago, 1964), (letter from Attorney General of Pennsylvania to Charles Boehm, Superintendent of Public Instruction, January 9, 1963), Pa. Const. art. III, § 18.
164. Scales v. Board of Education, 245 N.Y.S. 2d 449, 455 (Sup. Ct. 1963).
165. *Id.*
166. N.Y. Const. art. XI, § 4.
167. Scales v. Bd. of Education, *supra.* note 164 at 454.
168. Mo. Const. art. IX, § 8.
169. Ops. Att'y. Gen., February, 1963. Refusal by the Missouri State Board of Education to reimburse the St. Louis County Special School District for services to handicapped children in parochial schools is the subject of litigation begun in February, 1964. *Freedom in Education,* Vol. 6, No. 2 (published bi-monthly by Citizens for Educational Freedom).
170. Ops. Att'y. Gen., May 14, 1962.
171. Okla. Const. art. II, § 5.
172. Ops. Att'y. Gen. ———. Cited in "Liberty" (published bi-monthly by Religious Liberty Association of America), Volume 59, No. 4, July-August, 1964, p. 31.
173. Knowlton v. Baumhover, *supra.* note 111 at 727, 166 N.W. at 214 (1918).
174. NEA Research Bulletin, Vol. XXIV, No. 1 (1946) pp. 36-42.
175. Humble, "Religious Instruction and Activities in Texas Public Schools," 2 *Journal of Church and State,* 117, 129 (1960).
176. "Shared credits"—a system whereby a child can attend both public and private schools and secure credits in such subjects as Hebrew, Greek, Latin, Bible History, etc. which may be applied toward graduation from the public school—are discussed under Bible Reading in the Public Schools, *infra.* "Shared teachers" and "shared facilities" are discussed under Use of Public Facilities By Church-Related Schools, *supra.*
177. Pa. Const. art III, § 17.
178. Pa. Const. art. III, § 18.
179. Commonwealth v. Wehrle School District of Altoona, 241 Pa. 224, 88 A. 481 (1913).
180. April, 1963 letter from Assistant Attorney General Killian of Pennsylvania in the possession of the authors.
181. Utah Const. art. I, § 4.
182. Utah Const. art. X, § 13.
183. Utah Const. art. X, § 1.
184. Opinion of A. Pratt Kessler, Attorney General of Utah, requested by Walter D. Talbot, Deputy Superintendent, Department of Public Instruction, October 30, 1963.
185. Knowlton v. Baumhover, *supra.* note 111 at 727, 166 NW at 214; Iowa Const. art I, § 3.
186. Ops. Att'y. Gen., May 17, 1939.

Chapter Three

1. School District of Abington Township, Pennsylvania v. Schempp, Murray v. Curlett, 374 U. S. 203 (1953).
2. Id., Engel v. Vitale, 370 U.S. 421 (1962). In a recent case, a United States District Court has held that voluntary prayer, offered by public school children without any compulsion, and without being prescribed by law, would not tend to establish religion and school children were entitled to say such voluntary prayer, subject to reasonable rules and regulations of the school authorities. Stein v. Oshinsky, 224 F. Supp. 757 (1963). As of this writing, appeal has not yet been taken.
3. Fla. Const. Decl. of Rights § 6.

4. Brown v. Orange County Bd. of Public Instruction, 128 So. 2d 181, 185 (Fla. 1960).
5. Tudor v. Board of Educ., 14 N.J. 31, 100 A. 2d 857, cert. denied 348 U.S. 816 (1954).
6. N.J. Const. art. I, § 4.
7. Miller v. Cooper, 56 N.M. 355, 244 P. 2d 520 (1952); N.M. Const. art. XII, § 9.
8. Evans v. Selma Union High School, 193 Cal. 54, 222 P. 801 (1924).
9. Cal. Const. art. I, § 4.
10. People v. Board of Educ. of Dist. 24, 245 Ill. 334, 92 N.E. 251 (1910); Ill. Const. art. II, § 3.
11. Herold v. Parish Bd. of School Directors, 136 La. 1034, 68 So. 116 (1915); La. Const. art. I, § 4, art. IV, § 8.
12. State v. Scheve, 55 Neb. 853, 91 N.W. 846 (1902); Neb. Const. art VII, § 11.
13. Weiss v. Dist. Bd., 76 Wis. 177, 44 N.W. 967 (1890), Wis. Const. art. I, § 18, art. X, § 3.
14. Id.
15. Chamberlain v. Dade County Bd. of Public Instruction, 143 So. 2d 21 (Fla. 1962), judgment vacated and case remanded, 374 U.S. 487 (1963), affirmed, 160 So. 2d 97 (Fla. 1964), reserved, 375 U.S. 871 (1964); Fla. Const. Decl. of Rights § 5.
16. People ex rel. Vollmar v. Stanley, 81 Colo. 276, 255 P. 610 (1937); Colo. Const. art. II, § 4.
17. Chamberlain v. Dade County Bd. of Public Instruction, supra. note 15, Fla. Const. Decl. of Rights, § 5.
18. Wilkerson v. City of Rome, 152 Ga. 762, 110 S.E. 895 (1921), Ga. Const. art. I, § 1, par. XII.
19. Moore v. Monroe, 64 Iowa 367, 20 N.W. 475 (1884); Iowa Const. art. I, § 3.
20. Billard v. Board of Educ. of Topeka, 69 Kan. 53, 76 P. 307 (1904); Kan. Const. Bill of Rights, § 7.
21. Hackett v. Brooksville Graded School Dist., 120 Ky. 608, 87 S.W. 792 (1905); Ky. Const. Bill of Rights, § 5 & 189.
22. Donahoe v. Richards, 38 Me. 397 (1854); Me. Const. art. I, § 3.
23. Spiller v. Inhabitants of Woburn, 12 Allen 127 (Mass. 1866).
24. Pfeiffer v. Board of Educ. of Detroit, 118 Mich. 560 (1898); Mich. Const. art. IV, § 40 (Const. of 1850), art. 11, § 3 (Const. of 1908).
25. Kaplan v. Independent School Dist. of Virginia, 171 Minn. 142, 214 N.W. 18 (1927); Minn. Const. art. I, § 16.
26. Lewis v. Allen, 207 N.Y.S. 2d 862 (App. Div. 1960).
27. Cincinatti v. Minor, 23 Ohio State 211 (1872); Ohio Const. art I, § 7.
28. Stevenson v. Hanyon, 7 Dist. 585 (1898); Pa. Const. art. I, § 3, art X, § 2.
29. Carden v. Bland, 199 Tenn. 665, 288 S.W. 2d 718 (1956), Tenn. Const. art. I, § 3. In Scopes v. State, 154 Tenn. 105, 289 S.W. 363 (1927), decided under the same clause of the Tennessee Constitution, it was held that a statute forbidding the teaching of evolution in the public schools of that state was not unconstitutional as giving a preference to any religion.
30. Church v. Bullock, 104 Tex. 1, 109 S.W. 115 (1908); Tex. Const. art. I, §§ 6 & 7, art. VII, § 5.
31. North v. Bd. of Trustees of University of Illinois, 27 N.E. 54, 137 Ill. 297 (1891); Ill. Const. art. II, § 3.
32. Chamberlain v. Dade County Bd. of Public Instruction, 160 So. 2d 97, 99 (Fla. 1964).
33. Chamberlain v. Dade County Bd. of Public Instruction, 375 U.S. 871 (1964).
34. Ops. Att'y. Gen., August 20, 1963.
35. State v. Scheve, supra. note 12.
36. Neb. Const. art. VII, § 11.
37. People v. Board of Educ. of Dist. 24, supra. note 10.
38. Ill. Const. art. VII, § 3.
39. Moore v. Monroe, supra. note 19.
40. Iowa Const. art. I, § 3.
41. Pfeffer, Church, State and Freedom (Boston, 1953) 305-6.

42. State ex rel. Dearle v. Frazier, 102 Wash. 369, 379, 380 (1918). The litigated state constitutional clauses provide: "No public money or property shall be appropriated for or applied to any religious worship, exercise, or institution, or the support of any religious establishment," Art. I, § 11, and "All free schools maintained or supported wholly or in part by the public funds shall be forever free from sectarian control or influence." Art. IX, § 4.
43. Humble, Religious Instruction and Activities in Texas Public Schools, 2 J. Church & S., 117, 127 (1960).
44. State ex rel. Johnson v. Boyd, 217 Ind. 348, 370-71, 28 N.E. 2d 256 (1940).
45. O'Connor v. Hendrick, 184 N.Y. 421, 430, 77 N.E. 612 (1906).
46. Zellers v. Huff, 55 N.M. 501, 236 P 2d 949 (1951).
47. Knowlton v. Baumhover, 182 Iowa 691, 703, 166 N.W. 202 (1918).
48. State ex rel. Johnson v. Boyd, supra, note 44, Hysong v. Gallitzin Borough School Dist. 164 Pa. 629, 30 A. 482 (1894).
49. Rawlings v. Butler, 290 S.W. 2d 901, 60 A.L.R. 2d 285, 292 (Ky. Ct. of App. 1956).
50. Gerhardt v. Heid, 66 N.D. 444, 460, 267 N.W. 673 (1936).
51. Hysong v. Gallitzin Borough School Dist., supra. note 48.
52. Berghorn v. Reorganized School Dist. No. 8, 364 Mo. 121, 260 S.W. 2d 573 (1954).
53. N.M. Const. art. XII, § 9.
54. Zellers v. Huff, supra., note 46.
55. Commonwealth v. Herr, 227 Pa. 132, 78 A. 68 (1910).
56. Pa. Const. art. I, § 3.
57. Pa. Const. art. I, § 4.
58. O'Connor v. Hendrick, supra note 45.
59. Ops. Att'y. Gen. 1936, p. 629.
60. Knowlton v. Baumhover, supra. note 47.
62. Rawlings v. Butler, supra. note 49.
62. Rawlings v. Butler, 290 S.W. 2d 901, 60 A.L.R. 2d 285, 290 (Ky. Ct. of App. 1956).
63. Gerhardt v. Heid, supra. note 50.
64. Christian Century, July 28, Aug. 4, 1948.
65. State ex rel. Johnson v. Boyd, supra. note 44.
66. Stokes, Church and State in the United States, III, 177.
67. Humble, Religious Instruction and Activities in Texas Public Schools, supra. note 43.
68. Baer v. Kolmorgen, 14 Misc. 2d 1015, 181 N.Y.S. 2d 230 (1958). See also, Lawrence v. Buchmueller, 40 Misc. 2d 300, 243 N.Y.S. 2d 87 (1963).
69. Chamberlain v. Dade County Bd. of Public Instruction, 142 So. 2d 21 (Fla. 1962).
70. Id., Judgment vacated and case remanded, 374 U.S. 487 (1963), aff'd. 160 So. 2d 97 (1964), reversed 375 U.S. 871 (1964).
71 Rosenfield, Separation of Church and State in the Public Schools, 22 U. Pitt. L. Rev. 561, 572-73 (1961); V. T. Thayer, The Attack Upon the American Secular School (Boston, 1951) 150 ff.; Bennett, When Christmas Becomes Divisive, Christianity and Crisis, 162 (Nov. 24, 1958); Sherwin, Christmas in the Schools, 85 School and Society 331 (1957). The General Assembly of the United Presbyterian Church in the United States of America has gone on record as opposed to the use of public property for religious displays. General Assembly of the United Presbyterian Church in the United States, Relations Between Church and State in the United States of America (1963), pp. 7-8.
72. Rosenfield, id.; Thayer, id.; Ops. Att'y. Gen. of Mass., August 20, 1963.
73. Miller v. Cooper, 56 N.M. 355, 244 P. 2d 520 (1952). The pertinent state constitutional clause provides: "No religious test shall ever be required as a condition of admission into the public schools or any educational institution of this State, either as a teacher or student and no teacher or student of such school or institution shall ever be required to attend or participate in any religious service whatsoever." Art. XII, § 9.
74. Conway v. Joint School District, 162 Wis. 482, 156 N.W. 477 (1916). The Wisconsin constitution provides: "The right of every man to worship Almighty God according to the dictates of his own conscience shall never be infringed;

nor shall any man be compelled to attend, erect or support any place of worship, or to maintain any ministry, against his consent; nor shall any control of, or interference with, the rights of conscience be permitted, or any preference be given by law to any religious establishments or modes of worship; nor shall any money be drawn from the treasury for the benefit of religious societies, or religious or theological seminaries." Art. I, § 18. Another clause ordains that "no sectarian instruction shall be allowed" in the public schools. Art. X, § 3.

75. Chamberlain v. Dade County Bd. of Public Instruction, 143 So. 2d 21 (Fla. 1962).
76. Id, 374 U.S. 487 (1963).
77. Id., 160 So. 2d 97 (Fla. 1964).
78. Id., 375 U.S. 781 (1964).
79. *New York Herald Tribune,* June 6, 1950; Pfeffer, *Church, State and Freedom* (Boston, 1953), p. 419.
80. Ops. Att'y. Gen., August 20, 1963.
81. Hering v. Bd. of Education, 117 N.J.L. 455, 189 A. 629, (1937), aff. 118 N.J.L. 566, 194 A. 177, app. dis. 303 U.S. 624; Nicholls v. Lynn, 297 Mass. 65, 7 N.E. 2d 577, 110 A.L.R. 377 (1937); Leoles v. Landers, 184 Ga. 580, 192 S.E. 218 (1937), app. dis. 302 U.S. 656; Gabrielli v. Knickerbocker, 12 C. 2d 85, 82 P. 2d 391 (1938), app. dis. 306 U.S. 621; State v. Board of Education, 139 Fla. 43, 190 So. 815 (1939).
82. 21 F. Supp. 581.
83. 108 F.2d 683.
84. 309 U.S. 645.
85. 310 U.S. 586 (1940).
86. State v. Smith, 155 Kan. 588, 596-597, 127 P. 2d 518 (1942).
87. 41 F. Supp. 251.
88. 319 U.S. 624 (1943).
89. Id. at 642.
90. Id. at 634.
91. Pendley v. State, 77 Okl. Cr. 259, 141 P. 2d 118 (1943); Bolling v. Superior Court, 16 Wis. 2d 373, 133 P. 2d 803 (1943); Zavilla v. Massee, 112 Colo. 183, 147 P. 2d 823 (1944); see also Sheldon v. Fannin, 221 F. Supp. 766 (D. Ariz. 1963) where a Jehovah's Witnesses' refusal to stand during the singing of the national anthem at school was not such conduct which would "materially disrupt the conduct and discipline of the school" as to be grounds for denying the student admission to the public school.
92. Taylor v. Mississippi, 319 U.S. 583 (1942).
93. New Hampshire v. Hoyt, 84 N.H. 38, 146 A. 170 (1929).
94. Meyer v. Nebraska, 262 U.S. 390 (1923).
95. Pierce v. Society of Sisters, 268 U.S. 510 (1925).
96. Mississippi and South Carolina do not have compulsory school attendance laws.
97. Commonwealth v. Petersheim, 70 D & C 432, 14 Com. 329 (Pa. 1949).
98. Commonwealth v. Smoker, 177 Pa. Super. 435, 110 A. 2d 740 (1955); Commonwealth v. Beiler, 168 Pa. Super. 462, 79 A. 2d 134 (1951); see also Miller v. State, 77 Ind. App. 611, 134 N.E. 209 (1922) and State v. Def.-Amish, Independence Justice of Peace Ct. (Iowa, 1962).
99. Commonwealth v. Bev, 166 Pa. Super. 136, 70 A. 2d 693 (1950).
100. Shapiro v. Dorin 99, 99 N.Y.S. 2d 830, 839-40 (Dom. Rel. Ct. 1950).
101. 103 N.Y.S. 2d 757 (App. Div., 2d Dept. 1957).
102. Application of Auster, 198 Misc. 1055, 100 N.Y.S. 2d 60 (1950).
103. Myerkorth v. State, 173 Neb. 889, 115 N.W. 2d 585 (1962), appeal dismissed, 372 U.S. 705 (1963).

Chapter Four

1. Everson v. Board of Education, 330 U.S. 1 (1947); McCollum v. Board of Education, 333 U.S. 203 (1948).
2. Ariz. Const. art. II, § 12.
3. Md. Const. Decl. of Rts. art. 36.

4. N.H. Const. Part I, art. 5.
5. Idaho Const. art. I, § 4.
6. Mont. Const. art. III, § 4.
7. Utah Const. art. I, § 4.
8. Okla. Const. art. I, § 2.
9. 310 U.S. 296 (1940).
10. Jacobson v. Massachusetts, 197 U.S. 11 (1905).
11. Prince v. Massachusetts, 321 U.S. 158 (1944).
12. Anderson v. State, 84 Ga. App. 259, 65 S.E. 2d 848 (1951).
13. Commonwealth v. Green, 268 Mass. 585 (1929).
14. State v. Drew, 89 N.H. 54, 192 A. 629 (1937).
15. Gamble v. State, 206 Tenn. 376, 333 S.W. 2d 816 (1960).
16. Ga. Const. art. I, § 1, par. 12; N.H. Const. Part I, art. V; Tenn. Const. art. I, § 3.
17. Vonnegut v. Baun, 206 Ind. 172, 188 N.E. 677 (1934).
18. Mosier v. Barren County Bd. of Health, 308 Ky. 829, 215 S.W. 2d 967 (1948).
19. Sadlock v. Board of Educ., 137 N.J.L. 85, 58 A. 2d 218 (1948). But see Kolbeck v. Kramer, 202 A. 2d 889 (N.J. Super., July 23, 1964) where Rutgers University, which exempts Christian Scientists from vaccination requirements, was forced to admit the plaintiff, who refused vaccination for religious reasons, but was not a Christian Scientist.
20. In re Whitmore, 47 N.Y.S. 2d 143 (Dom. Rel. Ct. 1944).
21. State ex rel. Dunham v. Board of Education, 154 Ohio St. 469 (1950), cert. denied, 341 U.S. 915 (1951).
22. New Braunfels v. Waldschmidt, 109 Tex. 302, 207 S.W. 303 (1918).
23. Ind. Const. art. I, § 2; Ky. Bill of Rights, § 1 Second; N.J. Const. art I, § 6.
24. Fla. Decl. Rts. § 5.
25. Moore v. Draper, 57 So. 2d 648, 650 (Fla. 1952).
26. Holcomb v. Armstrong, 39 Wash. 2d 860, 239 P.2d 545 (1952).
27. Wash. Const. art. I, § 11.
28. Holcomb v. Armstrong, *supra.* note 26 (dissenting opinion).
29. Wis. Const. art. I, § 18.
30. Peterson v. Widule, 157 Wis. 641, 147 N.W. 966, 977 (1914).
31. Fealy v. Birmingham, 15 Ala. App. 376, 73 So. 296 (1916).
32. Smith v. People, 51 Colo. 270, 117 P. 612 (1911).
33. State v. Verbon, 167 Wash. 140, 8 P. 2d 1083 (1932).
34. State v. Harrison, 260 Wis. 89, 50 N.W. 2d 38 (1951).
35. Ala. Const. art. I, § 3; Colo. Const. art. II, § 4; Wash. Const. art. I, § II; Wis-Const. art. I, § 18.
36. People v. Pierson, 176 N.Y. 201, 68 N.E. 243 (1903).
37. N.Y. Const. art. I, § 3.
38. People v. Cole, 219 N.Y. 98, 113 N.E. 790 (1916).
39. In Re First Church of Christ Scientist, 20 C.C. 241, 6 Dist. Ct. 745 (1897), In Re First Church of Christ Scientist, 205 Pa. 543 (1903).
40. Pa. Const. art. I, § 3.
41. See Note, 109 U. Pa. L. Rev. 213-15.
42. See, generally, Annot., 43 A.L.R. 2d 453 (1955).
43. Kraus v. City of Cleveland, 121 N.E. 2d 311, affirmed 127 N.E. 2d 609 (Ohio, 1954), appeal dismissed, 351 U.S. 935 (1956); Teeter v. City of La Parte, 139 N.E. 2d 158 (Ind. 1956); Dowell v. City of Tulsa, 273 P. 2d 859, cert. denied 348 U.S. 912 (Okla. 1954); See, generally, Nicholas, Freedom of Religion and the Water Supply, 32 So. Cal. L. Rev. 158.
44. Baer v. City of Bend, 206 Ore. 221, 292 P. 2d 134, 141 (1956), noted, 55 Mich. L. Rev. 130.
45. N.D. Const. art. I, § 4.
46. McGurren v. Fargo, 66 N.W. 2d 207 (N.D. 1954).
47. There has been a good deal of litigation in the states, since the majority of states have statutes dealing with contraception. The cases are not decided under religion clauses, however, but uphold these statutes as an exercise of police power, Comment, Constitutionality of State Statutes Prohibiting the Dissemination of Birth Information, 23 La. L. Rev. 773 (1963) and cases cited therein.

48. Pfeffer, *Church, State and Freedom* (Boston: 1953), p. 201.
49. Mass. Const. Amend. XLVIII, § II.
50. Opinion of the Justices, 309 Mass. 555, 34 N.E. 2d 431 (1941).
51. Poe v. Ullman, 367 U.S. 497 (1961) (holding that the immediacy which is an indispensable condition of constitutional adjudication was not present in light of non-enforcement); noted, 33 Miss. L. J. 138 (1961); Tileston v. Ullman, 318 U.S. 44 (1943) (Doctor has not standing to raise the constitutional question of deprivation of life without due process in contesting contraception statutes); see also, State v. Nelson, 126 Conn. 412, 11 A. 2d 856 (1940) upholding the Connecticut contraception statute.
52. See, e.g., Pfeffer, *Church, State, and Freedom* (Boston: 1953) p. 201.
53. Annot. 30 A.L.R. 2d 1138 (1953).
54. Re Vasko, 238 App. Div. 128, 263 N.Y.S. 552 (1933). See also Santos v. Goldstein, 16 App. Div. 2d 755, 227 N.Y.S. 2d 450 (1962), Re Rotkowitz, 175 Misc. 948, 25 N.Y.S. 624 (1941).
55. Mitchell v. Davis, 205 S.W. 2d 812 (Tex. Civ. App. 1947).
56. Morrison v. State, 252 S.W. 2d 97 (Mo. 1952).
57. Hoener v. Bertinato, 67 N.J. Super. 517, 171 A. 2d 140 (1961).
58. Re Clark, 21 Ohio Ops. 2d 86, 185 N.E. 2d 128 (1962).
59. People v. Pierson, 176 N.Y. 201, 68 N.E. 243 (1903). See, generally, Cawley, Manslaughter Aspects and Criminal Liability in Faith Healing, 39 Minn. L. Rev. 48, Annot. 12 A.L.R. 2d 1047 (1950).
60. N.Y. Const. art. I, § 3.
61. People ex rel Wallace v. Labrenz, 411 Ill. 618, 104 N.E. 2d 769 (1952), cert. denied 344 U.S. 824 (1952).
62. Ill. Const., art. II, § 3.
63. State v. Perricone, 37 N.J. 463, 181 A. 2d 751, cert. denied, 317 U.S. 890 (1962), noted, 12 DePaul L. Rev. 342, 24 U. Pitt. L. Rev. 642, 8 Vill. L. Rev. 114.
64. N.J. Const. art. I, § 3.
65. Comment, 26 U. Chi. L. Rev. 471, 478 (1959). For Federal Authority See application of the President and Directors of Georgetown College, Inc., 331 F. 2d 1000 (D.C. Cir. 1964), reh. den., 1010 F. 2d 331.
66. Re Seiferth, 309 N.Y. 80, 127 N.E. 2d 820 (1955).
67. People v. Pierson, *supra* note 59 (concurring opinion).
68. Fitkin Memorial Hospital v. Anderson, 42 N.J. 421, 201 A. 2d 537 (1964).
69. Pfeffer, *Church and State, and Freedom* (Boston: 1953) p. 227.
70. Johnson and Yost, *Separation of Church and State*, (Minneapolis, 1948) pp. 220-222.
71. 29 Charles II, c. 7 (1677); the statute is set out in its entirety in Pfeffer, *supra.,* p. 228, Johnson and Yost, supra., p. 221, and in McGowan v. Maryland, 366 U.S. 420 (1961).
72. Everyman and woman shall repair in the morning to the divine service and sermons preached upon the Sabbath day, and in the afternoon to divine service, and catechising, upon pain for the first fault to lose their provision and the allowance for the whole week following; for the second, to lose the said allowance and also be whipt; and for the third to suffer death. See Johnson and Yost, *supra,* p. 224.
73. Massachusetts Bay Colony (1629), Rhode Island (1679), Maryland (1723); see 73 Har. L. Rev. 729-730 (1959).
74. Stokes, *Church and State in the United States* (New York, 1950) p. 170.
75. Shover v. State, 10 Ark. 259, 263 (1870).
76. Neuendorff v. Duryea, 69 N.Y. 557, 563 (1887).
77. Judefind v. State, 78 Md. 510, 516, 28 A. 405 (1894).
78. Pirkey Bros. v. Commonwealth, 134 Va. 713, 722, 114 S.E. 764 (1923).
79. 47 States at present have some type of Sunday law.
80. Vt. Const. Ch. I, art. 3.
81. Del. Const. art. I, § 1.
82. N.J. Stats. Anno. Chap. 171 et. seq.
83. Wests Ann. Calif. Code Bus & P., 18730; Colo. Rev. Stats. 129-1-16; Wy. Stats. 33.112; Laws 1961, ch. 100, sec. 3.
84. Colo. Rev. Stats. 1953, 40-12-20, 40-12-21; Rev. Code Mont. 99-5312.

85. E.g. Delaware restricts amusements, sports, etc. to the hours between 12:00 and 8:00, 28 Del. 906; Mississippi gives a local option between the hours of 1:00 and 5:00, see Miss Code 2370.5.
86. See Miss. Code 2371; Fla. Anno. Stats. 855.04, 855.05.
87. Conn. Gen. Stats. Anno. 53-303; Mich. Stats Anno. 18-855; see also, Ops. Att'y Gen. of Michigan, No. 1200, (Aug. 24, 1943) ruling that Jewish barbers are exempt from the law prohibiting the doing of business on Sunday; N. J. Stats. Anno. Ch. 171 et seq.; N.Y. Penal Law 2140 et seq.; N.D. Cent. Code 12-21-15; Ohio Rev. Code 3773.23 Okl. Stats. Anno. 907; Tex. Penal Code 284; Code of Va. 18.1-359; Rev. Code of Wash. 9.76.020; Minn. Stats. Anno. 614.28, 614.29; La. Acts 1962, 273, secs. 1 & 2, 5-1:194 of La. Rev. Stats.
88. Conn. Gen. Stats. Anno. 53-302; Ill. Rev. Stats. ch. 48, sec. 8a-L (Smith & Hurd, 1957); Wisc. Stats. Anno. 103.85 (1957).
89. N.J. Stats. Anno. Chap. 171 seq.; State v. Weiss, 97 Minn. 125, 105 N.W. 1127(1906).
90. See 30 Notre Dame L. Rev. 569 (1960).
91. Wisc. Stats. Anno. 103.85; Ill. Rev. Stats. Ch. 48, sec. 8a-L (Smith & Hurd, 1957); Anno. Laws of Mass. c. 136, 1 (1957).
92. See notes 83 and 84.
93. Since 1955 the following states have amended their Sunday laws: Illinois, Indiana, Louisiana, Missouri, New Jersey, Ohio, South Carolina, Texas, Vermont, Virginia, West Virginia, Wisconsin, Massachusetts, Oklahoma.
94. *Ala.*; Frolikstein v. Mayor of Mobile, 40 Ala. 725 (1867); *Ariz.*: Elliot v. State 29 Ariz. 389, 242 P. 340 (1926); *Arkansas*: Scales v. State, 47 Ark. 476, 1 S.W. 769 (1886); *Connecticut*: State v. Shuster, 145 Conn. 554, 145 A. 2d 1962 (1958); *Georgia*: Hennington v. Georgia, 90 Ga. 396 (1892) aff. 163 U.S. 299 (1896); *Illinois*: (No standing) Humphrey Chevrolet, Inc. v. City of Evanston, 7 Ill. 2d 402, 134 N.E. 2d 70, (1955) reh. den. Jan., 1956; Pacesetter Homes, Inc. v. Village of South Hallard, 18 Ill. 2d 247, 163 N.W. 2d 464 (1960); *Indiana*: Carr v. State, 175 Ind. 241, 93 N.E. 1071 (1910); *Kansas*: State v. Blair, 130 Kan. 863, 288 P. 729 (1930), and State v. Hainy, 131 Kan. 853 (1930); but a 1963 Kansas closing law was held unconstitutional, arbitrary and unreasonable. Cited in *Liberty* (Published Bi-monthly by Religious Liberty Association of America), Vol. 59, No. 4, July 1964, p. 31; *Kentucky*: State v. Judge, 39 La. Ann. 132, 132, 1 So. 437 (1887); and Commonwealth v. Phoenix Amusement Co., Inc., 241 Kv. 678, 44 S.W. 2d 830 (1931); *Maryland*: McGowan v. Maryland 220 Md. 117, 151 A. 2d 156 (1959), aff. 366 U.S. 420 (1961); *Minnesota*: 97 Minn. 125, 105 N.W. 1127 (1906), also State v. Petit, 74 Minn. 376, 77 N.W. 225 (1898), aff. 177 U.S. 164; *Missouri*: Komen v. City of St. Louis, 316 Mo. 9, 289 S.W. 838 (1926); *New Jersey*: State v. Fass, 32 N.J. 199, 160 A. 2d 265 (1960), see also State v. Fass, 62 N.J. Super. 265, 162 A. 2d 608 (1960), aff. 36 N.J. 102, 174 A. 2d 193, cer. den. & app. dis. 370 U.S. 47 (1961); *New York*: People v. Frieman, 302 N.Y. 75, 96 N.E. 2d 184, app. dis. 341 U.S. 907 (1950); *N. Carolina*: State v. McGee, 237 N.C. 633, 75 S.E. 2d 783; *N. Dakota*: State v. Barnes, 22 N.D. 18, 132 N.W. 215 (1911); *Ohio*: State v. Kidd, 167 O.S. 521, 150 N.E. 2d 413 (1958), and State v. Ulner, 600, O. 2d 262, *Oklahoma*: Ex parte Pappe, 88 Okla. 166, (1949); *Pennsylvania*: Specht v. Commonwealth, 8 Pa. 312, 49 Am. Dec. 518 (1848), and Commonwealth v. Bauder, 188 Pa. Super. 424; *S. Carolina*: Carolina Amusement Co. v. Martin, 236 S.C. 558, 115 S.E. 2d 273 (1960) app. dis. 367 U.S. 904 (1961); *Tennessee*: The validity of an act done on Sunday does not rest upon religious or moral grounds, but solely upon the question as to whether the same is a violation of the provisions of the law, either statutory or common. Knoxville v. Knoxville Water Co., 107 Tenn. 657, 74 S.W. 1075 (1901). The Common Law recognized the sanctity of the Lord's Day and this principle of the Common Law was adopted by the state of North Carolina and has become part of the law of Tennessee. State v. Reichman, 135 Tenn. 685, 188 S.W. 597 (1916); *Texas*: Ex parte Kennedy, 42 Cr.R. 148, 58 S.W. 129 (1900); *Utah*: Broadbent v. Bidson, 105 Utah 53, 140 P. 2d 939 (1943); *Vermont*: Lyon v. Strong, 6 Vt. 219 (1834); *Virginia*: Mendell v. Haddon, 212 Va. 979, 121 S.E. 2d 516; *Washington*: State v. Grabinski, 33 Wash. 2d 603.

206 P. 2d 1022 (1949) *West Virginia*: State v. Baltimore R. Co., 15 W. Va. 362 (1879).
95. Ex parte Neuman, 9 Cal. 502 (1858).
96. Id. at 505.
97. Ex parte Andrews, 18 Cal. 678 (1861).
98. Ex parte Bird, 19 Cal. 130 (1861); Ex parte Westerfield, 55 Cal. 552 (1880); Ex parte Carson, 59 Cal. 429, 8 P.C.L.J. 533 (1881); Ex parte Burk, 59 Cal. 6, 43 Am. R. 231, 8 P.C.L.J. 522 (1881); Ex parte Koser, 60 Cal. 177, 9 P.C.L.J. 163 (1882).
99. Wests Anno. Cal. Code, Bus & P. 18730.
100. Crown Kosher Supermarket, Inc. v. Gallagher, 176 F. Supp. 466 (D. Mass. 1959).
101. Id. at 475.
102. 366 U.S. 617 (1961).
103. Henderson v. Antonacci et. al., 62 So. 2d 5 (Fla. 1952).
104. State v. Graunerman, 132 Mo. 326 (1895).
105. State v. Morris, 28 Idaho 599, 155 P. 296, L.R.A. 1916D, 573 (1916).
106. McGowan v. Maryland, 366 U.S. 420 (1961); Two Guys From Harrison-Allentown, Inc. v. McGinley, 366 U.S. 582 (1961); Braunfeld v. Brown, 366 U.S. 599 (1961); for an earlier landmark decision holding the Sunday Law of Georgia not unconstitutional, see Hennington v. Georgia, 163 U.S. 299 (1896).
107. McGowan v. Maryland, *supra.,* note 106 at 465.
108. Sherbert v. Verner, 374 U.S. 398 (1963).
109. Torpey, *Judicial Doctrines of Religious Rights in America* (Chapel Hill, N.C.) at 203-207.
110. Idaho Const. art. I, § 4; Mont. Const. art. III, § 4; Okla. Const. art. I, § 2; Utah Const. art. III, First.
111. State v. Barlow, 107 Utah 292, 153 P. 2d 647 (1944).
112. Reynolds v. United States, 98 U.S. 145 (1878); Miles v. United States, 103 U.S. 304 (1880); Davis v. Beason, 133 U.S. 333 (1890).
113. Shepard v. Grimmett, 3 Idaho 403, 31 P. 793 (1888).
114. Utah Const. art. VI, § 3.
115. State v. Musser, 110 Utah 534, 175 P. 2d 724 (1946).
116. In re State in Interest of Black, 3 Utah 2d. 315, 283 P. 2d 887 (1955).
117. Torpey, *Judicial Doctrines of Religious Rights in America, supra,* note 109.
118. Quoted in Updegraph v. Commonwealth, 11 S & R 394, 398 (Pa. 1824).
119. Id. at 409.
120. People v. Ruggles, 8 Johns. 290, 5 Am. Dec. 335, 4 N.Y.R. 545 (1811).
121. Id. at 295.
122. Updegraph v. Commonwealth, *supra.,* note 118 at 407.
123. State v. Mockus, 120 Me. 84, 113 A. 39 (1921).
124. Ill. Const. art. II, § 3.
125. People v. Marquis, 291 Ill. 121, 125, 125 N.W. 757 (1919).
126. State v. Kramer, 49 S.D. 56, 206 N.W. 468 (1925).
127. Sweeney v. Webb, 33 C.A. 324, 76 S.W. 766 (Tex. 1903).
128. Tex. Const. art. I, § 6.
129. Hill v. State, 38 Ala. App. 404, 88 So. 2d 880 (1956).
130. Lawson v. Commonwealth, 291 Ky. 437, 164 S.W. 2d 972 (1942).
131. State v. Massey, 229 N.C. 734, 51 S.E. 2d 179 (1949), appeal dis. sub. nom. Bunn v. North Carolina, 336 U.S. 942.
132. Harden v. State, 188 Tenn. 17, 216 S.W. 2d 708 (1948), noted, 2 Vand. L. Rev. 694.
133. Kirk v. Commonwealth, 186 Va. 839, 44 S.E. 2d 409 (1947).
134. Ala. Const. art. I, § 3; Ky. Const. Bill of Rts. § 5; Tenn. Const. art I, § 3.
135. Lawson v. Commonwealth, *supra.,* note 130.
136. Harden v. State, *supra.* note 126 at 24.
137. State v. Big Sheep, 75 Mont. 219, 243 P. 1067 (1926). See also Oliver v. Udall, 306 F. 2d 219 (D.C. Cir. 1962), cert. denied, 372 U.S. 963 (1963) holding that such a restriction did not violate the Federal Constitution. **Mont.** Const. art. III, § 4.
139. People v. Woody, 40 Cal. Reptr 69, 394 P. 2d 813. (1964).
140. Permoli v. Municipality No. 1 of the City of New Orleans, 44 U.S. 598 (**1845**).

141. La. Const. art. I, § 4.
142. Mo. Const. art. II, § 5.
143. City of St. Louis v. Hellscher, 242 S.W. 652 (Mo. 1922).
144. Dill v. Hamilton, 137 Neb. 723, 728, 291 N.W. 62 (1940), Neb. Const. art. I, § 4.
145. N.Y. Const. art. I, § 3.
146. People v. Ashley, 172 N.Y.S. 282, 285-86 (App. Div. 1918).
147. People v. Brossard, 33 N.Y.S. 2d 369, 372 (County Court, 1942).
148. McMasters v. State, 21 Okla. Crim. 318, 207 P. 566, 569 (1922).
149. Wash. Const. art. I, § 11.
150. State v. Neitzel, 69 Wash. 567, 125 P. 939, 940 (1912).
151. Cal. Const. art. I, § 4.
152. In re Wedderburn, 66 C.A. 2d 70, 151 P. 2d 889 (1944).
153. State v. Delaney, 1 N.J. Misc. 619, 122 A. 890 (1923).
154. 322 U.S. 78 (1944).
155. Id.
156. Id. (Dissenting opinion of Stone, J.).
157. Id. (Dissenting opinion of Jackson, J.).
158. Coleman v. City of Griffin, 55 Ga. App. 123, 189 S.E. 427 (1936).
159. 302 U.S. 636.
160. Lovell v. City of Griffin, 55 Ga. App. 609, 191 S.E. 152 (1937).
161. 303 U.S. 444; the Georgia court adopted the ruling of the Supreme Court at 57 App. 901, 197 S.E. 347.
162. Commonwealth v. Anderson, 172 N.E. 114 (Mass. 1930); Maplewook v. Albright, 13 N.J. Misc. 46, 176 A. 194 (1935); Semansky v. Common Pleas Ct., 13 N.J. Misc. 589, 180 A. 214 (1935).
163. People v. Bohnke, 287 N.Y. 154, 38 N.E. 2d 478 (1941), cert. den. 316 U.S. 667; held also in City of Washburn v. Ellquist, 242 Wis. 609, 9 N.W. 2d 121.
164. Commonwealth v. Nichols, 301 Mass. 584, 18 N.E. 2d 166 (1938).
165. 308 U.S. 147.
166. Seevers v. City of Somerset, 295 Ky. 595, 175 S.W. 2d 18 (1943); Hibsman v. City of Madisonville, 295 Ky 601, 175 S.W. 2d 21 (1943).
167. State v. Woodruff, 13 So. 2d 704, 706-707, (Fla. 1943).
168. Hord v. City of Fort Myers, 13 So. 2d 809 (Fla. 1943); see also, State v. Woodruff, 147 Fla. 299, 2 So. 2d 577 (1941), and State v. Russel, 146 Fla. 539, 1 So. 2d 569 (1941).
169. Kennedy v. City of Moscow, 39 F. Supp. 26 (1941).
170. Brown v. Stillwater, 78 Okl. Crim. 399, 149 P. 2d 509 (1944); Emch v. Guyman, 75 Okl. Crim. 1, 27 P. 2d 855 (1942); Tucker v. Randall, 18 N.J. Misc. 675, 15 A. 2d 324 (1940); State v. Meredith, 197 S.C. 351, 15 S.E. 2d 678 (1941); Pool v. State, 154 Cr. R. 270, 226 S.W. 2d 868 (Tex. 1950); Ex parte Luehr, (Cr. Rep.) 336 S.W. 2d 375 (Tex. 1954).
171. Matter of Application of Dart, 172 Cal. 47, 55-56, 155 P. 63 (1916).
172. Rescue Army v. City of Los Angeles, 28 Cal. 2d 460, 171 P. 2d 8 (1946), app. dis. 331 U.S. 549; Gospel Army v. City of Los Angeles, 27 Cal. 2d 232, 163 P. 2d 704 (1945), app. dis. 331 U.S. 543; see also, American Mission Army v. City of Lynwood, 138 C.A. 2d 817, 292 P. 2d 533 (1956).
173. Hoover v. State, 161 Text. Cr. R. 642, 279 S.W. 2d 958 (1955).
174. State v. Cox, 91 N.H. 137, 16 A. 2d 508, aff. 312 U.S. 569 (1940); Darlington v. Stanley, 239 S.C. 139, 122 S.E. 2d 207 (1961).
175. State v. White, 64 N.H. 48, 5 A. 828 (1886).
176. Wilkes-Barre v. Parabed, 11 Pa. Super. 355 (1899).
177. Commonwealth v. Plaisted, 148 Mass. 375 (1888).
178. Hamilton v. Montrose, 109 Colo. 228, 124 P. 2d 757 (1942).
179. Brinkman v. City of Gainesville, 83 Ga. App. 508, 64 S.E. 2d 344 (1951).
180. People v. Smith, 259 N.Y. 48, 180 N.E. 745 (1932).
181. People v. Smith, 263 N.Y. 255, 188 N.E. 745 (1934).
182. People v. Kiernan, 26 N.Y.S. 2d 291, 308 (1940).
183. James v. City of Moultrie, 196 Ga. 15, 29 S.E. 2d 786 (1944).
184. 321 U.S. 158 (1944).
185. City of Portland v. Thornton, 174 Ore. 508, 149 P. 2d 972 (1944); People v. Ciocarlan, 317 Mich. 349 (1947).

186. In re Case of Frazee, 63 Mich. 396 (1886); Milwaukee Co. v. Carter, 258 Wis. 139, 45 N.W. 2d 90 (1950) (could not prohibit speech on religious subjects in public parks).
187. State v. Poulos, 97 N.H. 352, 88 A. 2d 860, aff. 345 U.S. 395, reh. den. 345 U.S. 978 (1952).
188. McBride v. McCorkle, 44 N.J. Super. 468, 130 A. 2d 881 (1957).
189. In Re Ferguson, 55 Cal. 2d 663, 12 Cal. Rptr. 753, 361 P. 2d 417, cer. den. 368 U.S. 864 (1961).
190. People v. Reid, 40 N.Y.S. 2d 793 (1943); see also Hotaling v. Dale, 47 N.Y.S. 2d 702 (1944); Commonwealth v. Palms, 141 Pa. Super. 430, 15 A. 2d 481 (1940).
191. State v. Martin, 199 La. 39, 5 So. 2d 337 (1943).
192. People v. Parker, 397 Ill. 305, 5 N.E. 2d 523, aff. 244 U.S. 816 (1947).
193. City of Louisiana v. Bottoms, 300 S.W. 316 (1927); Hollingsworth v. State, 37 Tenn. 518 (1858).
194. Mooney v. Village of Orchard Lake, 333 Mich. 389, 53 N.W. 2d 308 (1952); North Shore Unitarian Soc. v. Village of Plandome, 109 N.Y.S. 2d 803, 200 Misc. 524 (1951).
195. People v. Village of Morton Grove, 16 Ill. 2d 183, 157 N.E. 2d 33 (1959); State v. Item, 259 Minn. 77, 106 N.W. 2d 366 (1960).
196. Diocese of Rochester v. Panning Board of Town of Brighton, 1 N.Y. 2d 508, 136 N.E. 2d 827, 834 (1956); Semble: St. John's Roman Catholic Church Corp. v. Town of Darien, 184 A. 2d 42 (1962); State ex rel. Westminister Presbyterian Church v. Edgecomb, 108 Neb. 859, 189 N.W. 617 (1962); State ex rel. Roman Catholic Bishop v. Hill, 59 Nev. 231, 90 P. 2d 217 (1939); State ex rel. Synod of Ohio v. Joseph, 139 Ohio St. 229, 39 N.E. 2d 515, 138 A.L.R. 1274 (1942); State ex rel. Hiwell v. Meador, 109 W. Va. 368, 154 S.E. 876 (1930); Young Israel Organization of Cleveland v. Dworkin, 105 Ohio App. 89, 133 N.E. 2d 174 (1956); Congregation Committee of Jehovah's Witnesses v. City Council of Haltom City, 287 S.W. 2d 700 (Tex. Civ. App. 1956); Community Synagogue v. Bates, 1 N.Y. 2d 445, 154 N.Y.S. 2d 15 (1956).
197. Church of Latter Day Saints v. Porterville, 90 Cal. App. 656, 203 P. 2d 823 (1949); cert. denied 338 U.S. 805 (1950), rehearing denied 338 U.S. 839; Minney v. City of Azusa, 164 C.A. 2d 12, 330 P. 2d 255 (1958); Tustin Heights Assn. v. Board, 170 C.A. 2d 619, 339 P. 2d 914 (1959). And cf. Miami Beach United Lutheran Church v. City of Miami Beach, 82 S. 2d 880 (Fla. 1955); City of Chico v. First Ave. Baptist Church, 108 C.A. 2d 297, 238 P. 2d 587 (1951).
198. Congregation Temple Israel v. City of Creve Coeur, 320 S.W. 2d 451 (Mo. 1959) (city had no statutory power to exclude churches from residential zones).
199. Congregation Committee of Jehovah's Witnesses v. City Council of Haltom City, 287 S.W. 2d 780 (Tex. Civ. App. 1956).
200. Penn. Const. art. I, § 3.
201. Appeal of Stark, 72 D. & C. 168, 98 P.L.J. 361 (1950).
202. Willis v. New Orleans East Unit of Jehovah's Witnesses, Inc., 156 So. 2d 310 (La. 1963).
203. La Const. art. I, § 4.
204. Milwaukee Co. of Jehovah's Witnesses v. Mullen, 214 Ore. 281, 330 P. 2d 5 (1958); Appeal of Trustees, 183 Pa. Super. 219, 130 A. 2d 240 (1957); Galfas v. Ailor, 81 Ga. App. 13, 57 S.E. 2d 834 (1950). But compare Application of Garden City Jewish Center, 155 N.Y.S. 2d 523 (1956) (could not deny because insufficient parking space for *future* needs.)
205. West Hartford Methodist Church v. Zoning Bd. of Appeals, 143 Conn. 263, 121 A. 2d 640 (1956); Miami Beach United Lutheran Church of the Epiphany v. City of Miami Beach, 82 S. 2d 880 (Fla. 1955). Contra: Application of Garden City Jewish Center, *supra*, note 204, Rochester v. Planning Bd. of Brighton, *supra*. note 196.
206. Redwood City Co. of Jehovah's Witnesses v. City of Menlo Park, 335 P. 2d 195 (1959).
207. City of Miami Beach v. State ex rel. Lear, 128 Fla. 750 (1937); Catholic Bishop of Chicago v. Kingery, 317 Ill. 257, 20 N.E. 2d 583 (1939);

Roman Catholic Bishop v. Baker, 140 Ore. 600, 15 P. 2d 391 (1932); Cf. Roman Catholic Welfare Corp. v. City of Piedmont, 45 Cal. 2d 325, 289 P. 2d 438 (1955).

208. Diocese of Rochester v. Planning Board of Town of Brighton, *supra.* note 196.
209. State ex rel. Wisconsin Lutheran H.S. Conf. v. Sinar, 267 Wis. 91, 65 N.W. 2d 43 (1954), appeal dismissed, 348 U.S. 913 (1956).
210. St. John's Roman Catholic Church Corp. v. Town of Darien, 149 Conn. 712, 184 A. 2d 42 (1962).
211. Yanow v. Seven Oaks Park, 11 N.J. 341, 94 A. 2d 482 (1953); State ex rel. Hacharedi v. Baxter, 148 Ohio St. 221, 74 N.E. 2d 242 (1947), appeal dismissed, 332 U.S. 827.
212. Western Theological Seminary v. Evanston, 325 Ill. 511 (1927); City of Chicago v. Sachs, 1 Ill. 2d 342, 115 N.E. 2d 162 (1943); Concordia Collegia Institute v. Miller, 310 N.Y. 189, 93 N.E. 2d 632 (1950); Village of University Heights v. Cleveland Jewish Orphans' Home, 20 F. 2d 745 (C.A. 6th 1927); Jewish Consumptives Relief Society v. Town of Woodbury, 230 App. Div. 228, 243 N.Y.S. 686 (1930).
213. Church of Christ v. First Church of Christ, 200 Okla. 424, 195 P. 2d 276 (1948); Philomath College v. Wyatt, 27 Ore. 390 (1893); Bendewald v. Ley, 39 N.D. 272, 168 N.W. 693 (1917); Davis v. Scher, 356 Mich. 291 (1959); Wright v. Smith, 4 Ill. App. 2d 470, 124 N.E. 2d 363 (1955); Fussel v. Hail, 233 Ill. 73, 84 N.E. 42 (1908); State v. American Society, 132 Iowa 304, 109 N.W. 894 (1960); Kuns v. Robertson, 154 Ill. 394 (1895); Mack v. Kime, 129 Ga. 1, 59 S.E. 184 (1907); Connonly v. Smith, 255 Ky. 630, 75 S.W. 2d 222 (1934).
214. Cape v. Moore, 122 Okla. 229, 253 P. 456 (1927).
215. Reid v. Johnston, 241 N.C. 201, 85 S.E. 2d 114 (1954).
216. Stone v. Bogue, 238 Mo. App. 392, 181 S.W. 2d 187, 190 (1944).
217. Second Ecclesiastical Society of Portland v. First Ecclesiastical Society of Portland, 23 Conn. 255 (1854).
218. Swafford v. Keaton et al., 23 Ga. App. 238, 98 S.E. 122 (1919); Nance v. Busby, 91 Tenn. 303, 18 S.W. 874 (1892); U.S. ex rel. Johnson v. First Baptist Church, 13 F. 2d 296 (D.C. Cir. 1926).
219. Carter v. Papineau, 222 Mass. 464 (1916).
220. Hynes v. Lilles, 183 Mo. 190, 170 S.W. 396 (1914).
221. Chase v. Cheney, 58 Ill. 509, 11 Am. Rep. 95 (1871).
222. Feizel v. Trustees of the First German Society of the M. E. Church, 9 Kan. 402 (1872); McNeilly v. First Presbyterian Church, 243 Mass. 462, 137 N.E. 691 (1923); Greek Orthodox Community v. Malicourtis, 267. 472, 166 N.E. 863 (1929).
223. Schweiker v. Husser et al., 146 Ill. 399 (1893).
224. Parish of the Immaculate Faith v. Murphy, 89 Neb. 524, 131 N.W. 946 (1911).
225. Moustakis v. Hellenic Orthodox Society of Salem, 261 Mass. 462, 466 (1927).
226. Eranta v. Bohemian Roman Catholic Cent. Union of U.S.A., 164 Mo. 304, 63 S.W. 1100 (1901); Barry v. Order of Catholic Knights of Wis., 96 N.W. 797, 119 Wis. 362 (1903).
227. Hackney v. Vauter, 39 Kan. 615, 18 P. 699 (1888).
228. Church of Christ v. First Christ Church, 200 Okla. 424, 195 P. 2d 276 (1948); Cape v. Moore, 122 Okla. 229, 253 P. 506 (1927); Reid v. Johnston, 241 N.C. 201, 85 S.E. 2d 114 (1954); Presbyterian Church v. Cumberland Church, 245 Ill. 74, 91 N.E. 761 (1910); Feizel v. Trustees of First German Society of M. E. Church, 9 Kan. 402 (1872); Ramsey v. Hicks, 174 Ind. 428, 91 N.E. 344 (1910).
229. Bendewald v. Ley, 39 N.D. 272, 168 N.W. 693 (1917).
230. Ruthenian Greek Catholic Church v. Bilanski, 19 Del. Ch. 49, 162 A. 60 (1932).
231. Trustees of Pencader Presbyterian Church v. Gibson, 26 Del. Ch. 375, 22 A. 2d 782 (1941).
232. Kedroff v. St. Nicholas Cathedral, 344 U.S. 94, 120-21 (1952).
233. Presbytery v. Gordon, 68 S.D. 228 (1941).
234. Happy v. Morton, 33 Ill. 398 (1864).
235. Trustees of Pencader Presbyterian Church v. Gibson, supra note 231.
236. Watson v. Jones, 13 Wall. 679 (1871).

237. Bramlett v. Young, 229 S.C. 519, 538, 93 S.E. 2d 873 (1956).
238. Davis v. Scher, 356 Mich. 291 (1959).
239. Trustees of Pencader Presbyterian Church v. Gibson, supra note 231.
240. Kedroff v. St. Nicholas Cathedral, supra, note 232.
241. Reid v. Johnston, 241 N.C. 201, 85 S.E. 2d 114 (1954).
242. Fuchs v. Meisel, 102 Mich. 373 (1894).
243. Reid v. Johnston, 241 N.C. 201, 85 S.E. 2d 114 (1954); Hale v. Everett, 53 N.H. 9 (1868).
244. Sutter v. Trustees of the First Reformed Dutch Church, 42 Pa. 503, 511 (1862); Comparably, minorities will be permitted to retain the church name when majorities deviate. Purcell v. Summer, 54 F. Supp. 279 (E.D. S.C. 1944).
245. Wright v. Smith, 4 Ill. App. 2d 470, 124 N.E. 2d 363 (1955).
246. McGinnis v. Watson, 41 Pa. 9 (1861).
247. Seventh Elect Church in Israel v. First Seattle Dexter Horton Nat. Bank, 167 Wis. 473, 10 P. 2d 207 (1932); Bethanien Church v. Ochsner, 172 S.D. 150, 31 N.W. 2d 249 (1948).

Chapter Five

1. Stokes, Anson Phelps, *Church and State In the United States,* 3 vols., (New York, 1950); Cobb, Sanford H., *The Rise of Religious Liberty in America,* (New York, 1902); Thorning, Joseph F., S.J., *Religious Liberty in Transition,* (New York, 1931).
2. *E.g.,* the Congregationalists in Massachusetts and the Baptists and Presbyterians in Virginia.
3. Art. XIX; The complete texts of all earlier Constitutions cited in this chapter may be found in Thorpe, Francis N., *The Federal and State Constitutions,* 7 vols. (Washington, D.C., 1909).
4. Art. I, § 4.
5. Art. I, § 3.
6. Art. IV, § 10.
7. Art. X, § 4.
8. Art. I, § 6.
9. Art. III, § 11.
10. Proceedings of the Convention held at Williamsburg, 100-103; Hening Statutes at Large, IX, 109-12.
11. Art. II, § 4.
12. Art. I, § 3.
13. Art. I, § 4 (Iowa).
14. § 4 (Kansas).
15. Art. VIII, § 4.
16. Art. III, § 15.
17. Art. II, § 4.
18. Art. VI, § 3 (S.D.); Art. III, § 4 (Mont.).
19. Art. I, § 4.
20. Art. II, § 3.
21. Art. I, § 4.
22. Art. I, § 11.
23. Art. II, § 11.
24. Art. I, § 3 (Alaska); Art. I, § 4 (Hawaii).
25. Hroneck v. People, 134 Ill. 139, 24 N.E. 861 (1890); Commonwealth v. Busch, 80 Ky. 244, 3 R. 740 (1882); Percy v. Powers, 51 N.J.L. 432, 17 A. 969 (1889).
26. 367 U.S. 488 (1961).
27. Art. XXXV.
28. Art. XXXVI, (. . . the people called Quakers, those called Dunkers, and those called Mennonists . . . .").

29. Decl. of Rts., art. 34.
30. Art. I, § 2; Const. 1897, art. I, § 2.
31. Art. XXXVIII.
32. Art. VIII, § 3; Const. 1851, art. I, § 7.
33. Art. I, § 3; Const. 1851, art. I, § 5.
34. Art. I, § 5; Const. 1890, art. III, § 18.
35. Art. XIII, § 4; Const. 1870 protects this right by the more general type provision in art. II, § 3.
36. Art. I, § 6; Const. 1901, art. I, § 3; Me. Const. of 1820, art. I, § 3.
37. Art. I, § 4; Const. 1870, art. I, § 4.
38. Art. I, § 6, Const. 1909, protects right by more general type provision in art. II, § 3.
39. Art. IX, § 4.
40. Const. of 1874, art. I, § 4.
41. Art. I, § 3.
42. Art. I, § 4; Const. 1947, art. I, § 4.
43. Art. I, §.4; Const. 1857, art. I, § 4.
44. Art. I, § 19.
45. Art. I, § 7; Const. 1861, Bill of Rts., § 7.
46. Art. I, § 17.
47. Art. II, § 9; Const. 1872, art. III, § 11.
48. Art. I, § 5; Const. 1945, art I, § 1, para. XIV.
49. Art. IV, § 10.
50. Art. I, § 16; Const. 1875, art. I, § 4.
51. Art. I, § 12; Const. 1921, no specific clause.
52. Art. II, § 4.
53. Art. III, § 4.
54. Art. I, § 11.
55. Art. I, § 18.
56. Art. I, § 4.
57. Art. I, § 4.
58. Art. I, § 2.
59. Art. II, § 11.
60. Art. I, § 3.
61. Art. I, § 4.
62. State ex rel. Baker v. Bird, 253 Mo. 569, 162 S.W. 119, Ann. Cos. 1915 C, 353 (1913); Maxey v. Bell 41 Ga. 183 (1870).
63. Davidson v. Brice, 91 Md. 681, 48 A. 52 (1900).
64. Ops. Att'y. Gen. 1922, 486.
65. 223 Md. 49, 162 A. 2d 438 (1959).
66. 367 U.S. 488(1961).
67. Art. XIX, § 1 (1874); see Const. 1836, Thorpe, *supra*, I, 284; Const. 1864, art. VIII, § 3.
68. Art. I, § 4 (1874).
69. Art. I, § 4 (1876).
70. Art. I, § 4 & art IX, § 2 (1870).
71. Art. VI, § 8 (1868).
72. Art. XVII, § 4 (1895).
73. Stiener v. Darby, 88 C.A. 2d 481, 199 P. 2d 429, dis. sub. nom. Parker v. County of Los Angeles, 338 U.S. 327 (1948).
74. Miller v. El Paso Co., 146 S.W. 2d 1027 (Tex. Civ. App. 1940), rev. on other grds. 136 Tex. 370, 150 S.W. 2d 1000.
75. The earlier constitutional clauses banning clergyman from public office are set forth and discussed by Anson Phelps Stokes, *Church and State in the United States*, (New York, 1950) Vol. 1, 622 ff.
76. Const. 1778, art. XXI, Thorpe, Vol. 6, p. 3253.
77. Const. 1867, art. III, § 11.
78. Const. 1870.
79. Art. VIII, § 1, Thorpe, Vol. 6, p. 3420.
80. Art. III, § 11, Thorpe, Vol. 3, p. 1172.
81. Stokes, supra note 75, I, 622.
82. Torcaso v. Watkins, supra, note 26 with accompanying text.
83. Const. 1867, Decl. of Rts., art. 37 (Md.); Const. 1870, art. I, § 4, (Tenn.).

84. Curtiss v. Strong, 4 Day 51 (1809).
85. Id. at 55; see also Atwood v. Welton, 7 Conn. 66, 77 (1828).
86. Jackson, ex rel Tuttle v. Gridley, 18 Johns. R. 98 (1820).
87. Id. at 105.
88. Art. I, § 3; 1895 Const., art I, § 3.
89. Art. I, § 4; 1857 Const. art. I, § 4.
90. Art. I, § 19.
91. Art. I, § 4.
92. Art. I, § 7.
93. Art. I, § 7.
94. Id.
95. Clinton v. State, 33 Ohio St. 27 (1877).
96. Decl. of Rts. Art. 33; Const. 1864, Decl. of Rts. art. 36; same in Const. of 1867.
97. State v. Mercer, 101 Md. 535, 61 A. 220 (1905).
98. Art. I, § 7; Const. 1861, B.R. § 7.
99. Art. I, § 17.
100. Art. I, § 6.
101. Art. I, § 4.
102. Art. I, § 9; Const. 1945, art I, § 5.
103. Art. I, § 16; Const. 1875, art. I, § 4.
104. Dickinson v. Beal, 10 Kan. 233, 62 P. 724 (1900).
105. Id. at 724, 62 P. at 725.
106. State v. Peterson, 167 Minn. 216, 208 N.W. 761 (1926).
107. McClellan v. Owens, 335 Mo. 884, 745 S.W. 2d 570, 95 A.L.R. 711 (1934).
108. Art. II, § 26, art. XIX, § 1.
109. Farrell v. State, 111 Ark. 180, 163 S.W. 768 (1914); Mueller v. Cofforan, 132 Ark. 45, 200 S.W. 136 (1918).
110. Art. I, § 5.
111. Decl. of Rts., § 5.
112. Art. I, § 4.
113. Art. I, § 11.
114. Art. I, § 18.
115. Art. I, §§ 1, 4.
116. Art. II, § 17.
117. Art. II, § 12.
118. Blair v. Seaver, 26 Pa. 274 (1856); Cubbison v. McCreary, 12 W. & S. (Pa. 1841); Thurston v. Whitney, 56 Mass. (2 Weeks) 104 (1848).
119. Colter v. State, 37 Cr. R. 284, 39 S.W. 576 (1897); see also Fuller v. Fuller, 17 C. 605 (1872).
120. Tucker v. Reil, 51 Ariz. 357, 77 P. 203 (1938).
121. Davidson v. State, 39 Tex. 129 (1873); Cross v. State, 89 Fla. 212, 103 So. 636 (1925); People v. Delany, 52 Cal. App. 765, 199 P. 896 (1912).
122. Goodall v. State, 1 Ore. 333 (1861); but see State v. Yee Gueng, 112 P. 424 (1910), noted 24 Har. L. Rev. 484.
123. People v. Lim Foon, 155 P. 477 (Cal. App. 1915); but see People v. Sanford, 43 Cal. 29 (1887).
124. State v. Rozell, 225 S.W. 931 (Mo. 1920).
125. McClellan v. Owens, 335 Mo. 844, 74 S.W. 2d 570, 95 A.L.R. 711 (1934); Thornley v. State, 127 Cr. R. 583, 78 S.W. 2d 601 (Tex. 1935); Tucker v. Reil, 51 Ariz. 357, 77 P. 203 (1938); People v. Copsey, 71 Cal. 548, 12 P. 721 (1887); Fernandez v. State, 16 Ariz. 269, 144 P. 640 (1914); Ramirez v. State, 246 S.W. 2d 99 (Tex. 1953).
126. Clinton v. State, 33 O.S. 27 (1877).
127. Snyder v. Nations, 5 Block, 295 (Ind. 1840).
128. Searcy v. Miller, 57 Iowa 613, 10 N.W. 912 (1881).
129. Dedric v. Hopson, 62 Iowa 562, 17 N.W. 772 (1883).
130. Cambrell v. State, 92 Miss. 728, 131 Am. St. Rep. 549 (1908).
131. State v. Eisentein, 72 Ariz. 320, 235 P. 2d 1011 (1951).
132. Wright v. State, 24 Ala. App. 378, 135 So. 636 (1931) Reh. den. June 23, 1931.
133. Originally granted on May 26, 1931.
134. The Justice who authored the original per curiam opinion dissented.

135. Marshall v. Alabama, 21 Ala. 83, 121 So. 72 (1929).
136. Hroneck v. People, 134 Ill. 139, 24 N.E. 861 (1890) reversing Cent. Mil. Tract. Ry. Co. v. Rockafellow, 17 Ill. 541 (1856).
137. Perry v. Comonwealth, 3 Gratt (44 Va.) 632 (1846).
138. Commonwealth v. Bush, 80 Ky. 244, 3 R. 740 (1882); see also Louisville & N.R. Co. v. Mayes, 26 R. 197, 80 S.W. 1096 (1904).
139. Free v. Buchingham, 59 N.H. 219 (1879).
140. Percey v. Powers, 51 N.J.L. 432, 17 A. 969 (1889).
141. State v. Sevine, 109 N.J.L. 503, 162 A. 909 (1932).
142. Adopted 1947.
143. Wigmore on *Evidence*, Vol. III, sec. 936; Chadbaum, "Impeachment of Witnesses by Showing Religious Belief," 9 N.C.L. Rev. 77 (1930); Biggs, "Religious Belief As a Qualification of Witnesses", 8 N.C.L. Rev. 31 (1929); Swancara, "Religion in the Law of Dying Declarations", U.S.L. Rev. 192 (1932).
144. Decl. of Rts. Art. 33.
145. Art. I, § 6.
146. Art. I, § 5.
147. Art. I, § 6.
148. Art. III, § 11.
149. Art I, § 4.
150. Art. I, § 4.
151. Art. I, § 11.
152. Art. I, § 18.
153. Art. I, § 4.
154. Art. II, § 12.
155. People v. Chambers, 22 Cal. App. 2d 687, 72 P. 2d 746 (1937).
156. People v. Weitz, 42 C. 2d 338 [Main Vol.] 267 P. 2d 295, cer. den. 347 U.S. 993 (1954).
157. Smith v. Smith, 7 C.A. 2d 271, 46 P.2d 232 (1935).
158. Id. at 233.
159. In re Malrosi's Estate, 96 C.A. 204, 273 P. 1097, 1100 (1939).
160. McClure v. State, 9 Tenn. 206 (1829).
161. Cleage v. Hyden, 53 Tenn. (6 Heisk) 73 (1871).
162. Cosey v. Archbishop of Baltimore, 217 Md. 595, 143 A. 2d 627 (1958).
163. State v. Adams, 200 Md. 133, 88 A. 2d 556 (1952); but accord: Wasy v. State, 234 Ind. 52, 123 N.E. 2d 462 (1955) where court pointed out that the questioning was necessary in order to determine whether grounds for challenge for cause may exist.
164. State v. Mussen, 110 Utah 534, 175 P. 2d 724 (1946).
165. Rose v. Sheedy, 345 Mo. 610, 134 S.W. 2d 18 (1939).
166. Olliff v. State, 161 Cr. R. 336, 276 S.W. 2d 839, cer. den. 348 U.S. 981, (1955).
167. People v. Rollins, 179 Cal. 818, 179 P. 209 (1919); People v. Rogers, *supra;* State v. Leunch, 198 Wash. 331, 88 P. 2d 440 (1939); see also Commonwealth v. Leher, 17 S. & R. 155 (Penn. 1827).
168. Commonwealth v. Bently, 287 Pa. 539, 135 A. 310 (1926).
169. Ford v. O'Byrne, 25 N.Y.S. 1, 22 App. Div. 50.
170. State v. Levy, 187 N.C. 581, 122 S.E. 386 (1924); also McFadden v. Commonwealth, 23 Pa. 12 (1853).
171. State v. Maxwell, 151 Kan. 951, 102 P. 2d 109 (1940); Smith v. Sisters of Good Shepherd, 27 Ky. L.R. 1107, 87 S.W. 1083 (1905).
172. State v. Huff, 14 N.J. 240, 102 A. 2d 8 (1954).
173. Work v. Harp, 215 Miss. 5, 60 So. 2d 514 (1952).
174. In Re Jenison, 125 N.W. 2d 588 (Minn. 1963), reversing 120 N.W. 2d 515 (Minn. 1963), vacated and remanded, 375 U.S. 14 (1963).
175. 374 U.S. 398 (1963). See Ch. IV, note 108 and Text.
176. Stokes, *Church and State in the United States*, *supra*, note 1, I, 859.
177. Const. 1861.
178. Const. 1912, VII, 3.
179. Const. 1872, III, 11 (test oaths prohibited).
180. Const. 1874, II, 26.
181. Const. 1909, II, 3.

182. Const. 1857, I, 17.
183. Const. 1896, I, 4.
184. Innis v. Bolton, 2 Idaho 442, 17 P. 264 (1888).
185. 145 U.S. 642.
186. Art. VI, § 3.
187. Laws of Idaho, 1891.
188. Shepherd v. Grimmett, 3 Idaho 403, 31 P. 793 (1892).
189. Art. VI, § 4.
190. Whitney v. Findley, 20 Nev. 198, 19 P. 241 (1888).
191. Reynolds v. U.S., 98 U.S. 145 (1898), Davis v. Beason, 133 U.S. 333 (1890).
192. Hirst, *The Quakers in Peace and War*, p. 331 (1923).
193. Declaration of Rights, art. VIII.
194. Declaration of Rights, § 10
195. Art. XL.
196. Art. XIII.
197. Ch. 1, art. 9.
198. E.G., Ala. Const. art. IV, § 2 (1819), Ill. Const. art. V, § 2 (1816), Iowa Const. art. VI, § 2 (1846), Kan. Const. art. X, § 6 (1855), Ky. Const. art. VII, § 1 (1850), Me. Const. art. VII, § 5 (1819), Md. Const. art. IX, § 1 (1850), Miss. Const. art. IV, § 3 (1817), Mo. Const. art. XII, § 1 (1875), N.Y. Const. art. VII, § 5 (1821), N.C. Const. art. XII, § 1 (1868), Ore. Const. art. X, § 2 (1857), Pa. Const. art. VI, § 2 (1790), S.C. Const. art. XIII, § 1 (1868) Tenn. Const. art. VII, § 7 (1796), Tex. Const. art. VI, § 2 (1845), Va. Const. art. § 1 (1870).
199. Selective Service System, 2 Background of Selective Service (Special Monograph 1, 1947).
200. Lees v. Childs, 17 Mass. 351 (1821); Commonwealth v. Fletcher, 12 Mass. 441 (1815).
201. Doe v. Allen, 4 Me. 527 (1827).
202. Colo. Const. art. XVII, § 5, Fla. Const. art. XIV, § 1, Idaho Const .art. XIV, § 1, Ill. Const. art. XII, § 6, Iowa Const. art. VI, § 2, Kan. Const. art. VIII, § 1, Ky. Const. § 220, Me. Const. art. VII, § 5, Mich. Const. art. XV, § 1, N.H. Const. art. I, § 13, N.C. Const. art. XII, § 1, N.D. Const. art. XIII, § 188, Ore. Const. art. X, § 2, Pa. Const. art. XI, § 1, S.C. Const. art. XIII, § 1, S.D. Const. art. XV, § 7, Tenn. Const. art. VIII, § 3, Tex. Const. art XVI, § 47, Vt. Const. art. I, § 9, Wash Const. art. X, § 6, Wisc. Const. art. X, §|6, Wyo. Const. art. XVII, § 1.
203. Kansas, Michigan, North Carolina, South Carolina, and Wyoming Constitutions, *supra* note 202.
204. Colorado, Idaho, Illinois, Indiana, Iowa, New Hampshire, North Dakota, Oregon, Texas, Vermont, and Washington Constitutions, *supra* note 202.
205. Colorado, Idaho, Illinois, Iowa, North Dakota, Oregon, South Dakota, and Washington Constitutions, *supra* note 202.
206. Florida, Indiana, Kansas, Kentucky, Maine, Michigan, New Hampshire, North Carolina, Pennsylvania, South Carolina, Tennessee, Texas, Vermont, and Wyoming Constitutions, *supra* note 202.
207. Florida, Kentucky, Pennsylvania, and Tennessee Constitutions, *supra*, note 202.
208. E.g., Kansas and Michigan Constitutions, *supra*, note 202; cf. U.S. v. Seeger, 326 F. 2d 846 2d. Cir., 1964) holding that the federal statute limiting draft exemptions to conscientious objectors whose objections stem from belief in a Supreme Being violates the due process clause of the fifth amendment.
209. E.g., North Carolina and South Carolina constitutions, *supra*, note 202.
210. Maine Constitution, *supra*, note 202.
211. Gales (ed.) *Debates and Proceedings in the Congress of the United States*, I, 433 (1843); Perry, *Sources of Our Liberties*, p. 422 (1952).
212. Elliott's *Debates*, IV, 243, 244 (2d ed. 1836); *Debates*, I, 334, 335; *Debates*, II, 531.
213. Patterson, *The Forgotten Ninth Amendment* (Indianapolis, 1955) p. 181.
214. Jacobson v. Massachusetts, 197 U.S. 11 (1904) (dictum).
215. U.S. v. Macintosh, 283 U.S. 605 (1931).
216. Hamilton v. Regents of University of California, 293 U.S. 245 (1934). Accord, University of Maryland v. Cole, 165 Md. 224, 167 A. 54 (1933), app.

dis. 290 U.S. 597; Hanauer v. Elkins, 217 Md. 213, 141 A. 2d 903 (1957).
217. 325 U.S. 561, reh. den. 326 U.S. 807 (1945).
218. 325 U.S. 561, 576. In a 1918 New York case a Quakeress, dismissed from her position as a teacher became of her attitude on the war with Germany claimed that this attitude was based on religious scruples, and that her dismissal violated her religious freedom. The court affirmed her dismissal, not because she was a Quakeress, but because her views, albeit religious in origin, prevented the proper discharge of her duties. McDowell v. Bd. of Educ., 104 Misc. 564, 172 N.Y.S. 590 (1918).

Chapter Six

1. Cooley, *Taxation,* 3rd ed., p. 343.
2. U.S. Constitution, Art. 1, § 8; 16th Amendment.
3. Cf. Brushaber v. Union Pacific Ry. Co., 240 U.S. 1 (1916) Communist Party, USA v. Moysey, 141 F. Supp. 332 (D.C.N.Y., 1950); and Stanton v. Baltic Mining Co., 240 U.S. 103 (1916).
4. Paulsen, "Preferment of Religious Institutions in Tax and Labor Legislation," 14 Law & Contemp. Prob. 144 (1949); Leo Pfeffer, *Church, State and Freedom* (Boston, 1953), pp. 183-190; 4 Villanova Law Rev. 1; Note, 3 Rutgers Law Rev. 115 (1949); Note, 49 Columbia Law Rev. 968 (1949); see also 9 Stanford Law Rev. 366; 35 Calif. Law Rev. 352; Stimson, "The Exemption of Property From Taxation in the United States," 18 Minn. Rev. 411 (1934); Note, 64 Harvard Law Rev. 291.
5. Everson v. Board of Education, 330 U.S. (1947); McCollum v. Board of Education, 333 U. S. 203 (1948).
6. *Washington Post and Times Herald,* October 10, 1963.
7. See Joseph V. McKee and Charles Morrison, "Should Church Property Be Taxed?" (A debate) *Look,* Dec. 9, 1947, Vol. 11, p. 60; Lucy Winsor Killough, "Exemptions to Educational, Philanthropic, and Religious Organizations," in Tax Institute, *Tax Exemptions (Tax Policy League Symposium),* by James W. Martin, Lucy Winsor Killough and others. (New York: Tax Policy League, Inc., 1939), pp. 23-38.
8. Stimson, "The Exemption of Churches From Taxation in the United States," 18 *Taxes* 361 (1940).
9. Pfeffer, *Church, State and Freedom,* (Boston, 1953) p. 183; A major source for history of tax exemptions to churches and other institutions is Adler, *Historical Origin of Exemptions from Taxation of Charitable Institutions,* (New York, 1922); others include Stokes, *Church and State in the United States* (New York, 1950), Vol. 3, p. 418; Stimson, notes 4 and 8.
10. Stimson, *supra.* note 8 at 361.
11. Paulsen, *supra.* note 4 at 148.
12. Yale v. Town of New Haven, 71 Conn. 316, 332, 42 A. 87, 92 (1899).
13. Paulsen, *supra.* note 4 at 147.
14. See Pollack v. Farmers Loan & Trust Co., 157 U.S. 495 (1895) for an extensive treatment of the history of taxation by the federal government and its constitutional basis.
15. F. William O'Brien, S.J., "The Blaine Amendment: 1875-1876," Washington, D.C.: Georgetown University Law Center, 1963, (unpublished study for the Institute of Church-State Law).
16. *Id.*
17. *Id.* at 31.
18. See Int. Rev. Code of 1954, secs. 501(c)(3), (d) (2); 107(1)(2) (income taxes);secs. 31-1-3125, 3121(b)(8)(A)(B), (K)(1), secs. 3301-3308, secs. 3306(c)(8),(10)(A)(i), (employment taxes); religious organizations are exempt from District of Columbia Unemployment Cooperation Act, cf. D.C. Code Supp. V.T. 8, sec. 311(b)(7); Int. Rev. Code of 1954, secs. 4003, 4061-

4226(e)(3), 4221(a)(5)(excises); see also U.S. Customs Circular, Jan. 28, 1944, para. 1774 (Tariff Act of 1930) providing for duty free importation of certain religious articles; Int. Rev. Code 1954 secs. 4233(a)(1)(i)-(ii)(federal admissions taxes); 4294 (communications and transportation), 4421(2)(exemption from wagering taxes for bingo, etc.), 4473(3)(recreational facilities).

19. Pfeffer, *supra.* note 9 at 190.

20. Const. 1776, sec. 45, Thorpe, *The Federal and State Constitutions.* (Washington, D.C., 1909), p. 3091.

21. Const. 1790, art VII, §3, Thorpe, *supra.,* p. 3099.

22. Const. 1838, art. VII, § 3, Thorpe, *supra.,* p. 3112.

23. See 72 P.S., sec. 5020-204 exempting "regular places of worship," hospitals, universities, colleges, academies and other institutions of learning.

24. Philadelphia v. Barber, 160 Pa. 123, 28 A. 644 (1894); Parsonages taxes, 25 CC 570, 49 Pitts. 184 (1901); Northampton County v. St. Peter's Church, 5 CC 416, 1 North 236 (1888).

25. First Baptist Church v. Pittsburgh, 341 Pa. 568, 20 A. 2d 209, 134 A.L.R. 1169 (1941); Second Church of Christian Scientist v. Philadelphia, 398 Pa. 65, 157 A. 2d 54, 75 A.L.R. 2d 1103 (1959).

26. Pittsburgh v. Third Presbyterian Church, 10 Pa. Super. Ct. 302 (1899) where the court found that such use was not "necessary" to the "place of worship" as required by the statute (note 23 *supra.*) passed pursuant to this clause.

27. Moore v. Taylor, 147 Pa. 481, 23 A. 768 (1892); Pittsburgh v. Phelan, 11 Dist. 572 (1901); Dougherty v. Philadelphia, 112 Pa. Super. 570 (1934); Baptist Church v. Pittsburgh, 88 P.L.J. 477 (1941); Appeal of Baptist Church, 88 P.L.J. 625 (1941).

28. Philadelphia v. Overbrook Park Congregration, 171 Pa. Super. 581, 91 A. 2d 310 (1952); Appeal of Parmentier, 139 Pa. Super. 27, 11 A. 2d 690 (1940).

29. Northampton County v. St. Peter's Church, 5 CC 416, 1 North 236 (1888) which held in addition that the burden was on the tax collector to show that the parsonage actually did occupy the substantial part of the property.

30. Burd Orphan Asylum v. Upper Darby School Dist., 90 Pa. 21 (1880).

31. Episcopal Academy v. Philadelphia, 150 Pa. 565, 25 A. 55 (1892).

32. In re Assessment of Certain Real Estate, 387 Pa. 534, 128 A. 2d 773 (1957).

33. White v. Smith, 189 Pa. 222, 42 A. 125, 43 L.R.A. (1899); Goeser v. Vories, 41 C.C. 504, 5 Leh. 383 (1913); see also Haverford College v. Rhoads, 6 Pa. Super. Ct. 71 (1897).

34. Watchtower Bible & Tract Soc. v. Allegheny City, 14 Dist. 695, 52 Pitts. 222 (1904).

35. Young Men's Christian Ass'n Assessment, 24 Berks 55 (1931); Young Men's Christ. Ass'n v. Philadelphia, 139 Pa. Super. 332, 11 A. 2d 527 (1940); Appeal of Young Men's Christian Ass'n of Pittsburgh, 383 Pa. 176, 11 A. 2d 743 (1956).

36. Bethlehem Diocese v. Boyer, 20 Dist. 995, 4 Leh L.J. 213 (1911).

37. See *supra.* note 29.

38. Board of Missions of M.E. Church v. Philadelphia, 266 Pa. 405, 109 A. 664 (1920) Dougherty v. Philadelphia, 139 Pa. Super. 37, 11 A. 2d 695 (1940).

39. Mass. Const. 1780 rearranged in 1919 with amendments, Ch. 5, § 2.

40. M.C.L.A. c. 59, § 5, clause 11.

41. Trinity Church v. City of Boston, 118 Mass. 164 (1875).

42. All Saints Parish v. Brookline, 178 Mass. 404, 59 N.E. 1003 (1901).

43. *Supra.* note 27.

44. M.C.L.A. c. 59, § 5, clause 11.

45. Assessors of Boston v. Old South Soc. in Boston, 314 Mass. 364, 50 N.E. 2d 51 (1943).

46. Stat. 1953, c. 231.

47. Stat. 1954, c. 341.

48. South Lancaster Academy v. Inhabitants of Town of Lancaster, 242 Mass. 553 136 N.E. 626 (1922).

49. Assessors of Dover v. Dominican Fathers Province of St. Joseph, 344 Mass. 530, 137 N.E. 2d 225 (1951).

50. M.C.L.A. c. 59, § 5, clause 10.

51. Const. 1784, Thorpe, *supra.*, Vol. 4, p. 2467; earlier colonial constitution dated 1776 had no exemption clauses.
52. Const. 1792, § 83, Thorpe, *supra.*, Vol. 4, p. 2487.
53. Const. as amended in 1902, § 82, Thorpe, *supra.*, Vol. 4, p. 2510.
54. Const. as amended in 1955, Section II.
55. Const. of N.H., 1792, Part I, art. VI, Thorpe, *supra*, p. 2471 stating that the people may authorize the legislature and towns to support Protestant teachers at the people's expense.
56. 56 N.H. 508.
57. F. William O'Brien, "Government and Religion," 5 *Villanova Law Rev.* 335 (Spring, 1960), p. 349.
58. Ward v. Manchester, *supra.* note 56 at 509.
59. Opinion of the Justices, 99 N.H. 519, 113 A. 2d 114 (1955).
60. *Id.*, at 522, 113 A. 2d at 116.
61. St. Paul's Church v. Concord, 75 N.H. 420, 75 A. 531, 27 L.R.A. N.S. 910 (1910).
62. *Id.*, at 424-25, 75 A. at 533.
63. New Hampshire R.S.A. 72:23 as amended in 1957.
64. South Carolina Const. 1790, art. VIII § 2, Thorpe, *supra.*, Vol. 6, p. 3264. Although South Carolina had two colonial constitutions, dated 1776 and 1778, neither made any reference to tax exemptions for churches.
65. See *supra.* note 21.
66. S.C. Const. 1865, art. IX, § 9, Thorpe, *supra.*, Vol. 6, p. 3278.
67. Thorpe, *supra.*, Vol. 6, p. 3298.
68. S.C. Const. 1895, art X, § 1; art X, § 4.
69. E.g., schools, colleges, institutions of learning, churches, parsonages.
70. Wesley M.E. Church v. Columbia, 105 S.C. 303, 89 S.E. 641 (1916).
71. S.C. Code of Laws, 65-1512, clause 15.
72. *Id.*, clauses 28, 29, 30.
73. *Id.*, clause 13.
74. Ga. Consts. 1777 and 1789.
75. Ga. Const. 1798, art IV, § 3. Thorpe, *supra.*, Vol. 2, p. 800.
76. Samuel Gladney, et al. v. Deavors, 11 Ga. 79 (1851).
77. *Id.* at 90.
78. Ga. Const. 1877, art. VII, § 2, para. 2, Thorpe, *supra.*, Vol. 2, p. 864.
79. Ga. Const. 1945, art. I, § 1, para. 14.
80. Trustees of the First M.E. Church, South v. Atlanta, et al., 76 Ga. 181 (1886).
81. *Id.* at 191-192.
82. *Id.*
83. Atlanta v. First Presbyterian Church, 86 Ga. 730, 13 S.E. 252 (1891).
84. *Id.* at 734, 13 S.E. at 256.
85. Wardens of St. Marks Church v. Mayor of Brunswick, 78 Ga. 541, 3 S.E. 61 (1887). The question in the instant case was whether a parsonage was exempt from such an assessment. It was held that a parsonage was not a "place of worship", and therefore not entitled to the exemption as one.
86. Ga. Code Anno. 95-3105(C).
87. N.C. Const. 1868, art. IX, § 1, Thorpe, *supra.*, Vol. 5, p. 2817. North Carolina had two previous constitutions (1776 & 1861) but neither contained exemption clauses pertaining to religion.
88. N.C. Const. 1868, art. V, § 6, Thorpe, *supra.*, Vol. 5, p. 2814.
89. N.C. Const. 1876, art. V, § 6; art. IX, § 1.
90. Fuller v. Lockhart, 209 N.C. 61 (1935); Grade School Dist. v. Alamance Co., 211 N.C. 213, 189 S.E. 873 (1937).
91. G.S. N.C. 105-248.
92. 1776, 1830, 1850, 1861, 1864. Exemption was, however, granted by statute in 1800, see Va. Stats. at Large, Shepherd's Const. of Hening, p. 200.
93. Const. of Va. 1870, art. IX, § 3, Thorpe, *supra.*, Vol. 7, p. 3894.
94. Const. of Va. 1902, § 183.
95. Code of Va. Anno., 58-12.
96. Com. v. Lynchburg YMCA, 115 Va. 745, 80 S.E. 589 (1914).
97. *Id.* at 747-748, 80 S.E. at 590.
98. Del. Consts. of 1776, 1792, 1831.

99. Del. Code Anno. 9-8103, 8105.
100. Rettew v. St. Patrick's Church, 4 Penn. 593, 20 Del. 593, 58 A. 828 (1902).
101. Wilmington v. Monthly Meeting of Friends, 3 W. W. Harr. 180, 33 Del. 180, 133 A. 2d 88 (1926).
102. Wilmington v. Saint Stanislaus Kostka Church, 10 Terry 5, 49 Del. 5, 108 A. 2d 581 (1954).
103. Both had a number of earlier constitutions: New Jersey—Consts. of 1776, 1844; New York—Consts. of 1777, 1821, 1846, 1894.
104. See Laws of N.Y. 1896 C.908; Coles v. Platt, 24 *N.J.L.*108 (1853)
105. Coles v. Platt, *supra.* note 104 at 120.
106. N.Y. Const. 1894 (revised 1938), art. XVI, § 1.
107. N.J. Const. 1947, art. XIII, § 1, subd. 2.
108. *Ibid.*
109. N.Y. Tax Law, Sec. 4, subd. 6.
110. *Ibid.*, subd. 8—limited to assessed valuation of $3000.00.
111. *Ibid.*, subd. 10—limited to assessed valuation of $1500.00.
112. *Ibid.*, subd. 6-a—added 1939.
113. N.J.S.A. 54: 4-3.6.
114. Sisters of　Charity v. Chatham, 52 N.J.L. 373 (1890).
115. Sisters of Charity v. Cory, 73 N.J.L. 699 (1907).
116. Teaneck Township v. Southern Bible Institute, 20 N.J. 86, 188 A. 2d 809 (1955).
117. Gen. Laws of R.I., 44-3-3(5)—limited to one acre of land.
118. *Ibid.*, 44-3-3(6)—limited to assessed value of $10,000 and one acre of land.
119. *Ibid.* 44-4-4(7) (18).
120. Second Universalist Soc. v. Providence 6 R.I. 235 (1859); In re College St., 8 R.I. 474 (1867).
121. General Finance Corp. v. Archetto, 176 A. 2d 73 (R.I. 1961).
122. *Id.* at 77.
123. *Id.*
124. Atwater v. Inhabitants of Woodbridge, 6 Conn. 223 (1826).
125. *Id.* at 230.
126. Conn. Gen. Stats. Anno., 12-18(12)(13)(14)(16).
127. *Ibid.*, (15).
128. Town of Woodstock v. The Retreat, 125 Conn. 52, 3 A. 2d 232 (1939) (Unitarian ministers). Manresa Institute v. Norwalk, 61 Conn. 228, 23 A. 1088 (1891) (Jesuit retreat house).
129. Masonic Bldg. Ass'n v. Stamford, 119 Conn. 53, 174 A. 301 (1934).
130. Baltimore City v. Starr Church, 106 Md. 281, 67 A. 261 (1907).
131. Anno. Code of Maryland, Art. 81, § 9(4).
132. Morning Cheer, Inc. v. County Commissioners, 194 Md. 441, 71 A. 2d 255 (1950).
133. Const. of Vt. 177, ch. 2, § 41, Thorpe, *supra.*, Vol. 6, p. 3748.
134. Ch. 2, § 38, Thorpe, *supra*, p. 3760.
135. Ch. 2, § 41, Thorpe, *supra*, p. 3770.
136. Ch. 2, § 64 as amended.
137. 32V.S.A. 3802(4); 3832.
138. *Ibid.*
139. *Ibid.*
140. *Ibid.*, (6).
141. Grand Lodge v. City of Burlington, 104 Vt. 515, 518 (1932).
142. In re Estate of Curtis, 88 Vt. 445 (1915).
143. Consts. of 1792, 1799, 1850.
144. Ky. Const. 1890, § 170.
145. K.R.S.A. 140.060.
146. Broadway Christian Church v. Commonwealth, 112 Ky. 448, 454, 66 S.W. 32, 33 (1902).
147. Commonwealth v. Y.M.C.A., 116 Ky., 711, 719, 76 S.W. 522, 523 (1903).
148. Commonwealth v. Thomas, 119 Ky. 208, 83 S.W. 572 (1904) ". . . **an** exemption in favor of property devoted to the advancement of **any** particular belief is indirectly at least, a tax upon all the other property

owners of the Commonwealth to support that belief." at 214, 83 S.W. at 573.
149. Calvary Baptist Church v. Milliken, 148 Ky. 580, 147 S.W. 12 (1912).
150. Commonwealth v. Board of Education of M.E. Church, 166 Ky. 610, 179 S.W. 596 (1915).
151. Church of the Good Shepherd v. Commonwealth, 180 Ky. 465, 467, 202 S.W. 894, 895 (1918).
152. Preacher's Aid Soc. v. Jacobs, 235 Ky. 790, 32 S.W. 2d 343 (1930).
153. Ohio Const. 1802, art. VIII, § 3, Thorpe, *supra*, Vol. 5, 2910
154. Ohio Const. 1851, art. XII, § 2.
155. O.R.C.A. 5709.07; intangible property exempt, 5709.04.
156. Gurke v. Purcell, 25 O.S. 229 (1876).
157. In re The Bond Hill-Roselawn Hebrew School, 151 O.S. 70, 84 N.E. 2d 270, (1949); see also St. Paul's Evangelical Lutheran Church v. Bd. of Tax App. 114 App. 330 (1962) involving similar facts.
158. *Id.* at 72, 84 N.E. 2d at 272.
159. *Id.* at 73, 84 N.E. 2d at 272.
160. Cullen v. Schmidt, 139 O.S. 194 (1942).
161. Gerke v. Purcell, *supra* note 156.
162. *Id.* at 248, see also Ops. Atty. Gen. 1922, Vol. 2, p. 853.
163. *Id.*
164. Union v. Zangerle, 138 O.S. 246, 34 N.E. 2d 210 (1941).
165. Blach v. Board of Tax App., 144 O.S. 414 (1945); Rabbinical College v. Board of Tax App., 148 O.S. 654 (1947).
166. Gerke v. Purcell, 25 O.S. 229 (1876); Soc. of The Precious Blood v. Bd. of Tax App., 149 O.S. 62 (1948); Watterson v. Haliday, 77 O.S. 150, 82 N.E. 962 (1907).
167. Note: It was ruled in 1918 that dormitories for teachers in parochial schools or other institutions of purely public charity, were not subject to taxation. Ops. Atty. Gen. 1918, Vol. 1, p. 396; (Camp meeting property exempt even though charge made for its use) Davis v. Camp Meeting Asso., 57 O.S. 257 (1897).
168. Cleveland Bible College v. Board of Tax Apps., 151 O.S. 258, 85 N.E. 2d 284 (1949).
169. *Id.* at 271-72, 85 N.E. 2d at 290.
170. Stewart, J.
171. Church of God v. Board of Tax App., 159 O.S. 517 (1953) overruling Mussio v. Glarder, 149 O.S. 423 (1948).
172. Y.M.C.A. v. Spencer, 9 C.C. N.S. 351, 19 C.D. 249.
173. Holy Trinity P.E. Church v. Bowers, 117 O.S. 103, 173 N.E. 2d 682 (1961).
174. Consts. 1812 and 1845.
175. Const. of La. 1864, art. 124, Thorpe, *supra*, Vol. 2, p. 1443.
176. Const. of La. 1879, art. 207, Thorpe, *supra*, Vol. 3, p. 1505.
177. Cunningham v. Board of Assessors, 52 La. Anno. 233, 26 So. 872 (1889); also a priest's residence at a Jesuit College; parsonage held to include residence of minister in hospital who served chapel, Ops. Atty. Gen. 1940-42, p. 3999.
178. Const. of La. 1898, (as amended, Act 1902, no. 129, adopted Nov. 4, 1902, art. 230, Thorpe *supra*, Vol. 3, p. 1570.
179. La. Const. 1913, art. 230; La. Const. 1921, art. X, § 4.
180. Ops. Atty. Gen. 1920-22, p. 820.
181. Enout v. McGuire, 36 La. Anno. 804, 51 Am. Rep. 14 (1884) (property had been purchased with an eye to expansion of city and surrounding area, but it failed to expand as expected).
182. La Const. art. X, § 4.
183. *Ibid.*
184. Const. of Indiana 1816, art. IX, § 1, Thorpe, *supra*, Vol. 2, p. 1069.
185. Const. of Indiana 1851, art. X, § 1.
186. Anno. Ind. Sts. 64-201(6).
187. *Ibid.*, 64-201(9).
188. *Ibid.*, 64-201(5).

189. United Brethren Pub. Eestablishment v. Shaffer, 74 App. 178, 123 N.E. 697 (1919). The proceeds are devoted to one or another of the enumerated purposes.
190. Miss. Const. 1817, art. VI, § 16, Thorpe, *supra*, p. 2045; 1832, art. VII, 14 Thorpe, p. 2061.
191. Miss. Const. 1860, art. VIII, § 1, Thorpe, *supra*, p. 2080.
192. M.C.A. 9697.
193. Enochs v. Jackson, 130 Miss. 119, 144 So. 473 (1932).
194. Adams County v. Catholic Diocese of Natchey, 110 Miss. 890, 71 So. 17 (1916).
195. Ill. Const. 1818.
196. Ill Const. 1848, art. IX, § 3, Thorpe, *supra*, Vol. 2, p. 1004.
197. Ill. Const. 1870, art. IX, § 3.
198. People v. Deutches Geminde, 249 Ill. 132, 94 N.E. 162 (1911).
199. First Congressional Church of DeKalb v. DeKalb County, 254 Ill. 220, 98 N.E. 275, 39 L.R.A. N.S. 437 (1912); In re Walker, 200 Ill. 566, 66 N.E. 144 (1903); People v. Muldoon, 306 Ill. 234, 137 N.E. 863, 23 A.L.R. 857 (1935); People v. First Congregational Church of Oak Park, 232 Ill. 158, 83 N.E. 536 (1908).
200. First Congregational Church v. DeKalb County, *supra* note 199.
201. S.H.A. ch. 120, sec. 500.2 (adopted in 1959).
202. S.H.A. ch. 120, sec 500(2)(7); also People v St. Mary's Hospital, 306 Ill. 174, 137 N.E. 865 (1922).
203. In re Walker, *supra* note 199; People v. Muldoon, *supra* note 199.
204. First Congressional Church v. DeKalb, *supra*. note 199.
205. First M.E. Church v. Chicago, 26 Ill. 483 (1861); City of Lawrenceville v. Maxwell, 6 Ill. 2d 42, 126 N.E. 2d 671 (1955).
206. Swigert v. Anderson, 117 Ill. 50 (1886); People v. Watseka Camp Meeting Association, 160 Ill. 576 (1896).
207. People v. Salvation Army, 305 Ill. 545, 137 N.E. 430 (1922).
208. People v. Catholic Bishop, 311 Ill. 11, 142 N.E. 520 (1924) (included buildings, surrounding acres, a tree nursery, recreational playing fields, lake and wooded area.)
209. People v. Muldoon, *supra* note 199 (court noted that it made no difference that the public was admitted to a small outside chapel on the premises.)
210. *Id.* at 237-238, 137 N.E. at 864.
211. 311 Ill. 308, 163 N.E. 1 (1928).
212. *Id.* at 318, 163 N.E. at 4-5.
213. Chicago v. Baptist Theo. Union, 115 Ill. 245 (1885).
214. Publishing Soc. v. Board of Review, 290 Ill. 108, 125 N.W. 7 (1919).
215. Consts. of 1819, 1865, 1867.
216. Thorpe, *supra*, Vol. I, pp. 174-175.
217. Ala. Const. 1901, art. IV, § 91.
218. Code of Ala., Title 5, § 2 (a).
219. 160 Ala. 253, 48 So. 659 (1909); also Anderson v. Macedonia Bap. Church, 246 Ala. 398, 20 So. 2d 777 (1945).
220. *Id.* at 257-260, 48 So. at 661.
221. State v. Church of Advent, 208 Ala. 632, 95 So. 3 (1923); State v. First Presb. Church, 208 Ala. 635, 95 So. 6 (1923).
222. State v. Bridges, 246 Ala. 486, 21 So. 2d 316 (1945).
223. R.S.M.C. 91-A, sec. 10, II (b).
224. Baptist Missionary Convention v. Portland, 65 Me. 92 (1876).
225. R.S.M.C. 91-A *et. seq.*
226. Const. 1945, art. X, § 6.
227. Koeln v. St. Louis Y.M.C.A., 259 Mo. 233, 168 S.W. 589 (1914).
228. St. Louis Y.M.C.A. v. Gebner, 320 Mo. 1172, 11 S.W. 2d 30 (1928).
229. St. Louis Y.M.C.A. v. Gebner, 329 Mo. 1007, 47 S.W. 776 (1932).
230. Salvation Army v. Hoehn, 354 Mo. 107, 188 S.W. 2d 826 (1945); in this connection see also an earlier decision, Y.W.C.A. v. Bowman, 344 Mo. 898, 130 S.W. 2d 499 (1939).
231. *Id.* at 114.

232. Spillers v. Johnston, 214 Mo. 656, 113 S.W. 1083 (1908); Midwest Bible and Missionary Institute v. Sestric, 364 Mo. 167, 260 S.W. 2d 25 (1953).
233. Evangelical Luthern Synod v. Hoehn, 335 Mo. 257, 196 S.W. 2d (1946).
234. Bishop's Residence v. Hudson, 91 Mo. 671, 4 S.W. 435 (1887).
235. Thorpe, *supra*, Vol. I, p. 323.
236. 4 Ark. L.R. 433.
237. 86 Ark. 205, 110 S.W. 954 (1908).
238. *Id.* at 208.
239. Burbridge v. Smyra Baptist Church, 212 Ark. 238, 209 S.W. 2d 685 (1948) (An abandoned church not exempt).
240. 4 Ark. L.R. 433, 439.
241. Phillips County v. Sister Estelle, 42 Ark. 536 (1884).
242. Martin v. Reynolds, 124 Ark. 163, 188 S.W. 4 (1916).
243. Bensberg v. Parker, 192 Ark. 908, 95 S.W. 2d 892 (1936); Martin v. Reynolds, 124 Ark. 163, 188 S.W. 4 (1916); Ahern v. Texarkana, 69 Ark. 68, 61 S.W. 575 (1901).
244. Const. of Mich., art. X, § 2, Thorpe, *supra*, Vol. 4, p. 1139; 1850, art. XIII, § 11, Thorpe, Vol. 4 p. 1962.
245. Mich. Const., art. XI, § 1.
246. Public Acts 1893, no. 206; 211. 1-211. 157 compiled laws of 1948.
247. Ops. Att'y. Gen., 1917, p. 376.
248. Ops. Att'y. Gen., 1917, p. 376; 1928-1930, p. 367.
249. Ops. Att'y Gen., 1928-1930, p. 367.
250. Ops. Att'y Gen., Aug. 24, 1942, no. 23928.
251. Pub. Laws 1869, no. 169, Sec. 5, Clause 9.
252. St. Joseph's Church v. Detroit, 189 Mich. 408 (1915); see also, Ops. Att'y. Gen., 1914, p. 247.
253. Lefevre v. Detroit, 2 Mich. 586 (1853); see also Ops. Att'y. Gen., 1921-1922, p. 92; 1926-1928, p. 595; May 9, 1940.
254. Const. of Mich. 1963, (effective January 1, 1964), art. IX, § 4.
255. Const. of Fla., art. XVI, § 1, Thorpe, *supra*, Vol. 2, p. 718 (previous Consts. 1838, 1861, 1865).
256. Const. of Fla. 1885.
257. Const. of Fla. 1868, art. XVII, § 24, Thorpe, *supra*, Vol. 2, p. 725.
258. See Thorpe, *supra*, Vol. 2, p. 73.
259. Const. of Fla., art. XVI, § 16.
260. Ops. Att'y. Gen. 058-185, June 16, 1958.
261. Lummus v. Miami Beach Congregational Church, 142 Fla. 657, 195 So. 78 (1940).
262. Fla. Stats. Anno. 192.06.
263. Burbridge v. St. John, 143 Fla. 544, 197 So. 131 (1941).
264. See Ops. Att'y Gen. 058-251, Aug. 26, 1958 where it was ruled that vacant lots owned by an unincorporated church are subject to the tax, where in the case of incorporated churches, they may be exempted if used for some religious purpose. *Id.*
265. Ops. Att'y. Gen. 061-105, June 30, 1961.
266. Const. of Texas, 1845, art. VII, § 27, Thorpe, Vol. 6, p. 3562; 1866, art. VII, § 17, Thorpe, Vol. 6, p. 3585; 1868, art. XII, § 19, Thorpe, Vol. 6, p. 3614.
267. The statutory language is the same in substance; see Vernon's anno. Cir. Sts., art. 7150, *et. seq.*
268. Trinity M.E. Church v. San Antonio, 201 S.W. 669 (Tex. Civ. App. 1918) (citing previous decisions).
269. Acts Nov. 6, 1928.
270. Ops. Att'y Gen. 1942, No. 0-4713.
271. Houston v. Cohen, 204 S.W. 2d 671 (Tex. Civ. App. 1947).
272. Radio Bible Hour, Inc. v. Hurst-Euless Indep. School Dist., 341 S.W. 2d 467 (Tex. Civ. App. 1961).
273. Act 1913, p. 153.
274. San Antonio v. Y.M.C.A., 285 S.W. 844 (Tex. Civ. App. 1926).
275. Act 1928.

276. Act 1937, p. 401, ch. 201, § 1.
277. 64 Tex. 673 (1885).
278. Id.
279. St. Edward's College v. Morris, 82 Tex. 1, 7 S.W. 512 (1891).
280. Little Theater of Dallas v. Dallas, 124 S.W. 2d 863 (Tex Civ. App. 1939).
281. Const. 1846.
282. Const. of Iowa, 1857, art. IX, § 3.
283. See Iowa Code Anno. 427.1(9) et seq.
284. 46 Iowa 275, 26 Am. Rep. 138 (1877).
285. 46 Iowa at 282.
286. Id. at 280.
287. Id. at 283.
288. Lutheran Mutual Aid Soc. v. Murphy, 223 Iowa 1151, 274 N.W. 907 (1937).
289. W.S.A. 70.11, et. seq.
290. R.S. 1849, c. 204.
291. Laws 1955, c. 660.
292. Laws 1949, c. 643.
293. Laws 1955, c. 130.
294. W.S.A. 71.01(3) ; 72.04, 72.045.
295. Reynolds v. Nusbaum, 17 Wis. 2d 148, 115 N.W. 2d 761 (1962).
296. W.S.A. 70.11 (10) (11).
297. Calif. Const. of 1849.
298. Const. of Calif. 1879, art. XI, § 1, Thorpe, supra, Vol. 1, p. 431.
299. Thorpe, supra, Vol. 1, p. 441.
300. Adopted Nov. 6, 1900.
301. Adopted Nov. 7, 1944, numbered sec. 1c of art. XIII.
302. Adopted Nov. 7, 1944.
303. Laws of California 1952; nullifying the holding in First Baptist Church
     v. Los Angeles, 113 C.A. 2d 392, 248 P. 2d 101 (1952) decided contra just
     prior to the adoption of this amendment.
304. Laws of California 1956; the exemption of such property had been per-
     mitted earlier under the "convenient use and occupation" phase of the
     constitutional exemption of art. XIII; see, Immanuel Presb. Church v.
     Payne, 90 C.A. 176, 265 P. 547 (1928).
305. Serra Retreat v. County of Los Angeles, 35 C. 2d 755, 221 P. 2d 59 (1950).
306. 35 C. 2d at 758.
307. Church of the Brethren v. City of Pasadena, 17 Cal. Rptr. 30, 34, 196
     A.C.A. 192 (1962).
308. Fellowship of Humanity v. Alemeda, 315 P. 2d 394, 409 (Cal. 1957).
309. Serra Retreat v. Los Angeles, 35 C. 2d 755, 758, 221 P. 2d 59 (1950).
310. Church of Divinity School v. Alemeda, 152 C.A. 2d 496, 314 P. 2d 209
     (1957).
311. House of Rest v. Los Angeles, 312 P. 2d 392 (1957).
312. Serra Retreat v. Los Angeles, supra note 309.
313. Fellowship of Humanity v. Alemeda, 153 C.A. 2d 673, 315 P. 2d 394
     (1957).
314. Watch Tower Bible & Society v. Los Angeles, 30 C. 2d 426, 182 P. 2d
     178 (1947), cert. den. 332 U.S. 811.
315. Lutheran Hospital Society v. Los Angeles, 25 C. 2d 254, 153 P. 2d 341
     (1944).
316. Supra note 298.
317. Adopted Nov. 6, 1894, amending art. XIII, § 1, Consit. of 1879.
318. Adopted Nov. 6, 1900, added as § 10 of art. XI, Const. of 1879; another
     act of the legislature adopted the same year exempted "the California
     School of Mechanical Arts," and in 1905 another private institution known
     as the Cogswell Polytechnical College was exempted (both of these latter
     institutions were located in San Francisco.)
319. Walters Bill, No. 3383; a similar measure had been introduced in 1933,
     but was not successful.
320. Laws 1944, numbered sec. 1c of art. XIII (known as the "Enabling Act.")
321. Section 214.
322. 108-3 (Senate 33-3, Assembly 75-0).

323. Proposition No. 3.
324. For background on Proposition No. 3, see the following: Ted LeBurton, "Trouble in California," *Commonweal*, 68:299-301 (June 20, 1958) with a discussion at 68:424-425 (July 25, 1958); Anthony T. Buscaren, "Schools and Taxes in California," *America*, 87:306-08 (July 21, 1952); Al. Antczak, "This Makes it Forty-Eight," *America*, 88:206-08 (Nov. 22, 1952).
325. Lundberg v. California, 46 C. 648, 298 P. 2d 1 (1956) (Rehearing Denied, July 5, 1956).
326. Heisy v. California, 352 U.S. 921 (1956).
327. Proposition No. 16.
328. For background on this campaign see Ted LeBurton, "Trouble in California," *Commonweal*, 68:229-301 (June 20, 1958) with a discussion at 64:424-425 (July 15, 1958); Al. Antczak, "California's proposition 16," *America* 100:233 (Nov. 22, 1958); Kenneth Worington Carey, "Protestant Strategy in California," *Christianity Today* 3:6-8 (Oct. 27, 1958); Edward Augustus Fitzpatrick "California Defeats a Proposal to Tax the Private Schools," (Editorial), *Catholic School Journal*, 59:32 (February 1959); Lawrence T. King, "Bigotry in California," *Commonweal*, 69:514-516 (February 13, 1959); Charles Oxten, "School Crisis in California," *Catholic Digest*, 22:5-8 Sept., 1958).
329. Al. Antczak, "California's Proposition 100" *America*, 100:233 (Nov. 22, 1958).
330. Const. of Colo. 1876, art. X, § 5.
331. Colo. Rev. Stats. 137-1-17(2)(3).
332. Bishop & Chapter v. Treasurer of Arapahoe County, 29 Colo. 143, 68 P. 272 (1901).
333. 29 Colo. at 146.
334. *Id.*
335. Kemp v. Pillor Fire, 94 Colo. 41, 27 P. 2d 1036 (1933).
336. 94 Colo. at 45.
337. McGlone v. First Baptist Church of Denver, 97 Colo. 527, 51 P. 2d (1936); see also 97 Colo. 427, 50 P. 2d 547 (1935).
338. 97 Colo. at 431.
339. *Id.* at 432.
340. *Id.* at 433.
341. Const. of Minn., 1857, art. IX, § 1.
342. See Thorpe, *supra*, Vol. 4, p. 2012 (numbered art. IX, § 3).
343. Ramsey v. Macalester College, 51 Minn. 437, 53 N.W. 704 (1892).
344. St. Peter's Church v. Board of Commrs., 12 Minn. 395 (1866); In re Groce, 27 Minn. 503, 8 N.W. 761 (1881) (when the playground of a Catholic grammar school was exempt, but not the parsonage located next to it); Ramsey County v. Church of the Good Shepherd, 45 Minn. 229, 47 N.W. 783 (1891).
345. Petition of the Bd. of Foreign Missions of Augustana Synod, 22 N.W. 2d 642 (Minn. 1946).
346. *Id.*, see also State v. Second Church of Christ Scientists, 185 Minn. 242, 240 N.W. 532 (1932); State v. Union Congregational Church, 173 Minn. 40, 216 N.W. 326 (1927).
347. State v. Union Congregational Church, 173 Minn. 40, 216 N.W. 326 (1927); State v. Church of Incarnation, 158 Minn. 48, 196 N.W. 802 (1924); Ops. Att'y Gen. 1934, No. 786, p. 1114, where an exemption was granted for an assembly hall owned by a church and used by young people for both religious and social meetings, even though it was not on same lot as the church and even though it was rented out to other groups when not in use.
348. State v. Seabury Mission, 90 Minn. 92, 97, 22 N.W. 882 (1903).
349. State v. Carlton College, 154 Minn. 280, 284 (1923).
350. Petition of Bd. of Foreign Missions, 22 N.W. 2d 642 (1946).
351. *Id.* at 646.
352. *Id.*
353. Ops. Att'y. Gen. 414-D-6, April 5, 1955.

354. M.S.A. 272.02
355. State v. Church of Incarnation, *supra* note 347.
356. Ops. Att'y. Gen. 408 C, Aug. 22, 1956.
357. Const. of Oregon, 1851, art. IX, § 1; Const. of Nevada, 1864, art. VIII, § 2, art. XI, § 1; Const. of W. Va. 1861-63, art. VIII, § 1, Const. of W. Va. 1872, art. X, § 1.
358. Ore. Rev. Stats. 307.140; Nev. Rev. Stats. 361.105; W. Va. Code 1961, § 678.
359. Central Realty Co. v. Martin, 126 W. Va. 915, 30 S.E. 2d 720 (1944).
360. *Supra* note 358.
361. State v. Kittle, 87 W. Va. 526, 105 S.E. 775, 17 A.L.R. 1030n, 1041n (1921).
362. Sisters of Mercy v. Lone County, 123 Ore. 144, 261 Pac. 694 (1927).
363. Const. of Neb. 1875, art. VIII, § 2.
364. Central Union Conference Assn. v. Lancaster City, 109 Neb. 106, 189 N.W. 982 (1922); In re St. Elizabeth's Hospital, 109 Neb. 104, 189 N.W. 981 (1922) . . . the use must be a present one. First Christian Church v. Beatrice, 39 Neb. 432, 58 N.W. 166 (1894); Scott v. Society of Russian Isrealites, 59 Neb. 571, 81 N.W. 624 (1900).
365. Nebraska Conference Ass'n. of Seventh Day Adventist v. County of Hall, 166 Neb. 588, 90 N.W. 2d 50 (1958).
366. Academy of the Sacred Heart v. Gray, 51 Neb. 755, 71 N.W. 752 (1897).
367. Masonic Temple Craft v. Bd. of Equalization, 129 Neb. 293, 261 N.W. 569 (1935).
368. Scottish Rite v. Board of County Commissioners, 122 Neb. 586, 241 N.W. 93 (1932) overruling 101 Neb. 274, 162 N.W. 639.
369. In re St. Elizabeth's Hospital, *supra.* note 364.
370. Const. of Kan., 1859, art. XI, § 1.
371. See Const. of Kan., 1855, art. XI, § 1, Thorpe *supra*, Vol. 2, p. 1191; 1858, art. XI, § 1, p. 1234.
372. Gen. Stats. of Kansas 79-201.
373. Const. 1858, *supra* note 371.
374. Vail v. Beach, 10 Kan. 214 (1872).
375. *Id.;* Nuns of St. Dominic v. Younkin, 118 Kan. 554, 235 P. 869 (1925).
376. Gen. Stats. of Kan. 79-202.
377. Sunday School Bd. v. McCue, 179 Kan. 1, 293 P. 2d 234 (1956) . . . the Board failed to sustain the burden of proving its right to exemption.
378. Rev. Code of Wash. 84.36.020; Idaho Code 63-105.
379. Unoccupied land not to exceed 100 X 120 Ft.; parking lots, *e.g.* are "occupied land," Ops. Att'y. Gen. 51-53, No. 295.
380. Wesley Foundation v. King Co., 185 Wash. 12, 52 P. 2d 1247 (1936).
381. Const. of N.D. 1889, art. XI, § 176 as amended in 1914.
382. N.D. Cent. Code 57-02-08.
383. Same two acre limitation applies.
384. See Engstad v. Grand Forks County, 10 N.D. 54, 84 N.W. 577 (1900).
385. Const. of S.D. 1918, art. XI, § 6.
386. S.D. Code of 1939, 57.0311.
387. *Ibid.*
388. In re Dakota Wesleyan University, 48 S.D. 84, 85 (1925) (emphasis added).
389. Scottish Rite Ass'n. v. Bd. of Comrs., 62 S.D. 204 (1934); Eveland v. Erickson, 44 S.D. 63, 182 N.W. 315 (1921).
390. 44 S.D. at 68.
391. Quoted by the court in McFarland v. Keeson, 77 S.D. 39, 84 N.W. 2d 884 (1957).
392. Mont. 1889, art. XII, § 2.
393. Rev. Code of Mont., 84-202.
394. See Montant Catholic Missions v. Lewis & Clark Co., 13 Mon. 559, 35 P. 2 (1893); see also State v. King Colony Ranch, 137 Mon. 145, 350 P. 2d 22 (1960) when it intended that a license tax on the agricultural activities of a ceremonial religious society did not violate the religious

freedom clause because this type of property did not qualify for the exemption granted to "places of worship" or "public charities."

395. Wyoming Const. 1840, art. XV, § 12.
396. Utah Const. 1895, art. XIII, § 2.
397. Wy. Stats. 39-7; Utah Code 1953, 59-2-1.
398. Odd Fellows Bldg. Assn. v. Naylor, 53 Utah 111, 177 P. 214 (1918).
399. Rev. Laws of Haw. 128-18(a) *et seq.*
400. Const. of Okla. 1907, art. X, § 6, art. X, § 9; Okla. Stats. Anno. 68:1.52 (exempt property).
401. State v. Alumnae of Tau Beta Chapter of Chi Omega Fraternity, 176 Okla. 186, 55 P. 2d 134 (1936).
402. Const. N.M. 1911, Art. VIII, § 3.
403. Church of The Holy Faith v. State Tax Com., 39 N.M. 403, 48 P. 2d 777 (1935).
404. Trustees of P.E. Church v. State Tax Com., 39 N.M. 419, 48 P. 2d 786 (1935).
405. Const. of Ariz. 1910, art. IX, § 2.
406. Ariz. Rev. Stats. 42-271.
407. Verde School v. Yavopoi Co., 90 Ariz. 180, 367 P. 2d 223 (1910).
408. 90 Ariz. at 182.
409. Const. of Alaska, 1959, art. IX, § 4.
410. Cooley, *supra* note 1 at 343-344.
411. 18 Acts 1831.
412. Yale University v. Town of New Haven, 71 Conn. 316, 42 A. 87, 92 (1886).
413. People ex rel. Seminary of Our Lady of Angels v. Barber, 42 Hun. 27, 30 (1886).
414. St. Barbara's Church v. City of New York, 243 App. Div. 371, 277 N.Y.S. 538 (1935); cf. Connecticut Junior Republic Assn. v. Town of Litchfield, 119 Conn. 106, 124 A. 304, 95 A.L.R. 66 (1934) wherein relatively the same language was employed.
415. Y.M.C.A. v. Douglas County, 160 Neb. 642, 646, 83 N.W. 2d 924, 926 (1900).
416. Zollman, "Tax Exemptions of American Church Property," 14 Mich. Law Rev. 646 (1916).
417. Cooley, *supra* note 1 at 198.
418. Paulsen, *supra* note 4 at 155.
419. *Id.* at 148.

TOPICAL INDEX

References Are To Pages

275

References Are To Pages

References Are To Pages